D1602751

Village Governance in North China

華北村治

李懷印 著

Village Governance in North China

1875–1936

HUAIYIN LI

Stanford University Press

Stanford, California

2005

Stanford University Press
Stanford, California
www.sup.org

Library of Congress Cataloging-in-Publication Data

Li, Huaiyin.
    Village governance in North China : 1875–1936 / Huaiyin Li.
        p.   cm.
    Includes bibliographical references and index.
    ISBN 0-8047-5091-2 (alk. paper)
        1. Land—Taxation—China—Huolu Xian.   2. Huolu Xian (China)—
Politics and government.   I. Title.
HJ4406.L52 2005
336.22'0951'152—dc22   2004013447

Printed in the United States of America on acid-free, archival-quality
paper.

Original Printing 2005

Last figure below indicates year of this printing:

14   13   12   11   10   09   08   07   06   05

Designed and typeset at Stanford University Press in 10.5 / 12 Bembo.

For Guiyun, Daniel, and Cathy

Contents

Maps and Tables

Preface

This book is about village governance in late nineteenth- and early twentieth-century China. It draws on the historical archives of Huailu county, Hebei province in North China. Compared to many other county archives in northern, southeastern, and southwestern China where most collections of the Republican period were limited to the late 1930s and 1940s, as I realized during my travels in three consecutive summers from 1994 to 1996, the Huailu archives are probably the best collection on land taxation and village administration that have consistent coverage of the late Qing and Republican periods. Of particular interest to me were case records that document disputes between villagers over local affairs, such as community service, tax payment, village government, and education during the late Qing and Republican years. These files permit in this book an up-close look at the everyday experience of the villagers in running their communities and dealing with the government. Instead of the familiar image of Chinese peasants engaged in popular protest, collective violence, and mass mobilization, what emerges from the materials is a picture of villagers cooperating for the good of the whole community while conflicting with each other over their respective rights and obligations.

Equally remarkable was the nonviolent, cooperative, and conciliatory relationship between the villagers and the government. The archives show persistent efforts by rural leaders to bargain with bureaucrats through collective petitions and deliberative organs at different levels in the early twentieth century, acts that repeatedly forced the government to make concessions. These legitimate *and* effective actions once again contrasted sharply with armed resistance against taxation found in many parts of rural China that often ended in a crackdown by government. Although collective violence is part and parcel of rural politics during the time of disorder and upheaval, this study calls for attention to the consensual dimensions of intra- and inter-village politics, which in my opinion are essential for understanding *everyday* village governance under normal circumstances and are as important as the contentious areas for a balanced grasp of the peasant society and village-state relations.

The main body of this book is divided into two parts. The five chapters in the first part explore the operational realities of endogenous institutions pertaining to community service and land taxation. The focus of this part is on the hows and whys of the persistence of cooperative practices in the peasant communities and their implications for understanding the peasant, the peasant community, and rural governance. Chapter 2 surveys the ecological and socioeconomic settings in which the cooperative arrangements came into being. Central to my analysis is a demonstration of south-central Hebei, where Huailu county is located, as a core zone of the North China "macroregion." Chapter 3 discusses the emergence and actual operation of the cooperative practices in a comparative perspective, and underscores the importance of peasant values, in particular reciprocity and survival ethics, that bolstered those practices. To understand peasant behavior and explain the durability of the communal institutions, Chapter 4 scrutinizes disputes over the rotating service of villagers as tax agents and local administrations, focusing on the changing motives and strategies of ordinary villagers and local notables in different circumstances. Chapters 5 and 6 examine various practices in the collection of land taxes and the taxation of land deeds, respectively, and explicate their significance for identifying the traditional pattern of village governance.

The second part of this book centers on changes in the village society caused by the implementation of nationwide administrative systems and modernizing measures after 1900. My purpose is to assess the effects of "state-making" on local communities. Chapter 7 examines disputes over the newly created village government offices in a context in which official systems and state discourse interacted with local institutions to shape the new process of village politics. Chapter 8 moves to the creation and maintenance of primary schools, another project imposed on the villagers by the state. My emphasis is on how the villagers' cooperative tradition continued in the new undertakings of the community, and how local elites combined their traditional privileges with new resources obtained from the state to aggrandize their symbolic and material interests. Chapter 9 discusses the responses of rural elites to the increased tax burden, focusing on their petitions and negotiations with the government in the first three decades of the twentieth century. Chapter 10 turns to the reorganization of village administration after 1930 under the Guomindang state. The spotlight is on discursive and institutional changes during the new wave of state-making as well as continuity of local arrangements in the everyday practice of village governance. To evaluate the actual effects of administrative institutionalization in different periods of the early twentieth century, Chapter 11 focuses on the investigation of untaxed illegal landholdings in the county, especially the campaigns in the early 1930s, which showed both the breakthroughs and limits of government modernization during the Guomindang era. Readers who have no interest in the empirical details in these chapters can refer to Chapter 1 for an outline of major issues addressed in this study and my preliminary findings, and then go to Chapter 12 for a summary of my arguments and further deliberations on those findings.

For my intellectual journey in the United States that led to this book, I owe my greatest debt to Philip Huang, my principal adviser at UCLA and still a warm, untiring mentor. His astute comments, wise counsel, and unfailing support were crucial to the completion of my doctoral dissertation, on which this book is based. I offer my sincere thanks to Kathryn Bernhardt, who greatly helped improve the dissertation with her careful reading and insightful comments. My writing of this book also benefited from several other scholars during my graduate years. David Sabean was helpful in introducing me to studies of peasant communities in European countries. His own studies of German villages inspired my analysis of Chinese peasants in this book. My study of European economic history with Robert Brenner and Japanese history with Fred Notehelfer opened my eyes to new ways of looking at subjects ranging from the agrarian roots of capitalism to modern state-making. Yunxiang Yan offered unwavering support when I was in need. His own ethnographic studies of Chinese villages are a constant source of inspiration to my research.

While revising the manuscript for this book, I received generous help from a number of distinguished historians and colleagues. Lucien Bianco, Joseph Esherick, and Odoric Wou read the whole manuscript at different stages and offered me detailed, very helpful suggestions for improvement. My special thanks are due to Bradly Reed, who generously donated his time and energy on two drafts of the entire manuscript. His incisive comments on both theoretical and empirical issues substantially improved the manuscript. Stephen Averill, Jack Goldstone, Christoph Harbsmeier, Daniel Little, Edward McCord, William Rowe, and Frederic Wakeman commented on individual chapters or journal articles and conference papers on which some chapters of this book are based. I am particularly grateful to William Rowe for his enthusiastic support and encouragement, and to Daniel Little, whose perceptive critiques of existing theoretical constructs for understanding Chinese peasants benefited my analysis of village politics. Many of my friends in China and the United States, as well as my fellow graduate students at UCLA, contributed to this book by providing input on individual chapters or moral support; they include, among others, Joel Andreas, Cong

Xiaoping, Clayton Dube, Thomas Dubois, Hu Chuansheng, Margaret Kuo, Eugenia Lean, Liu Chang, Lu Xiaobo, David Moore, Mark Lupher, Meng Yue, Jennifer Neighbors, Yang Nianqun, Elizabeth VanderVen, Zhang Jiayan, Zhang Renshan, and Zhao Gang. Needless to say, I am solely responsible for any defects and flaws that remain. With professional care and skillful assistance, Muriel Bell and Carmen Borbón-Wu of Stanford University Press guided me through the publishing process. Janet Mowery copyedited the manuscript with meticulous attention. My debts also go to Mr. An Shuguo, mayor of Luquan municipality (formerly Huailu county), for his generous help; and to my colleagues in the History Department at the University of Missouri-Columbia for friendship and encouragement that have made my research and teaching there more enjoyable.

I particularly wish to thank Yueying Zhong, my good friend and an acclaimed artist of Chinese painting, now living in San Francisco. He astonished me with his drawing for this book, appearing on the cover, which deftly and appealingly depicts the landscape of a village on the piedmont in Hebei province. I would also like to thank my brother, Li Huaiqin, my host in Nanjing for two summers of research.

For financial support, I am grateful to the UCLA History Department for a dissertation fellowship; to Sun Yet-sen Cultural and Educational Foundation for the Ou Jou Yi scholarship; to the China Times Cultural Foundation for the Young Scholar Award; and to the Chiang Ching-kuo International Scholarly Exchange Foundation for a postdoctoral grant. A Research Board grant from the University of Missouri system enabled me to return to Shijiazhuang for additional research materials. A summer fellowship and Research Council grant from the University of Missouri-Columbia allowed me to concentrate on completing the final draft of the book and facilitated its publication. Some of the materials contained in this book were published in my articles in *Ershiyi shiji* (no. 55, 1999), *Modern China* (vol. 26, no. 1, 2000), *Lishi yanjiu* (no. 6, 2001), *Twentieth-Century China* (vol. 28, no. 2, 2003), and *Zhongguo xiangcun yanjiu* (no. 1, 2003).

Finally, a few words to my family. My wife, Guiyun Zhao, could not have been more supportive as I sacrificed countless weekends bringing this book into its final form. In the years since we moved to the United States, we have shared joys and hardships watching the growth of our two children, Daniel Zhaobai Li and Cathy Shuqin Li, who endlessly make us proud parents. I lovingly dedicate this book to my wife and our two children.

H.L.
Columbia, Missouri
August 2004

Village Governance in North China

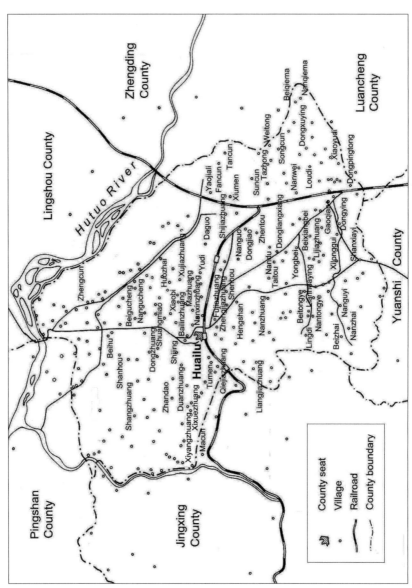

Map 1. Huailu County in the 1920s

CHAPTER 1

Introduction

It is widely observed, and indeed true, that a simple peasant in prerevolutionary China had little contact with government officials. Unless involved in a lawsuit or criminal case, he never visited the office of the county magistrate, the lowest-level appointee of the regular bureaucracy who oversaw hundreds of villages and an average of 250,000 people.[1] This was even true for landowners who owed taxes to the government, for they seldom traveled to the county seat to pay a tax in person, or to obtain a deed directly from the yamen when buying land. Instead villagers usually turned to unofficial agents in their own or neighboring communities for those purposes. Noting the limited effectiveness of the city-based imperial administration, which barely extended beyond the city walls, Max Weber remarked that a Chinese village was nothing less than a "self-governing settlement without a mandarin!" (Weber 1951 [1922]: 91). Sidney D. Gamble, who conducted fieldwork in rural North China in the early 1930s, found that the government lacked any interest in the villages "beyond receiving their tax payments." The peasants were still able to "keep a varying amount of control over their local affairs and usually to recover gradually any that had been taken from them by reform programs developed in the capital"(Gamble 1963: 8).

But the villages were not totally out of the government's reach; nor was the subcounty administration necessarily chaotic, inefficient, and open to malfeasance. In fact, during most of the imperial times, the state was able to extract enough taxes to meet its normal needs and maintain social order in most of the country. What made this possible was a wide variety of informal institutions in local communities that grew out of the interaction between government demands and local initiatives to carry out day-to-day governmental functions. Therefore, I prefer to use the term *governance* in this book to describe the operational realities of those informal institutions rather than *government*, which denotes the state imposition of control through formal agents and systems. Governance, in other words, was a shared process between state authorities and rural dwellers, involving predominantly endogenous arrangements that satisfied the needs of both the rulers and the villagers during the imperial period, and a combination of the formal and informal systems after 1900. The purpose of this book is to offer a detailed account of the actual operation of those institutions in Chinese villages in the late nineteenth and early twentieth centuries.

Focusing on Huailu county in Hebei province of North China, this study seeks to shed light on three major issues. The first is the traditional patterns of rural governance and their implications for understanding the nature of the Chinese state before the twentieth century. The prevailing perceptions of the imperial Chinese state have centered on the bureaucratic system, ranging from the imperial court to the yamen of the county magistrate, including its formal organizations as well as informal and illicit elements.[2] Few, however, have paid attention to the administrative process below the county office, especially governing activities in peasant communities. Owing in large part to the unavailability of documentation at the village level, much of the conventional wisdom on village administration remains limited to the statutory frameworks and methods of rural control attempted by the early Qing rulers and their deterioration in the late seventeenth and early eighteenth centuries (Hsiao 1960; Ch'ü 1962; Watt 1972). With regard to land taxation, likewise, we know most about the official representation and elite discourse on the methods, legal or illegal, used in tax collection and long-term changes in the tax burden during the imperial and Republican periods (Wang 1973a and 1973b; Zelin 1984). Without access to local records on land taxation, however, few have systematically examined the process of tax collection and administration at the bottom of society. To get a complete and more realistic picture of the Chinese state and its interactions with village society, it is necessary to shift attention from the state apparatus to informal institutions at the grassroots level that performed everyday government functions.

An empirical study of the local governing process will also permit a deep look into the inner workings of village communities and patterns of peasant behavior. Despite the many studies on rural China that have focused on the peasant economy and collective action in the nineteenth and early twentieth centuries, we know very little about the motives and strategies of the villagers in daily community affairs; much is to be done to alter the old view of Chinese peasants as ignorant, docile individuals vulnerable to the abuse and tyranny of the powerful with in and outside their community.[3] This study examines the peasants in a social context in which established practices, shared assumptions, and power relations combined to motivate and constrain the villagers in their pursuit of self-interest and collective goals. This approach will enable us to obtain a picture of the villagers that enriches as well as revises the traditional images of Chinese peasants and village communities.

A third objective of this book is to scrutinize changes in rural administration after 1900. Studies of village politics in late Qing and Republican China have overwhelmingly concentrated on protests, revolts, and revolutions of rural dwellers in defiance of abusive elites and government officials. This focus on contentious politics in rural society has much do to with scholars' overriding concern with social unrest that led to the sweeping triumph of the Communist revolution in the first half of the twentieth century. This study instead turns to the orderly changes intended by the government and rural elites in that period, most noticeably the installation of the formally elected village government, the founding of primary schools, and new measures in land taxation. While competition and conflict were unavoidable when those reforms were introduced to the rural society, their successful implementation in the villages entailed consensual efforts among all participants, including the government, the elites, and ordinary villagers. In this study, I analyze these changes in a discursive context in which traditional values and assumptions about power and leadership interacted with a new set of political notions and concepts that accompanied the advent of the formal institutions to shape the consciousness of rural dwellers. My emphasis is on how changing values and popular notions about authority and legitimacy were translated into action to form the strategies of both the notables and the ordinary in village politics. A close examination of both the institutional and discursive changes will help us understand whether the villages under study underwent a transition from the traditional pattern of governance based on informal, indigenous practices to a new one under externally imposed, formal institutions before the Japanese invasion and the subsequent Communist revolution in the late 1930s and 1940s.

South-Central Hebei as a Core

An important reason I chose Huailu county as the locality for this study is its location in the south-central Hebei plain, a core area of the North China "macroregion."[4] In his discussion of regional development of Chinese cities in imperial times, Skinner depicts agrarian China as composed of nine "physiographic macroregions" corresponding to the country's drainage basins (Skinner 1977: 210–49, 275–351).[5] For all its defects and inaccuracies, this concept is still useful and valid for understanding the regional patterns of economic and social formations in imperial China, given the undeniable facts that the country comprised ecologically and culturally distinct regions and that within each macroregion conspicuous distinctions in population density, land fertility, and commercialization existed between core and periphery.[6] Past studies have examined in varying detail the rural conditions in different macroregions.[7] Most studies of North China, however, have focused on its peripheral areas. These include the Huaibei region (Perry 1980), the Japanese (Mantetsu)-surveyed villages located mainly in northeastern Hebei and northwestern Shandong (Myers 1970; P. Huang 1985; Duara 1988), northwestern and southwestern Shandong (Esherick 1987), and the Hebei-Henan-Shandong boarder area (Pomeranz 1993; Thaxton 1997).[8] These studies show that the ecological settings, social conditions, and popular culture varied widely in North China. In general, however, the dominant view of this region has been associated with the image of an insecure natural environment, low-yield dryland farming, and villages of predominantly owner-cultivators. It has been observed that the harsh farming conditions and the consequent scarcity in areas such as Huaibei and northeastern Hebei made peasants vulnerable to the repeated ravages of natural disaster, which often stripped them of all means of subsistence and forced them to migrate. The high rate of migration in and out of villages in turn resulted in weakened lineage organizations, evident in the fact that most villages were multiple-surname communities. In contrast, south-central Hebei has consistently been a core area of the North China macroregion. Located in the piedmont plain east of the Taihang Mountains, south-central Hebei was relatively secure from the frequent droughts, floods, and waterlogging that had long threatened many other parts of the North China plain. This ecological security, coupled with a highly developed well-irrigation system, permitted a high level of land fertility and population density in the region.

What interests us here is the correlation of ecological settings with the pattern of human activities. Elizabeth Perry, in her study of peasant revolts in Huaibei, an area she equates with the periphery of North China, argues that there is a close connection between natural environment and human choices. She finds that difficult and insecure conditions tended to give rise to collective violence, or "aggressive survival strategies," because of heightened competition over scarce resources. It is thus her central proposition that "peripheral zones may have been especially prone to enduring traditions of rural unrest. Defined by inhospitable ecological circumstances, peripheral areas could well have set the stage for violent forms of peasant adaptation [to the local environment they inhabited]" (Perry 1980: 261). What remains unidentified are the characteristics of social arrangements in the ecologically stable areas. My examination of the peasants' strategies for coping with natural and social environments in the core zone of North China reveals a pattern of village communities and village-state relations that differed substantially from that in the peripheral areas. In general, the villages in south-central Hebei displayed greater collectivity and solidarity than those in the rest of North China. One of the central purposes of this book thus is to show how ecological security and social stability in the core area gave rise to cohesive village organizations and communal practices in local governance.

Given the regional differences in local ecological and social conditions and administrative practices, throughout this study I warn against making national-level generalizations without fully considering regional variations. I frequently compare the area under investigation with other areas, in particular Southeast China and the Yangzi delta, in order to highlight the contrasts between the core and peripheries within North China and to obtain a more precise and complete picture of village society.

County Government Archives

In addition to its location in the core area, an equally important reason to study Huailu county is its rich collection of archives pertaining to village administration. Currently preserved at Hebei Provincial Archives in Shijiazhuang city, the "old regime" archives of Huailu county government include over 5,000 files (*juan*) on a wide range of issues concerning land taxation and local administration. The files I have used in this study date from the beginning of the Guangxu reign (1875) to the eve of the Japanese occupation (1936), a period that witnessed the transition from imperial control of rural society to the vigorous state-making process under the Guomindang government.[9] These materials fall largely into two broad categories. One is documents generated by different levels of official agencies, including the provincial government, the county magistrate (the county head after 1928), his yamen offices, and gentry-controlled "self-government" bodies of the early twentieth century. These records provide details on the workings of every aspect of local administration. They allow us to see, for example, how the tax burden was determined by negotiation between the government and local elites, how the county yamen maximized its tax revenue by investigating illegal deeds and unregistered land, and how the state taxed people through formal and informal agents.

The vast majority of the Huailu archival files, however, are records of administrative cases. Unlike civil disputes over land, debt, marriage, inheritance, and the like that involved common people of the peasant society, administrative disputes mainly had to do with local administrative service and occurred primarily between the administrative agents on the one hand and community members on the other. Chinese archivists thus classify these cases into the general categories of *neizheng* (internal administration), *xingzheng* (administration), or simply *tianfu* (land taxation). Archival records on these disputes include plaints and counterplaints filed by villagers and petitions from village leaders. These files thus allow us to see how the disputes were adjudicated by the county court or mediated by peasant communities. They also permit an up-close examination of village practices pertaining to local governance, such as the selection of village agents, their relationships with local communities and with the county yamen, the taxation of land deeds, the investigation of unregistered "black land," the transfer of tax liabilities, the creation of village government and local schools, and so forth.

Other sources I refer to in this study include local gazetteers of the imperial, Republican, and contemporary periods, the *wenshi ziliao* or recollections of local history published in recent decades by "renmin zhengzhi xieshang huiyi" (People's Political Consultative Conference) at different levels, as well as government statistics and research papers by scholars of the 1930s. It is noteworthy that the field survey reports produced by researchers of the Japanese Southern Manchurian Railway Company (Mantetsu), a major source that has informed past studies of North China, also include data on the farming conditions in two villages of Huailu county, Macun and Dongjiao (Hokushi keizai chosajo 1940; Kahoku sogo chosa kenkyujo 1944). Although these two surveys contain no data about the social and political institutions in the villages, their detailed records of labor use, cropping patterns, land output, and peasant income nicely supplement the archival materials that I have used in this study.

Village Governance

VILLAGE AUTONOMY VERSUS STATE DOMINANCE

Two contrasting approaches have shaped traditional interpretations of village-state relations in imperial China. One presumes an autocratic state capable of penetrating all the way down to every village and household through the imposed groupings of rural households known as *baojia* for neighborhood surveillance and *lijia* for adult male registration and tax collection (see Chapter 3 for full explanations). These devices, we are told, allowed the state to use the rural agents as its tool to exert authority in local society. By putting all aspects of rural life under its direction and supervision, the state successfully prevented the growth of any forms of local autonomy or self-government.[10]

The other approach presumes autonomous communities operating against government control. The idea that Chinese society functioned autonomously was quite popular in the early twentieth century in both Western scholarship and Chinese writings. In his analysis of Chinese social organizations, for example, Max Weber consistently emphasized the existence of communal autonomy and its tension with the patrimonial monarchy. According to Weber, the autonomy and cohesion of Chinese villages stemmed from local self-governing bodies, which carried out duties such as road improvement, river dredging, local defense, criminal control, schooling, and funeral and burial services; no less important were the clan organizations in community life, as evidenced in the supremacy of clan elders' power and ancestral halls. It was clan solidarity based on the cult of ancestors that "withstood the ruthless encroachments of the patrimonial administration," resulting in a constant clash between patrimonial rule from above and the clans' strong counterbalance from below (Weber 1951: 86–87).

Despite their contrasting views of local administration, the above two approaches have one assumption in common—that is, the dichotomous opposition between state and society. Local governance was perceived as a realm of either omnipresent state influence or predominantly local autonomous practices. To a degree, this paradigm of binary opposition between state control and local autonomy may be ascribed to the fact that earlier scholarship on local government was largely based on traditional source materials, mainly official documents, local gazetteers, and private writings. As Kung-chuan Hsiao complained, these sources are marred with "possible biases, inaccuracies, partiality, dishonesty, or carelessness," for they were written from the standpoint of either the government or the literate, particularly the gentry (Hsiao 1960: vi–viii). It is no wonder that one often finds in those writings a juxtaposition of the idealized image of state control with various counter-ideals that were depicted as full of flaws.

Moreover, in the absence of reliable empirical studies, scholars could only perceive and interpret the different forms of village governance in the context of theoretical constructs then available and appealing to them. The very absence of a formal government below the county level and the prevalence of self-governing bodies in local society prompted scholars to treat them as forms of self-government in opposition to the autocratic state. Likewise, in the 1950s and 1960s when the theory of "oriental despotism" was prevalent (e.g., Wittfogel 1957), scholars tended to perceive the Chinese state as despotic and penetrative, and dismissed baojia and its variants merely as tools of state control that had nothing to do with autonomy and self-government (Hsiao 1960; Ch'ü 1962; Balazs 1964; Watt 1972; and Fu 1993).

Dissatisfaction with this paradigm has caused scholars to seek a sophisticated alternative construct for understanding the complexity of village-state relations in imperial China. The constant tension and conflicts between state and society, as recent studies have revealed, did not preclude their mutual dependence in local administration.[11] In the resolution of civil disputes in Qing China, for instance, many disputes were resolved by neither the informal method of community or kin mediation nor formal court adjudication, but instead by the working of a "third realm" of civil justice, in which both the formal and informal systems participated and interacted with each other (P. Huang 1993b). In the day-to-day operation of the county government, for another example, the ostensibly "formal" county court employed a large number of "informal" or illicit clerks and runners who were not subject to any statutory administrative regulations. While acting as agents of the state, they were simultaneously an occupational group rooted in the local community, thus functionally mediating between state and society (Reed 2000). For Chen Hongmou, a model bureaucrat in eighteenth-century China, effective administration rested on communal self-management as well as heightened government efforts; local initiative and state activism were complementary rather than incompatible in the actual practice of governance (Rowe 2001).

Together, these recent findings suggest a new direction in which we can explore a more dynamic and complicated relationship between state and society. The dichotomy between state control and local autonomy that prevailed in earlier studies of local administration was inadequate to explain the complex realities of rural governance; we need an alternative conceptual framework built on solid empirical researches. For this purpose, this study moves attention from the activities of the bureaucrats and their underlings at and above the county level, which have concerned the aforementioned studies in recent years, to the governing process in village communities.

PRACTICES IN HUAILU VILLAGES

Villages in late nineteenth- and early twentieth-century Huailu county adopted neither the original statutory baojia and lijia systems that were officially promoted in early Qing nor illegal arrangements banned by the government. What prevailed in the local communities was a form of voluntary cooperation among villagers who shouldered administrative tasks that had been performed by the baojia and lijia personnel. The key position in the cooperation was the *xiangdi*, who acted as an intermediary between the county yamen and his village. Chosen from local dwellers by annual rotation, the xiangdi performed a variety of tasks delegated by the county magistrate. He was required, for example, to report local crimes and help yamen runners to arrest criminals or bring summoned disputants to court. He was also responsible for issuing official deeds, prompting the payment of deed taxes, and investigating untaxed deeds and unregistered land. And it was his duty to collect irregular levies and provide facilities on the magistrate's instruction. The xiangdi, as shown in Chapter 3, performed the same functions as the rural agents under the previous baojia system.

However, the xiangdi was not just an agent of the government. He also served the needs of fellow villagers and represented his community before the county yamen. This was evident in his roles in all activities pertaining to land taxation. Unlike the statutory tax system that required villagers to pay taxes individually, a common practice in Huailu and neighboring counties was for the xiangdi to pay in advance all of the taxes of the community members during the collection period, using public village funds or loans; he then collected his monies from individual households after the taxes had been paid. The villagers preferred this cooperative arrangement because the xiangdi's collective payment of taxes saved them the time and expense of delivering the taxes individually. Moreover, it precluded the intrusion into local communities of tax-prompting yamen runners under the official tax system and also made it impossible for tax farmers from outside to extort additional taxes from individual taxpayers, a phenomenon not uncommon in many parts of North China.

Subcounty administration in Huailu was characterized by a variety of cooperative arrangements among community members. The key to understanding the prevalence of cooperation in local governance, I will argue, lay in the fact that most villages in the area under study were highly cohesive communities of predominantly owner-cultivators. Endowed with a secure ecological setting where the absence of frequent natural calamities minimized migration, the villagers developed over time tight kinship networks and a strong identity with the community. With the support of village conventions and shared principles, they cooperated in community projects that benefited all members. Such cooperative practices were of course not limited to the villages in Huailu and other counties of south-central Hebei. We will find that similar cooperation existed in other areas as well, such as the lower Yangzi region and southeastern China, where comparable ecological conditions, property relations, and social networks prevailed.

SUBSTANTIVE GOVERNMENT

My examination of local administrative disputes shows that the magistrate rarely interfered with the working process of village institutions when they functioned to generate the expected taxes and social order. He stepped in only when disputes arose that disrupted the normal operation of those institutions and when the community failed to mediate on its own. And the magistrate acted on those occasions only as an arbitrator. In fact, this noninterference approach was not limited to Huailu county, but was a standard method of conducting government widely seen in imperial and early Republican China, despite variations in the ways local communities interacted with the government. What we can find from the case of Huailu county, however, is an accurate picture of how the magistrate routinely dealt with villages and how local arrangements worked to benefit both the government and the community.

From the rulers' point of view, the government's assignment of tasks to local communities and the promotion of cooperative practices in the villages had two obvious advantages. First, it freed them from the mundane task of dealing with individual villagers in tax collection and police control and saved them the expense of hiring additional underlings to perform those tasks. Second and more important, it reduced illicit practices in administrative activity. A deeply rooted conviction among the ruling elites throughout the imperial period was that the involvement of yamen underlings in local administration would inevitably result in malfeasance, for the self-interested and underpaid underlings were always in a position to engage in wrongdoing to enrich themselves at the cost of local people. Allowing the community to shoulder those official duties instead could solve the problem because local agents were always subject to the scrutiny of the community, and their abuses, if any, could be handled by the community itself.

Therefore, the imperial rulers preferred to minimize government intervention in local governance and to encourage villagers' voluntary cooperation in fulfilling their duties to the government. As long as the informal institutions of local communities proved able to meet the government's need for tax income and local control, the state showed no inclination to extend its reach further down than the county level; instead it allowed local communities and their own agents to assume all administrative tasks of the government. The communal arrangements in Huailu villages fell well within the scope of voluntary cooperation the state promoted.

In this study, I use the term *substantive government* to characterize the government's noninterference, laissez-faire orientation and the predominance of informal practices in subcounty administration. This term emphasizes the fusion of government purposes into local, unofficial arrangements and distinguishes this reality from the long-used standard practices that prevailed in the formal, centralized bureaucratic system at and above the county level. Unlike formalistic administration, which ideally precludes informal elements and nonstandardized practices, substantive government was a realm in which both the government and society participated and where governmental functions intermeshed with local arrangements.[12] The primary goal of the state in this realm was to ensure that the public order be maintained and its financial needs be met to the extent that they would not jeopardize local stability. So long as these demands were satisfied, the state felt no need to involve itself in the process of local governance. Instead, in order to achieve its goals, the state opened the realm to local communities and encouraged their participation when local initiatives did not infringe on state interests. Local society, too, found it to their advantage to develop cooperative, self-governing arrangements to deal with the government and minimize its disruptive intrusion. We thus find in substantive government a common ground where the interests of the state and the village society converged. This was a realm, however, that must be distinguished from various illegal practices in local administration that encroached on the prerogatives of the state and therefore suffered its ceaseless attacks and prohibitions. It should also be distinguished from forms of local "autonomy" that ruled out government influence from the community.

The Chinese Peasant

There has been a substantial amount of scholarly literature on Chinese peasants in recent decades, dealing with issues such as peasants' engagement in family farming for self-consumption, their involvement in domestic and international markets, their social mobility and dislocation, and their participation in rebellious and revolutionary movements in the modern era. What remains largely obscure, however, is the everyday experience of the peasants in community life, especially their strategies for survival in the context in which communal norms and values were interwoven with individual interests and power relations. By and large, past studies of village politics in imperial and Republican China have tended to concentrate on elites, be they gentry, clan elders, or headmen of endogenous village associations, rather than ordinary peasants.

This study shifts the focus from the dominant to the dominated. My account of peasant behavior is based on a variety of "administrative cases" from Huailu villages, which involved disputes over two sets of issues. One had to do with the collection and payment of land taxes, surcharges, middlemen's commissions, and school contributions or tuition. The other pertained to the election and appointment of villagers to local positions, including the xiangdi, village heads, schoolmasters, and teachers. These cases permit a close look at the functioning of various cooperative arrangements, administrative institutions, kinship organizations, and power relations, as well as the less visible aspects of community life, such as communal norms, values, and beliefs. Together, they bring to light a peasant world in which the villagers cooperated on the basis of institutional arrangements and shared assumptions, and at the same time engaged in rivalry and even assault in the face of competition and conflicts of interest.

MORAL COMMITMENT VERSUS SELF-INTEREST

The social behavior of the peasants may be seen as combining their pursuit of self-interest with their moral commitment to community norms and conventions. I propose that both the rational calculation of personal gain and the constraints of normative requirements played a significant role in shaping their strategies for involvement in community activities. This is especially clear when we look at the working realities of established practices and conventions pertaining to cooperation in administrative and self-governing activities.

Known to local residents as "village regulations" (*cungui*), "local regulations" (*xianggui*), or "old regulations" (*jiugui*), such arrangements had existed in local communities for generations and varied widely in different localities, reflecting the diversity of social ties, interest patterns, and power configurations in the peasant society. Although acknowledged by all community members, these regulations usually lacked codified texts. They were publicly discussed and came to the attention of the government only when disputes broke out. Indeed, it is primarily in plaints and petitions from the villagers that we find the concrete stipulations of those regulations.

The central importance of such regulations was most evident in the handling of administrative cases. When filing a complaint, for example, a plaintiff typically started with a statement about relevant cungui and went on to accuse his opponent of violating the regulations. In his initial reaction to the complaint, the magistrate normally instructed the community leader (usually the village head) to mediate the dispute in accordance with local regulations. If the mediation was successful, the village head would report back that the dispute had been settled in compliance with the village regulations. If the disputes evolved into a court session, the magistrate would invariably adhere to local regulations in making a ruling.[13] In no dispute did I find any villagers who openly challenged their cungui; instead, they unanimously acknowledged the central importance of the regulations in community life. When they quarreled, it was usually not the regulation itself but about their own qualifications or lack of qualifications for serving the xiangdi or other offices. By and large, these conventional regulations remained effective in the 1910s and 1920s.

The village regulations are critical to our analysis of the peasant society, for they not only guided economic practices and social exchanges in peasant communities, but also reflected the shared principles and normative commitments of community members. Two basic principles stand out as common to these village regulations: reciprocity and the right to subsistence. By the cungui in most Huailu villages, the xiangdi had the duty to pay in advance taxes on behalf of his fellow villagers; in return, the villagers had the obligation to repay him before a designated date. Likewise, according to the cungui, the xiangdi was responsible for all of the costs associated with his payment of the taxes, and the villagers compensated the xiangdi by allowing him to act as a middleman in the sale of all kinds of commodities and paying him a commission. In most communities, the cungui also linked the burden of xiangdi service to one's landholding or tax liability. The more land a person owned, the more years he served as the xiangdi. Households with less than the minimum amount of land required for one-year's service were exempted from the burden, obviously because they could not afford the expenses involved in performing the xiangdi duties. This arrangement brings to mind the "subsistence ethic" that James C. Scott explicated in his study of peasant society in Southeast Asia. This ethic assumes that all members of a community have a presumptive right to a living so far as local resources will allow. As a moral principle, it enables peasants to create and maintain a social practice that insures the weakest against crisis by making certain demands on better-off villagers. This right to subsistence, Scott argued, produces a redistributive effect and works as a shock absorber during economic crises in peasant life (1976: 40–41).

The villagers in Huailu, however, were not always committed to community norms and regulations; they were goal-directed, calculating agents as well, who chose strategies that best served their individual ends after taking into account all factors, symbolic and material, that concerned their interests and evaluating all alternative routes of action. Thus, while the villagers cooperated to achieve collective benefits that they could not obtain as individuals and accepted communal arrangements that served their purposes under normal conditions, they might turn to alternative options when circumstances changed. For example, some villagers competed for the position of xiangdi when it was very profitable; when providing the service became burdensome, however, they tended to evade it, using whatever pretexts were available to them. My examination of disputes over tax payment also demonstrates that the villagers tended to repay the xiangdi in a timely manner for the tax duties he had advanced on their behalf where the village regulation prescribed their mutual obligations in this regard. Disputes took place more often where the communities fell short of such cooperative conventions. And taxpayers were most likely to be derelict when the tax collector was from outside the community, feeling no normative obligation to outsiders or other communities. The actions of the villagers thus varied under different circumstances; they could be at once moral community members subject to normative constraints, and self-interested individuals focused on maximizing material gains. Despite their seemingly contradictory propositions, both the "moral economy" thesis and the "rational-choice" theory are partly applicable to the analysis of village politics in late Qing and Republican Huailu, but neither of them could fully explain the complexity of peasant behaviors.[14]

UNDERSTANDING PEASANT BEHAVIORS

To understand the patterns of peasant actions, this study considers two sets of factors that influenced their strategies for participation in collective events. One was the social context of the community that comprised a wide array of institutions, ranging from kinship ties, power structure, and property relations to explicit regulations and implicit norms, values, and principles, of which the most important was no doubt the perceived supremacy of cungui in the community. Together, these institutions informed the villagers' "durable dispositions" or *habitus*, to borrow from Pierre Bourdieu, which shaped their perceptions and attitudes, and made their motives and actions readily intelligible to all members of the community (Bourdieu 1976; 1977: 72 and 80). The other was the immediate situation that confronted individuals, which changed from time to time and from person to person. Serving as village head or schoolmaster, for example, could be an honorable and lucrative opportunity at one time and a thankless burden at another. A household of average means, in another instance, could well afford to serve the community as a xiangdi under normal conditions. However, if misfortune struck, continuing the service could lead to disaster for the whole family. Therefore, what defined the possibilities and limits of a person's strategies, I will argue, were not only the shared principles or dispositions embedded in the community but also the specific situations in which the individual deliberated and acted.[15]

It is in this context that the actions of ordinary villagers as well as the notables could be properly explained. The villagers chose to abide by local regulations under normal conditions because conformity to such arrangements was necessary to maintain one's social standing and economic security in the community. Anyone who failed to perform his duties as prescribed by the regulations ran the risk of being denounced by and isolated from the rest of the community, and consequently being denied access to the collectively produced goods of the group. It follows that to fulfill one's obligatory duties was in itself the most important means of ensuring subsistence in the village. It was not uncommon, to be sure, for a villager to deliberately shirk his duty or vie for a profitable job in violation of community conventions. To do so, however, he had to couch his action in the language of observing or defending village regulations and limit his wrongdoing to a degree that minimized the damage to his standing. Overt denial of normative duties and flagrant violation of community conventions rarely occurred in such circumstances.

Much the same can be said about the powerful in the community. Living in a social network that comprised many forms of patron-client relationship, people of means and influence were always in a position to abuse their power by protecting those they favored at the expense of others. Nevertheless, as community leaders whose status rested mainly on their reputation and the trust of community members, the powerful were subject to the same community norms and informal sanctions in the form of rumor, gossip, ridicule, and even open denunciation as ordinary villagers. They could not afford to brazenly abuse their influence or openly breach established rules, for fear of losing their reputation. Quite the contrary, the notables had to actually or at least ostensibly support the accepted norms and practices in order to uphold their prestige, which was indispensable for maintaining their leadership in the community.

Obviously, the moral obligation to adhere to community norms or the rational calculation of self-interest alone cannot explain peasant actions and village solidarity. For most villagers, conformity to community regulations should be seen as the optimal strategy for maintaining their well-being, rather than merely the result of internalizing community norms and values. However, unlike a rational actor in the highly developed market economy who can base decisions on personal preferences or utility maximization, individuals in the precapitalist community had to take into account normative constraints and commitments linked to the specific group as well as their private interests and personal goals (North 1998). Villages in Huailu, after all, were social spaces where explicit institutions were interwoven with implicit principles and diffuse sanctions to empower and constrain the actors in their pursuit of private gain and collective goals. It was the interaction between shared group principles and personal circumstances that shaped their strategies for the production and reproduction of both material and symbolic capital. We cannot fully understand the Chinese peasants and their diverse strategies unless they are perceived in this context.[16]

"State-Making" in the Village

North China villages underwent many institutional changes as a result of the implementation of the New Policy (*xinzheng*) for economic, educational, and administrative modernization after 1900. By and large, we can identify two distinct phases in which these changes took place. The first was the late Qing and early Republican period from 1904 to 1927. The most important development during those years was the introduction of the "self-government" (*difang zizhi*) program, especially the creation of the village head (*cunzheng* or *cunzhang*) position and the establishment of new-style primary schools in many villages. The second was the late 1920s and early 1930s, when the Guomindang government took further measures to penetrate rural society such as the installation of a formal government at the ward (*qu*) level and the reorganization of village government into artificial administrative units called *xiang*. As the administrative apparatus expanded at the subcounty level, government expenditures mounted, entailing increases in the tax burden in the form of multiplying surcharges.

THREE VIEWS OF STATE-MAKING IN RURAL CHINA

Recent studies have identified three patterns of political changes under the rubric of "state-making" in early twentieth-century rural China. The first was the breakdown of traditional communities owing to the increasing pressure of state penetration, as evidenced by the withdrawal of local elites from village government, who had spoken in behalf of local communities. It occurred when the tax burden increased and village leaders felt unwilling to perform their thankless duties of tax collection at the risk of alienating themselves from fellow villagers. Many thus resigned from office, leaving a political vacuum that permitted the rise of "village bullies and tyrants," a phenomenon that became prevalent in North China villages in the 1920s and 1930s (P. Huang 1985: 264–74, 289–91; Duara 1988: 159–60, 181, 252). Whereas the breakdown of traditional village leadership took place mainly in disaster-prone areas where community ties were tenuous, in solidary villages based on strong lineage organizations and/or strong elite leadership a pattern of community "closure" prevailed. To resist bureaucratic intrusion and multiplying impositions, the elites in these localities organized their communities as a "united community front" (P. Huang 1985: 259–64). As the tension between state and village increased, they assumed the leadership of armed resistance, which often involved the participation of the entire village (see also Perry 1980: 163–207 and Prazniak 1999: 45–91).

Unlike the two views described above that highlight the failure of state-making and its disruptive impact on the countryside in the early twentieth century, the third underscores the growing capabilities of the state in regulating political and economic activities in local society. In his study of the Hebei-Henan-Shandong border region, Kenneth Pomeranz describes the government as both a "more successful donor," able to provide and improve police, public health, and other key services to local society, and a "more successful extractor." The result of state-making in this region thus was the simultaneous strengthening of state and society (Pomeranz 1993: 272). Susan Mann observes that there were compromises between state and society in the course of state-making, as seen in tax-farming in the collection of *lijin* (transit tax) in the early twentieth century. Rather than treating these profiteering businesses in taxation as signs of the state's inability to penetrate local society, Mann interprets their acceptance as "useful compromises" that contributed to the historical process of state-building in all societies and were "essential steps on the road to success" for China's modern state-builders. In general, proponents of this approach identify state-making in early twentieth-century China as a successful process, comparable to that in early-modern Europe (S. Mann 1987: 6).

It must be acknowledged that the process of state-making in different areas of early twentieth-century China varied in different local ecological and social settings. Therefore the above three patterns of state-village relations were likely to prevail in regions with different conditions. Exactly how these trends affected the everyday operation of power structures and popular perceptions of local leadership, however, has not been made clear in previous studies. Moreover, despite recent scholarship on rural North China that has discussed the enforcement and malfunctioning of newly instituted administrative agencies and popular protests against internal decay and external intrusions, much of the scholarly attention has concentrated on either the late Qing period when the New Policy took effect or the Guomindang period when state penetration accelerated. Almost no research has been done on changes in village politics during the interim between 1912 and 1927. The dominant image of Chinese politics during this period is one of disunity, corruption, and chaos under warlordism. This image is largely true of political and military competition between rival warlords. However, once we shift attention from the obvious national phenomena to local political process, a different picture emerges that shows many significant and meaningful developments. My examination of village politics after 1900 thus concentrates on the early Republican years and their differences from the Guomindang era in order to highlight continuity and change in village leadership in the early twentieth century.

OBVIOUS CHANGES

One significant change in the local power structure in early twentieth-century Huailu was the formalization of local leadership. Before the twentieth century, informal leadership in rural China usually rested with those who built prestige and influence on the basis of their literacy, seniority, wealth, or social connections. After 1900 the introduction of the self-government movement allowed the rural elites to formalize their leadership through their control of village government and primary schools. Those who were most active even extended their influence beyond the village and joined urban elites to hold positions in county-level institutions, such as the deliberative assemblies and offices in charge of police, education, and financing.

This change in village leadership no doubt gave the rural elites greater influence in their localities and more opportunities for self-aggrandizement. They abused their power where social constraints and public sanctioning were weak or nonexistent. However, in tight-knit communities such as those of Huailu, where cooperative arrangements remained untouched and where they identified themselves with the rest of the community as landowners and taxpayers, the elites had to speak on behalf of the village before the government in order to defend their own interest and reproduce their reputations among the villagers. Not surprisingly, the village heads, though formally appointed by the county government, owed their loyalty primarily to the community rather than the magistrate. It was in their capacity as village heads that the local notables mobilized to combat tax escalation and abuses in the 1910s and 1920s. In the campaign to investigate unregistered and un-taxed holdings ("black land") in the early 1930s, likewise, the *xiangzhang* (head of the *xiang*) normally reported only a nominal amount of black land in his village, although the actual amount could be substantial. These facts implied that the village communities in the core area remained as solidary as before and were far from the verge of breakdown in the 1920s and 1930s. And elite leadership in behalf of local interests effectively prevented the ten-sion between village and state from mounting to the point of violent protest in Huailu county before the Japanese occupation in 1937. This reality con-trasted sharply with the withdrawal of community leaders from local gov-ernment and the resultant political decay, a phenomenon that prevailed in ecologically unstable areas.

Another significant development in local politics was the state's growing ability to assert itself in rural society. This is especially evident when the early Republican and Guomindang periods are compared. In the 1910s and 1920s, when the government was yet to extend its formal reach to the village, the magistrate relied heavily on the elites, especially urban elites active at the county seat, to start self-government projects and extract more resources from the countryside. To maintain a working relationship with them, the practical magistrate in Huailu county had to yield to the elites when the lat-ter, who were usually the largest landowners, resisted tax increases or the in-vestigation of black land. The magistrate often acted as a mediator between the provincial government and local elites, rather than as a representative of the state.

This situation, however, came to an end after 1928 when the Guomin-dang government took resolute steps to weaken the presence of urban elites and to extend the formal bureaucracy below the county level. In addition to dissolving the county assembly, a stronghold of the urban elites, and creating the formally elected xiang and supra-village *qu* (ward) governments that an-swered more directly to the county head, the new regime took radical meas-ures to update tax administration. It took back the tasks of tax transfer, tax-roll updating, land-deed writing and investigation by unofficial agents and handed them over to the newly created ward government offices. These moves signified a departure from the traditional methods of rural gover-nance relying on local, informal personnel. Thus in Huailu villages during the successive waves of state-making before 1937 we find a concurrence of tighter state control over local society and the formalization of local admin-istration that enhanced the leadership of rural elites.

PERCEPTIONS AND REPRESENTATIONS

Modernization in local administration caused not only conspicuous development in local leadership and village-state relations, but also subtle yet significant changes in the way people perceived the changing power structures and articulated their interests. The establishment of village government and primary schools in the late Qing and Republican years, for example, was accompanied by the intrusion of a nationwide discourse on "self-government," which presupposed the priority of national goals over the objectives of the community and individuals, the supremacy of "modern" national systems over traditional local institutions, and the legitimacy of formal legal principles instead of informal moral norms.

Rural elites who embraced the imposed institutions as new opportunities for personal gain enthusiastically mastered the new language of official discourse and used it to fashion their public exchanges with the government and among themselves. We thus found in disputes over village leadership that the traditional notion of the diffuse power of community leaders based on their seniority and reputation gradually yielded to a new assumption that village headship should be based on legal, formal election and the principle of division of duties, as well as proper age and education. It was also publicly accepted, for instance, that the new-style primary schools were not only more "scientific" than the traditional private school (*sishu*) for eliminating illiteracy, but also a critical means of training modern citizenry and saving the Chinese nation from the perils of imperialism. State-making, in this light, was not only the creation of a formal national system in place of local institutions, but also the establishment of the dominance of the national political discourse in public debate at the local level.

This is not to suggest, of course, that external ideas superseded or prevailed over traditional assumptions of the villagers in the early twentieth century. Quite the reverse; the villagers often reacted to the enforcement of new institutions by expressing their own values and notions. While the village head or the schoolmaster may have used the external language to legitimize and disguise his own self-interested actions, the ordinary villagers expressed their anger and resentment by the various means available to them, including private chatting, cursing, spreading rumors, and even revenge. The "hidden transcripts" or "discourse that takes place 'offstage,' beyond direct observation by powerholders" is equally important for understanding peasant reactions to state penetration (Scott 1990: 4).

Village discourse in early twentieth-century Huailu county thus was often a mix of old notions rooted in the community and new concepts borrowed from outside. The elites, as the primary beneficiaries of the new institutions, could use both the vocabulary of official discourse on state-making to justify their newly obtained privileges and popular values to legitimize their power within the community. Likewise, the ordinary villagers, while adhering to traditional values to justify their claims, did not hesitate to appeal to exogenous concepts to defend their interests. Thus was a transition in the popular vision of power and legitimacy already under way in early twentieth-century rural society.

To understand the changes and continuity in village governance in the early twentieth century, then, we must expand our attention from institutional changes to symbolic areas where the discursive hegemony of imposed systems interacted dynamically with the legitimizing power of embedded assumptions. Village communities in early twentieth-century China, in other words, were places where endogenous institutions coexisted with the newly created systems, and where the shared values, attitudes, and assumptions mixed with the invading ideas and rhetoric of the state. State-making in the core area of rural North China was neither a lineal development nor a complete failure during the late Qing and Republican periods, but a gradual process in which national systems and ideas penetrated the village to coexist with or replace local arrangements and popular values and to refashion the strategies and perceptions of both the notable and the ordinary in the village.

PART ONE

Local Practices

CHAPTER 2

The Setting

The economic and social institutions in village communities are closely related to local ecological settings, such as climate, topography, water supply, land yield, population density, and residential patterns. To understand why cooperative practices existed in south-central Hebei villages and why the peasant communities showed extraordinary stability and solidarity during the imperial and early Republican periods, an examination of the natural environment and its relationship with human activities in this area is indispensable.

The villages in south-central Hebei, like those in the rest of the North China Plain, were predominantly communities of owner-cultivators. However, unlike the disaster-prone, low-yield peripheral areas in North China, south-central Hebei was free of constant natural catastrophe due to its piedmont topography and a developed well-irrigation and drainage system. This, together with a warm climate and moderate precipitation, allowed a diversified cropping pattern and high-level land fertility, which further supported a high population density and economic commercialization.[1] These favorable circumstances characterized south-central Hebei as a core of the North China macroregion and distinguished it from the peripheral areas.

The Locality

Hebei province, as well as the whole North China Plain, comprises ecologically different regions. Outside of the mountain areas on the western and northern sides of the province and the highland in the northwest, most of Hebei territory is vast plain area, part of the larger North China Plain. This plain area may be further divided into three distinct parts: the piedmonts to the east and south of the mountain areas, the coastal plain, and the lowland between the piedmonts and the coastal area. The piedmont east of the Tai-

Map 2. Hebei Province in 1932

hang Mountains covers approximately forty counties along the Beijing-Hankou railroad in south-central Hebei province. The core of this area, however, is the twenty-four counties surrounding Shijiazhuang city (see Map 2 and Table 4 for a list of these counties). These counties make up Shijiazhuang municipality and Shijiazhuang prefecture after 1949 (Hebei renmin chubanshe 1984: 4). Chinese agronomists term this area a "two-crops-a-year zone" to distinguish it from the "one-crop-a-year zone" of the northern and northeastern Hebei regions and the "three-crops-every-two-years zone" of coastal Hebei (HBSZ 1993, 3: 435–65).[2]

Huailu county, located in the western vicinity of today's Shijiazhuang city, had a particular place in south-central Hebei (see Map 1). Historically known as a "dry dock" (han matou), the county seat of Huailu had been a hub of local market networks that connected external markets in northern and northeastern Hebei and Shanxi provinces. The construction of the vertical Beijing–Hankou railroad in 1902 and of the horizontal Shijiazhuang–Taiyuan railroad in 1907, the two most important trunk lines in North China that intersected in Shijiazhuang (then a village of only 150 households and slightly more than 600 people in Huailu county), quickly transformed it into a bustling city of 166,700 by 1940 (Xu Zhen'an 1984; Liang Yong 1986; Yang Junke 1986; Tian Bofu 1997); after 1949 it became the capital and economic center of Hebei province.

The villages in Huailu county were mainly communities of owner-cultivators. The survival of over 230 volumes of cadastres (shence) between 1706 and 1771 from most villages of Huailu county have made it possible for Chinese historians to reconstruct its landholding pattern in the eighteenth century. These materials detailed the number of ding (adult male) of each taxpaying unit called hu (literally, "household") and the tax quotas associated with each ding, as well as the amount of land listed under the name of the ding. As their studies have revealed, owner-cultivators and landlords with ten mu or more of land made up 38.2 percent of the total number of ding (one standard mu equals ⅙ of an acre or 1/15 of a hectare). The landless (either tenants or wage laborers) accounted for 25.5 percent of the ding. The rest (36.3 percent), with holdings ranging from 1 to 9 mu, were presumably part-tenants and part-laborers (Pan and Tang 1984; see also Shi Zhihong 1984). Landowning ding thus made up 74.5 percent of all those listed on the cadastres. It should be noted that the ding used in the cadastres was not equal to a household. Although ding in many cases meant a household (in other words, one household had just one ding), some households had two or three or even more ding (Pan and Tang 1984). Therefore, households with 10 mu or more of land were definitely more than 38.2 percent of all households in the county.

The predominance of owner-cultivators in Huailu village remained unchanged in the early twentieth century. Take, for example, Macun and Dongjiao, for which we have the most detailed data regarding landholdings produced by researchers of the Japanese South Manchurian Railway Company (Mantetsu) in 1939 and the North China General Investigation Institute (Kahoku sogo chosa kenkyujo) in 1944, respectively. Macun had a population of 1,707 in 308 households, of which 67 were nonagricultural and 241 lived on farming. The arable land in this village totaled 4,209.8 mu, of which 3,192.8 mu (75.8 percent) was cultivated by landowners and 1,017.0 mu (24.2 percent) by tenants. The composition of the 241 farming households was as follows: 134 households (55.6 percent) were owner-cultivators having a total of 2,422.7 mu of arable land (57.6 percent), or 18.1 mu per household; 80 households (33.2 percent) were part-tenants with 1,532.8 mu of land (36.4 percent), or 19.2 mu per household; and 27 households (11.2 percent) were tenants with 254.3 mu of land (6.0 percent), or 9.4 mu per household (Hokushi keizai chosajo 1940: 81−87). Together, the landowning (and theoretically taxpaying) households, including owner-cultivators and part-tenants, made up 89 percent of all the farming households, each having 18.5 mu of land on average.

Dongjiao village was 2.5 kilometers west of the railway station of Shimen (Shijiazhuang) and 0.5 kilometer to the bus line that linked Shimen and the Huailu county seat. This village had been a part of Huailu county until 1939, when the Shimen municipality was created to include the former Shijiazhuang city and its vicinity. As a suburban community, this village had a much larger portion of the population living on nonagricultural activities than Macun, amounting to 50 (31.6 percent) of the 158 landowning households in 1939. Of the remaining 108 farming households, 73 (46.2 percent of the 158 households) were owner-cultivators, having a total of 1,079 mu (60.2 percent) of the arable land, or 14.8 mu per household. Thirty households were part-tenants (18.9 percent) and held 340.6 mu of land (19.0 percent), or 11.4 mu per household. There were only five (3.1 percent) tenant households with a total of 17.1 mu (1.0 percent) of land. Thus, households with varying amounts of land totaled 153 (96.8 percent) of all households in this village. The fragmentation of land ownership was obvious (Kahoku sogo chosa kenkyujo 1944: 25−28).

There are no detailed statistics available to show landholding patterns in the whole county. According to a gross estimate by the county government, 30,000 households, or 67.6 percent of the rural households in the county, were owner-cultivators who possessed a total of 600,000 mu of farming land in the early 1930s, an average of 20 mu per household. The remaining 32.4 percent (14,410 households) were part-tenants who possessed 170,782 mu of land in total, or 11.9 mu per household (Hebei tongzhi gao 1993: 1815). The Japanese researchers reported roughly the same figures: 44,374 farming households owned a total of 770,782 mu, an average of 17.3 per household in 1933 (Tenshin jimusho chosaka 1936: 14).

Taking into account all of the evidence, we may estimate that 60 to 70 percent of the households in Huailu villages were owner-cultivators with an average farm size of 15 to 20 mu. In addition, 20 to 30 percent of households were part-tenants owning a farm of roughly 10 mu on average. This predominance of owner-cultivators in Huailu county showed no significant difference from the pattern of land distribution in the North China Plain as a whole, where owner-cultivators made up 62 percent to over 71 percent of rural households.[3]

Land Use

FARMING PATTERNS

The topography, climate, and resulting farming patterns of Huailu county, and south-central Hebei as a whole, are quite different from those in the peripheral areas of the North China macroregion, in particular northeastern Hebei.[4] The piedmont plain in south-central Hebei shows a gradient varying from 1/1,000 (one foot per 1,000 feet) to 1/10,000. This gradient, combined with the ample fresh water lying only two to ten meters below ground, provides perfect conditions for well irrigation in this area, where the scarcity of river water does not permit canal irrigation (HBSZ 1993, 3: 454–56; Hou Jianxin 2001a). In addition, farming in this area benefited from warm weather favorable to most crops and a long frost-free period that permitted a diversified pattern of rotation.[5]

By comparison, northeastern Hebei is composed mainly of mountainous areas that are generally unsuitable for cropping. Cultivated land is scarce and concentrates in basins and valleys. A local saying thus characterizes this area as "*bashan yishui yifentian*," or eight-tenths mountains, one-tenth water, one-tenth land (HBSZ 1993, 3: 440). The piedmont plain to the south of Yanshan Mountain has most of the cultivated land in northeastern Hebei. Yet unlike the piedmont in south-central Hebei, where underground water was close to the surface, here the water is as deep as 100–150 meters and therefore beyond the technical abilities of peasants to gain access to. The result was a negligible portion of irrigated land in this area: only 1 percent of the cultivated land was irrigated, whereas in south-central Hebei the proportion was as high as 35 percent of cultivated land (Zhang Xingyi 1933: 13–18).[6] Moreover, the cold winter in northeastern Hebei restricted the area of winter-crop cultivation and produced a low-yield cropping pattern.[7]

To perceive the difference in cropping patterns between the two regions, consider, first, the winter crop of wheat. In the early 1930s, wheat occupied

TABLE I

Cropping Patterns in South-Central and Northeastern Hebei, the Early 1930s

Crop	South-Central Hebei			Northeastern Hebei		
	Percentage of cultivated land	Yield per mu (catties)	Cash equivalent[a] (yuan)	Percentage of cultivated land	Yield per mu (catties)	Cash equivalent (yuan)
Wheat	27.46	146	7.14	10.75	105	5.13
Barley	3.33	133	6.12	6.35	106	4.88
Cotton	17.55	30	9.60	3.20	21	6.72
Soybeans	6.50	119	5.25	9.90	115	5.07
Maize	5.63	118	3.82	17.10	146	4.73
Sorghum	11.67	132	4.32	31.30	114	3.73
Millet	33.21	168	8.05	18.05	111	5.32

SOURCE: Zhang Xingyi 1933: 20–40.

[a] The prices of the crops listed here in the major markets of Hebei province in 1931 were as follows (per 100 catties): wheat, 4.887 yuan; millet, 4.786 yuan; maize, 3.237 yuan; sorghum, 3.265 yuan; soybeans, 4.406 yuan; and cotton (ginned), 32 yuan (HBSZ 1991: 30, 52). The price for barley was 4.6 yuan per 100 catties (*Hebei tongzhi gao*: 1788–1853).

as much as 27 percent of all cultivated land in south-central Hebei, whereas in northeastern Hebei only 10.75 percent of cultivated land was devoted to that crop. At the same time, farm yield under wheat was 146 catties per mu, which was 39 percent higher than in the northeast (one standard catty [jin] equals 1.1 pounds or 0.5 kilograms) (see Table 1). Today, over half of the land planted with wheat in the province is in this area, which generates more than 60 percent of the province's total output of wheat (Hebei renmin chubanshe 1984: 404). What made possible the widespread wheat cropping and its high yield in south-central Hebei is primarily the warm weather, which allows wheat to grow through the winter in safety. In contrast, the harsh winter in northeastern Hebei (as low as -17 to -6°C in January) prohibits the planting of wheat in its mountainous area. Winter in the plain area south of Yanshan Mountain, though a bit warmer than in the mountainous area, is still too cold to grow wheat well. The weather thus greatly affects output and limits the planting area in northeastern Hebei.

Cotton was, and today remains, another major crop in south-central Hebei, owing to the area's ample heat and security from soaking and flooding. The precipitation in this area is modest, averaging 450–500 mm (millimeters) annually, while the gradient of the land provided a good condition for drainage. By contrast, in the plain area of northeastern Hebei, where cotton was rotated with other crops, cotton cultivation suffered heavy precipitation (630–820 mm per year) and waterlogging because of poor drainage (HBSZ 1993, 3: 135–37, 453, 456). Thus only 3.20 percent of cultivated land was under cotton in northeast Hebei, yielding twenty-one catties per mu, while the figures for south-central Hebei were 17.55 percent and thirty catties, respectively (see Table 1). With perfect conditions for cotton cultivation, south-central Hebei started cotton cropping as early as the Ming dynasty (1368–1644). By the Qianlong reign of the Qing (1736–95), cotton was planted in 20 to 30 percent of cultivated land here. As a result, Hebei province even surpassed most southeastern provinces in both its per unit output and the techniques of spinning and weaving. A local gazetteer claims that "eight to nine out of every ten households grew cotton" (Xie Qinglin 198; HBSZ 1995, 16: 194). During the Republican period, south-central Hebei produced fully 70 percent of the cotton in the province, and the province stood head and shoulders above all other provinces in the country in cotton output (Hebei renmin chubanshe 1984: 405).

In contrast with the preponderance of the high-yielding crops of wheat and cotton in south-central Hebei, the major crops in the northeastern area were sorghum, maize, and millet. Together, the three crops occupied two-thirds of the cultivated land in the northeast. Although the per unit yields of maize and sorghum were low in comparison with that of wheat (see Table 1), their relatively stable yields nevertheless provided peasants security of subsistence under harsh conditions. Understandably, few peasants were willing to take a risk on wheat and cotton, for they required high investment of both labor and capital and precise heat and drainage conditions.

The wide cultivation of high-yielding crops, together with a frequent rotation system, supported a higher level of land productivity in south-central Hebei than in the northeastern region.[8] In general, the net farm income after deducting all expenses (normally accounting for 57 percent of the gross income) was 4.74 yuan per mu in south-central Hebei and 3.17 yuan per mu in northeastern Hebei in the early 1930s.[9]

COMMERCIALIZATION

Cropping patterns and land productivity dictated the level of commercialization. Cotton as the major cash crop in south-central Hebei was planted primarily for market rather than family consumption. Winter wheat, another major crop in this area, was also a highly commercialized product. For personal consumption, peasants grew millet and other supplementary crops. The high percentage of farmland under cotton and wheat (totaling 45 percent of all the cultivated land) in south-central Hebei drove agricultural commercialization to a level much higher than in northeastern Hebei, where cotton and wheat occupied only 3.20 percent and 10.75 percent respectively, and their per unit farm yield was one-third lower than in south-central Hebei.

It is worth emphasizing here the role of cotton cultivation in the commercialization of rural economy in south-central Hebei. The three counties surrounding Shijiazhuang, namely Huailu in the west, Zhengding in the north, and Luancheng in the southeast, were especially known for the quantity and quality of their cotton in North China. Located in the Hutuo River region, these counties are endowed with the warm weather and clay soil that are particularly suitable for cotton growth. By 1920, farms under cotton had increased to 260,000 mu, or 40 percent of the arable land in Huailu; 240,000 mu or 50 percent in Zhengding; and 210,000 mu or 43 percent in Luancheng. The output of cotton varied from 80 or 90 to 100 catties per mu. The price of unginned cotton ranged from 12 to 15 yuan per 100 catties, whereas ginned cotton was usually priced at 25 to 30 yuan per 100 catties. The peasants sold most of the cotton they produced to local markets and kept a small amount for the production of "native cloth" for their own use and for sale. The handwoven cloth sold to local and regional markets totaled 400,000 bolts in the three counties in 1920. Huailu county alone had sixteen companies engaged in trading cotton and native cloth (Bai Jing'an 1988). The construction of Daxin Cotton Mill in Shijiazhuang in 1922 and the mushrooming cotton purchasing stations in the neighboring counties further stimulated cotton cultivation. By 1930, farms under cotton had expanded to an unprecedented 80 percent of the arable land. At the same time, the rapidly shrinking acreage of farms devoted to grain necessitated the importation of a large amount of grain to this area. However, the booming cotton and grain trade ended abruptly after 1931, when the Japanese occupied Manchuria and closed the largest cotton market in south-central Hebei by levying exorbitant import duties and at the same time dumped its cotton textile goods in North China markets. Consequently most farms quickly switched from cotton to grain in the 1930s (Jiao Shouzhi 1987). As Table 1 shows, less than 20 percent of the arable land in south-central Hebei still grew cotton in the early 1930s.

The degree of commercialization in south-central Hebei may be demonstrated by the case of Macun village in Huailu county, for which the Mantetsu investigators provided detailed data. Macun was located between the county seat of Huailu and Shijiazhuang city, with a distance of four *li* (one standard li equals 0.31 miles or 0.5 kilometers) to a railway station that connected the two cities. The cropping pattern in this village in 1939 (the year of the Mantetsu survey) was typical of the general cropping pattern in this piedmont plain. Here the villagers devoted 23.5 percent of farmland to cotton and 21.3 percent to wheat. Both crops were highly commercialized:

TABLE 2

Cropping Pattern and Commercialization in Macum Village, Huailu County, 1939

Crop	Cultivation Area per Household (mu)	Percent	Yield per Household (yuan)	Marketed Product per Household (yuan)	Percentage of Yield
Cotton	9.5	23.5	247.89	224.62	90.61
Wheat	8.6	21.3	164.57	75.25	45.73
Millet	11.2	27.7	195.96	29.06	14.83
Other	11.1	27.5	185.02	30.24	45.27
Total	40.4	100.0	793.44	359.17	45.27

SOURCE: Hokushi keizai chosajo 1940.

90.61 percent of cotton and 45.73 percent of wheat entered the market. In comparison, only 14.83 percent of millet and 16.34 percent of other miscellaneous grains were sold in the market. Cotton was the biggest source of cash income for peasant families: 62.54 percent of their cash income (247.89 yuan out of the total cash income of 359.17 yuan per household) came from the sale of cotton. Next was the sale of wheat, which generated 20.95 percent of the total cash income. Peasants in Macun thus earned 83.49 of their cash income from their cultivation of cotton and wheat (see Table 2).

The high yields from the two cash crops and their high level of commercialization in Macun created an economic surplus considerably above basic subsistence needs. Here each household, with an average of 16.78 mu of land (or 3.17 mu per capita, see Hokushi keizai chosajo 1940: 81–85), earned a yearly gross income of 1,357.76 yuan (including farm income). The net income after deducting all productive and nonproductive expenses (including tax and rent) was 1,015.71 yuan per household. Of this net income 699.40 yuan was needed for daily household expenses, leaving a surplus of 316.31 yuan per household (Hokushi keizai chosajo 1940: 7–19).

Detailed data exist for the northeastern Hebei village of Shajing in Shunyi county, north of Beijing. This village was typical of the region in its ratio of population to cultivated land and its cropping pattern. Here farmland averaged 4.1 mu per capita, very close to the average size in northeastern Hebei as a whole (3.92 mu per capita). The major crops were the low-yielding maize and sorghum, which accounted for 37.45 percent and 25.11 percent of all the cultivated land, respectively. But only 13.64 percent of

TABLE 3

Cropping Pattern and Commercialization in Shajing Village, Shunyi County, 1942

Crop	Cultivation Area per Household (mu)	Percent	Yield per Household (yuan)	Marketed Product per Household (yuan)	Percentage of Yield
Maize	10.2	37.45	218.29	41.35	18.94
Sorghum	6.8	25.11	96.59	51.18	52.98
Beans	1.4	4.98	119.47	52.65	44.07
Wheat	3.7	13.64	59.82	21.88	36.58
Millet	2.9	10.82	62.12	0	0
Cotton	0.1	.22	5.65	2.82	50.00
Others	2.1	7.78	51.24	28.00	54.65
Total	27.2	100.00	613.18	197.88	32.27

SOURCE: Chugoku noson kanko chosa kankokai, 2: 273–91.

NOTE: It is important to keep in mind, when comparing Shajing village here with Macun village in Table 2, that prices in 1942 in North China under the Japanese occupation were 2.64 times the prices in 1939 (Jia Xiuyan 1992; Zhongguo nongmin yinhang jingji yanjiuhui, n.d.).

farmland was under wheat, and cotton cropping was almost absent here. Except for millet, all of which was kept for self-consumption, a substantial portion of all other crops entered the market. The marketed produce thus accounted for 32.27 percent of total farm output, compared with 45.27 percent in Macun (Table 3).

What is important here is why the peasants in Shajing marketed their produce. To explain this, we need to consider the peasant household's budget. On average, each household earned a gross income of 613.18 yuan from farming. This income, together with income from other sources, made up a total gross income of 840.53 yuan per household. The household's annual expenditure (including cultivation and living expenses), however, amounted to 966.58 yuan. Instead of an economic surplus, this expenditure resulted in a deficit of 126.05 yuan per household (Chugoku noson kanko chosa kankokai 2: 290–91). Unlike cultivators in Macun village in south-central Hebei, who cropped and marketed wheat and cotton to maximize their economic surplus, here the peasants sold their crops primarily to pay their rent and taxes and to purchase household necessities.

I have not intended here to develop a complete characterization of commercialization in northeastern and south-central Hebei. Yet the comparison between the two villages, each representative of its own area in ecological constraints and cropping patterns, is indicative of the remarkable gap between the two regions in marketization. In general, it is safe to say that the low percentage of cash crop area in northeastern Hebei resulted in a corresponding low level of commercialization. And peasants there sold crops, mostly subsistence ones, to meet their cash needs for taxes, rent, and family living expenses. This kind of commercialization could not generate an economic surplus above the peasants' basic subsistence needs. The reverse was true in south-central Hebei. There the cultivators devoted a high percentage of farmland to cash crops (cotton and wheat), which allowed them to derive a substantial surplus above subsistence. These differences in land yield and economic surplus between the two areas were the key to the striking differences in their population density and tax burden.

POPULATION DENSITY

Population density is the most important difference between the core and the periphery of a macroregion (Skinner 1977). The contrast between the south-central and northeastern Hebei regions was particularly conspicuous in this regard. In general, the plain areas of North China were more densely populated than the hilly areas, and so were the areas with better irrigation and drainage systems than those prone to flooding, waterlogging, or drought. Reflecting its ecological security, cropping diversity, and high land yield, south-central Hebei had the highest population density in rural North China. The plain area of this region had an average of 436.43 people per square kilometer, much higher than 166.74 in the mountain area in the western side of south-central Hebei. Huailu county had 276,592 people living in a territory of 476 square kilometers, or a density of 580.77 per square kilometer, second only to the 598.15 per square kilometer of Anguo county, the most densely populated county in Hebei province. On the whole, south-central Hebei had an average of 278.14 people per square kilometer. Northeast Hebei had a much lower level of population density than south-central Hebei. The plain area south of Yanshan Mountain had an average of 304.88 people per square kilometer, which was 69.86 percent of the density in the plain area east of Taihang Mountain. The population in the Yanshan Mountain area of this region was as sparse as 131.76 people per square kilometer, or 79.02 percent of that in the mountainous area of south-central Hebei (see Table 4). The population in northeastern Hebei as a whole averaged 214.49 per square kilometer, which was 77.12 percent of that in south-central Hebei.

TABLE 4

Population Density of Counties in Hebei Province, 1930 (Per Square Kilometer)

South-Central Hebei				Northeastern Hebei			
Plain area		Mountain area		Plain area		Mountain area	
Anguo	598.15	Jingxing	158.57	Baodi	224.66	Changping	152.08
Baixiang	340.50	Lingcheng	116.91	Changli	327.58	Funing	140.21
Dingxian	371.73	Lingshou	174.06	Fengrun	285.21	Huairou	134.91
Gaocheng	377.86	Neiqiu	151.27	Jixian	249.51	Lingyu	153.60
Gaoyi	359.84	Pingshan	117.95	Leting	360.19	Miyun	108.73
Huailu	580.77	Quyang	211.35	Luanxian	414.94	Qian'an	145.04
Jingxian	450.47	Tangxian	237.71	Ninghe	142.60	Zhunhua	101.29
Luancheng	311.93	Xingtang	279.32	Pinggu	207.52		
Shenze	488.06	Yuanshi	196.54	Sanhe	316.92		
Shulu	481.46	Zhanhuang	118.34	Shunyi	308.05		
Wuji	502.66			Tongxian	362.64		
Xinle	293.57			Xianghe	418.65		
Zhaoxian	440.38			Yutian	387.36		
Zhengding	491.73						
Average	436.43		166.74		304.88		131.76

SOURCE: *Hebei tongzhi gao*: 2866–71.

Land Taxation

THE TAX BURDEN

A given piece of land was usually taxed according to its grade of fertility. Higher-grade land shouldered higher tax rates (Yeh-chien Wang 1973b: 31–32). Predictably, different land productivity in the northeastern and south-central regions of Hebei province dictated their different level of taxation. The high land yield resulted in high tax quotas in the twenty-four counties of south-central Hebei, averaging 0.25 yuan per mu or 5.27 percent of net farm income in the early 1930s. The figure for northeastern Hebei was just 0.10 yuan per mu, or 3.15 percent of net income from land (Li Hongyi 1977 [1934]: 6382–92).

The land tax in Huailu county at the beginning of the twentieth century consisted of two parts. One was the statutory land tax (*diliang*), which had been a fixed quota (23,160 taels for the whole county) ever since the early eighteenth century. This tax was augmented with three informal charges, namely, the melting fee (*huohao*) of 3.3 percent, the clerk's stipend (*guishu zhizhang fanshi*) of 2.18 percent, and the administration subsidy (*bangong pingyu*) of 17 percent. These three charges totaled about 5,200 taels a year. The actual land tax thus was 28,360 taels in total. The other part was sur-taxes. The only surtax in Huailu before 1915 was the so-called *chaiyao* (liter-ally, "labor service"), which was 17,700,000 wen in copper cash, or 4,400 taels. In addition, the county yamen also charged taxpayers a receipt fee (*chuanpiao*) of 3 wen per receipt, which totaled approximately 1,000 yuan or 666 taels a year (656.1.103, 1913; 656.1.243, 1914).[10] The real tax burden in Huailu County before 1912 thus was 33,426 taels in all, which can be alter-natively expressed as 0.075 yuan per mu of land,[11] or 2.44 yuan per tael of land tax quota (see Table 5).

For peasants cultivating irrigated farmland, this tax burden accounted for 1.07 percent of their gross farm income, or 2.5 percent of their net farm in-come. For those living on dry land, it accounted for 2.14 percent of gross farm income, or 5 percent of net farm income.[12] By and large, this tax bur-den was in accordance with Yeh-chien Wang's estimation that land tax in the last quarter-century of the Qing fell "within the range between 2 and 4 per-cent of the land produce in most districts and provinces" (Wang 1973b: 128).

After entering the Republican era, the land tax peaked in two periods, 1914–16 and 1930–34, which coincided with the two waves of state expan-sion. The first occurred during Yuan Shikai's presidency (1912–15), when he made great efforts to strengthen the power of the central state. A major step taken by his government was to abandon the traditional silver tael system used in tax assessment and replace it with the silver yuan system. According to a 1914 statute issued by the Zhili provincial government, each tael of the land tax together with all the informal charges attached to it was to be assessed at 2.3 yuan, which was now called the main tax (*zhengshui*, although sometimes still referred to as diliang or land tax) (656.1.396, 1915). Contemporaries widely observed, however, that the conversion rate of taels to yuan was much higher than the statutory one (Li Hongyi 1977 [1934]: 6351). The result thus was an increase in the real tax burden. As the Huailu case indicates, each tael of land tax together with various informal charges before 1914 equaled 1.84 yuan. The new system brought about an increase of 25 percent. In the ensu-ing two years, two new surtaxes (*hegong juan* or the "water work levy," which amounted to 0.23 yuan per tael, and the police fee, which was 400 wen or 0.31 yuan per tael) were created, bringing the total tax burden to 3.04 yuan per tael, which was 46 percent higher than the 1913 figure (see Table 5).

TABLE 5

Land-Tax Rate in Huailu, 1910–1936

Year	Main Tax	Chai-yao	Water Work	Police Fee	Ward Fee	Const. Fee	Edu-cation Fee	Self-Gov. Fee	Militia Fee	Mili-tary levy	Total
1910	1.84	0.60									2.44
1911	1.84	0.60									2.44
1912	1.84	0.20									2.04
1913	1.84	0.20									2.04
1914	2.30	0.20									2.50
1915	2.30	0.20	0.23								2.73
1916	2.30	0.20	0.23	0.31							3.04
1917	2.30	0.20	0.23	0.31							3.04
1918	2.30	0.20	0.23	0.31							3.04
1919	2.30	0.20	0.23	0.27							3.00
1920	2.30	0.20	0.23	0.27							3.00
1921	2.30	0.20		0.26							2.76
1922	2.30	0.20		0.26							2.76
1923	2.30	0.20		0.26							2.76
1924	2.30	0.20		0.10							2.60
1925	2.30	0.20		0.40							2.90
1926	4.60	0.20		0.40							5.20
1927	2.30	0.20		0.40						2.30	5.20
1928	2.30	0.20		0.40							2.90
1929	2.30	0.20		0.40							2.90
1930	2.30	0.20		0.40	0.450	0.25	0.15				3.75
1931	2.30	0.20		0.40	0.450	0.20	0.15	0.60			4.30
1932	2.30	0.20		0.40	0.450	0.20	0.15				3.70
1933	2.30	0.20		0.40	0.450	0.20	0.15				3.70
1934	2.30	0.20		0.40	0.345	0.20	0.15		1.06		4.655
1935	2.30	0.20		0.40	0.345	0.20	0.15		1.06		4.655
1936	2.30	0.20		0.40	0.345	0.20	0.15		1.06		4.655

SOURCE: Huailu archive file 656.1.426, 1910–36.
NOTE: In addition to the main tax and all the surtaxes listed above, the county government charged taxpayers a receipt [*chuanpiao*] fee, which was 3 wen per receipt before 1933. After that, each kind of tax was charged a receipt fee of 0.01 yuan.

The tax burden in the ensuing decade (1916–25) was quite stable, and even decreased slightly, owing to the ending of the water work levy in 1920 and the decreasing conversion rate of copper cash to silver yuan. This rate had declined to such a degree by 1924 that the county government had to substitute the silver yuan system for the old copper cash system in collecting the police fee (now assessed at 0.4 yuan per tael of land tax) (see Table 5).

The two years of 1926 and 1927 were exceptional, when the county was torn by successive wars, first among the northern warlords and then between the leading northeastern warlord (Zhang Zuolin), who controlled the Beijing government, and the Guomindang's Northern Expedition Army. Beginning in 1926, the warlord government collected in advance the next year's main tax. In 1927 it further assessed the so-called "anti-Reds military special levy" (*taochi junshi tejuan*), which was equal to the land tax quota, resulting in a skyrocketing tax burden.

The establishment of the Guomindang regime in 1928 was followed by a sharp escalation of imposts on land. Five new surtaxes were added in 1930–34, namely, the ward office fee, the construction fee, the education fee, the *baoweituan* (local militia) fee, and the *zizhi* (self-government) fee (which was levied only in 1931). The total tax burden in Huailu soared to 4.66 yuan per tael of land tax quota or 0.17 yuan per mu of most common land in 1934.[13] An average cultivator working on irrigated land thus had to pay 2.43 percent of his gross income or 5.67 percent of his net income in taxes. For a peasant cultivating the unirrigated "dry" land, the figures are 4.86 percent and 11.33 percent, respectively. This tax rate was quite close to that of Michang village in Shunyi county, northeast of Beijing, where middle-income and rich peasants paid approximately 3 to 5 percent of their gross income in taxes until the Japanese occupation in 1937 (P. Huang 1985: 280).[14]

In general, then, the land tax in Huailu more than doubled over the early Republican years (from 2.04 yuan per tael of land tax quota or 0.07 yuan per mu of land in 1912 to 4.66 yuan per tael or 0.17 yuan per mu in 1934). The main tax remained quite stable throughout the Republican decades. Increases in the real tax burden resulted from the creation of surtaxes, which accounted for only 11 percent of the main tax in 1912 and rose to 103 percent in 1934 (see Table 5).

It should be noted that, while the surtax in Huailu (0.09 yuan per mu) was above the average surtax level in Hebei province (0.077 yuan per mu in 1934), the surtax rate (as a percentage of the main tax) was not as high as in other regions.[15] It was 34 percent of the main tax under the Beijing warlord governments (1912–25), and remained less than 89 percent in 1930–33. It was only after 1934 that the surtaxes came to exceed the main tax by 9.8 percent.

In addition to the regularized land tax and surtaxes, taxpayers in Huailu

TABLE 6

Tax Payment in 24 Counties of South-Central Hebei, 1931

County	Tax paid (% of tax quota)
Yuansi	100.00
Zhanhuang	100.00
Xingtang	100.00
Lingshou	100.00
Pingshan	100.00
Jingxing	100.00
Huailu	99.94
Quyang	99.89
Jingxian	99.53
Gaocheng	99.52
Dingxian	99.31
Luancheng	99.31
Zhaoxian	99.18
Baixiang	99.16
Xinle	98.86
Wuji	98.58
Neiqiu	98.39
Tangxian	98.35
Shulu	98.09
Zhengding	97.46
Lingcheng	97.00
Gaoyi	96.60
Shenze	95.11
Anguo	92.25
Average	98.61

SOURCE: Li Hongyi 1977 [1934]: 6412–24.

also shouldered irregular and temporary levies. During the late Qing period, these imposts were collected as *paijuan* (the shared contribution), *huangchai* (service to the royal court), or *juanban jiguo* (contribution to grain reservation [for famine relief]) in Huailu on rare occasions (655.1.913, 1882;

TABLE 7

Fulfillment of Tax Quotas in South-Central and Northeastern Hebei, 1930–1933

Year	South-Central Hebei (% of tax quota)	Northeastern Hebei (% of tax quota)
1930	96.09	55.58
1931	98.61	60.28
1932	86.95	34.32
1933	83.68	12.98

SOURCE: Li Hongyi 1977 [1934]: 6412–24.

655.1.997, 1884). In the Republican years, especially the 1920s, the most no-torious one was *bingchai*, a military levy, which was imposed by passing troops or when the government was at war. In addition to sums of cash, vil-lages were required to supply carts, fodder, and peasant labor. According to an observation made by the elite-controlled Huailu County Assembly (*xian yi / canshihui*) in 1928, the bingchai charged to the villages had skyrocketed in recent years as the wars between warlords intensified; it could be as high as hundreds and even thousands of yuan for a village each year (656.2.1120, 1928). In a petition for the exemption of part of the advance collection of taxes, the assembly claimed that the bingchai attached to land taxes in 1927 amounted to 100 yuan per tael, or more than thirty-four times the land taxes (656.2.1118, 1928). However, such charges were limited to villages within the battle area (in particular, those surrounding the county seat) and were levied on an exceptional rather than a regular basis.

Past studies have observed the proliferation of special levies (*tankuan*) in certain North China villages in the 1930s and 1940s, when local authorities faced increasing needs to finance local self-government enterprises, such as the police force, new-style schools, local militia, and the ward and village government. The tankuan (also known as *mujuan*) was imposed on the whole village rather than on individual taxpayers, and its collection was sep-arate from that of the land tax. In some localities, the tankuan even surpassed the land tax and became the biggest source of tax income for local govern-ment (P. Huang 1985: chap. 15; Duara 1988: chap. 3).

In Huailu county, however, these levies took the form of regularized sur-taxes and were collected together with the land tax. They included the po-lice fee collected since 1916 and five other fees since 1930 to support the ward government, local construction, education, self-government activities, and the militia. Funds for local education and other institutions in Huailu before 1930 came mainly from increased sales taxes (*maimai qishui*) on land

and housing and did not necessitate the creation of irregular special levies. By the 1919 regulation of Huailu county, for example, one-third of the sales tax (6 percent of the sale price) was allotted as *zizhi jingfei* (funds for self-government) and 5 percent of the sales tax as *xuewu gongyi* (education and public welfare). Of the tax on conditional sales (*diantui qishui*, 2 percent of the sale price), 35 percent was used as *zizhi jingfei* and 5 percent as *xuewu gongyi* (656.1.967, 1917–19. See also 655.1.876, 1904; 655.1.884, 1905).

TAX PAYMENT

In Huailu county, as well as in all twenty-four counties of the south-central Hebei plain, taxes had been paid almost in full at the beginning of the 1930s. In 1931, for example, the counties met an average of 98.61 percent of their tax quotas, and six counties met 100 percent of their quotas (see Table 6 for details). In contrast with the nearly full payment of taxes in south-central Hebei in 1931, tax shortages in northeastern Hebei were as high as 40 percent to 50 percent of their tax quotas, although their tax quotas were less than half the quotas of south-central Hebei counties. And the shortages increased drastically as the tax burden increased after 1932 (Table 7). Thus the actually paid taxes in relation to farm size in south-central Hebei were more than four times those in northeastern Hebei.

The low yield and low per capita income in northeastern Hebei were undoubtedly the primary reasons for the villagers' limited taxpaying ability. The preponderance of subsistence crops (sorghum and maize) and the limited growing of cash crops (wheat and cotton) in that area made it impossible to generate sufficient surplus for taxpayers to meet their tax duties. The fact that people fulfilled only 60 percent of their quotas in 1931 may well indicate that the preexisting tax burden in northeastern Hebei before the 1930s had already threatened the peasants' subsistence; any further increase in the tax burden would only result in corresponding increase in tax shortage. In contrast, most taxpayers in south-central Hebei had little difficulty fulfilling their duties despite the sharp tax escalation in the early 1930s. The wide cultivation of cash crops and the relatively high farm yield generated a net farm income of 4.74 yuan per mu, one-third more than that of the northeastern counties. This income permitted a standard of living above the subsistence level for most households and enabled them to pay taxes in full.

However, land productivity was not the only factor that determined the peasants' capacity to pay taxes. Tax collection was a process involving intense interactions between the state and rural society. The methods used by the government to collect taxes and the ways in which villagers organized themselves to cope with the government were as important as land yield in shaping the outcome of land taxation. The next chapter therefore turns to the emergence and functioning of village institutions pertaining to local control and land taxation in Huailu county and south-central Hebei as a whole.

CHAPTER 3

Cooperation and Control in the Peasant
Community

The Xiangdi System

The villagers in Huailu and neighboring counties had a long tradition in the Qing and Republican years of cooperation in tax payment and village administration under various communal arrangements, which I call the *xiangdi* system because of the xiangdi's central role in those activities. This chapter examines the origins of that system, community regulations that supported its operation, and its persistence and adaptations in the early twentieth century. We will see that the ecological and social settings in south-central Hebei had a profound impact on the way local communities interacted with the government. The relatively homogeneous social structure coupled with strong kinship ties enabled the villagers to cooperate in providing the xiangdi service and paying taxes. At the same time, the stable natural environment also made it possible for such cooperative practices to persist for centuries. To understand the xiangdi system in the larger context of rural governance in China, I will also compare the practices in Huailu with those in other parts of the country.

Origins of the Xiangdi

The statutory tax system in the early Qing period was known as *lijia*, which was introduced during the Ming (1368–1644) and reestablished at the beginning of the Qing. Under the lijia, ideally 110 households were arranged into a *li*, in which the heads of the ten households having the largest number of adult males were selected as the *lizhang* (head of the li) candidates, and the remaining 100 households were divided into ten *jia*. The *lizhang* post rotated each year among the ten largest households. Its job was to urge the households within the li to pay taxes and to assist the government in updating adult-male registers (*dingce*) (Hsiao 1960: 96–98; Sun Haiquan 1994).

In south-central Hebei, however, the lijia had never been implemented according to this official format. Here each county was divided into approximately a dozen li (or *she*) (*Lingshou xianzhi* 1874, 1: 16; *Luancheng xianzhi* 1872, 2: 4; *Jingxing xianzhi* 1875, 9). Huailu county had fourteen li in early Ming, and eighteen li by the sixteenth century (*Huailu xianzhi* 1990 [1522–66]: 539–40). The eighteen li remained unchanged throughout the Qing. The size of the li varied, covering from a few to as many as twenty-four villages (*Huailu xianzhi* 1985 [1876]: 70). The lizhang's actual role in tax collection also differed from official regulations. Instead of prompting tax payment, many lizhang engaged in tax-farming (*baoshou*). This illegal business was believed to "have threatened the livelihood of the people," because the tax farmers were able to exact additional monies from ordinary "small households" and at the same time exempt those they favored from taxation (*Jingxing xianzhi* 1730, 2: 14).

In 1726 the Qing state decided to merge the poll tax (*ding*) with the land tax and terminated the periodic compilation of adult-male registers. It thus abandoned the lijia system in actuality, for the basic purpose of the lijia had been to update the adult-male records and facilitate tax collection. The official tax collection method thereafter was known as *zifeng tougui* (literally, "self-sealing [the tax bag] and delivering into the collection chest"). In official discourse, this self-delivery system was believed to work for the good of both the government and the taxpayers, for it would do away with any intermediaries who might either embezzle the government's tax income or extort extra monies from taxpayers.

The smooth working of this self-delivery system, however, entailed the government's effective control over rural society. The local police-control organization introduced in the early Qing was called *baojia*. Officially, under the baojia, ten households were arranged into one *pai*; every ten pai constituted a *jia*; and every ten jia formed a *bao* (Hsiao 1960: 28; Hua Li 1988). After the abolition of the lijia, the state shifted the functions of tax collection previously assumed by the lijia to the baojia (Luo Yuandao 1994; Sun Haiquan 1994). Local baojia practice, needless to say, always deviated from the state's design and varied from place to place. So far the most reliable picture of the baojia system in practice comes from Baodi county in northeastern Hebei. Philip Huang (1985) and Wang Fuming (1995), both drawing on the archives of nineteenth-century Baodi county, find that the lowest-level quasi-official was called a *xiangbao*, each of whom oversaw about twenty villages. Both studies demonstrate that this person was nominated by local notables to serve as a buffer between themselves and the government. His main duty was to prompt the households in his charge to pay taxes and to make good on tax shortages (P. Huang 1985: 224–31; Wang 1995: 17–41). In many parts of the empire, however, the baojia was never put into effect. According to T'ung-tsu Ch'ü, the baojia had been "on the whole ineffective" and "remained a formality" for several centuries after it was introduced, for the magistrates had only half-heartedly executed and supervised the baojia administration: "In the nineteenth century, despite the many decrees issued by the emperors and provincial officials to enforce the *pao-chia* [baojia], it was seldom carried out and on the few occasions when it was, it produced no effect" (Ch'ü 1962: 152).[1]

Where the baojia deteriorated and state influence waned, the official tax system inevitably ceased to work or failed to generate sufficient tax revenue, giving rise to various nonstatutory practices. Three different types of local practices developed in reaction to the demise of the baojia system.

The first is tax-farming (*baoshou*), a business prevalent in many parts of China. It tended to occur where the government failed to collect taxes on its own and where the community was too weak to pay taxes collectively. The tax farmer was often the so-called *lishu* or *sheshu* at the subcounty level, whose basic duty was to record changes in tax liabilities.[2] A magistrate was willing to contract with the sheshu to collect taxes for two reasons. First, the county yamen had great difficulty getting tens of thousands of individual households to pay taxes where the baojia had deteriorated. This was particularly true where the taxpayers' real names differed from their registered taxpayer's titles (*huaming*). Second, the sheshu was the only person who knew the actual taxpayers and how much they owed. To reduce tax delinquency and thereby avoid punishment in the periodic merit evaluation, the magistrate would find it expedient to farm out part or all of the tax quota of his county despite the state's prohibition. To maximize their profits, however, the tax farmers would employ any available means to extort the delinquent extra tax monies, such as creating surcharges and manipulating the conversion rate between the silver taels used in the tax quota and the copper coins used for actual payment. This practice harmed the taxpayers more than it did the government (Jiang Shijie 1944: 60–66; Wang 1973: 43–44; Prazniak 1980; Chen Zhenhan 1989: 281–83). Tax-farming was a common catalyst of collective resistance in North China in the late nineteenth and early twentieth centuries (Zhang Youyi 1957: 695–99; Perry 1980: chap. 5; Prazniak 1980).

The second new business was proxy remittance (*baolan*). It prevailed in areas where a strong landed elite dominated the rural society, such as the Lower Yangzi region. As degree holders, the gentry elites were exempted from the poll tax (*ding*) and all other labor imposts during the imperial period. In other words, they were privileged to pay less tax than commoners with the same amount of land or tax quota. By assuming the responsibility of tax payment for the unprivileged who desired to lessen or evade their tax duties, the gentry obtained a considerable amount of unlawful profit from the transaction. Because the government, rather than the taxpayers, suffered as a consequence, it objected strenuously to this practice by "evil gentry" (Hsiao 1960; Wang 1973; Nishimura 1976; Yamamoto 1977; Bernhardt 1992). In the North China plain, however, the gentry landlords were relatively few and less active than in the highly stratified southern regions, and consequently their engagement in the illegal baolan was much less common than in the south.

A third practice that emerged after the breakdown of the baojia system was for the village community to choose a representative to deliver taxes to the government on behalf of all households. In communities where most members were small owners and each owed just a trivial amount of tax, it was neither convenient nor economical to deliver their taxes individually to the county yamen. Instead, a single representative took on the baojia agents' duties in tax collection and even assumed their functions in police control.

This might be what had occurred in villages of the south-central Hebei plain. The Huailu archives, most of which came from the late Qing and Republican periods, provide no details on the origin of the xiangdi system. But I do find some clues from the nineteenth-century gazetteers of south-central Hebei counties (*Zhili Dingzhou chi* 1849, 7: 52–56; *Jingxing xianzhi* 1875, 9; *Lingshou xianzhi* 1874, 1: 17; *Luancheng xianzhi* 1872, 2: 4; *Baixiang xianzhi* 1932, 2: 73). According to the gazetteer of Jingxing county (west of Huailu):

Since the merger of the poll tax with the land tax and the abolition of the lizhang in the fourth year of Yongzheng [1726], the tax-liable households were required to deliver taxes in person [*zifeng tougui*]. . . . The zifeng tougui might be feasible for rich households with large tax quotas. However, it was inconvenient for the poor who had just a small tax quota. Consequently, every village selected a *xiangzhang* from those who were impartial and wealthy. . . . It was the duty of the xiangzhang alone to prompt and collect taxes and deliver them to the treasury. . . . This benefited both those above and those below and is still abided by today. (*Jingxing xianzhi* 1875, 9)

This passage reveals three facts about the xiangdi (or xiangzhang) system.[3] First, the taxpayers voluntarily created it in response to the imposed official self-delivery system after the abolition of the lizhang system in 1726. Second, this cooperative system benefited all taxpayers by saving them the trouble of delivering the taxes themselves. Third, the xiangdi existed at the village level rather than the supra-village level as did the xiangbao in nineteenth-century Baodi. Huailu county had around 200 villages in the late nineteenth and early twentieth centuries.[4] About two-thirds of them had a single xiangdi. The remaining third were further divided into several pai, and each pai had a xiangdi.[5] The total number of the village or subvillage xiangdi in Huailu hovered around 500 in this period and peaked at 514 in 1931, when they were abolished (656.3.431, 1931).

There were two types of tax-collecting xiangdi in Huailu. One, the tax-prompting xiangdi (*cuiliang xiangdi*), was responsible for getting taxpayers in his charge to deliver their tax payments by a specified deadline. If the tax-payers failed to pay the full amount by the closing date, the xiangdi had to make up the shortage for the defaulters or face punishment, usually detention in jail (656.1.392, 1915; 656.1.419, 1915). When the xiangdi paid the balance due, he would take the payment receipt (*liangchuan*) to each delinquent's house and ask the latter to repay him (655.1.997, 1884; 656.1,419, 1915; 656.1.1091, 1919).[6]

The majority of the xiangdi in Huailu, however, were tax-advancing xiangdi (*diankuan xiangdi*). By local arrangement, they had to pay all the tax-payers' statutory taxes and miscellaneous levies in advance. In many localities they set up a special fund or designated public land for rent to facilitate the xiangdi's advance payment. The amount of the xiangdi fund ranged from 30,000 to 40,000 wen, or approximately 20 to 30 yuan.[7] The public land was in the neighborhood of 10 mu (656.1.1216, 1920). This was a size that could generate a rent close to the xiangdi fund.[8] However, the xiangdi fund or the rent collected from the public land could only alleviate the xiangdi's burden; by no means could it cover the full advance payment.[9] In places where no special fund or land was reserved, the xiangdi had to borrow from a local moneylender. And it was up to the xiangdi alone to pay the interest on the loan (656.1.1232, 1922). At the end of the year, when the xiangdi was to hand over his job to his successor, he would invite a literate person in the village, usually a teacher, to help him determine how much each taxpayer owed him so that he could be repaid (656.2.406, 1924; 656.2.1120, 1928; 656.3.57, 1929; 656.3.434, 1931). A magistrate of the county described this custom in 1921: "In most villages in Huailu County, the xiangdi would first borrow money and make advance payment of taxes. He then distributes the receipts to each taxpaying household in his charge and gets his money back" (656.1.1232, 1922).

The advantages of this cooperative practice were twofold. First, the xiangdi's advance payment benefited the taxpayers, allowing them to avoid a trip to the tax collection station (which was usually located at the county seat); they also escaped the extortion by tax farmers conducting the illegal baoshou business. The xiangdi himself, though, could not make a profit from advancing the tax payments, for his activities were under the close surveillance of fellow villagers, who knew well each other's landholdings as well as their tax quotas. What he advanced and what the taxpayers reimbursed him were exactly the amounts that appeared on the tax roll (*hongce* or *hongbo*, which was sent to him before the tax collection season). Under normal circumstances the xiangdi had no way to overcharge taxpayers or pocket any of the money (see Chapter 5). In fact, serving as the xiangdi was usually a thankless burden, although the xiangdi was allowed to draw fees as a middleman to help him recoup the loss he incurred by advancing the taxes.

The xiangdi system also benefited the government, because it was more expedient for the yamen to deal with the entire village or a subvillage neighborhood through its agent, the xiangdi, than to deal with individual taxpayers directly. It is not surprising therefore that this practice was allowed and actually safeguarded by the county government, although it deviated from the statute that required taxpayers to deliver their own taxes. Consider the official handling of the following case, in which the xiangdi, along with the village head, filed a complaint against four fellow villagers for breaching village regulations in 1929. According to their charge, the four men opposed the xiangdi's advance payment of taxes for all households in the village and insisted that they be allowed to pay their taxes themselves. However, since most villagers were illiterate, the plaint went on, they did not want to change the regulation. The accusers therefore petitioned to punish the four violators in order to defend the village regulation. The magistrate responded by ordering the head of the ward police to look into the matter and settle it by requiring compliance with the village regulation (656.3.57, 1929). The county government defended the xiangdi system because the villagers' compliance with local regulations would ensure the full and timely payment of taxes, and the fulfillment of tax quotas was traditionally the most important criterion in the regular evaluation of the magistrate's performance (T'ung-tsu Ch'ü 1962: 34). It was probably because of this practice that the compiler of *Huailu Xianzhi* asserted that "it was easy to collect the government taxes (*guanfu yi wan*)" in this county (1985 [1876]: 72).

To understand how the taxpayers in Huailu villages formed their own cooperative practices for tax payment, we need to examine various local arrangements that governed the selection of the xiangdi and defined the mutual obligations between the xiangdi and his fellow villagers.

The Selection of the Xiangdi

Social scientists have offered two different interpretations of the genesis of cooperative institutions. One emphasizes the importance of a shared sense of identity that leads to cooperation as a group. According to this theory, people are willing to identify themselves as members of a unified group when they have lived in circumstances that require direct, repeated face-to-face relations and have had to defend their integrity and interests. Human emotional ties embedded in the networks of mutual obligation and loyalty provide a foundation for a "system of solidarity" in which cooperation takes place. Once individuals perceive a collective identity and collective interests, and consequently develop a sense of fellowship and membership, they begin to favor coordinated action in order to realize the common good (Mayhew 1971).

An alternative interpretation of institutional genesis views cooperation as a product of collective endeavors by people who share some common ends and who are subject to a set of obligations and consciously designed mechanisms of enforcement and controls. Cooperative institutions emerge and persist where individuals with roughly equal power agree on some common end and accept joint obligations. And they begin to demand cooperation when they encounter adverse events such as wars, invasions, epidemics, and natural disasters and share the desire to consume "jointly-produced private goods" (or joint goods) that cannot be obtained by following individual strategies (Hechter 1987, 1990). This common end, therefore, is more important than the shared sense of identity that leads to the formation of cooperative institutions.

These two theories, contrasting as they seem to be, are not incompatible. In fact, both shared identity and shared interest played an important role in the creation and maintenance of the xiangdi system. This is evident from the way the xiangdi was selected.

To govern the selection of the xiangdi, the villagers in Huailu created informal rules, locally known as "village regulations" (cungui, xianggui, or ji-ugui). These regulations, which varied from village to village, specified the way the xiangdi was to be selected and the date the outgoing xiangdi was to hand over his duties to the incoming one. A widely accepted principle underlying those regulations was that all qualified households of the community took turns serving as the xiangdi in annual rotation. According to the xiangdi of Beixiangbei village, for example, each household in his village had to furnish the xiangdi service by rotation in an endless cycle (lunliu menhu, zhou er fu shi) (656.1.717, 1917). In another instance, seven xiangdi asserted in a collective petition in 1922 that all the taxpaying households in their respective villages supply a xiangdi in annual rotation (lunliu menhu, annian huanchong) (656.1.1232, 1922; see also 656.2.15, 1921; 656.2.406, 1924).

The most important factor in villagers' cooperation in providing xiangdi service was their kinship ties. Where the community comprised a single lineage or descent group, it was usually the individual branches (fang) of the lineage or individual households of the lineage that took turns providing a xiangdi for the whole village. Yaojiali village, for instance, had about 180 households in the 1920s, all bearing the surname of Yao. These households belonged to eight branches, each of which had to supply by turn a xiangdi for the village for one year (656.1.1099, 1919). Nangucheng, too, was a single-surname village of the Yangs. Its regulations demanded that all households of the lineage provide a xiangdi for the whole clan in rotation and that the incumbent xiangdi hand over his office to the next xiangdi on the first day of the tenth month of the lunar year (656.2.27, 1921).

Local regulations governing xiangdi service for multi-surname villages fell largely into three types. Under one type, individual taxpaying households served as the xiangdi for an entire community by rotation regardless of their descent group. Alternatively, different descent groups rotated annually to offer a xiangdi for the whole village. Nanguo village, for example, comprised two descent groups, the Wangs and the Lis. Its village regulation prescribed that the two groups alternate to supply a xiangdi for the village. The Lis' one-year xiangdi service was to be followed by two years as the village head, while the Wangs' one-year xiangdi service was to be followed by two years as vice-village head. The head of each descent group then chose from his group the candidates for the xiangdi post and village office according to their landholdings (656.2.1120, 1928).

More often than not, however, each descent group in a village tended to form a subvillage unit, the pai, and each pai chose its own xiangdi from within the group. Fantan village, for instance, consisted of two descent groups, the Fans and the Tans. While sharing the same tax roll, the two groups made up "Front Pai" and "Back Pai" respectively, and each pai had its own xiangdi to serve the households within the pai (656.3.230, 1930). The number of descent groups in a village varied, and so did the number of pai, which ranged from two to as many as fourteen (see, e.g., 656.1.419, 1915; 656.1.1216, 1920; 656.2.15, 1921; 656.2.23, 1921; 656.2.139, 1921; 656.1.1232, 1922; 656.2.406, 1924; 656.3.911, 1934).

Whether the xiangdi was chosen by annual rotation among different lineages, lineage branches, or individual households of the village or subvillage pai, the nomination of the xiangdi within the cooperative group was invariably based on his household's tax duty or landholding. Usually the larger the tax quota a household owed, the earlier and longer it was to furnish the xiangdi service. In many villages, people thus created a list of xiangdi candidates according to their tax quotas, and each household on the list had to take turns serving as the xiangdi (656.2.852, 1926; 656.2.967, 1927). Alternatively, the villagers based the sequence and duration of their xiangdi rotation on landholdings. This was especially true where the tax quotas of individual households deviated from their actual landholdings, resulting in the unequal distribution of the tax burden among the landowners. To alleviate the burden of small landowners and ensure the smooth working of the village regulation, it was necessary to base the xiangdi service on landholdings rather than on tax quotas. The minimum amount of land that necessitated one-year's xiangdi service ranged from 10 to 20 mu. In Nanzhuang village, for example, the village regulation stipulated that households having 20 mu of land serve as xiangdi for one year, those with 40 mu for two years, those with 60 mu for three years, and so forth (656.2.6, 1921). The village regulation of Mazhuang was more sophisticated. Here households with 100 mu of land or more were to serve as xiangdi for one year. Households with less than 100 mu, but more than 10 mu, had to form groups that together owned 100 mu in total and serve as the xiangdi collectively. If any one household wanted to be exempted from xiangdi duties, he had to subsidize the one who held the office. The amount of the subsidy would be set by the person who had acted as xiangdi before. Anyone who considered the subsidy excessive could propose a lower figure. The xiangdi post would fall to the one who offered the lowest figure (656.1.1212, 1920).

It is clear that the community members' shared identity and shared interest both contributed to the emergence of the xiangdi system. People of the same lineage or the same branch were inclined to cooperate because they were subject to the same leadership by clan elders and had cooperated in matters concerning the welfare of the descent group. This identity provided a natural basis on which they were ready to cooperate in xiangdi service. Equally important, however, was the fact that the villagers had the same need to cooperate in tax payment in order to avoid individual tax delivery, which cost them much more than joining the xiangdi service rotation. It was this common end, more than anything else, that brought together different descent groups or individuals of different surnames in the community under the cooperative system.

The issue that needs to be further clarified is the extent to which the villagers participated in the xiangdi service. The principle that all members of the community rotate annually to serve as the xiangdi was practicable only when two conditions existed. First, the community had to be small enough so that every household had the opportunity to serve as the xiangdi in the foreseeable future of, say, fifteen or twenty years. In other words, the community must be a small group of no more than fifteen or twenty households. For villages of more than fifty or even 100 households, letting *all* of them take part in the annual service for the whole community was completely impracticable, for no one could predict what would happen to any household decades or a century later. That is probably one of the reasons why a large village was often broken into a number of subgroups (pai) so that each of the households in the pai had a chance to serve as the xiangdi during the coming years. Second, all members of the group must be households of roughly equal landholding and tax duty. Since the major task of the xiangdi was to advance taxes for community members, it was unreasonable for landless or land-poor households to share the same burden of the xiangdi service as villagers of average or better-than-average means. We can thus safely say that the equal participation of *all* group members in xiangdi service was usually limited to small, undifferentiated communities: small hamlets or subvillage pai made up of a descent group or a branch of a large clan.

More complicated was the situation in stratified villages. As discussed in the preceding chapter, most villages in Huailu were communities of pre-dominantly landowners with farms of 10 to 20 mu or more, who usually met the minimum requirement for one-year's xiangdi service. Most villagers thus were involved in the xiangdi service. Landless or land-poor peasants with farms smaller than 10 or 20 mu, who accounted for 10 to 40 percent of all households, were not included among the xiangdi candidates. The ques-tion that arises is, what was the implication of the minimum requirement on landholding for villagers of different means? Did it offer the poor a free ride to enjoy the collective goods of xiangdi service, or only enable the rich to monopolize the xiangdi position for their prerogatives?

An obvious fact was that where the frequency of annual xiangdi service was linked with landholding, those with plenty of land served more often than those of poor means. This, however, should not be interpreted as the rich excluding the poor from the xiangdi's privileges. In fact, under most cir-cumstances, serving as a xiangdi entailed a burden rather than a profiteering opportunity, for the cost of xiangdi service normally outweighed the com-pensation it was allowed. Exempting the poor from the xiangdi service while allowing them to take advantage of the xiangdi's advance payment of taxes, therefore, was a beneficial arrangement rather than a deprivation.

The poor were able to free-ride under the xiangdi system for two rea-sons. Their financial circumstances made it impossible for them to pay ad-vance taxes for their fellow villagers or to pay the interest out-of-pocket, as required by many villages. Forcing the poor to serve as xiangdi thus would jeopardize the smooth working of the cooperative system, which would in turn threaten the joint benefit enjoyed by the rest of the community. Free-riding was thus a "rational" option. But this is not a sufficient explanation for their free-riding, for we may ask why other landowners or contributors to the xiangdi system did not simply exclude the poor from their cooperative system. We must remember that those with less land were not outsiders or strangers to the majority in the community. They were the neighbors, friends, and kinsmen of the contributors. It was morally unjustifiable for the relatively wealthier households to limit the joint goods to themselves, disre-garding the disadvantaged in their neighborhood. The individual payment of taxes by the poor would be even more uneconomical since their number was even fewer and many were already on the verge of subsistence. To en-sure their survival and the solidarity of the community, it was morally nec-essary to give the poor access to the joint goods even though they did not contribute to their production.

Clearly, what was at work under the xiangdi system was a survival ethic embedded in the homogeneous communities of mainly kinsmen and owner-cultivators. By imposing more duties on those of means and at the same time allowing those in poverty to share the benefits of cooperation at no cost, the community produced a "redistributive effect" among the community members (Scott 1976: 40–41). Contrary to the rational-choice assumption that an effective and durable cooperative system must do away with free-riding, the regulations of peasant society such as the villages of Huailu constituted both a rational arrangement for producing collective goods that could not be achieved by individual efforts and a redistributive method of protecting the disadvantaged and maintaining village cohesiveness.

The Xiangdi as a Middleman

To offset the xiangdi's costs, especially the interest he paid on loans for tax payment and his travel expenses to the county seat to deliver the taxes, the villages in Huailu developed local regulations to define the taxpayers' obligations to the xiangdi. The most common one was to allow the xiangdi to draw a commission on his services as a go-between in local transactions. The xiangdi's duties as the middleman typically included: first, seeking out a buyer or a seller for fellow villagers who wanted to sell or buy property; second, facilitating negotiations between the two parties in working out a price acceptable to both; third, inviting both parties to the plot or house to be sold and measuring the property using a public measuring stick of the village; and finally, drawing up a deed using the official deed form.[10] To ensure the xiangdi's prerogatives as a middleman, the village regulations usually required the seller or the buyer to ask the xiangdi to be his middleman, and the xiangdi, in turn, had the right to demand a commission from the seller or the buyer regardless of whether he actually acted as middleman in the sale.

Two examples of such village regulations illustrate how the xiangdi's privilege as a middleman was related to his service in advancing taxes. In his petition against a local villagers' nonpayment of a sale commission, Wu Delian, the xiangdi of Dongying village, stated in 1924:

In our village, [the villagers] rotate to serve as the xiangdi and handle taxes as well as all miscellaneous imposts. All the monies needed for the payments are shouldered by the xiangdi, who apportions his advanced monies to individual taxpaying households and collects his expenses at the end of the year when he is to hand over his duties [to the next xiangdi]. This is the harm the xiangdi suffers. Whoever in the village sells outright or sells conditionally his housing and land has to turn to the xiangdi to make the transaction and allows him to draw a commission. This is the benefit the xiangdi enjoys. This is the village's old regulation, which has existed for a long time. (656.2.406, 1924)

A similar statement is found in a petition submitted in 1926 from three taxpayers of Liangjiazhuang village against their xiangdi for overcharging them:

Our Liangjiazhuang village has a regulation: the xiangdi service is to be rewarded with certain benefits; he is allowed to make transactions and draw commissions on sales of land and housing as well as sales of all commodities, including trees and fruits. However, he is strictly prohibited from engaging in malpractice in weighty matters like [the collection of] official taxes and miscellaneous levies, as well as the transfer of tax liabilities and taxation of land deeds. The xiangdi who violates the village regulation is to be dismissed immediately upon accusation. (656.2.852, 1926)

The connection between the xiangdi's service as tax agent and his right as middleman is quite clear in these village regulations. Not surprisingly, transactions without the xiangdi as middleman were treated as "illegitimate sales and purchases" (*simai simai*). One villager, named Zhang Taoqi, was thus accused by a xiangdi of illegitimately selling 3.5 mu of land for 146,000 wen and of selling his house for 88 yuan. In that xiangdi's opinion, "it is downright intolerable in both human feeling and reasoning [*qingli nanrong*] that I suffered the harms [of advancing his taxes] while I was kept from enjoying the benefits [to be his middleman]" (656.1.419, 1915). Disputes between the xiangdi and the villagers were thus inevitable when the xiangdi found such evasions and failed to collect a fee. Without exception, as we will find in the following cases, the xiangdi would appeal to "village regulations" to justify his charge against the violators and his request for the fee.

On February 24, 1919, Liu Fuzhi, the xiangdi of Yudi village, filed a plaint against his fellow villager, one Xie Yongtai. "By the old regulation of the village [*cunzhong jiugui*]," he stated at the beginning of his petition, "it has been the xiangdi's duties to make a deal for the two parties in a transaction and to write deeds for the sales and purchases of housing and land." Xie, however, had secretly made a deal with another fellow villager and sold him 1.5 mu of land at the price of 75,000 wen. According to the xiangdi, he discovered the private sale when the two parties were measuring the plot. He therefore accused the two of "illegitimate sale and purchase" and of evading deed taxes. The magistrate responded by sending out a clerk to verify the accusation. Ten days later, the village head reported to the magistrate that, "as a friend to both parties," he could not "stand by with folded arms" and had investigated and settled the matter. Feng had paid the xiangdi a middleman's fee and both now were willing to end the lawsuit (656.1.1093, 1919).

In a similar case, Ji Fuhong, the xiangdi of Beixiangbei village, who by local regulations had the right to "bring the two parties together and talk into agreement" in land and housing sales, charged Ji Erni of his village with "attempting to evade the middleman's fee and deed tax," for Erni had bought 10 mu of land from a fellow villager and had "stealthily written" (*touxie*) a deed without informing the xiangdi of the sale. A policeman soon came to the village to prompt the payment of the deed tax and middleman's fee on the magistrate's instruction. Two fellow villagers, who claimed themselves to be "local friends" (*xiangyi*) of the disputants, immediately mediated the dispute. As a result of their mediation, the two parties finally paid the xiangdi the middleman's fee in accordance with the local regulation (656.1.1095, 1919).

The importance of village regulations is also evident in the dispute between Wu Delian, the xiangdi of Dongying village, and his fellow villager Wu Liande, who sold 5 mu of land to another fellow villager without telling Wu Delian. On January 20, 1924, the xiangdi filed a petition against the seller. After laying out the village regulation, the xiangdi complained, "it is unfair that the xiangdi suffers harm while the benefits go to others." He therefore asked the magistrate to issue an instruction to assert his right to handle the ongoing sales, in order to forestall "violation against village regulation" (*wenluan cungui*). Upon receiving the petition, the magistrate instructed the disputants to "check and comply with the old regulation" (*chazhao jiuzhang*) and to settle the dispute on their own. A month later, the xiangdi filed another petition, complaining of Wu Liande's "illegitimate selling" despite the mediation of the village head as well as friend-villagers. The ensuing proceedings of the lawsuit involved a yamen runner's investigation and a formal court session. According to the xiangdi, Wu Liande had trusted the xiangdi to sell his land, and the xiangdi had found a potential buyer. Later, however, Wu turned to another villager to be his middleman and sold his land at 20 yuan to one of his relatives. To avoid paying the deed tax and middleman's fee, both parties denied this sale in court. Because of the lack of written evidence about the sale, the xiangdi could not win the magistrate's support, despite the fact that Wu's relative was actually cultivating the plot. The magistrate dismissed the case by asking both parties to pledge to cease the dispute (656.2.406, 1924). Although the xiangdi failed to demand a fee from the claimed sale, no party involved in the lawsuit (the seller, the buyer, the mediator, or the magistrate) denied the xiangdi's right as middleman in local sales. The "village regulation" on the xiangdi's right as middleman was beyond dispute.

It is clear, then, that two sets of village regulations bolstered the xiangdi system. One set, regarding the selection of the xiangdi, linked xiangdi service with taxpayers' landholding or tax liability. The other set of regulations had to do with the mutual rights and obligations between the xiangdi and taxpayers. It must be emphasized, however, that although such regulations existed in almost every community in Huailu county and were acknowledged by all community members, they usually lacked codified texts and were orally passed on from generation to generation of local dwellers. They surfaced in public discussion and came to the attention of the government only when disputes arose among the villagers. To the extent that these local regulations, as well as the villagers' shared beliefs about their roles in com-

munity life, formed a body of knowledge that was linked with a specific locale, we may label them as a sort of "local knowledge" (Scott 1983).

To understand how this indigenous knowledge affected the communica-
tion between the local residents and administrators from outside, we have a
telling case from Beigucheng village. The incumbent xiangdi of this village,
a certain Zhang Xigui, filed a plaint on March 18, 1925, charging that a fellow villager, Zhang Shuanbao, "disrupted local regulations" (*wenluan xianggui*) by selling a loom to another villager, Huo Xixiu, without asking him to
be the middleman. According to that plaint, this village had an old regulation by which every household, when selling or buying land, house, trees,
and implements, had to ask the incumbent xiangdi to handle the transaction
and pay him a fee. However, the plaint went on, the seller not only refused
to pay him a fee when asked, but insulted him with slanderous words. The
accuser thus requested a summons of Zhang Shuanbao in order to "uphold
local regulation" (*yi zheng xianggui*). The magistrate's comment: "In Zhang
Shuanbao's sale of his loom to Huo Xixiu, there is no need to let this xiangdi draw a commission. [However] since there is such a regulation [*guize*],
submit it to me for a check and final decision." Obviously, the magistrate had
no knowledge of the regulation, for he denied the xiangdi's request, and the
petitioner could not submit such a "regulation" because it did not exist in
written form. The magistrate soon received a petition from the head of that
village to close the case. The village head reported that he, as a friend of both
parties, had mediated the dispute and that the seller had paid the xiangdi the
commission in full in compliance with the local regulation (565.2.569, 1925).
Obviously, the regulation, though unknown to the magistrate, was nevethe-
less in effect and defended by the village leader.

Village Regulations versus Customary Law

Let us consider at this point the differences between the village regulations
described here and various customary laws discussed in previous studies of
Chinese villages. In general, we can safely say that customary law regulated
contractual activities in peasant society (e.g., Fu-mei Chen and Ramon Myers 1976 and 1978; Duara 1990; Liang Zhiping 1996). However, the foregoing analysis of the xiangdi's role as middleman also sheds light on the importance of village regulations in local transactions. In several aspects, village
regulations departed from customary law on contractual activities.

First, unlike middlemen under customary law whose activities covered a
wide range of contractual arrangements, such as loans, land rentals, land sales
and purchases, and even marriage and adoption, the xiangdi's role as middleman was confined to local sales, especially land and housing transactions.
The xiangdi avoided involvement in loans and land rentals because those

businesses often entailed burdens such as mediation and dispute resolution, while the only purpose of the xiangdi's role as middleman, by village regulation, was to draw commissions in order to offset his expenses in advancing taxes. In fact, to ensure the xiangdi's gains from commissions, his role as middleman was often extended to sales that did not need a go-between, such as the sale of agricultural produce including cotton, fruit, and trees, and even to the "sale of all commodities" as the case of Liangjiazhuang village indicated. The important thing was to allow the xiangdi to draw a commission from local sales, whatever his actual role in such activities.

Second, in addition to facilitating transactions, the most important function of a middleman by customary law was to mediate disputes and even to act as a guarantor in formal loans when needed (P. Huang 1996: 52–58). In contrast, the xiangdi's duty as middleman was limited to facilitating transactions; mediation and guaranteeing loans were left to other community members.

Third, the middlemen in other localities under customary law were often people with an excellent reputation or wealth in the community, for only such persons with "face" and wide connections could be trusted to mediate when a dispute arose. Unlike the professional broker, however, such middlemen usually did not receive money for their service. Instead, their services were usually remunerated in symbolic forms such as a gift or a meal. The local elite usually treated their service as a way to regenerate their authority rather than to profit (Duara 1990; P. Huang 1996: 52–61). In Huailu, in contrast, the xiangdi who offered middleman service were ordinary villagers. Acting as a middleman in local sales was, by village regulation, strictly the duty of the xiangdi and he was to be paid in money. Not to ask him or not to pay him a commission was treated as a violation of village regulation and could result in a formal petition.

These differences between the xiangdi and ordinary middlemen reveal how village regulations depart from customary law. Customary law, existing almost everywhere to govern contractual activities, did not necessarily bespeak the collectivity of peasant communities (Chen and Myers 1976; Duara 1988: 182–92; P. Huang 1996: 52–58). The village regulations described here, however, were an integral part of the communal arrangements that supported the xiangdi system. Aimed at securing the xiangdi's prerogative as middleman to draw a fee, those regulations contributed to the smooth working of community cooperation in taxation. Together with other institutions, they made it possible for village communities to act as a collectivity in dealing with the state. Village regulations as seen in Huailu thus outweighed customary law in governing local transactions. As the preceding instances indicate, normal conduct under customary law, such as asking friends or relatives to be middlemen, was treated as illegitimate under the village regulations.

Continuity and Changes after 1900

LAND TAXATION

Traditionally, the xiangdi in Huailu villages advanced not only the well-defined land tax for his community, but also all kinds of surcharges, such as the *chaiyao* (literally, "labor service"), as well as temporary special levies, such as *paijuan* (the allocated contribution) and *juanban jiguo* (the grain reservation) during the late Qing period (655.1.913, 1882; 655.1.997, 1884). After 1900, surtaxes in the county proliferated from just one (the chaiyao) to five by 1930 (see details in Chapter 2). All of them were collected at the same time as the land tax (the so-called *suiliang daizheng*), and it remained the xiangdi's responsibility to advance all of the surtaxes together with the land tax (656.2.1120, 1928).

The xiangdi's burden was extraordinarily heavy during the turbulent years of warlordism in the late 1920s, when he had to join the village head in paying an irregular military levy (*bingchai*) in addition to the land tax and surtaxes. Sometimes this levy would be as much as several times the regular taxes and well beyond their ability to pay them in advance. Consequently, most villages in this county developed a new practice in the 1920s: the xiangdi remained responsible for the land tax and regular surcharges, and rich households (*fuhu*) were to advance the payment of the military levies. As the deliberative assembly of Huailu county stated clearly in 1928:

In recent years, military levies have become frequent and exorbitant, often amounting to as much as several hundred or even several thousand [yuan per village]. It is practically impossible for the xiangdi to handle their payment in advance. Therefore, it has always been up to the wealthy households to make advance payment temporarily and then to allocate [their advanced monies to individual taxpayers] according to their land tax liabilities. The allocation and recollection, however, cannot be delayed too long. It is usually made three or six months later. Such arrangements, though not yet established regulations, have prevailed in every village without exception. (656.2.1120, 1928)

Here again we find the survival ethic at work in peasant society. As the military levies skyrocketed, requiring the xiangdi to advance both the land taxes and military levies would have driven him to bankruptcy. It was thus necessary to change the time-honored village regulations by shifting the heaviest burden of advancing military levies to the rich. However, so burdensome was this task that even the rich households were unable to wait until the end of the year to collect their advanced monies from the villagers, as the xiangdi had usually done. To reduce their interest payments on the money they had borrowed to make the advance payment, the waiting period had to be shortened to only three or six months. Thus both the ordinary taxpayers and the wealthy families made a concession under the pressure of the subsistence ethic, in order to survive the crisis caused by warfare and to avoid the breakdown of the cooperative xiangdi system. Making necessary changes to the village regulation in times of crisis reflected the perpetual solidarity of the villages rather than the weakening of the peasant communities.

LOCAL ADMINISTRATION

In addition to his tax-related duties, the xiangdi traditionally also shouldered many tasks pertaining to local administration. The county government required the xiangdi "to investigate and report to the government unlawful activities in his village such as theft, gambling, and prostitution; to help the runner to bring to court all parties and witnesses involved in a lawsuit when they were summoned; and to investigate and mediate ongoing disputes in his village under the magistrate's instruction" (*Zhili Dingzhou zhi*, 7: 54–56). As a quasi-official, the xiangdi performed the same duties as the original baojia agents.[11]

What needs clarification is the xiangdi's role in local administration after 1900 when the village head position (*cunzhang* or *cunzheng*) came into existence (see Chapter 7 for details about the village government). The state's real purpose in installing the village office was to extend its reach into local society by displacing the old-style quasi-officials (including the xiangbao and the xiangdi) with the formally sanctioned village head. This institutional change has led to the assumption that the old baojia (or xiangbao) agents disappeared entirely after 1900 when the new means of local control (the village government and ward police) were supposedly in full swing (Wang Fuming 1995: 40, 58, 102). However, archival records from Huailu county show a different picture of village politics after 1900. Here the position of xiangdi existed until 1931, when it was formally replaced by the newly created xiangzhang post. There was thus a "dual" village office in which the xiangdi coexisted with the village head. What interests us therefore was the relationship between the two, and whether the creation of the formal village government brought to an end the xiangdi's traditional role as administrative agent in the manner of the xiangbao.

To be sure, the creation of the formal village office inevitably weakened the administrative functions previously performed by the xiangdi. The village head, as an administrative agent at the lowest level, was responsible for "all the public affairs ongoing in the village" (656.2.438, 1924). For example, he took care of all matters concerning "self-government" (656.2.139, 1921), of which the most important was the establishment and maintenance of primary schools (see Chapter 8). In many instances, the village head was also the schoolmaster (656.1.1099, 1919). The xiangdi shouldered tasks mainly in connection with the land tax.

In practice, however, the division of duties between the two was not so clear. In many villages, the xiangdi continued to act as an administrative agent in place of the village head. This was especially true where the village head existed only in name or proved incapable of taking care of village affairs. One village head, for example, claimed that he "spent most of the year out of the village on personal business and found no time to handle village affairs" (656.1.733, 1917; a similar instance is found in 656.1.561, 1916). Some village heads were too old to supervise public activities and therefore petitioned to resign their service (656.1.70, 1913; 656.1.377, 1915; 656.1.1158, 1919). In such instances, the xiangdi had to take on the village head's tasks. In some villages, "to serve as xiangdi was to be the leader of the village" (chongying xiangdi, xi yixiang zhi lingxiu) (656.2.967, 1927). Therefore the state had to continue to rely on the old-style xiangdi to carry out some administrative duties.

The xiangdi's continuing role as an administrator after 1900 was particularly evident in the establishment of primary schools. As required by the county magistrate, the village head and the xiangdi together shouldered all of the tasks of founding a school in their villages, such as choosing or constructing school buildings, nominating schoolmasters and teachers, and collecting the school's operating funds (xuekuan) (656.1.175, 1913; 656.1.301, 1914; 656.1.292, 1914). In reality, it was usually the xiangdi's duty to collect the school funds. His cooperation was indispensable if the village head and the schoolmaster were to build and run the school smoothly. Because of this, the xiangdi was able to exert much influence on the management of the school, including matters such as choosing and paying the teacher (656.1.499, 1915; 656.1.1012, 1918). When he and the village head or schoolmaster disagreed, the xiangdi would refuse to collect the school funding from the villagers (656.1.163, 1913). A dispute thus broke out in Shijiazhuang village in 1913 between the village head and the schoolmaster on one side and the four xiangdi of their village on the other. According to the plaint from the village head and the schoolmaster, the four xiangdi's collection of school funds had enabled them to control the school for many years; the village head and the schoolmaster played only a nominal role in the school and had no real power. When the schoolmaster tried to hire a native villager as the teacher instead of an outsider whom the four xiangdi supported, they immediately decided not to collect the school monies, saying, "we will not collect the monies unless we hire the teacher" (656.1.155, 1913). A similar dispute took place in Shuangmiao village, where the xiangdi (also an acting schoolmaster) and the village head argued with each other over the qualifications of two teachers they each nominated (656.1.817, 1917).

As an administrator, the xiangdi also played an important role in the appointment and removal of the village head. Normally, when the village head's post was left vacant, the magistrate would send out a bailiff to order the xiangdi of the village to "elect a proper person" (*lingju tuoren*), or to "[call on] the entire village to elect [a suitable person]" (*hexiang lingju*) to fill the post (656.1.70, 1913; 656.1.377, 1915; 656.2.814, 1926; 656.1.561, 1906; 656.2.2, 1921). In Qiejiazhuang village, the xiangdi quarreled with the village head over the sale of a piece of public land in 1921. So influential was the xiangdi that he was able to convene a meeting of more than one hundred village households in the temple and elect a new village head (656.2.23, 1921). Sometimes the xiangdi invited several villagers of high prestige to nominate the new village head, instead of gathering all the villagers to vote (656.2.139, 1921). In all these activities, the xiangdi was able to influence the selection of the village head to some degree.

The xiangdi's attitude became even more important when the village head petitioned for retirement. On receipt of this request, the magistrate typically noted that he would not allow his retirement until the xiangdi of that village nominated an appropriate person to take over his position. In that case, the xiangdi might obstruct the process or make trouble for the village head simply by foot-dragging and not finding a candidate. If the xiangdi reported that no candidate could be found, the magistrate would require the current village head to continue in office (656.1.561, 1906). In a case from Zhengcun village, for example, the xiangdi foiled the village head's attempted retirement simply by nominating the village head himself (656.1.377, 1915). In a similar case from Beitongye village, both the village head and deputy head petitioned for retirement in 1917 on the pretext that their businesses left them no time to take care of village affairs. The magistrate suspected that there might be other reasons behind the story and sent a policeman to instruct the xiangdi to investigate the case. Four weeks later, the policeman reported back that the xiangdi had mediated the case and asked the village head and deputy head to reassume their offices (656.1.733, 1917). The xiangdi's obvious influence on these occasions suggests that he was not merely a tax agent serving his own community but continued to act as a quasi-official in local administration after 1900.

How Effective Was the Xiangdi System?

The survival of the xiangdi post in Huailu villages after 1900 well suggests the vitality of the cooperative tradition in tax payment and village administration in the peasant communities. The xiangdi system even continued in a modified manner after 1930, when the Guomindang government reorganized local administration and replaced the xiangdi with the formally appointed xiangzhang at the village level (see Chapter 10). As it turned out, however, the xiangzhang did not differ much from the former xiangdi in the

TABLE 8

Formally Filed Disputes over Xiangdi Service in Huailu County, 1912–1929

Year	Formally Filed Disputes
1912	0
1913	1
1914	2
1915	4
1916	2
1917	3
1918	2
1919	4
1920	1
1921	3
1922	2
1923	0
1924	4
1925	2
1926	0
1927	1
1928	1
1929	2
Total	34
Average	1.9

SOURCE: Historical archives of Huailu county, Hebei Provincial Archives.

way he served his community and dealt with the government.

To further evaluate the effectiveness of the xiangdi system in the early twentieth century, let us look at the incidence of disputes over xiangdi service. The incidence should be low when the xiangdi system worked well, and vice versa. Table 8 indicates that there were on average two formally filed disputes over xiangdi service each year in Republican Huailu, or only one for every 200 xiangdi posts (the county had approximately 400 xiangdi positions). There were of course many more disputes over xiangdi posts that were mediated within communities and did not go to court. However, even if there were ten times as many mediated disputes as there were formally

TABLE 9

Fulfillment of the Tax Quota in Huailu County and Hebei Province

	Huailu County			Hebei Province
	Tax quota (yuan)	Tax collected (yuan)	Percentage	Tax collected (% of tax quota)
1915	53,448	53,343	99.80	n.a.
1930	54,119	54,043	99.86	76.50
1931	53,915	53,881	99.94	81.09
1932	53,915	53,453	99.14	66.47
1933	53,915	50,905	94.42	67.53

SOURCE: The figures for 1915 are from 656.1.396, 1915. Data for 1930 to 1933 are from Li Hongyi 1977 [1934]: 6412–24.

filed ones, there would have been just one dispute for every twenty xiangdi posts per year. This implies that village regulations on xiangdi rotation were well observed by the villagers.

We may also take the fulfillment of tax quotas as an indicator of the effectiveness of the xiangdi system. Tax quotas were most likely to be met in full when the system worked well; tax delinquency rose when it malfunctioned. Huailu county had long been known for its good record in tax payment, as noted in the late nineteenth-century Huailu gazetteer (*Huailu xianzhi* 1985 [1876]: 72). Statistics from the early Republican years substantiate that comment. During those years for which data are available, this county fulfilled tax quotas almost in full. A Huailu magistrate reported to the Hebei provincial government in 1923, "this county has always paid its taxes in full every year and the people left no delinquency" (*xiang xi nian qing nian kuan, bing wu minqian*) (656.2.288, 1923). That statement was even true in the early 1930s when Huailu suffered a new wave of state intrusion and tax escalation (see Table 9). It is thus safe to say that the xiangdi system or village regulations on xiangdi service remained largely valid in the early twentieth century.

The Xiangdi System in Comparative Perspective

To further explicate the nature of the xiangdi system, we may compare the practices in Huailu with the administrative institutions in other parts of rural China during the late Qing and Republican periods. Let us begin with a comparison between the xiangdi in south-central Hebei and two different systems in northeastern Hebei, namely, the *xiangbao* in Baodi county and the *banpai* in Changli county.

The xiangdi system was coupled with an unstratified social structure in south-central Hebei, where over 90 percent of the rural households owned farms and hence were taxpayers. This social homogeneity laid a basis for communitywide participation in xiangdi service. However, low stratification and a predominance of owner-cultivators were not unique to the core area but quite common in the rest of the North China Plain. And homogeneity does not necessarily produce shared identity, which was indispensable for people in the precapitalist community to cooperate in pursuit of shared interests. What distinguished south-central Hebei from the peripheral areas of rural North China and made it possible for cooperative institutions to prevail were primarily the strong kinship ties that characterized the villages. It was on the solid basis of kinship organizations that the villagers cooperated to pursue their common ends in dealing with the government. The predominance of descent groups, in turn, was a result of ecological stability and land fertility. These favorable conditions allowed the descent groups to flourish and develop into tightly knit communities and made it possible for their cooperation to endure in a secure environment.

In sharp contrast, the xiangbao system in nineteenth-century Baodi county involved no cooperation among the taxpayers. Unlike the villagers in Huailu, who rotated annually to provide xiangdi service, in Baodi it was the wealthy and prestigious in local communities who nominated xiangbao candidates from households of average means and even the landless to shoulder the burden of tax collection and to serve as the buffer between themselves and the government. Although the state held the sponsors responsible for helping the xiangbao to make up tax shortages, few did so. Furthermore, unlike the xiangdi, whose advance payment of taxes directly benefited his fellow villagers, the xiangbao only did what he was assigned by the government—that is, to prompt taxpayers and to make good on tax deficits after the deadline. This system had no protective effects on the taxpayers. And unlike the villages in Huailu that set up a public fund or public land to facilitate the xiangdi's advance payment, the Baodi villages had no such security institutions. Finally, unlike the villagers in Huailu, who provided the xiangdi with substantial compensation for the service they received, there were no such reciprocal arrangements under the xiangbao system. Therefore it is difficult to view the xiangbao system in Baodi as a cooperative practice.[12]

The contrast between the xiangdi and xiangbao is also evident in their fates in the late nineteenth and early twentieth centuries. Unable to fulfill their duties in making good on tax deficits, many xiangbao simply ran away when they failed to do so (P. Huang 1985: 224–31). In many places, illegal tax-farming occurred when the traditional xiangbao system failed to meet the state's increased need for taxes.[13] Overseeing as many as twenty villages, the xiangbao also failed to reach the bottom of village society. Consequently, the xiangbao system disappeared altogether in the early twentieth century. This contrasts sharply with the survival and effective operation of the xiangdi system in Huailu.

Another institution that is worth mentioning is the so-called banpai organization found in nineteenth-century Changli county in northeastern Hebei. The banpai normally comprised as many as ten or fifteen villages. Under this arrangement, every village contributed to a fund that the banpai agents used to handle local matters, including bribing the yamen functionaries and paying miscellaneous fees. The villages were also responsible for the agents' salaries, which were paid every six months. It is likely that the banpai functioned to protect local interests, but the materials currently available lack details showing how these agents worked. Duara's study shows no involvement of the banpai personnel in tax payment, the most important task in local administration. Given the insularity of most villages in the North China Plain, I doubt the effectiveness and durability of such trans-village organizations. The peasants in Changli county did attempt to create trans-village defensive organizations such as green crop associations. However, without effective coordination among different villages, these efforts all ended in failure (Duara 1988: 53). No evidence of substantial cooperation in tax payment has been found so far in the peripheral areas of North China.

The villages in south-central Hebei, a core area of the North China Plain, had a much higher level of communal solidarity than their counterparts in the peripheral parts. It is worth repeating that the solidary arrangements in Huailu villages resulted from their homogeneous social structures and strong kinship ties embedded in a relatively stable environment. Again, this contrasted with the situation in localities of northeastern Hebei, where the weak lineage organizations and disaster-prone environment made it difficult, perhaps even impossible, for cooperative institutions to emerge and endure in local administration.

SOUTH CHINA

Needless to say, the homogeneous village structure, stable ecology, and close kinship ties that nurtured the xiangdi system were not limited to the south-central Hebei plain. Where similar conditions prevailed, cooperative practices in tax payment and village administration were also likely to occur. The strong kinship ties in the ecologically stable Canton delta, for example, allowed the prevalence of cooperative practices in tax collection in descent-group villages. There people of the same clan tended to reside together in single-surname villages. Such communities developed sophisticated, hierar-chical kinship organizations with the *zuzhang* (clan elder) at the top. At the center of such organizations was the "ancestral hall" (*citang*), which was led by the zuzhang and supported by public land of the clan (which often accounted for as much as 40 percent of all the cultivable land). The ancestral hall was in-variably involved in tax collection. It either prompted its members to pay taxes by a due date or directly collected taxes from individual kinsmen and then remitted them together to the government. Some ancestral halls also paid taxes in advance for all their members and then collected the prepaid monies from the latter with a 5 percent surcharge. It was not uncommon in such cases for strict "clan regulations" (*zugui*) to be formulated and enforced to ensure full and prompt tax payment or repayment. Those who failed to fulfill their tax duties were often excluded from sharing the sacrifices to clan ancestors by these clan regulations (Ye Xian'en and Tan Dihua 1985; Liu Zhi-wei 1988, 1997; Chen Zhiping 1988: 139–60; Katayama 1982a, 1982b).

Of all forms of cooperation in taxation, the closest to the xiangdi system in Huailu was the *yitu* (voluntary *tu*) found in some parts of South China. Under this system, as a typical case reveals, taxpayers with landholdings to-taling up to 3,000 mu or so formed a tax unit called a *tu* (usually a natural village), which was further divided into a number of subunits called *zhuang*. The tax agent of the zhuang was chosen from villagers with the largest land-holdings, who further rotated each year to serve as the tax agent for the whole tu. During the tax collection period, the zhuang agent first collected taxes from individual households under his charge and then turned the pro-ceeds over to the tu agent. The latter further delivered the taxes of his tu to the county government. Both the zhuang and tu agents were responsible for taxes in arrears occurring in their own units (Wan Guoding et al. 1971; Chen Dengyuan 1938). Obviously, the yitu had much in common with local prac-tices in Huailu, for both were cooperative arrangements aimed at protecting village communities from intrusion by yamen runners and tax farmers. Both functioned to satisfy the state's financial needs and therefore received official encouragement. Yet there were also significant differences between the two. Unlike the xiangdi, whose service was rewarded with certain privileges, the tu agent (*xianbao* or *zhinianyuan*) fulfilled his duties without any remunera-tion or compensation ("*you yiwu er wu quanli*") (Wan Guoding et al., 1971: 86). Moreover, in comparison with village regulations in Huailu, the yitu in-volved an even greater role by local government. The government had pro-posed the yitu in the nineteenth century as a means of combating the illegal baolan business (Faure 1976; Kuhn 1979; Morita 1976, 1981). In the 1930s, lo-cal government again attempted to restore and consolidate the yitu in order to secure its tax income. As a result of greater government involvement, each tu stipulated its own *tugui* (regulations of the tu) in written form to detail the duties of tu agents and taxpayers. However, this greater role of the state might also explain why the yitu declined in the late Qing and early Republican years as state influence in the countryside deteriorated (Wan Guoding et al. 1971). The xiangdi system, by contrast, was primarily a product of the initiatives of village communities and therefore showed greater longevity than the yitu system.

To conclude, the xiangdi system illustrated the cooperative institutions in the core area of the North China macroregion. Like the rest of North China, south-central Hebei was dominated by communities of owner-cultivators, which made possible villagewide cooperation in tax payment and local administration. However, unlike the ecologically unstable areas where weak kinship ties made it difficult for villagers to form effective and endurable cooperation in tax payment, south-central Hebei was endowed with a secure environment and fertile land, which nourished stable communities, strong descent groups, and a wide array of cooperative institutions. These characteristics made this area more similar to the southern regions of China than to the rest of North China. In state-village relations, the xiangdi system departed from practices in both the peripheral areas of North China and the core area in the southern regions of China. Without protective arrangements, the peasants in peripheral North China were exposed to the intrusion of predatory yamen runners and tax farmers, which often caused tensions between the village and the state, especially after 1900 when the government raised the tax burden substantially. The single-surname communities in South China, on the other hand, were so strong that their cooperative arrangements often overwhelmed influences of the state, as seen in the supremacy of "clan regulations" in village life (Fei Kangcheng 1998). Unlike any of these institutions, the working of the xiangdi system relied on support from both the government and community members. As an endogenous cooperative institution, the xiangdi worked primarily to facilitate the villagers' tax payment and to protect village communities from external intrusions under the otherwise official system or illegal practices by predatory yamen runners or rapacious tax farmers. Communities under the xiangdi system thus showed a high level of cohesiveness. At the same time, however, this endogenous system did not exclude government influence. Instead, the xiangdi assumed certain official duties in village administration, thus bringing government authority all the way down to village communities. More important, the smooth working of the xiangdi system ensured the prompt and full payment of land taxes. Therefore the government accepted this local institution as a desirable substitution for the deteriorating and malfunctioning baojia system. The xiangdi system, in a word, registered both a high level of community solidarity and a relatively strong presence of the state in the rural society.

CHAPTER 4

Rules, Self-Interest, and Strategies

Disputes over the Xiangdi Service

The xiangdi system, as shown in the preceding chapter, was quite effective in Huailu villages as late as the 1920s. The question that needs to be further addressed here is why it was so enduring in the peasant communities and how the villagers complied with or deviated from established practices and rules under that system. Focusing on disputes over the xiangdi service, this chapter analyzes the factors that shaped the villagers' behaviors, such as their collective interests, group identity, shared experiences and assumptions, as well as property relations and power configurations that defined the specific interests of each individual in the community. All these factors combined to form a context in which the villagers thought about their interests, interpreted the actions of others, and chose their own strategies.

Social Contexts of the Disputes

The Huailu archives contain a fairly complete record of thirty-four lawsuits over xiangdi service occurring between 1912 and 1929.[1] These disputes fell broadly into two categories, one about competition for the xiangdi post (five cases) and the other evasion of xiangdi service (twenty-nine cases). The taxpayers competed for the xiangdi post when its advantages outweighed its disadvantages. Xiangdi service could be lucrative. The fees a xiangdi drew as middleman from local transactions were substantial. It was common in Huailu that, aside from serving as tax agent, a xiangdi also acted as the go-between in the sale of land, housing, and other commodities. The statutory commission the xiangdi drew from the sale was 2 percent of the selling price in the Qing period and 1.5 percent in the Republican period (656.1.947,

1918). But in practice, a xiangdi could get a fee much higher than this official rate. He might, for example, enter on the land deed a price much lower than the actual one so that the buyer would pay a deed tax less than he should have paid. In turn, the xiangdi would receive a fee higher than the statutory figure (656.1.749, 1917).

The subsidy for xiangdi service could also be attractive. To compensate the xiangdi for his advance payment of taxes, many villages provided the post with a subsidy (*jintie* or *gongshiqian*). In Xujiazhuang village, for example, the subsidy was 8,000 wen or 2.06 yuan (656.2.814, 1926). In another instance, the subsidy amounted to 23,000 wen or 15.3 yuan (656.1.1212, 1920), which equaled the net income a cultivator could earn from 7 mu of the most common type of land. Such significant earnings from the middleman's fee and / or the subsidy, therefore, could easily trigger competition for the xiangdi office.

The majority of the disputes, however, had to do with attempts to avoid xiangdi service. The villagers did so when the xiangdi's burden outweighed the benefits he would receive. This evasion became frequent in the late 1920s, when military conflicts among the warlords in North China intensified and Huailu, as a strategically important location, bore the brunt of their damages. Miscellaneous charges imposed on the xiangdi skyrocketed, while local commercial activities declined and most of the xiangdi's commissions disappeared. Serving as xiangdi became an unbearable burden in many localities.

The peasants thus appeared to be rational actors interested in maximizing their self-interest to the extent that they were inclined to compete for the xiangdi service when the post was profitable and avoid it when the costs of service outweighed its benefits. Likewise, community leaders either helped those under their patronage to shirk their duties or seize the xiangdi position, depending on its undesirability or profitability. However, few in the village community openly violated the established rules regarding the xiangdi system. Instead, all disputants used the asserted village regulations to justify their actions, whether they had complied with or deviated from them in actuality. There was often a disjunction between their intention and representation.

To understand the complexity of the social contexts in which the villagers calculated and made decisions, we need to take into account the objective conditions that informed the villagers' shared assumptions and attitudes, as well as the immediate circumstances that influenced their individual decisions. Let us first consider the social contexts that shaped the peasants' collective consciousness and dispositions as seen in Huailu villages.

Living in a community of mainly owner-cultivators and kinsmen, the villagers were involved in the same social relations and subject to the same regulations that governed their mutual obligations in cooperative activities. They all knew, for example, who would take the next turn as xiangdi, when and how he would take his post, and what the job entailed. As neighbors, friends, or kinsmen living in proximity or intimacy, the villagers also knew each other well—the limits and potential of their abilities, the purposes of their actions, the strategies they were likely to choose, and the results they wanted to achieve. This homogeneity of objective conditions produced a "homogeneity of habitus" that made their practices and expressions readily apprehensible (Bourdieu 1980: 58).

The villagers also shared a broad understanding of village institutions and the mechanisms that enforced them, of which the most conspicuous was a consensus on the supremacy of village regulations in community life. In most villages or subvillage *pai*, the villagers unanimously agreed on the utmost importance of village regulations (*cungui*) about the xiangdi service. All parties involved in disputes over this service, for example, used the cungui to justify their respective claims. When submitting a plaint, the accuser invariably charged his opponent with "violating the village regulation" (*pohuai cungui*). His petition typically began with a summary of the regulation on the selection of the xiangdi, and ended with a request for a just ruling in order to "remedy the [disrupted] village regulation" (*yi zheng cungui*) or to "preserve the old regulation" (*baocun jiugui*). Needless to say, the villagers built and continued this consensus because compliance with relevant regulations was critical to the successful production of the collective good of the community and each individual, while any violation could be disastrous to the whole community. As one villager put it in his complaint about a xiangdi candidate who refused to serve: if the breach of village regulations were tolerated, then "it will be inevitable that all villagers follow the bad example and it will be extremely difficult to handle the succession to the xiangdi service" (656.1.554, 1916). Similar words are found in almost every petition for a court inquiry into the matter (e.g., 656.2.6, 1921; 656.2.967, 1927). This strong consensus on village regulations explained at least in part why they did not have to be written or codified in most communities where the obligatory fulfillment of xiangdi service was taken for granted (see also H. Li 2000a).

Another factor that shaped the dispositions of the villagers was the correlation of one's social standing with the fulfillment of prescribed roles in the community. For ordinary peasants in Huailu villages, serving as the xiangdi was not merely a duty for the production of the collective well-being, but also necessary to maintain membership in the community. Not surprisingly, anyone who violated the village regulations would find himself under immense pressure from public opinion. One villager who was involved in a dispute observed that, if he failed to comply with the old regulation, he would be denounced by all other villagers (*yinghuai jiugui, kong ren tuoma*) (656.2.967, 1927). Community leaders, too, had to defend and conform to village regulations in order to reaffirm and reproduce their prestige and authority in the community. For both the notables and ordinary members, social standing and reputation were as critical as material interests when the source of their influence or means of survival were largely limited to the community. Thus, although the ordinary as well as the powerful had the urge to disobey village regulations in order to minimize their material loss or maximize their gains, their violation had to be disguised and limited so as to prevent their reputations from being damaged.

Also important in shaping the peasants' perceptions and actions were the attitudes of external authorities. The legitimacy of village regulations, to be sure, rested primarily in the recognition and consensus of the local residents and did not await the endorsement of external forces. When disputes occurred, village regulations invariably served as the basis for community mediation. However, as the examples examined below reveal, the regulation or the consensus on it alone was sometime not enough to reach a resolution acceptable to all disputants. Once the quarrel was brought to an external agency, be it the county magistrate or the county assembly, the attitude of those outside the community became critical. In the absence of any official regulations applicable to the essentially indigenous practices in dispute, the magistrate naturally relied on the village regulations to render his decision. This method in return reinforced the validity of the local regulations and enhanced the shared understanding of its supremacy among the villagers.

Last but no less important were past experiences shared by all members of the community. The dispositions of community members not only reflected existing circumstances but also integrated their memories of previous experiences that reinforced and reaffirmed their attitudes toward community undertakings. When a dispute over the xiangdi service arose, the accuser invariably emphasized the relevant regulation's long history and validity in the community. Frequently seen in those plaints are statements such as: "the old regulation of the village has an origin that is not traceable" (656.1.1212, 1920); "the old regulation has a long history in the village" (656.2.406, 1924); "the regulation has continued in the village for hundreds of years and has been well observed by all" (656.2.6, 1921); or "village regulation has been transmitted for a long time and no confusion has ever occurred" (656.1.1216, 1920).⁷ These statements, of course, do not necessarily mean that their village regulations had operated without disruption or violation throughout their history. Rather, they reflected the villagers' disposition that past experiences had an important place. Habitus, as Bourdieu put it, is the "principle of . . . continuity and regularity," or "a past which survives in the present and tends to perpetuate itself into the future by making itself present in practices structured according to its principles" (1977: 82).

These factors thus formed a social and historical context in which all members of a community interacted with one another to pursue their individual and collective ends. It was the homogeneous living conditions, the consensus on community institutions, the same way they interacted with external forces, and the shared experience and memory that informed and shaped how the villagers thought and acted, enabling them to harmonize their expression and orchestrate their actions.

However, to understand the action of every individual in the community, we cannot limit our attention to the aforementioned factors that constrained the villagers. Equally important were individuals' changing circumstances, which influenced their different motivations and actions. The most obvious was the degree of group solidarity and the position of an individual in relation to the group. The cohesiveness of peasant communities varied. Some were stable and strong, as seen in their elaborated and entrenched institutions and social sanctions against deviation from community rules. In such places, the individual had to be scrupulous in making a decision or exercising power when he found it difficult to deviate from the norms and regulations. The reverse was true in a weak community where institutional constraints and social sanction were absent. Equally important was one's position in the community. For example, a villager who had a short history of residence in the locale and had been treated as an outsider would be eager to fill the xiangdi position in order to establish his membership in the community and would not easily give up if his opportunity were threatened by other competitors. Likewise, a powerful person would tend to abuse his influence if he was an outsider and therefore not subject to its rules.

The other is one's status in the power configuration of local society. By and large, we can classify the villagers into three categories: the weak or those of less-than-average means and outside the network of patronage of the powerful; the ordinary or those of average means; and the powerful, whose strength and power were based on their wealth, office, or social status. When a dispute took place between two villagers of roughly equal strength, each would tend to focus on their justification in accordance with the village regulation. The village regulations worked best under such circumstances, for no one was powerful enough to misrepresent or distort them to his advantage. Where gross inequities in power existed, however, a powerful person might manipulate the village regulation to his advantage. A weaker villager might give up his claim after attempting to defend his rights or accept a compromise without trying to defend himself. One's options varied depending on his strength in the community.

Therefore, to understand peasant behaviors, we have to consider not only the social conditions that produced the dispositions or habitus common to all members of the peasant community, but also their individual concerns with material and symbolic interests as well as their individual positions in the power structure. It was the interaction between these two sets of factors that caused the peasants' strategies to vary from person to person yet rendered them readily understandable and even predictable to the rest of the villagers.

To illustrate how the villagers deliberated and took action, the following examination focuses on six cases, each describing a typical situation and a specific strategy employed by the villager involved in the dispute.[3] These disputes are put into three groups that represent the strategies of the ordinary, the weak, and the powerful in the community, respectively.

Strategies of the Ordinary

As in other parts of the North China Plain, most villages in Huailu remained communities of low-level stratification. Not surprisingly, in most instances the disputants were peasants of roughly equal strength. They had a similar economic status and the same resources and options available to them. Therefore, the strategies they chose also showed a similar pattern. The following two cases reveal the kinds of decisions they made when involved in a dispute.

SHANXIAYI VILLAGE

Shanxiayi village consisted of eleven pai for tax-collecting purposes. Most of them were single-surname neighborhoods. Each neighborhood or descent group had its own xiangdi and regulation (*paigui*) on the recruitment of the xiangdi. According to the regulation of the first pai, for example, its households, all bearing the surname Zai, were to serve as its xiangdi in annual rotation on the basis of the tax each household owed. Those with the largest taxes had to serve first. The incumbent xiangdi was to nominate his successor at the beginning of the twelfth month of the lunar year and ask the xiangyue of the pai to inform the nominee of his turn to serve.[4] If the nominee found another household who had a tax quota higher than his, the latter would supply the next year's service.

On January 30, 1927, a xiangyue of the ninth pai of the village reported a dispute to the magistrate. According to his petition, villager Zai Ziyou, who was nominated by the current xiangdi of the first pai, refused to accept the office when the xiangyue informed him of the nomination. According to the xiangyue, Ziyou claimed that he owed tax of just 1.4 taels while Zai Qinghe owed more than 2 taels. Therefore, Ziyou insisted that it should be Qinghe's turn to be the xiangdi. Worrying about the probable delay of tax payment in the coming year, the xiangyue requested that the magistrate summon the two Zais and decide who should take the office. Following the xiangyue's petition, Qinghe submitted a plaint, charging Ziyou with "disrupting the old regulation" (*wenluan jiugui*) by nominating him as the xiangdi. He asserted that, if the order of service was to be determined by the size of the tax owed, he should not serve as the xiangdi until three years later, but he failed to specify how much his tax quota was. His plaint provoked Ziyou's counterplaint, which likewise accused Qinghe of "not obeying the village regulation" (*buyi xianggui*), claiming that Qinghe had a tax quota much higher than his and therefore should offer the service first.

To clarify the facts, the magistrate sent a policeman to the village to investigate the matter jointly with the village head. On February 22, the village head (Qinghe's uncle) reported to the magistrate that he had investigated the matter and that "by village regulations" Ziyou should take over the xiangdi office. The magistrate commented accordingly: "Since Zai Ziyou should take over the position by the village custom, [I] would trust this village head to instruct [Ziyou] to observe [the regulation]."

Three days later, however, Ziyou filed another petition, insisting that his tax quota was lower than Qinghe's and that Qinghe had not served as xiangdi in the past fifty years as far as he could recall. He went on to charge that the village head, "ganging up with the xiangyue" (*cunzhang xiangyue langbei weijian*), protected his nephew and helped him evade his service. He warned that if he were compelled to take over the office it would "destroy the old regulation and [he would] be reproached [by other villagers]." Ziyou therefore asked the magistrate to summon Qinghe to court and order him to be the xiangdi. After the magistrate's rejection of his request, Ziyou filed a third petition, repeating his claims. This time the magistrate ordered the ward police, instead of the village head, to look into the matter. The police soon reported back that it was Ziyou who should take over the job in conformity with the village regulations.

Following the police report, the xiangyue, together with another xiangyue, one Zai Guanbao, filed three consecutive petitions. In the first two, they reported a chain reaction resulting from Ziyou's refusal of his service: following Ziyou's example, Feng Erni refused to serve as the xiangdi of the ninth pai as well. What made things even worse, the two xiangyue claimed, was that "the xiangdi of other pai also refused to perform their duties upon seeing the fact that those two xiangdi could reject their duties. Now the ward has ordered our village to supply straw, and no one has taken up the task." The two xiangyue reasserted this point in the third petition: "If he [Ziyou] refuses to assume the post, others will follow his bad example, and the xiangdi office will no longer exist. When there comes a demand from the government, who will take up the public responsibility?" The two xiangyue's petitions prompted a counterpetition from Ziyou, who merely re-

peated his claims. At this point, the magistrate summoned Ziyou, the two xiangyue, and the village head to court. At the court session, the magistrate
found for the xiangyue and ordered Ziyou to serve as the xiangdi.

The case turned in Ziyou's favor only after the persistent villager filed his
fifth petition following the court hearing. In that petition Ziyou repeated his
claim and even challenged the magistrate: "during the court session, [you]
ordered me to serve as this year's xiangdi without allowing me to make an
explanation. Nor did [you] give me a reason why [you] made such a decision. I really cannot understand." Ziyou further pointed out the possible result of such a decision: "If I assume this year's office, by what kind of village
regulations, for what reason, and to whom should I hand over my duty in
the next year? Disputes will inevitably arise." He therefore asked the magistrate to withdraw his ruling, and to "preserve the old regulations" (*baocun
jiugui*) by reordering Qinghe to be the xiangdi. "If [you] order me to be
the officeholder," Ziyou insisted, "give me an explicit explanation of how
this order was made. Otherwise, I will not be able to hand over the job next
year. . . . " The magistrate responded by asking Ziyou to provide his registered name as it appeared on the "red books" (*hongbu*, the official copy of the
tax roll), because the magistrate wanted to determine whether Ziyou's tax
quota was really lower than Qinghe's as he repeatedly asserted. After checking Ziyou's tax quota, the magistrate noted: "On verification, [I found that
the tax quota as Ziyou claims] tallies with [the record on] the red book. Wait
for instructions to order Zai Qinghe, who has a higher tax quota, to assume
this pai's xiangdi post this year."

But the dispute did not end here. Two weeks later, the xiangyue of the
first pai reported to the magistrate that Zai Ziyou, together with his two
brothers, had a tax quota of over 4 taels, which was much higher than Zai
Qinghe's. "In order to evade serving as the xiangdi, Ziyou purposefully divided their shared tax quota into three portions . . . so each has only slightly
over 1 tael. This, however, is only a cunning trickery and calculation." The
magistrate decided to hold another court session, commenting that the three
brothers' taxes, if combined, were higher than Qinghe's but lower if divided.
"They disputed with each other by adhering to the custom and each does
have his own rationale." In the court session, the two parties repeated their
justifications. The magistrate's final decision was a compromise; he ordered
both Ziyou and Qinghe to serve as the xiangdi (656.2.967, 1927).

The xiangdi service was obviously an unwanted job in Shanxiayi village.
To avoid this duty, however, no one in the dispute violated the village regulation by overtly rejecting his duty. Instead, both Ziyou and Qinghe justified
their refusal of the service by adhering to the village regulation. For Ziyou,
the best strategy for shirking his duty was to divide the tax liability among
the three brothers to make his own lower than Qinghe's, so that Qinghe had

to serve as xiangdi first by the village regulation. For Qinghe, the only choice was to deny the legitimacy of this division and stress Ziyou's evasive division of his tax liability, which in Qinghe's opinion was immoral. In fact, however, legally Ziyou had done nothing wrong, for no rule or regulation prohibited him from doing so. And since his tax after the division was indeed lower than Qinghe's, the latter had to take his turn first. That was why the magistrate accepted Ziyou's petition after verifying his tax liability. But the act of dividing his tax liability right before his turn to serve as xiangdi was indeed a deliberate evasion of his duty, which, from the magistrate's point of view, was legal but a violation of the moral code. When he realized this upon reading the xiangyue's report and the second court session, the magistrate changed his original decision and ordered the two disputants to share the burden equally. In doing so, he took into account both Ziyou's legal action and Qinghe's moral appeal.

It is clear, however, that despite the different approaches used by the two disputants, there was a strong consensus on the central role of the village regulation throughout the dispute. The two disputants adhered to the village regulation when defending themselves and accusing each other, and those in power, including the village head, the two xiangyue, and the county magistrate, all purportedly made their judgments and decisions in accordance with the village regulation. Reflecting the strong solidarity of the descent group, this consensus made it impossible for anyone in the community to deviate from the regulation in an overt manner. The strategy of those who attempted to resign their duties was to take advantage of the "legal" techniques allowed by social practices, which was in perfect compliance with the village regulation.

The two disputants persisted not only because both had valid grounds to defend themselves but also because both had the necessary resources to pursue the litigation. Although Ziyou's land after the division was 30 mu, less than Qinghe's 40-plus mu, it was far above the average landholding in rural North China. The wealth allowed him to persist, submitting a total of five petitions in his defense. Qinghe's wealth may have been a bit greater than Ziyou's, but his real strength lay in the support of his uncle, the village head, and the two xiangyue. The village head was clearly a person of strength in his village, for he was able to mobilize two xiangyue from their respective pai of the village to sue Ziyou, the xiangdi nominee. It was the repeated petition from the xiangyue that made it possible for Ziyou to share the xiangdi service with him. The result of the dispute thus reflected not only their equally valid claims, but also their respective strength.

NANZHUANG VILLAGE

Nanchuang was a small community of twenty-three households from five descent groups. To cooperate in village administration and tax payment, the villagers ranked all households in order of the size of their landholdings and formulated a list of xiangdi candidates on a folded piece of paper (*zhezi*). By village regulation, the xiangdi for the coming year was to go to the incumbent xiangdi's home on the fifteenth day of the twelfth month to acquire the bronze gong and other tools of office from the outgoing xiangdi, and then commence his xiangdi service on lunar New Year's Day. According to the xiangdi candidates' list, a household headed by Wang Kejian, 80 years old, was to serve as the xiangdi in 1920. But Wang argued with the outgoing xiangdi, named Geng Yunfang, over the handover procedure and refused to go to Geng's house to pick up the tools of office.

The suit was brought to court on April 4, 1920, by Geng, who accused Wang of "not taking over [the xiangdi post] according to the list." He submitted with his plaint the list of xiangdi candidates. The magistrate responded simply by returning the list to the village head and instructing him to order Wang Kejian to assume the post immediately "in accordance with the village regulation"(*anzhao cungui*). Four days later, however, the village head returned the list to the magistrate with a report saying that Wang stubbornly refused to take over the office. At the court session held on April 14, Wang Faying, the son of Kejian speaking on behalf of his 80-year-old father, claimed that his father was not unwilling to take over the post; he had not done so because Geng had failed to inform him of his turn on the fifteenth day of the twelfth month of the last lunar year as the village regulation specified and because Geng had refused to give him the bronze gong, a tool used by the xiangdi to convene villagers and therefore a symbol of the xiangdi office. On the magistrate's instruction, Wang Faying submitted a pledge, stating his willingness to assume the post in place of his father and to receive the gong at Geng's home.

The two disputants, however, continued their quarrels over the transfer of the gong. Wang accused Geng of occupying the post and refusing to give him the gong, and Geng, in turn, charged Wang with not taking over the gong despite his several promptings. As a compromise, the magistrate asked the village head to hand the gong to Wang. The village head, however, refused to do so on the pretext that three rooms of his house had been burned because of his report to the magistrate, suspecting Wang to be the arsonist. As a counterattack, Wang submitted a plaint accusing Geng and the village head of making several illegal purchases of housing and land; he said that they had used plain sheets of paper instead of the designated official forms to draw up contracts in order to evade the deed tax. Wang also accused the two of illegal involvement in several transactions that allowed them to pocket all the fees they had drawn as middlemen. The case came to an end when the magistrate pressed Wang to take over the gong directly from Geng and held him solely responsible for failure to do so, while encouraging him to file a separate complaint detailing Geng's abuses (656.1.1216, 1920).

The main reason that Wang disputed with Geng, as his final plaint revealed, was that the outgoing xiangdi and the village head had encroached on the material benefits that Wang would have received as the only legitimate and exclusive middleman, a privilege granted to the xiangdi by village regulations. To avoid paying a middleman's fee to Wang, Geng and the village head had illegally conducted their own transactions without using Geng as the middleman. Even more intolerable for Wang was that they further acted as illegal middlemen for other transactions and drew fees that were rightfully his. However, failure to receive a middleman's fee was not a justifiable reason for Wang to reject the xiangdi service. And indeed Wang had no intention of doing so; the xiangdi service in the early 1920s was not yet as onerous as it became several years later. Wang's only goal was to vent his resentment against the outgoing xiangdi and the village head, and Geng's failure to inform him of the handover procedure on the fifteenth day of the twelfth month in compliance with the village regulation offered him a perfect excuse. This was why Wang tenaciously refused to go to Geng's house to receive the gong until he received a threatening instruction from the magistrate.

Like the preceding case, this dispute was couched in the language of compliance with village regulations. Each party to the dispute accused the other of violating the cungui while defending himself with it. Beneath the surface of the dispute over the hand-over of the bronze gong, however, was a rivalry between two households of roughly equal strength. The Wang household held over 80 mu of land, which was far above the average level in the village, and behind him was his descent group of five households. Geng held only about 40 mu of land. However, Geng's descent group was the same size (five households) as Wang's, and more important, he was backed by the village head, the most influential person in the community. These differences in their resources shaped the approach and results of the lawsuit. Wang's wealth enabled him to maintain his stance until the magistrate intervened and to pose a threat to the xiangdi and the village head by bringing their abuse to light. But Geng eventually won the battle owing to the support of the village head.

Together, these two cases have some meaningful implications for understanding the actions and motivations of the villagers. There is no doubt that the disputants were self-interested actors who were concerned primarily about their own material interests. The loss caused by xiangdi service or the failure to reap the benefits of this service drove them to sue each other. But the villagers were at the same time members of communities that showed a high level of solidarity, as seen in the valid working of village regulations, a strong consensus on the supremacy of these institutions, and the resulting social sanctions imposed for deviating from them. Therefore, no one in the disputes dared to completely ignore the regulations in their pursuit of private goals. This was especially true when the two parties were of equal strength. To protect themselves from attack and to avoid social sanction, they had to represent their actions in line with the cungui. As strategic, calculating actors, they had to strike a careful balance between attempting to maximize their own material gains and the constraints of community regulations, moral obligations, and public opinions.

Strategies of the Weak

I define the weak in a peasant community as those who were living on the verge of subsistence, those who were socially disadvantaged because they lacked the support of kinsmen or protection from the powerful, or those who were in dire straits owing to unexpected mishaps. The weak or poor, however, were not necessarily passive, docile, and helpless. Like the rest of the community, they formed their own strategies using the resources available to them. The following two cases illustrate the actions they could take in different situations.

NANGUO VILLAGE

Nanguo village comprised two descent groups, the Wangs and the Lis. According to its cungui, the two groups alternated annually to supply a xiangdi for the whole community. When any of them was to take turn, the head of the descent group (zuzhang) would nominate a xiangdi from among the households owning more than 20 mu of land in his clan according to the amount of their land holdings. The xiangdi would begin his service at the start of the lunar New Year when he received a bronze gong and other "public items" from the outgoing xiangdi. In 1928, when the Lis were to provide a xiangdi, their head appointed the grandfather of Li Shengqun to take the post. Because Shengqun's grandfather was already over 90 years old and unable to fulfill his duties in person, Shengqun's two elder brothers acted in their grandfather's name. However, just two weeks after the Li household took the position, the two brothers were killed by armed bandits. The Li household thus gave up the position of xiangdi, and Li Shengqun, the third grandson, who had been adopted out, returned the office items to the zuzhang. Without a xiangdi in office, the head and the deputy head of Nanguo village took over the xiangdi's duties and prepaid over 200 yuan in taxes for fellow villagers over the following few months. But they could not be reimbursed because there was no xiangdi to collect the taxes from the individual households. Therefore, they filed a plaint on April 11, claiming that Li Shengqun "disrupted village regulations" (*wenluan cungui*) not taking on the job after the accidental death of his two brothers. The magistrate sympathized with the grieving Shengqun and instead of asking him to take the office just required Shengqun to "assist" the two village heads in collecting the money they had advanced. Shengqun refused, however, and defended himself at a court hearing held at the village heads' request. According to Shengqun, the xiangdi post should have gone to his grandfather. Having been adopted out, he had no obligation to take over the duties of his birth family. The magistrate, taking into account "his grief in losing two brothers," asked Shengqun to ask his zuzhang to choose from the Li lineage a proper person to fill the post. He also instructed the village heads to "show sympathy for Li Shengqun's deep sorrow and to assist him in managing local affairs or in finding a suitable person to take over his job." When the village heads reported back that Shengqun refused to consult the zuzhang, the magistrate simply asked the village heads either to nominate another appropriate person for the job or continue to temporarily hold the post themselves.

This put the two village heads in a difficult position. They were of course unwilling to shoulder the xiangdi task. But they could not compel Shengqun to resume the post, and they would have difficulty persuading anyone else to do so. Their only option was to turn to the zuzhang of the Lis to nominate a new xiangdi. The zuzhang's opinion was that "if another person is needed to serve as the current xiangdi, it should be Li Qingcheng by the order of landholdings." However, this proposition could not be justified because, according to the village regulation, Qingcheng should take over xiangdi service on the next lunar New Year's Day. Realizing the difficulty of persuading Qingcheng to accept the xiangdi post more than half a year in advance, the village heads turned to the County Assembly, a deliberative organization at the county seat, asking it to discuss the matter and decide who should be the xiangdi for the current year. The assembly soon held a meeting and concluded that Qingcheng should be the xiangdi. The magistrate thus issued an order accordingly.

Upon learning of the appointment, Qingcheng ran away. On May 28, Qingcheng's son, Koude, submitted a plaint against the village heads, alleging that although Qingcheng had 50 mu of land registered under his name, his three sons had in fact divided the household, and each had less than 20 mu of land. Therefore neither they nor their father was obligated to fill the xiangdi post.

At this, the magistrate sent a ward policeman to the village to "clarify the facts" and to make sure that the post was filled "in line with the old regulations of the village." The policeman soon reported back the result of his mission. The zuzhang of the Li lineage, according to the report, insisted that

Qingcheng should serve as the xiangdi in place of Shengqun's grandfather and that he knew nothing about Qingcheng's household division. If they had divided their household when their turn came around, asserted the zuzhang, others would also do so to shirk service. Therefore he could by no means sanction such a division. Although Qingcheng should fill the post by local regulations, the report went on, he stubbornly refused to do so. As a result, the policeman brought all the parties concerned to court.

At the court session held on June 11, Koude insisted that the middle of the year was not the right time for his father to take over the office. If he was compelled to assume the post, he should not have to pay taxes in advance, but do legwork only. Moreover, he should not be held responsible for the "harm" (*hai*, a specific term referring to the irregular levy of *bingchai*, or military service) for the first half of the year. Taking the claims of both parties into consideration, the magistrate ruled that Li Qingcheng be the xiangdi for the year, but that the advance payment of taxes would be equally shared by the three parties: the village head, the deputy head, and the xiangdi (656.2.1120, 1928).

This dispute was difficult to handle because the village regulations could not be applied to any of the parties involved. Although the village head accused Shengqun of "violating village regulations" when his birth family abandoned its duty in the middle of xiangdi service, Shengqun felt justified in not taking over the task, for he was no longer a legal member of his natal family and no regulation obligated him to shoulder the xiangdi duties in place of his deceased brothers. The head of the Li lineage was no doubt correct to nominate Qingcheng as the successor to the deceased xiangdi, for Qingcheng did follow Shengqun's grandfather in the established sequence of xiangdi candidates. Qingcheng, however, could call on two reasons to reject the nomination: it was not the correct time as required by the cungui to take over the service, and his landholding after the division of household was not large enough to qualify him for that service. Obviously, the source of the dispute was not so much that they violated village regulation as that the village regulation did not apply to any of the disputants.

The final resolution of the dispute suggests the effective functioning of the survival ethic in the peasant community. After the unexpected death of Li Shengqun's two elder brothers, their elderly grandfather remained the only adult male in the household. Unable to perform the xiangdi duties, the old man had no choice but to reject the job, an action that indeed constituted a breach of cungui. Taking into account the Lis' misfortune, the county head did not require him to continue his birth family's duty. After Shengqun firmly refused to take over the xiangdi duties from his birth family as the village leaders initially requested, no authorities in and outside of the village further pressed him to do so; his birth family thus successfully got rid of its xiangdi duties. Communal ethics played a critical role in settling the dispute.

MAZHUANG VILLAGE

Mazhuang was a community of four descent groups. The village regulation that guided their cooperation was quite complicated. By that regulation, households having 100 mu of land or more had to serve as xiangdi for one year. Households having less than 100 mu but more than 10 mu had to band together to bring their lands to 100 mu in total and serve as the xiangdi collectively. However, if any of them wanted to relinquish xiangdi duties, the regulation demanded, he had to subsidize the others. The amount of the subsidy should be set by the person who had acted as xiangdi before. If anyone considered the subsidy excessive, he might propose a lower figure. The post would go to the one who offered the lowest figure. Unlike many communities, where households with less than 10 or 20 mu were exempted from the xiangdi service, here all land-owning families were included.

A dispute between Wang Maishou, the "would-be" xiangdi of Mazhuang village, and Ma Baozi, another competitor for the xiangdi of the current year, came to the county magistrate's attention on February 15, 1920, when Wang filed a plaint along with two outgoing xiangdi, charging Ma Baozi with "unsettling village regulations (*raoluan cungui*) and impeding the handover of the xiangdi post." The plaint first recounted the aforementioned village regulation regarding the recruitment of the xiangdi. According to Wang, seven households with a total of 100 mu of land had banded together to perform the xiangdi's responsibilities. Five of them were willing to provide subsidies for relinquishing their xiangdi service. Ma Baozi, who had served as xiangdi before, therefore proposed a subsidy of 23,000 wen for the would-be xiangdi. In order to seize the post, Wang Maishou put forth a subsidy of 16,000 wen, much lower than Ma's. All the parties agreed that Wang should be the xiangdi, except Ma. Because of Ma's opposition, the plaint went on, the outgoing xiangdi could not hand over the job, and Wang could not take over the post. The petitioners asked the magistrate to issue a summons for a court inquiry.

On receipt of this plaint, the magistrate made a standard response. He instructed the accusers to "invite the village head to settle [the dispute] peacefully in compliance with the village regulation, and do not come to court." Three days later, however, Wang filed a prompting petition, repeating his charge against Ma. At this, the magistrate directed one policeman to go to the village and instruct the village head to "clarify the facts and have [the dispute] settled properly."

The village head reported back on March 12, claiming that by village regulations Ma should be the one to fill the post and that the other five households had agreed to provide subsidies for Ma's service, but Wang objected and insisted on his claim to this post. Following the village head's report, Ma submitted a counterpetition against Wang. Ma put forth his own version of the village regulation regarding the selection of the xiangdi. According to Ma, the regulation required that villagers with more land assume the office first. Since he had "a lot of land," he should take over the position. He further asserted that the village head had agreed on his assumption of the post, and that, as a compromise, the village head also had allowed Wang to act as an assistant to the xiangdi. But Wang had rejected this offer, insisting that he alone be the xiangdi.

The magistrate's reaction to the village head's report was predictable. On the basis of the "facts" the head provided, he ruled that Ma Baozi should be the xiangdi for the current year and that Wang Maishou should be prohibited from interfering. The magistrate closed the case when the village head petitioned to end the suit (656.1.1212,1920).

We have found in this dispute two different versions of the village regulation in this community, represented by Wang and Ma, respectively. The village head's mentioning in his report to the magistrate the fact that other taxpayers agreed to subsidize the xiangdi candidate implied that Wang's version of the village regulation might be true. In contrast, Ma's story was not really credible, for if the xiangdi was chosen according to landholdings, it would seem unnecessary to subsidize the xiangdi, as we found in most other villages. Moreover, if Ma's story was true and he was the right person to fill the post, the village head should have made a clear-cut settlement on the selection of the xiangdi; there was no reason for him to agree to Wang's post as assistant to the xiangdi. More likely was that Ma first proposed the xiangdi subsidy and wanted to be the xiangdi. When Wang offered a lower subsidy to gain the post, Ma ganged up with the village head to block Wang and secure the position for himself. Ma likely colluded with the village head to endorse his claim in the report to the magistrate.

Compared to his rival, who had plenty of land and the support of the village head, Wang was poor and weak, unable to force the issue and to insist on a court session in the manner of Zai Ziyou from Shanxiayi village, who stuck to his claim by tenaciously appealing to the cungui. Furthermore, Wang had no grounds to appeal to the subsistence ethic, for his motive was to compete for the position and to enrich himself rather than to avoid a survival crisis. Not surprisingly, he quickly gave up after receiving the magistrate's initial response, which was merely based on the village head's report.

These two cases demonstrate the different strategies available to the weak. Where the community was cohesive, comprising only one or two descent groups, the disadvantaged would very likely turn to its survival ethic for a resolution in their favor. However, this appeal to communal principle could be fruitful only when the xiangdi position entailed a financial burden that threatened their subsistence. Where the position was profitable, that ethic did not work at all, and the service was more likely to be subject to the competition of fellow villagers and the abuse of the powerful. This was especially true in loosely organized communities, where social sanctions against abusers were weak. Nevertheless, the powerful could never totally ignore the *cungui* when the community remained largely intact and where cooperative arrangements stayed on; he had to minimize the possible impact of his misconduct on his own reputation, making some concessions to his victim when necessary. At any rate, his abuse had to be concealed by his ostensible compliance with village regulations.

Strategies of the Powerful

The power one could wield in his community rested in the resources, abilities, and qualifications that he had amassed or could mobilize. Monetary and material wealth, or economic capital, were critical sources of well-being and social influence. No less important, however, were social capital or "the aggregate of the actual or potential resources which are linked to possession of a durable network" and cultural capital in the form of educational qualifications such as academic degrees and other achievements (Bourdieu 1986: 248–49, 243ff.). All these, Bourdieu told us, can be readily translated into "symbolic capital," as manifested in the prestige and renown attached to a family and a name. As perhaps the most valuable form of accumulation in a precapitalist society, symbolic capital is convertible back into economic capital and, therefore, is a transformed and disguised form of the physical "economic" capital (1977: 179, 183).

In Huailu villages, the most powerful were invariably those who possessed one or a combination of different forms of capital. It was their social networks of kinship, friendship, and patronage, or educational background, or their prestige and status as clan leaders and village heads that generated their influence and prestige in the community, which in turn enabled them to pursue self-interests. The following two cases reveal how the notables employed the capital available to them to maximize their social and material gains and to prevail in rivalries with their competitors.

SUNCUN VILLAGE

This village was divided into seven "gates" (*men*, a variant of the standard term *pai*), and each gate supplied a xiangdi for the entire village by turns. Within each gate, those who had already served as xiangdi were labeled *jiuding* (literally, "the old adult male"), the rest *xinding* ("new adult male").

When nominating the xiangdi at the end of the lunar year, the seven gate heads (*mentou*) would as a rule give priority to the xinding households with at least 20 mu of land.

In 1920 a dispute broke out between two lineages in Suncun village, the Liangs and the Rens. The former had a long tradition of better education than the rest of the community. Their ancestors had been degree holders. One current member of the clan was a *shengyuan* (entry-level degree holder). The three schoolmasters of the village all came from the Liang lineage. Because of its ancestor's gentry status, this lineage had been exempted from xiangdi service during imperial times. Yet the Liangs had a relatively short history in the community, having immigrated to the village just about hundred years earlier. Because of their relatively recent arrival, combined with their exemption from the xiangdi service, many fellow villagers treated them as outsiders. The Liangs strived to hold the xiangdi post precisely because they saw that service as a way to achieve full membership in the community. The Rens, on the other hand, were a native lineage in the community. Although their educational background was not comparable to the Liangs', their large clan and entrenched social networks outranked the Liangs. These differences in strength directly affected their respective strategies in competing for the xiangdi service.

The case went to court on January 17 when Liang Guanfeng, the would-be xiangdi of the Liang lineage, filed a plaint against Ren Changqing of the Ren lineage. According to Liang, his lineage, despite having lived in the village for more than one hundred years, had never served as the xiangdi. As a xinding with over 30 mu of land, he should assume the office according to village regulations. However, the plaint continued, Ren Changqing, who was greedy for the middleman's fees resulting from the burgeoning sale of cotton and straw in recent years, "attempted to destroy local regulations and occupy the xiangdi post by force," although he had already served as the xiangdi several times. Afraid of Ren's ire, the charge went on, both the village head and deputy head dared not say a word about his breach of the regulations. Liang therefore asked the magistrate to summon the violator for an inquiry "in order to maintain the local regulations." Regarding this plaint, the magistrate noted: "it is up to the village head and deputy head as well as gentry-villagers [*shenmin*] to discuss and handle the issue of whether Ren Changqing is to be replaced and who is to take over the post. It is definitely unacceptable that you alone come forward and rashly ask for a summons and inquiry." On January 29, Liang filed another petition, repeating his charge against Ren. The magistrate responded by instructing him "not to annoy [the court] any more."

The county yamen took the case seriously only when the village head filed a statement on January 31, just two days after the magistrate's rejection of Liang's second petition. "According to the village regulation," asserted the village head, "Liang should be the one to take over the xiangdi post. However, Ren Changqing, an audacious person who is determined to mess up the village regulation, brazenly insists on his claim to the post. I am afraid that the hand-over procedure of the post which is scheduled for the lunar New Year's Day would thus be delayed." The magistrate's comment: "Since the village heads claim that by the village regulation it should be Liang Guanfeng who is to assume [the office], [I will] permit [this arrangement] in order to forestall a dispute." Five days later, the village heads reported back, claiming that Ren persisted in occupying the post and refused to hand it over to Liang. In response, the magistrate sent a policeman to the village to have the matter properly settled. "If Ren Changqing dare refuse to hand it over, bring him in immediately," instructed the magistrate. On February 15, three schoolmasters (*xuedong*) from the Liang lineage collectively filed a prompting petition, repeating their charge of Ren's "unreasonable infringement of local regulations." They urged that "if we, the Liang lineage, do not serve as xiangdi, the rascals in the village would assert that we are not Suncun villagers. When public issues arose, they will not allow us to have a voice."

The magistrate held a court session on February 15 and again on March 2. On detailed cross-examination, he found that certain points of Liang's accusation did not tally with the facts. The preceding year's xiangdi, it turned out, was a Du, rather than Ren as Liang asserted. And it was not that Ren himself occupied the xiangdi post and refused to hand it over, but that Ren attempted to bar Liang from being the xiangdi and instead put his trusted follower, a Zhang, in the position. Liang insisted on his turn to serve as the xiangdi simply because he believed he was a xinding, and Zhang a jiuding, who had given up three chances to fill the post.

But the court hearing also brought Ren's bullying deeds to light. As it turned out, when the seven gate heads met together with most villagers in a temple on the night of the twentieth day of the twelfth month to nominate the new xiangdi as the village regulations demanded, Ren, himself a gate head, successfully controlled the nomination and put Zhang in the desired position by intimidating those from other lineages and keeping them from having a say. The gate heads of other lineages, as they testified at the court session, said nothing during the nomination. The village head and deputy head, complaining that Ren's action "did not jibe with the old regulation," refused to attend Zhang's feast for celebrating his assumption of the post. Believing that Zhang's assumption of the office "ran counter to the village regulation," Du, the former xiangdi, refused to give the bronze gong and other instruments of the xiangdi office to Zhang as well. On the thirtieth day of the twelfth month, however, when the xiangdi's job was to be handed over on the next day by the village regulation, Ren assembled dozens of his followers and came to Du's house, pressing him to hand the items over to Zhang. Fearful of Ren, Du escaped to an inn outside the village in the night. The next day, when the transfer came due, Ren gathered his followers again and broke into Du's house, taking all of the xiangdi's things away and handing them over to Zhang.

In spite of Ren's flagrant manipulation of the nomination and his resort to violence, the magistrate nevertheless founded for Zhang in his ruling after the two court sessions on the grounds that Zhang was formally "nominated" in a meeting in which the seven gate heads and the two village heads were all present. In the magistrate's view, that procedure conformed to the village regulation, no matter how the village bully twisted it to suit his own designs (656.2.6, 1921).

Clearly, each party in this dispute had its own advantage over the other. The Liangs' strength lay in their gentry background and better ability to represent themselves, while the Rens' strength resided in their entrenched lineage power in the community. This power configuration shaped the strategy each took to fight the other. The Liangs fully utilized their writing abilities. They brought the dispute to court first and dominated the representation of the dispute during the early stage of the lawsuit. To justify his claim to the xiangdi post, Liang Guanfeng talked about the cungui or village regulations repeatedly in his petitions against Ren and blamed the latter for violating the regulations. In fact, the Liangs were not alone in battling the Rens. The village heads, too, accused Ren of "destroying the cungui" in their report to the magistrate. The outgoing xiangdi refused to hand his job to Ren precisely because of his conviction that the nomination was at odds with the cungui.

Situated in this discursive context, people even as reckless as Ren had to avoid flagrant violation of the cungui. As a jiuding who had already served as xiangdi, Ren himself was of course not eligible for that post. The only way for him to block his adversary from the post was to let Zhang, his follower, be the officeholder. Doing so, in his opinion, did not violate the cungui, for Zhang had never been an actual xiangdi and therefore was still a xinding or fresh candidate, despite the fact that he had given up three chances to serve. Ren, however, could in no way put his man in the desired post by force. To "legitimize" this action, Ren took advantage of his lineage strength and easily dominated the nomination procedure, which was ostensibly done in line with the cungui, and no one opposed the result before Ren. Although Ren eventually bent the working of village regulations to his will, he had to hide his misconduct when public opinion in support of the village regulation was strong.

Village heads played a conspicuous part in the settlement of conflicts over xiangdi service. Normally, the head had to mediate between the disputants. If the dispute evolved into a lawsuit, he had to act as an intermediary between the magistrate and the litigants, reporting to the government his investigation of the facts and carrying out the magistrate's instructions. The possibility that he would abuse his power existed throughout that process, given the fact that the village head, as a member of the peasant community, lived in a social network of kinship, friendship, and neighborhood ties. We have seen in the dispute from Shanxiayi its village head's attempt to help his relative evade xiangdi service. In the following case from Weitong village, a village head attempted to help his friend seize the xiangdi position in the face of strong opposition from the local community.

Weitong village consisted of three pai, East Pai, Middle Pai, and West Pai. Each pai had approximately seventy households and had its own xiangdi. Unlike most other places where the xiangdi position rotated among villagers, here the *paigui* (regulations of the pai) demanded that the xiangdi be collectively nominated by the taxpaying households of his pai and that the outgoing xiangdi transfer the bronze gong to the new xiangdi on the lunar New Year's Day.

The dispute was first brought to court by Li Dengxian, the village head, who filed a petition on February 3, 1925. Li requested the removal of Xing Luoxiang from the xiangdi post of East Pai, for the reason that Xing purportedly had a record of misappropriating public funds during his previous service. Instead, Li nominated a Hou Liubao as the xiangdi of East Pai, who, according to the village head, was from a well-to-do family and had a good reputation among the villagers. The magistrate accepted Li's petition and ordered Hou to be the new xiangdi.

Xing Luoxiang, however, rejected the magistrate's order. He refused to give the gong to Hou Liubao even when the magistrate issued a prompting notice at the village head's request. The reason Xing refused to hand over the gong, according to a report submitted by Middle Pai's xiangdi, was that he had received the gong from the households of East Pai who had nominated him and therefore he would not give the gong back until all the households of his pai asked him to do so.

Meanwhile, as many as twenty-one villagers from East Pai submitted a collective petition to the magistrate, charging Village Head Li with "disrupting the local regulations" for his nomination of Hou as their xiangdi. According to that petition, the villagers of East Pai had nominated Xing as their xiangdi on the lunar New Year's Day and handed him the bronze gong in line with their own paigui. The reason Li had nominated another person, the petition went on, was that the village head had long hated Xing, and the new xiangdi he nominated (Hou) was merely his "running dog," who was too young to assume xiangdi duties. "To safeguard the local regulations," the petition continued, "we would ask you [the magistrate] to allow Xing Luoxiang to be the xiangdi as usual."

The magistrate thus had to ask Middle Pai's xiangdi to look into the matter and to clarify who should be East Pai's xiangdi. The xiangdi soon reported back that all the households in East Pai were unhappy with the village head's arbitrary nomination of Hou Liubao, and that the village head, in turn, was also dissatisfied with their nomination of Xing Luoxiang. The magistrate's comment: since Li's nomination was not endorsed by the public, another xiangdi should be elected.

On April 26, the xiangdi of West Pai, one Hou Mengqi, reported to the magistrate that he, together with Middle Pai's xiangdi, had consulted East Pai's households and had nominated a Xing Luoping to be the xiangdi of that pai for the current year. The magistrate agreed immediately. It should be noted, however, that Hou Mengqi had most probably sided with the village head, for not only did they both reside in West Pai, but Hou Mengqi was the brother of Hou Liubao, the person nominated by the village head. Their relationship was further confirmed by the fact that the handwriting of Hou Mengqi's petition was the same as the village head's. It implied that Mengqi's petition was actually prepared by the village head. They almost certainly acted in cahoots to prevent Xing Luoxiang from filling the xiangdi post.

The ensuing struggle between the village head and Xing Luoxiang occurred mainly between their respective representatives, namely Hou Mengqi (West Pai's xiangdi) and Xing Ruke (a resident of East Pai), and centered on the transfer of the gong. On May 16, Hou Mengqi submitted a prompting petition, charging Xing Luoxiang with occupying the gong. This resulted in the magistrate's order to prompt Xing Luoxiang to hand it over. Xing Luoxiang rejected the magistrate's order, and his action was supported by Xing Ruke and three other residents from East Pai. According to their petition, "It was not that Xing Luoxiang refused to give the gong, but that they, the taxpayers of East Pai, prohibited him from doing so." They asserted that Xing Luoxiang, as the incumbent xiangdi nominated unanimously by the taxpaying households of his pai, had advanced all the tax monies for the taxpayers of the pai and had not yet been reimbursed. They further accused the village head of "destroying the local regulations and arbitrarily nominating the xiangdi" (*pohuai xianggui, lanju xiangdi*). The new xiangdi recently nominated by the village head (one Xing Pingsan), according to the petition, was an utterly destitute village teacher who had previously been charged by the very same village head with embezzling school funds. However, the petition went on, they now colluded for reasons unknown. All the households of East Pai would never accept Li's new nomination, asserted the petition.

A week later, Xing Ruke, with still more people from East Pai (thirteen in total), filed yet another petition, repeating their charge against the village head. In their opinion, Li was a resident of West Pai and had no right to "interfere in affairs of East Pai." His nomination of Xing Pingsan was "a violation of the village custom."

The petitions and counterpetitions between the two parties resulted in the magistrate's second court hearing. During that session, the magistrate blamed Xing Luoxiang for ignoring his repeated orders and refusing to relinquish the gong, and he ordered Xing Luoxiang to file a pledge to turn the gong over to Hou Mengqi, West Pai's xiangdi. However, the magistrate did not sanction the village head's new nomination of Xing Pingsan either. "Xing Pingsan can take over the xiangdi post only when the majority of the people [of that pai] agree."

The magistrate's instruction, far from ending the dispute, opened the way for further contestation. On June 14, Hou Mengqi filed yet another prompting petition, complaining that Xing Luoxiang refused to give the gong to him despite the magistrate's ruling. Hou Mengqi's petition was soon followed by a counterpetition from Xing Ruke, who claimed that Xing Luoxiang refused to give the gong to Hou Mengqi because Hou was from West Pai and therefore had no right to intervene in East Pai's affairs. Instead, the petition went on, Xing Luoxiang had returned the gong to the taxpayers of his pai, who rotated to keep the gong. Moreover, claimed the petitioner, the residents of East Pai had taken a vote to elect a new xiangdi and Xing Luoxiang had won most votes. The same facts were reasserted in the ensuing two petitions from Xing Shitai, a member of the Xing clan who had had business outside the village and had just come back, and from eight "representatives" of East Pai, respectively. Skeptical, the magistrate sent a policeman to the village to investigate. The policeman came back with a report from Hou Mengqi. As might be expected, Hou Mengqi denied that an election had taken place and asserted that the gong was still in Xing Luoxiang's hands.

The magistrate thus had to convene a third court session on July 7, in which he ruled that the xiangdi of East Pai for the current year should be chosen by ballot from the residents of that pai but excluding Xing Luoxiang, and that Xing Luoxiang file a pledge not to serve as the current year's xiangdi. To ensure that the election be done fairly and that the result be recognized by the government, the magistrate sent a policeman to supervise the election upon the request of the eight representatives.

To the magistrate's surprise, the policeman reported back on July 24 that Xing Luoxiang had won forty-one of the forty-two votes. The magistrate had no option but to endorse the result. The dispute ended with the villagers' petition to replace the village head and the magistrate's approval of a newly elected village head (656.2.568, 1925).

The village head's abuse was obvious in this case. As a person of West Pai and therefore an "outsider" to East Pai, Village Head Li felt less constrained by the regulations of East Pai than a native leader would have. He abused his power in a flagrant manner that we have not seen in the previous cases. The village head would have succeeded had he encountered no resistance from East Pai. Here, however, he dealt with a group of people with strong solidarity, evident in their numerous petitions and their repeated election of Xing Luoxiang as the xiangdi. Their collective efforts eventually aborted the village head's attempts to block Xing's xiangdi service. Although the magistrate agreed with the village head's initial petition, he soon changed his decision, realizing that the village head's nomination "received no consent from the public" (*wei de dazong tongyi*). More interestingly, although the magistrate forbade people of East Pai to reelect Luoxiang as their xiangdi, he tolerated the result of the second election, which contradicted his ruling. The village head's open violation of local regulations and the community's resistance were equally evident in this case.

Together, these two cases suggest the possibilities and limits of abuse by the powerful in the peasant community. As purposive individuals, those in power were always ready to pursue their self-interests by using their strengths, such as education, social networks, or official positions. However, the social constraints imposed on them were equally obvious. Where the powerful were from within the community and therefore subject to the social sanction and scrutiny of fellow villagers, they had to hide or justify their abuses, for their reputations were closely linked with conformity to communal arrangements. A powerful outsider could be less scrupulous and succeed if the community was weak. However, where the villagers showed strong cohesiveness, he would risk losing his reputation in and outside the community and eventually the position he had held. To form an optimal strategy for self-aggrandizement a powerful person had to consider not only the immediate gain and loss of his material interests but also the production and reproduction of his symbolic capital.

Conclusion

This chapter discusses three patterns of strategic behavior used by villagers involved in disputes. Two rivals of roughly equal means or strength would attempt to avoid misrepresenting the village regulation or manipulating the working of the regulation because neither was powerful enough to overwhelm the other. Instead, they would agree to abide by the same village rules and focus their dispute on the disqualifications of their competitors. Furthermore, as equals they tended to persist in their litigation, often resulting in several court sessions or on-the-spot investigations by the county magistrate's agent. Neither would give up until a compromise satisfied them both or until a mandatory ruling was issued in favor of one or the other.

A weak or poverty-stricken individual would most likely act in a way that deviated from the village regulation yet was allowed by the survival ethic of the community. However, this option was viable and acceptable only when the service in dispute entailed a burden and a threat to his subsistence and when the community itself was cohesive enough to enable the working of the survival ethic. If the service was profitable, the villager would likely use the village regulation, rather than the survival ethic, to secure the desired position. In communities where the villagers failed to show solidarity, the person of strength would find more room to abuse his influence. And the weak would likely give up when his initial defense failed.

When both of the individuals involved in a litigation were powerful, possessing or monopolizing different forms of capital in the community, the conflict might be fierce. Each in the dispute would use and mobilize whatever resources he could. Depending on the means available to him, a disputant would maximize his abilities of representation, mobilize the support of his social network, or use his position as village head to dominate the litigation. Violation of village regulations became unavoidable. However, in a peasant community where village regulations were held supreme, any abuse of them had to be covert and not threaten the standing of the powerful in the community or impair the "legitimacy" of their influence. Those who attempted to get around their obligations of xiangdi service had to disguise their intentions in the language of the cungui or paigui, when conformity with the collective norms was deemed a necessary "virtue" of the powerful and an essential of maintaining and reproducing their authority.[5]

Clearly, what shaped the litigants' strategies was neither the simple "rational" calculation of private gain nor commitment to village regulations, but the interaction between contextual factors such as collective norms, shared rules, consensus, and social sanctions on the one hand, and the disputant's personal situation on the other, such as the economic, social, cultural, or symbolic capital that defined his position in the community, as well as his calculation of gain or loss of different forms of capital in specific circumstances. The interaction of individual abilities and motivation with contextual constraints produced a number of principles that allowed the villagers to use a variety of strategies. While the individual's motive and desire to maximize capital might lead him to deviate from village regulations, the social context was a strong constraint. The actual strategy was thus often chosen after taking all factors into account. Villagers tended to conform to the regulation when the constraints were strong and when the resources available to them were limited; they were more likely to distort, abuse, or manipulate the regulation when the constraints were weak and when they had enough resources to prevail over others. And they would become self-interested actors, ignoring the established rules, where such constraints were absent.

It is in this context that we can understand why the xiangdi system was effective and long-lasting in Huailu county. Most villages there were stable, homogeneous communities of mainly owner-cultivators and members of the same descent group, where a strong sense of group identity enabled community members to safeguard and socially sanction the operation of co-operative institutions. With these constraining mechanisms at work, the villagers, whether the powerful or the ordinary, had to limit their pursuit of self-interest to an extent allowed by external contexts; their deviation from established practices and norms had to be disguised and limited. Such constraints would remain in force until the community broke down or was incorporated into a national system that did not have room for local institutions. These changes, however, did not occur in south-central Hebei until the late 1930s and 1940s, when the Japanese occupation and then the Communist revolution fundamentally transformed the village institutions and social structure.

CHAPTER 5

Tax Collection

Three different tax systems prevailed in different parts of Qing and Republican China, namely, the informal practice of voluntary cooperation in tax payment, which was most common in Huailu villages; the official system of self-delivery of taxes to the collection station (*zifeng tougui*), which was less popular in the county; and the illegal business of tax-farming, which in Huailu was limited to local landholders who owed tax duties to a neighboring county or nonresident taxpayers who had land in Huailu. This chapter will show how these methods operated in the county. Tax payment was most efficient where the village regulations obliged the xiangdi to advance taxes for his community and compelled community members to repay the xiangdi by a deadline. It was less smooth where people paid taxes individually under the xiangdi's prompting. Least efficient was tax-farming, which caused most disputes between the tax collectors and taxpayers in the absence of both village regulations and community mediation.

This chapter begins with an analysis of the xiangdi's performance in delivering taxes and the county yamen's prompting. My examination of disputes between the tax-advancing xiangdi and local taxpayers shows how village regulations functioned in land taxation. The last two sections examine tax collection in villages under the tax-prompting xiangdi and on tax enclaves, respectively, which contrast with the cooperative practices in most villages. My concern is primarily with the changing relationships between the government and the village under different tax systems, as well as their implications for understanding the nature of governance in North China villages.

The County Government and the Xiangdi

Each year the land tax was collected in two periods. The first tax period (*shangmang*), in which half of the tax quota was to be collected, normally began on the second day of the second month of the lunar year and ended on the fifteenth day of the fourth month. The second tax period (*xiamang*), with another half of tax quota to be fulfilled, lasted from the second day of the eighth month to the fifteenth day of the tenth month. The deadline for the second period sometimes varied; it could be advanced to the first day of the tenth month or delayed to the first day of the twelfth month, depending on the actual process of tax collection as well as the government's need for revenue (656.1.366, 1915–27).[1]

To start the collection season, the Revenue Office (*hufang*) (or the First Section during the Republican period) of the county government routinely prepared a notice on behalf of the magistrate and posted it on the gates of the wall surrounding the county seat as well as at public sites in market towns.[2] At the same time, the office also sent to the xiangdi in each village a copy of the updated tax roll (*zhengliang hongbo*, literally, "tax-collecting red book"), and an official announcement of the tax-collecting method (*zhengliang banfa*) for the current year. The tax roll only listed the tax quotas of individual taxpaying households in the form of how many taels a household owed. It was the tax-collecting method that informed the taxpayer how many silver dollars or copper coins were to be assessed for each tael of his tax quota. Both the notice and the announcement were to be posted at a public site in the village (656.1.426, 1915–34).

During imperial times as well as in the first two Republican years, all taxes in Hebei (then Zhili) province were paid in copper cash. The tax quota listed in silver taels on the tax roll thus needed to be converted into copper cash. Since the conversion rate changed every year, so did the actual amount of taxes paid by landowners. It was widely believed that this method of tax payment, and the possible manipulation of the conversion rate, created opportunities for the collection of extra tax monies (e.g., Huang Hanliang 1918; Li Hongyi 1977 [1934]). It is also worth noting that, aside from the statutory land tax quota, taxpayers had to pay a number of additional charges attached to the land tax. In Huailu county, it had been an established practice since 1831 that for each tael of the land tax a surcharge of 0.175 tael was assessed to cover the "melting fee" (*huohao*, the fee to cover the loss after melting irregular pieces of silver into standard bullion), the remittance fee, and the administration fee, and another surcharge of 0.0218 tael to cover the collectors' expenses for stationery and meals. In addition, the taxpayer needed to pay three wen as a tax-receipt fee (656.1.103, 1913).

To simplify tax payment, the Zhili provincial government decided to collect land taxes in silver dollars (yuan) instead of copper cash (wen), beginning on April 1, 1914. The taxpayers now needed to pay 2.30 yuan for each tael of tax quota; all the surcharges mentioned above were abolished, except

TABLE 10

Monthly Reports of Cumulative Land Taxes Collected in Huailu County, 1914, 1917, and 1920

	1914			1917			1920		
Month	Annual Tax Quota	Tax Col- lected	Percent Col- lected	Annual Tax Quota	Tax Col- lected	Percent Col- lected	Annual Tax Quota	Tax Col- lected	Percent Col- lected
	54,878			53,272			53,167		
Jan.		0	0		0	0		0	0
Feb.		0	0		0	0		0	0
March		14,605	26.61		1,026	1.93		0	0
April		18,055	32.90		9,959	18.69		1,481	2.79
May		26,951	49.11		19,063	35.78		16,431	30.90
June		0	0		26,624	49.98		26,631	50.09
July		0	0		0	0		0	0
Aug.		0	0		0	0		0	0
Sept.		0	0		0	0		0	0
Oct.		42,131	76.78		0	0		0	0
Nov.		—	—		32,120	60.29		35,407	66.59
Dec.		54,403	99.68		38,361	72.01		41,778	78.58

SOURCE: *Jingzheng diliang yuebaocegao* (Draft monthly report on the collection of land tax) (656.1.216, 1914; 656.1.719, 1917; 656.1.1204, 1920).
NOTE: Data on taxes collected in the third month of the second period in 1917 and 1920 (i.e., January of the next year) are not available.

the receipt fee (656.1.216, 1914; 656.1.396, 1915; see Chapter 2 for details). But small taxpaying households with a tax of less than one yuan still needed to pay in copper cash. Every day the local Chamber of Commerce announced the conversion rate between the silver tael (liang) and silver dollars (yuan). It is hard to judge the extent to which the government clerks may have profited by manipulating the daily conversion rate at a cost to the taxpayers. The Huailu magistrate simply denied any extra collection of taxes resulting from the conversion rate in his report to the Financial Department of Zhili province in 1920. According to his assertion, the clerks' activities during the collection season were under his frequent and close surveillance (656.1.1203, 1920).

THE XIANGDI'S DELIVERY OF TAXES

The majority of the xiangdi in Huailu delivered the tax monies promptly. Table 10, based on the monthly reports of tax collection available to me, shows the cumulative amount of taxes collected each month. In 1914, for example, the first tax period started on February 24. By the end of March, 26.61 percent of the county's tax quota had been met. In other words, the xiangdi of the county had delivered 53.22 percent of the taxes in the first month for the first tax period. By the end of April, the county had met 32.9 percent of the tax quota for the whole year or 65.8 percent for the first period. The first period ended on May 6; it is hard to judge how much the xiangdi had paid by that deadline. By the end of that month, however, the xiangdi had turned in 49.11 percent of the whole year's taxes or, in other words, almost all of what was owed for the first period. The same was true for the second tax period of that year. By the end of the first month (October), the xiangdi had delivered 76.78 percent of the taxes for the whole year or over 55 percent for the second period. Data for the next month are not available. However, by the end of December (the third month), the taxpayers in Huailu had paid almost all of the taxes owed. The data of 1917 and 1920 show no big difference from that of 1914, except that the two tax periods started later in 1917 and still later in 1920 (almost one month later than in 1914).

In general, the taxpayers, primarily the xiangdi, delivered in the first two months of a collection period approximately 30 percent of their tax quotas for the whole year or 60 percent of their duties for the collection period. As a rule, by the end of the third month they had met almost 50 percent and even more of the whole year's tax quotas or almost all of what was due in a given period. We may then surmise that by the middle of the third month— that is, the end of a collection period—the taxpayers had paid 40 percent of their taxes for the whole year or 80 percent for the period. Since the xiangdi usually delivered all of the money due in a single visit to the county seat during a collection season rather than in several visits, it is safe to say that the vast majority of xiangdi in Huailu advanced land taxes for his village or his pai before the deadline.

TAX PROMPTING BY THE COUNTY GOVERNMENT

In order to collect as much tax as possible by the due date, the county government took several steps. Two months after the start of collection, the magistrate normally instructed village heads in his county to "supervise and hasten" (*ducui*) the xiangdi's tax payment by the deadline. If the xiangdi remained inactive, the village head had to report the situation to the magistrate. However, few village heads abided by the magistrate's instructions at the expense of their relationship with the xiangdi; in fact I found no case in which the village head accused the xiangdi of delinquent tax payment (656.1.953, 1918–21).

As a second step, the county office in charge of the land tax would submit to the magistrate a list of villages that had not yet paid their taxes. The magistrate would summon in batches all those dilatory xiangdi (usually one collective summons for five villages) to court, where he "instructed and urged" (yucui) them to pay the tax promptly. This method, however, again proved to be ineffective. In an extreme case, the xiangdi of Fujiazhuang village, who was responsible for a tax quota of 41 taels for his village, was named in as many as six collective summonses during the first tax period of 1920 but never once went to court. Consequently, the tax office advised the magistrate to detain the xiangdi. The xiangdi immediately paid the taxes upon receipt of the notice, alleging that he had failed to obey the earlier collective summons because "he had been ill for over two months and just recovered only recently" (656.1.953, 1918–21).

The magistrate also used the officers of the eight policing wards of the county, instructing them to send policemen to villages in their charge to "watch and prompt" (shoucui or zuocui) the xiangdi's tax payment. If the xiangdi failed to pay the taxes in full by the deadline, the policemen then might either submit to the magistrate a list of the delinquent xiangdi or bring them to court outright (656.1.953, 1918–21).

After the closing date of the collection period, the magistrate would use his own bailiff (fajing or zhengwu jing in the 1930s) instead of the ward police to deal with delinquent xiangdi. Each bailiff was assigned several xiangdi to prompt (hence called jingcui). Those who failed to clear their debts were invariably accused. On receipt of the accusation, the magistrate always responded with a summons to the accused. In fact, to make their promptings effective, the bailiff often first asked for a summons on the delinquent xiangdi and then went to the village with the summons in hand to collect the tax (this was called piaocui or "to prompt with a summons"). And most xiangdi paid off their duties upon receiving the summons (656.2.1, 1921; 656.3.916, 1934). Those who failed to do so were without exception brought to court and detained there. Jia Jiren, the xiangdi of Zhuangke village, for example, was detained on September 16, 1917, for failing to meet his obligation for the first collection period. The magistrate required him to pay what was due within five days. Three days later, the xiangdi was released when his relatives paid all the taxes in arrears (656.1.757, 1917).[3]

The tax-prompting steps taken by the county government as delineated above do not mean that delinquent tax payment was widespread in Huailu. In fact, as Table 10 shows, the majority of the xiangdi in this county delivered the taxes in a timely manner. Those who failed to meet the deadline accounted for only one-fifth of all the xiangdi in the county. And these delinquent xiangdi also paid off their taxes shortly after the deadline under the tremendous pressure of government prompting. This pressure, however, was not the only reason behind the xiangdi's full payment of taxes. Equally important was the effective functioning of cooperative arrangements for tax payment in the villages.

Village Regulations on Chaiyao

We have seen in Chapters 3 and 4 a variety of local regulations (known to villagers as *cungui*) concerning the recruitment of the xiangdi in Huailu villages during the late Qing and early Republican periods. In tax collection, likewise, various cungui regulated the xiangdi's advance payment of taxes for his fellow villagers and the latter's repayment to the xiangdi. Let us first consider village regulations on the supply of chaiyao during the late Qing period.

The chaiyao was the only surtax in Huailu during the late Qing period.[4] It was to cover the county government's expenses in supplying services to the imperial court (locally known as *dachai*, major service, or *huangchai*, royal service) as well as its expenses for local projects (*xiaochai*, minor service). The amount of the chaiyao varied every year, depending upon the magistrate's actual needs and the year's harvest. The collection of chaiyao was separate from that of the land tax. Unlike the land tax, which was always a fixed quota (listed in taels) for individual taxpaying households and was collected regularly, the chaiyao could be levied at any time and was assessed directly in copper cash (wen) (see Chapter 9 for further discussion).

In most Huailu villages, it was the xiangdi's duty to advance the chaiyao for his community. Because of the irregularity of the chaiyao, disputes between the xiangdi and his fellow villagers were much more likely to occur over this surtax than over the regularized land tax. In fact, all of the late-Qing records of disputes over tax collection available in the Huailu archives pertain to the chaiyao. Villagers thus felt it necessary to create village regulations to govern their activities in advancing and repaying the chaiyao and to reduce related disputes.

In general, those village regulations fall into two types. In one type, rich households were obliged to assist the xiangdi in his advance payment of the chaiyao. In Dongpingtong village, for example, all households with more than 80 mu of land were required to help the xiangdi advance the chaiyao. In 1875, four rich villagers refused to do so on the grounds that the xiangdi had not asked four other households with 80 mu of land to share the collective duty; they argued that he had violated the "old custom" (*jiuli*). At the court session, the magistrate simply ruled that all the households in that village with a tax quota of 1.5 taels and above had to help advance the chaiyao. He chose to use the tax quota instead of actual landholding as the criterion for sharing the xiangdi service because the magistrate had the information on all households' tax liabilities readily available from the records of his ya-men, whereas the actual landholdings of the villagers involved in the dispute were difficult to verify (655.1.901, 1875). Another village, Lianhuaying, had an "old regulation" (jiugui) that all the rich households had to assist the xi-angdi to meet the "royal service" when imposed. According to a petition from the xiangdi of the village, a rich villager, named Li Er Pangniu, refused to honor his obligation in 1875. Li was immediately summoned to the court, where he promised to help (655.1.978, 1875). A third case comes from Gao-qian village. Its regulation demanded that, in addition to the xiangdi (locally known as hongming xiangdi, "the xiangdi in red name"), six more villagers were to be appointed each year as bangban xiangdi (assistant to the xiangdi) according to their landholdings. The six bangban, mostly the rich in the vil-lage, had to share the xiangdi's duty of advancing land taxes as well as the chaiyao. If any failed to do so, the xiangdi had to make good on the tax shortage and then collect his money from the delinquent bangban. In 1884 a xiangdi named Du Yuanyuan had to do so for one of his bangban, one Liang Youren, and later brought suit against Liang for failing to repay him 44,000 wen (655.1.977, 1884).

Another type of regulation required the xiangdi to advance the chaiyao on his own and then collect the money owed by individual households ac-cording to their landholdings, exactly as he did with the land tax. A case in point came from Xiumen village. By the "old regulation" of this village, the xiangdi had to advance all the chaiyao for his fellow villagers and then ap-portion his duties to them according to their landholdings (andi paichai). In 1882, each mu of land in that village was to share 81 wen of the chaiyao the xiangdi had advanced. A 9 mu plot in this village, however, had recently been sold to Yao Yongqing of the neighboring Shijiazhuang village. Yao re-paid the xiangdi of Xiumen village only 900 wen in land tax (100 wen per mu) but refused to reimburse 729 wen in the chaiyao. The xiangdi thus sued Yao for "not acting in accordance with the regulation of [his] village" (bu an xiaode cungui xingshi). The magistrate issued a summons to Yao upon receipt of the plaint. Yao's son, who appeared at the court session on behalf of his fa-ther, promised to repay the advanced chaiyao after returning home. Three days later, the xiangdi filed a petition to close the case, claiming that Yao had asked the elderly in the village to mediate the quarrel, had paid off all his chaiyao dues, and had pledged to "abide by the old regulation" (zunshou ji-ugui) in the coming years (655.1.913, 1882).

Clearly, by the late nineteenth century, these sorts of "village regulations" had been firmly established in many Huailu villages to govern the payment of the chaiyao, a surtax that was much more likely than the land tax to cause disputes between the xiangdi and his fellow villagers because of its irregularity. Any of the two parties in dispute who violated the regulation was thus subject to the accusation of the other in the language of cungui. The county yamen, likewise, always honored local regulations in its adjudication of disputes over the chaiyao.

Village Regulations on Land Tax

VILLAGE REGULATIONS

The county assembly's decision in 1912 to freeze the rate of chaiyao and to collect it together with land tax (see Chapter 9 for details) eliminated disputes resulting from the irregular levying of that surtax and ended the working of related village regulations. Disputes over tax collection during the Republican period bring to light the role of the cungui in the collection of the land tax.

As described in Chapter 3, in most Huailu villages the xiangdi advanced tax monies for all his fellow villagers during the collection season and then collected them from individual taxpaying households on a designated date at the end of the lunar year. The operation of this cooperative arrangement, however, necessitated the support of village regulations. Without an effective cungui, both the xiangdi's advance payment and the villagers' reimbursement were unimaginable. The purpose of the cungui was to define the mutual obligations between the xiangdi and his fellow villagers; it demanded the former to advance taxes incumbent on the whole village or the pai during the collection season, using the village fund or money he had borrowed, while requiring the taxpayers to repay the xiangdi by the due date.[5]

The imposition and subsequent suspension of the *shanhou liangjuan* ("levy for postwar rehabilitation"; see Chapter 9 for details) illustrate how the cungui worked. In compliance with the decision of the Zhili governor, the Huailu magistrate announced on September 2, 1921, the collection of that levy together with the land tax, which brought the tax burden to 2.99 yuan per tael. Many xiangdi thus advanced their taxes at that rate. On November 29, however, the governor, in response to resistance from the elite, decided to postpone the collection of the liangjuan to the next year; all the overcharged taxes, by the governor's order, were to be applied to the coming year. The Huailu government ceased the collection of the liangjuan accordingly and restored the collection rate to the original 2.50 yuan per tael.

This midstream change in the collection rate put all those xiangdi who had paid tax in advance in a difficult situation. First, although the xiangdi had advanced taxes at 2.99 yuan per tael, the taxpayers now insisted on repaying him at the reduced rate of 2.50 yuan per tael. Since in most villages the xiangdi used loans rather than public funds of the community to advance taxes and had to pay interest on the loan, repayment at the reduced rate would mean that he would be unable to pay off his loan. Second, in most Huailu villages the xiangdi service rotated annually among the taxpaying households. The incumbent xiangdi was only responsible for advancing the taxes for the current year and thus needed to collect all his monies at the end of the year. If the overcharged monies were applied to the next year as the provincial government required, much confusion would arise in tax advancement and repayment in the next year.

Therefore many xiangdi delivered petitions to the magistrate for immediate reimbursement. Most of those petitions cited the "old regulation" on the xiangdi's advance payment of taxes in their respective villages and then emphasized the two reasons described above for prompt reimbursement of the overpaid taxes. The magistrate's initial reaction to those petitions was simply to instruct the xiangdi to collect the advanced monies at the new rate (2.99 yuan per tael). After so many petitions arrived, however, the magistrate changed his opinion and reported the matter to the Financial Department of the province on December 14, requesting a reimbursement of the overcharged taxes as the xiangdi had requested. Three weeks later, the department approved the request and all the xiangdi received their overpaid taxes back from the government (656.1.1232, 1922). It is obvious from this case that village regulations on the advance payment of taxes by the xiangdi remained effective in most Huailu villages and were respected by the government in the early 1920s.

NONCOMPLIANCE

However, there was no shortage of instances in Huailu villages in which the taxpayers violated the village regulations. Those violations generally fell into three categories: some villagers simply rejected the old cungui and insisted on the statutory method of tax payment; some xiangdi overcharged the taxpayers; and some taxpayers refused to repay the xiangdi. Let us begin with an example of the first category.

Although the xiangdi system worked for the overall good of taxpayers, protecting them from potentially abusive outsiders, on occasion the villagers disregarded the preexisting cungui requiring advance payment by the xiangdi. This was especially true after the state reasserted the self-delivery system. In 1929 the Guomindang government announced the abolition of the sheshu system for the purpose of eradicating the ill-favored tax-farming business, which was widespread in the country and was often the monopoly of the sheshu. At the same time, it reaffirmed the self-delivery system in tax collection, as the Qing state had repeatedly done. This step, though aimed at wiping out the entrepreneurial tax farmers, nevertheless offered a pretext for some villagers to challenge village regulations and to shirk their duties in tax collection and repayment. A dispute thus erupted in Nanxinzhuang village in October 1929, when Xue Deyu, the village head, accused four fellow villagers of "violating the local regulation" (*pohuai xianggui*). According to his plaint to the magistrate, it had long been a practice in his village for the xiangdi to advance taxes at collection time and then distribute the tax receipts to individual households with the help of a teacher to collect the money owed him. However, the petition went on, the four villagers, all "rascals and ruffians" (*wulai guntu*) and "determined to change the local regulation" (*fei gai xianggui bu yi*), insisted on "delivering taxes individually" (*ge na ge liang*) and prevented the xiangdi from advancing taxes for all the villagers. However, most taxpayers in the village, the village head contended, were illiterate and unwilling to change the regulation. The four villagers' violation had impeded the xiangdi's discharge of his public duties. Upon receipt of the plaint, the magistrate instructed the ward police to look into the matter and to settle the dispute in accordance with the local regulation (656.3.57, 1929).

The threat to village regulations came not only from the taxpayers. The xiangdi could also violate established practices when collecting taxes. I found two cases in which the xiangdi overcharged taxpaying households. On December 27, 1926, three Liangs from Liangjiazhuang village submitted a plaint against Liang Jifu, the incumbent xiangdi of that village. They asserted that the government had announced a collection rate for the current year of 2.9 yuan or 11,252 wen (copper cash) per tael of tax quota. However, the xiangdi had assessed them extra amounts varying from 30 or 40 to 200 or 300 wen per tael. The magistrate asked the ward police to investigate. The police reported that, according to the village head, the xiangdi had made an accounting error. As a friend of both parties, claimed the village head, he had mediated the dispute and done the accounting again, and all the overcharged money had been returned to the accusers (656.2.852, 1926).

A similar event occurred in Zhengjiazhuang village. In 1920, Wu Weiyi, the xiangdi of that village, received a court instruction at the beginning of the first tax period to set the collection rate for the year at 2.3 yuan per tael of quota plus 0.20 yuan per tael as the chaiyao (totaling 2.50 yuan per tael, with the police fee and water-work contribution on top of that). On December 18, four villagers, all surnamed Shi, filed a petition complaining that the xiangdi had failed to post the new rates at a public site. After advancing all the taxes, they said, the xiangdi collected his monies at 2.53 yuan per tael, which was 0.03 yuan higher than the announced rate, and declined their request for a reimbursement. On the magistrate's instruction, the village head mediated the dispute and had the overcharged monies repaid to the four accusers (656.1.1243, 1920).

It was possible, therefore, for the xiangdi to overcharge taxpayers when collecting his advanced monies. But this kind of abuse was not the rule. Under normal conditions, the xiangdi was unable to profit from tax collection, for his activities were under the close surveillance of his fellow villagers; not only did they know each other's tax quotas, but the official notice of the collection rate was normally posted in a public place as required by the government. Everybody thus knew exactly how much they needed to repay the xiangdi. Those who paid the xiangdi's overcharge would not hesitate to request a refund, and the xiangdi's refusal to provide it would lead to a lawsuit.

In these two cases the overcharges were quite minor, 0.26 to 2.6 percent of the taxes due in the first instance and 1.2 percent in the second. When the xiangdi demanded a higher surcharge, the taxpayers would simply refuse to repay the xiangdi. That was exactly what happened with the suspension of the shanhou liangjuan in 1921. In that instance, the taxpayers unanimously refused to repay the xiangdi at a rate almost 20 percent higher than the recently reduced one. Thus the xiangdi's opportunities to profit from overcharging the taxpayers were limited.

The incidence of taxpayers' nonpayment was even lower. I found just one such case. In 1915, the xiangdi of Bailinzhuang village, who had advanced all the taxes for his fellow villagers, accused one Wang Xinshun of refusing to pay back the tax money the xiangdi had advanced. The magistrate summoned the accused immediately. Wang pledged at the court to pay his debt to the xiangdi and was released on bail (656.1.424, 1915).

By and large, tax payment proceeded quite smoothly where the villagers cooperated under local regulations. Disputes resulting from the xiangdi's extra collection or taxpayers' nonpayment were rare and, when they did happen, were quickly mediated and adjudicated on the basis of the regulations.

The Tax-Prompting Xiangdi

Aside from most Huailu villages where the xiangdi advanced taxes for households in his charge, in a small number of villages the xiangdi only prompted his villagers to pay taxes; individual households paid their own taxes according to the official requirement of "self-delivery" (*zifeng tougui*). Needless to say, the burden of the tax-prompting xiangdi was much lighter than that of the tax-advancing xiangdi, for he did not have to borrow money for the advance tax payment or collect his repayment from individual households. However, his obligation to the government was the same as that of the tax-advancing xiangdi. Like the latter, he was to see that all taxpaying households in his charge paid taxes in full and within a time limit. If any villager failed to pay taxes by the deadline, the xiangdi had to make good the shortage. Failure to do so would result in a court hearing and possible detention.

The tax-prompting xiangdi's relationship with the government thus was no different from that of the tax-advancing xiangdi. Both were held responsible for full payment of the taxes imposed on fellow villagers. Under either arrangement, the government dealt only with the single xiangdi rather than with individual taxpayers.

Where the two kinds of xiangdi differed was in their relationship with taxpayers. Unlike the tax-advancing xiangdi, who seldom argued with his fellow villagers where village regulations worked smoothly, the tax-prompting xiangdi faced great tensions in his relationship with local taxpaying households. To avoid the burden of making good any tax shortage after the deadline, the xiangdi resorted to every means available to prompt his fellow villagers to pay their taxes before the deadline. After that deadline, the xiangdi had to advance any taxes still due, so that he could avoid a court hearing and, if summoned to court, get released from detention. In the absence of communal cooperation in tax payment, no regulation was formulated to define the mutual obligations between the xiangdi and his fellow villagers, as we have seen under the tax-advancing xiangdi. Therefore, the tax-owing villagers also felt no pressure to repay the xiangdi on time. Instead, they would delay repayment as much as possible, and, in some instances, simply denied it completely. It is no wonder that the incidence of disputes involving this type of xiangdi was exceptionally high, accounting for 72 percent of all the disputes over tax collection in Huailu county (thirty-four of forty-seven cases, excluding disputes over enclave taxes). These disputes resulted from either the xiangdi's prompting or the taxpayers' nonrepayment. Let us first consider the former.

The tension between the tax-prompting xiangdi and his fellow villagers started at the very beginning of the tax collection season. To avoid advancing taxes for delinquent taxpayers after the closing date, the xiangdi would strongly urge his villagers to pay their taxes. However, not every villager was able to pay on time, and, similarly, not every xiangdi was able to advance taxes for the delinquent households. Unlike the tax-advancing xiangdi, here the xiangdi lacked institutional support and a stable source of money to make the payment, such as public land or a village fund. For poor xiangdi who lacked sufficient credit, it was also difficult to ask for a loan to cover tax shortages. Thus there were always a number of xiangdi unable to fulfill their duties by the deadline and they were summoned and detained. Zhang Yongtai, a xiangdi of Lingdi village, was thus detained in December 1915, owing to his failure to pay off the tax balance for a villager named Zhang Taoqi. He was released only after his relatives and friends helped him clear the deficit (656.1.419, 1915).

Given the trouble that tax shortages caused, the xiangdi urged taxpayers in his charge to pay taxes by any means. And the tension between the two

parties escalated as the deadline approached. An effective way to press dilatory taxpayers to pay on time was to file a plaint against them before the
closing date. Thus, on January 8, 1919, Liu Shunxing, the xiangdi of Yongbei
village, filed a petition claiming that Wang Wenzai and another fifteen taxpayers in his village refused to pay taxes and ignored his repeated promptings
in an insulting way. He therefore found it difficult to perform his public
tasks. The magistrate responded with a summons to all sixteen villagers, who
promptly paid their taxes upon receiving the summons (656.1.1084, 1919). In
another instance, Shi Yutai, the xiangdi of Zaicheng, accused twelve fellow
villagers of nonpayment. The taxpayers immediately paid what they owed
after receiving the summons from the magistrate (656.1.965, 1918). Although
filing a petition proved here to be an effective way to prompt tax payment,
it inevitably undermined the xiangdi's relationship with his fellow villagers.

More often than not, the disputes between tax-prompting xiangdi and
taxpayers resulted from the latter's nonrepayment of money owed. In most
cases, a delinquent villager quickly paid his debt to the xiangdi after the xiangdi submitted a plaint.[6] Those who refused to reimburse the xiangdi, as
the latter often complained, were the "bully-like" villagers. Such persons, according to the petition from a xiangdi of Dongtongping village, were "always reckless and did unlawful things. And no one dare to offend them."
Every year, claimed the xiangdi, they delayed tax payment, forcing the xiangdi to advance their taxes. And as a rule, they refused to reimburse the xiangdi (656.1.599, 1915). In Nantongye village, a villager named Wang Yulin
not only refused to repay the xiangdi himself, but encouraged others to delay their repayment. When asked to repay his debt to the xiangdi, Wang
claimed that he would repay nothing until he received a court ruling requiring him to do so (656.1.392, 1915). In such cases, the xiangdi had no option but to file a complaint to recover his money.

Together, these two kinds of cases illustrate the tension between the tax-
prompting xiangdi and local community members in the absence of cooperative arrangements. Unlike the tax-advancing xiangdi who paid all of the
households' taxes in advance and therefore had no tax-prompting conflicts
with them, the tax-prompting xiangdi found himself in intense conflicts
with local residents; he had either to use all possible means to press the taxpayers to meet their obligation before a deadline or make good on the tax
shortages out-of-pocket. Because of the lack of cooperative arrangements,
however, the taxpayers felt no obligation to repay the xiangdi in a timely
manner; some even denied their debts to the xiangdi. The incidence of disputes involving the tax-prompting xiangdi thus was much higher than that
involving the tax-advancing xiangdi. And naturally, villages with a tax-
prompting xiangdi were much less solidary than those with a tax-advancing
xiangdi.

Nevertheless, we should not exaggerate the extent of such disputes. In fact most disputes over tax payment and repayment were settled through community mediation (*xiangzhong paijie*) before the xiangdi had to file a plaint; disputes that led to a lawsuit accounted for just a small proportion of all those disputes.[7] And such lawsuits quickly came to an end after the magistrate's initial reaction in the form of a notice to prompt tax payment or repayment or the issuing of a summons, in which the magistrate also instructed the village head to help handle the case. Once the village leader received the magistrate's order, he had to look into the causes of the dispute and persuade the accused to pay his debt. Then he would report to the magistrate the result of his handling and ask for the case to be closed (e.g., 656.1.392, 1915). Community mediation thus played an important part in the resolutions of disputes involving the tax-prompting xiangdi.

The Collection of Enclave Taxes

In Huailu, most land was owned by local residents and taxed by the county government. Yet there existed numerous nonresident enclaves (*jizhuangdi*) of varying sizes owned by people of neighboring counties but still taxed by the Huailu government. A 1913 statistic indicates that the nonresident enclaves within the county totaled 13,435 mu, with a sum of 484 taels of tax quota, which accounted for only 2 percent of the total taxable land in the county and almost 2 percent of the county's total tax quota (656.1.103, 1913).[8] There were also numerous enclaves outside Huailu owned by Huailu residents and taxed by neighboring counties.[9]

In spite of the small amount of enclave land in Huailu county, conflicts between tax-collecting outsiders and local taxpayers were much more frequent than disputes between local xiangdi and their fellow villagers. The Huailu archives contain forty-one records of disputes between local enclave owners and outside collectors and twenty-two between Huailu collectors and enclave owners in neighboring counties. Together, the two kinds of disputes, totaling sixty-three, accounted for over 57 percent of the 110 formally filed disputes over tax payment between 1912 and 1936. And again most such disputes involved enclave owners in villages under the tax-prompting xiangdi system, where no xiangdi advanced the enclave taxes to the collector.

The person responsible for collecting enclave taxes was usually the sheshu (a semi-official clerk at the supra-village level, who recorded changes in tax liabilities and helped the government compile tax rolls), for he was the only person who knew the real names and exact locations of taxpaying households on the tax roll. Occasionally the county government relied on its bailiff (*fajing*) to collect taxes from the delinquent enclave owners as it often did with tax-owing taxpayers under its direct jurisdiction.

At the beginning of the collection period, the county government usually issued to the sheshu or the bailiff a joint-notice (*huipiao*), which was also stamped by the neighboring county government, authorizing him to go to the neighboring county and prompt the enclave owners there to pay their taxes. Aware that the taxpaying households often "refused to pay their taxes, counting on its outside location" (*yiyi geshu, kang bu wanna*), the magistrate always allowed the prompters to report delinquent taxpayers to him for summons and even detention (655.2.12, 1921–27).

However, the sheshu and the bailiff had tremendous difficulty prompting tax payment. When the deadline came due, they themselves often had to make good all the tax shortages for the delinquent enclave owners. Then they faced similar difficulty recovering the money they had advanced. One obvious reason for the taxpayers' nonrepayment, as mentioned in almost every petition from the sheshu, was that the taxpayers took advantage of him as an outsider; (*zhangdi qiyi*) in their home places they were under the jurisdiction of a different government (*zhangshi geshu*) (e.g., 656.3.1102, 1919; 656.2.439, 1924). As an outsider, the sheshu could not collect their monies by force, for the debtor was backed by his relatives and friends and even the whole community. The sheshu thus frequently complained that "being in the strange land, [they] could not demand repayment by force [*shenju yidi, weibian yingtao*]" (e.g., 656.3.455, 1931). Nor could the sheshu resort to community mediation to settle his dispute with a local debtor, for he was not a member of the community. To hasten the enclave owners' tax payment and to avoid advancing taxes for them, many sheshu opted to submit a plaint against the taxpayers before the deadline, just as a tax-prompting xiangdi might do in dealing with his fellow villagers. This was especially true of sheshu who were in charge of villages with numerous enclave owners.[10]

When disputes with the delinquent taxpayers occurred, the only way for the sheshu or the bailiff to get his money back was to file a complaint. The incidence of filing a formal plaint against the enclave owners thus was exceptionally high. In the absence of community mediation, the magistrate usually issued a straight summons, instead of a repayment-prompting notice, to the delinquent taxpayer, at the request of his colleague in the neighboring county to whom the sheshu had filed a petition. In most cases, upon receiving the summons the delinquent taxpayer quickly traveled to the neighboring county to pay what he owed.[11]

The xiangdi's role varied in such cases. In some villages, he was not held responsible for fellow villagers' nonpayment. In other cases, the xiangdi had to share with the fellow villagers the duty of repayment. For instance, when the summoned taxpaying households failed to go to court, the xiangdi had to appear at the court for them. Zhang Ruiheng, the xiangdi of Tazhong village, was thus brought to court on April 4, 1916, when the policeman failed to find a delinquent villager, who owed 0.07 tael of tax money to a sheshu of Luancheng county. The xiangdi was released after pledging to find the missing villager and report back to the court within ten days (656.1.597, 1916). Sometimes the xiangdi was expected to assist the sheshu or a bailiff to collect his advanced monies. Not surprisingly, some xiangdi were reluctant to help the outsider and were charged with noncooperation (e.g., 656.1.968, 1918; 656.2.101, 1921).[12] Han Luozhang, the xiangdi of Nanqiema village, even suffered detention for refusing to cooperate with Liu Heng, a sheshu from Luancheng county, who was to collect the taxes of all seventy-seven households in that village (totaling 20.973 taels).[13]

These cases show that disputes over the payment of enclave taxes occurred either between an outside collector (the sheshu or the bailiff) and enclave taxpaying households who refused to repay the collector, or between the outside collector and the xiangdi who was in charge of the delinquent enclave taxpayer yet refused to assist the outsider.[14] What drove the incidence of such formally filed disputes so high was not merely the fact that the two disputing parties were under different jurisdictions, but the lack of community mediation that resolved most disputes between the local xiangdi and his fellow villagers. For the outsider, unable to count on local mediation to settle the dispute, the only way to get his money back was to file a plaint against the delinquent taxpayer. The incidence of formally filed disputes between the sheshu and enclave taxpayers thus was even higher than that between the tax-prompting xiangdi and his fellow villagers. In the latter case, disputes that were brought to court were greatly reduced by community mediation.

Conclusion

Three tax systems existed simultaneously in local villages, namely, the voluntary cooperation under tax-advancing xiangdi, the official system of self-delivery under the supervision of tax-prompting xiangdi, and the sheshu's tax-farming business in enclaves that owed taxes to a neighboring county. The incidence of disputes over tax payment varied under different systems. Disputes were rare in cooperative communities where the xiangdi paid all taxes in advance on behalf of his fellow villagers and the latter repaid the xiangdi on time in accordance with local regulations. Disputes were more likely where the villagers paid taxes individually at the prompting of the xiangdi. The incidence was the highest where the taxpayers refused to cooperate with tax farmers from outside.

The different incidence of disputes on land taxes entailed different degrees of government involvement in local administration. Under normal conditions, the magistrate left tax collection to informal agents and did not step in until the taxpayers failed to deliver taxes by a deadline or until the tax collectors disputed with the taxpayers. His role thus was minimal in villages under the cooperative xiangdi system where disputes were rare because of the effective working of local regulations. The magistrate's involvement increased accordingly as disputes mounted under the tax-prompting and tax-farming systems.

The contrasting effects of different systems on the relationship between the government and the village explain why neo-Confucian authors since the Song dynasty (960–1279) had vehemently advocated voluntary cooperation as the best way of governance. They believed that such cooperative institutions, when working properly, would serve the interests of both the community and the government, for they reduced the government's administrative costs while protecting local people from abusive outsiders. When disputes arose among local residents, the self-governing community could easily work out a compromise through mediation, which further reduced the scope of official involvement. The best form of government, they argued, was one that minimized its interference with local affairs and let the people govern themselves on the basis of voluntary cooperation (Wu Ding'an 2000; Cao Guoqing 1997; Wang Gaoxin 1995).

Counter to this ideal of self-governance, of course, was the situation in which the government devolved all its administrative tasks to profiteering agents, such as tax farmers or yamen runners, whose only concern was to enrich themselves at the expense of the people and even the government, and whose predatory activities inevitably incurred conflicts with local people, which could never count on community mediation for a resolution, thus causing the government's frequent involvement. Compared to the desired method of cooperative self-governance and the counterideal of entrepreneurial practices, the official system of self-delivery was depicted as a compromise aimed at ensuring the government's tax revenues while precluding the profiteering activities of any third party between the government and taxpayers. However, the weakness of this system—that is, its reliance on the government's effective control of rural society—often caused local magistrates to turn to local initiative, either self-governing or abusive practices, when the government failed to penetrate the countryside through the bao-jia network.

The coexistence of the self-governing cooperation under the tax-advancing xiangdi with the formally imposed self-delivery system and the officially denounced tax-farming practice in Huailu villages, then, can be seen as a microcosm of different methods of governance in rural China. Although these methods had different images in official representations and Confucian discourse on local control, a pragmatic magistrate had no difficulty allowing their concurrent existence in village communities. From his point of view, these different systems were actually supplementary, rather than contradictory, for each occurred in a certain context, and together they worked to secure the government's tax revenues. The magistrate's usual approach to local government thus was to tolerate and even encourage local initiatives so long as these informal practices met the expected goals of tax collection and social control. Although the informal practices emerged seemingly as a result of the government's inability to impose its own designs on the villages, from the magistrate's point of view, doing so was both financially unnecessary (and even counterproductive) and ideologically against the neo-Confucian doctrine of a minimal government and a self-governing society.

It is in this context that we can understand the intriguing relationship between state law and village regulations on taxation. From the viewpoint of village communities, any action that deviated from their established rules was deemed unacceptable. "*Ge na ge liang*," or individual delivery of taxes, though exactly what the state stipulated, was nevertheless seen as a violation of local regulations. For the pragmatic magistrate, the village regulations were perfectly compatible with the state law when they facilitated tax collection, no matter how the local cungui deviated from the statutory method. This was why the magistrate endorsed the cungui, rather than the statutory practice, in his handling of disputes resulting from the villagers' insistence on self-delivery. The substitution of village regulations for state law was, then, indicative of the substantive approach of local government, an approach that remained unchanged in land taxation as late as the early twentieth century.

CHAPTER 6

Land and Tax Administration

Land taxation comprised a series of administrative activities. Aside from tax collection, it involved the administration of land sales, the investigation and taxation of unofficial land deeds, the transfer of tax liabilities resulting from changes in land ownership, the compilation and updating of tax rolls, and the uncovering of untaxed land. This chapter examines all of these activities except the investigation of untaxed land, which is discussed in Chapter 11.

The county government in Huailu, as discussed in Chapter 5, relied mainly on the unofficial xiangdi to collect taxes throughout the late imperial and Republican periods. This chapter shows that the magistrate again delegated his tasks in land taxation to unofficial agents in local society, including the xiangdi, who was responsible for all duties in connection with land sales and land deeds, and the sheshu, who managed land cadastres and updated tax rolls. This reliance on local agents, characteristic of the traditional method of rural administration, continued in the early Republican years when the state's demand on tax revenues rapidly increased. Instead of handling the administrative tasks by itself, the government terminated the xiangdi's official duties and farmed them out to entrepreneurial agents at the supra-village level, which caused disturbances in local communities and protests from rural elites. A close examination of malfeasance and local protests in the early Republican years will help us understand why the Guomindang regime took radical measures to reorganize the rural administrative system after 1928, a topic explored in Chapters 10 and 11.

This chapter first examines the xiangdi's role as a government agent in the investigation and taxation of illegal deeds before 1916. It then focuses on the early Republican state's efforts to install new agents in deed taxation, abuses associated with the profiteering agents, and local resistance. Finally, I examine the activities of the sheshu in transferring tax liabilities and updating tax rolls.

The Xiangdi as a Government Agent

Deed tax (qishui), or the tax levied on land and housing sales, was an important source of government revenue during the late Qing and Republican periods. In Huailu county, it amounted to approximately 1,500 to 2,000 taels a year, which equaled 6 percent to 9 percent of the statutory quota of land tax for the county.[1] Unlike the land tax, which was remitted to the provincial treasury in full, however, most of the deed tax was kept by local government and other institutions to cover their daily expenses in the early twentieth century.[2] The deed tax was the biggest source of revenue to finance local modernizing projects. The provincial ordinance on deed taxation stipulated that one-third of the deed tax was to be used as exclusive funds for "self-government" enterprises (such as the creation and maintenance of local assemblies, new-style schools, and modern police).[3]

The major concern of local government in deed taxation had long been widespread evasion. By state law, after each transaction, both the seller and the buyer had to visit the county yamen to have the title of the property transferred and pay a deed tax. This officially verified deed, stamped with the red government seal, was called the "red deed" (hongqi). In practice, however, few people went to the county seat for an official stamp. Usually they possessed unofficial deeds drawn up by the middlemen (in Huailu, the xiangdi). Such deeds were called "white deeds" (baiqi), for they bore no official stamp.[4] To increase its tax income, local government tried to uncover the unofficial deeds throughout the late Qing and the Republican periods. An examination of government activities in this area and local responses to deed taxation will offer us a different vantage point from which to view the interactive relationship between the state and rural communities.

WRITING DEEDS

Before 1900, the xiangdi was the only quasi-official at the bottom of peasant society and the only personnel available to the magistrate to carry out his instructions. Therefore, it was up to the xiangdi to write a "draft deed" (caoqi, which needed to be verified by the county government in order to be a legal document—that is, a red deed) for the new owner after each transaction, to prompt the new owner to pay deed taxes to the county government, and to help the yamen investigate untaxed deeds. This reliance on the semiofficial xiangdi did not change until 1915, when the government created new agents to take over the xiangdi's official duties in deed taxation.

The paper used by the xiangdi to write draft deeds was, by law, the official deed form (*qizhi*) issued by the financial commissioner (*buzhengshi*) of the provincial government. To put deed tax under its control and to prevent county yamen from embezzling tax monies, each year the financial commissioner of Zhili province required the counties in his jurisdiction to obtain the deed forms from his office and at the same time return the unused forms from the previous year. He also required the county yamen to report to him every quarter (and every month after 1905) the amount of deed taxes collected.[5]

The Huailu yamen nonetheless had its own way to embezzle deed taxes. Beginning in 1884, its office in charge of deed tax (*jianfang*), upon the approval of the magistrate, printed its own deed forms (known as "small deeds") in lieu of the official forms issued by the commissioner (655.1.827, 1884–1902). This reduced the number of official forms the county received from the province.[6] The commissioner was well aware of this practice and articulated his concern in an instruction to the Huailu magistrate in 1895: "This county has a vast territory and is densely populated. Land and housing sales therefore must boom. But why have the deed forms this county receives been decreasing in recent years? . . . It is not impossible that there is the private use of small deeds affixed with the county's own stamp (*shuyin xiaoqi*)." Such "small deeds," he warned, would be treated as white deeds when uncovered (655.1.835, 1888; 655.1.853, 1895; 655.1.880, 1905–8). On most occasions, however, the county yamen treated such instructions as mere formalities and continued printing small deeds as usual.

Reducing the use of official deed forms was just one side of the county yamen's embezzlement of deed taxes; the other side was to maximize the use of its self-printed deed forms. The xiangdi, as its agent in deed taxation, faced immense pressure from the yamen to use the small deeds. Since printing its first small deed forms in 1884, every year the Huailu yamen urged the xiangdi in the county to receive its so-called "officially printed deed forms" (*guanban qizhi*) and, at the end of the xiangdi's yearly service, to submit a report of all the sales he had handled in his village, which should list the names of both sellers and buyers as well as the prices of properties transacted. At the same time, the xiangdi needed to return to the yamen all the unused deed forms. However, the xiangdi seldom responded to the magistrate in a timely manner. A magistrate named Xie thus remarked in an instruction to all the xiangdi in May 1901 that in the previous year the xiangdi who came to the yamen to receive the forms were "very few" (*liaoliao wuji*), though people who purchased land and housing were "numerous." Because of the xiangdi's dereliction, the magistrate pointed out, the propertied households "have suffered a shortage of official forms to pay deed taxes." He thus demanded in the middle of the year that all those delinquent xiangdi come to the yamen to receive the forms, a routine that should have taken place at the beginning of the year (655.1.827, 1884–1901).

The magistrate's instructions did not improve the situation; the xiangdi remained reluctant to use the deed forms. Every year, therefore, the magistrate complained in his instruction that "few xiangdi" had abided by his order to report to the yamen the sales occurring in their villages and to return the unused forms. As a rule, the magistrate concluded his notice with a threat to summon those who had delayed their work. There is no indication in any of the successive magistrates' instructions that the xiangdi's performance had improved (655.1.827, 1884–1901). In 1898 the magistrate, named Liu, even asked the xiangdi to record the transactions they handled in a booklet and deliver it to the yamen on the first day of every month, rather than once a year. Not surprisingly, no xiangdi was willing to visit the county seat so frequently, and the magistrate soon gave up this idea (655.1.859, 1898).

The xiangdi's dereliction in deed taxation contrasted sharply with his efficiency in the advance payment of land taxes. As a community member, the xiangdi advanced land taxes promptly in accordance with village regulations. The task of receiving, writing, and returning deed forms, however, was imposed from outside the community. He therefore shirked that duty whenever he could. The xiangdi, after all, was not an officer appointed by the magistrate but chosen by fellow villagers according to local regulations. Therefore he was primarily responsible to his community rather than the government.

PROMPTING DEED-TAX PAYMENT

The Qing code prescribed severe punishment for those who evaded deed taxes. It stipulated that people who purchased land and housing without paying taxes were to receive fifty lashes with the light bamboo and were to pay a fine equal to half of the sale price of the property (*Daqing lüli*, 9: hulü). However, there was always a large number of people who purchased land and housing without paying deed taxes. In fact, few paid them without prompting. In 1885, after issuing the self-printed deeds, Huailu county yamen repeatedly urged the xiangdi to prompt white-deed holders to pay taxes. The magistrate warned in his instruction that any xiangdi who failed to do so would be summoned to the yamen, and once again most xiangdi neglected this order and even refused to attend the hearing upon receiving a summons.

A change then took place in 1887. In his notice to prompt deed-tax payment, the magistrate warned that "those proprietors who delayed their deed-tax payments would be summoned and punished together with the xiangdi who was in charge of the sale." As this notice implied, it was now the buyer rather than the xiangdi who assumed the primary responsibility for the delayed deed-tax payment. Beginning in 1891, the yamen further turned to its own runners to prompt the deed-tax payment and only asked the xiangdi to assist the runner. The xiangdi thus actually got rid of much of the burden of deed-tax prompting.

INVESTIGATING WHITE DEEDS

Investigating white deeds was normally the sheshu's duty. The main duty of the sheshu, a semiofficial clerk, was to record changes in land-tax obligations. He was also the only person who knew the details of land and housing sales in his *she* (a subcounty division for the purpose of tax-liability management, consisting of approximately a dozen villages), for although a buyer might be reluctant to pay deed tax, a seller had to immediately inform the sheshu of the sale in order to transfer his tax liability to the new owner. Therefore every year the magistrate instructed the sheshu to go to his villages along with records of land-tax liability changes and investigate whether the newly propertied households had paid deed taxes. The xiangdi had to assist the sheshu in this process (see, e.g., 655.1.871, 1903; 655.1.874, 1904).

Nonetheless, there were occasions when the magistrate charged the xiangdi directly with the task of white-deed investigation. In 1892, for example, a magistrate named Zhang, noticing that there were always "ignorant simpletons" (*wuzhi xiangyu*) who hid their deeds from taxation and that some even had held untaxed deeds for several decades, required all the xiangdi in Huailu to report on white deeds in their own villages, with a warning to summon and punish all those xiangdi who failed to come to the yamen on the date due. Eight xiangdi thus were brought to court on October 8, and all pretended that they had failed to report to the yamen on time because "they were sick and unable to move." After submitting a pledge, vowing to "take care of public tasks diligently hereafter" (*jinhou haohao bangong*), all of them were released without any punishment. In fact, so many xiangdi failed to attend to white-deed investigation that it was practically impossible for the magistrate to put them in custody, a form of punishment he often applied to the small number of xiangdi who failed to fulfill their tax quotas by the deadline. These circumstances encouraged the xiangdi's dereliction.

The ineffectiveness of the xiangdi lay in the very nature of his post. The xiangdi was selected by the villagers to serve their needs (advancing taxes and being middlemen in local sales), rather than by the magistrate to answer to the county government. Situated in a social network of kinship, friendship, and neighborhood, the xiangdi could not afford to rigorously carry out official tasks in deed taxation at the expense of his relationship with his community. Therefore, few xiangdi accused their fellow villagers of not paying their deed taxes.[7] The xiangdi sued his fellow villagers only when they refused to reward him with a middleman's fee, a matter that had to do with the xiangdi's personal gain.

The Official Middlemen, 1916–19

The xiangdi's ineffectiveness led the government to create a new post, that of *tianfang guanzhong* (official middleman in land and housing) or *guanzhong*. He took over the official duties previously shouldered by the xiangdi in 1916. The guanzhong received no salary. He was to pay to the county government a sum of 80 yuan to obtain an annual guanzhong license and a levy of 20 yuan on this license. A guanzhong thus needed to pay the government a total of 100 yuan a year. Huailu county was allowed 20 guanzhong posts in 1916, which should have generated an income of 2,000 yuan. However, only sixteen licenses were sold in that year, which brought to the government a total of 1,600 yuan. By regulation, the guanzhong could earn a fee or commission for each new deed he wrote, which was 1.5 percent of the sale price of the property (656.1.967, 1917–19; see note 3 for details). In actuality, however, the guanzhong could obtain a fee much higher than the statutory one through various abuses of the system.

It should be noted that those who purchased the guanzhong title were not necessarily rich and powerful individuals; usually they pooled money with others to become joint license holders. In fact, local gentry members avoided this position for its risk and its brokering nature. As we will see below, the relationship between the profiteering guanzhong and local gentry was full of tension and hostility, which finally led to the end of the guanzhong system in 1919.

Like the xiangdi before 1916, the guanzhong's job was to investigate white deeds and write official deeds. However, unlike the xiangdi, the guanzhong did not serve as a middleman in local sales. In fact, because the average guanzhong was in charge of twenty-odd villages, it was far beyond his capacity to act as a middleman for all of the sales taking place in the villages in his charge. In addition, few people trusted the guanzhong to seek out a buyer or a seller and to make a deal, for the guanzhong was an outsider to people in most villages. Therefore, it remained the xiangdi's task to serve as the go-between in transactions in his community. And he was now called *sizhong* (unofficial middleman) in official documents (renamed *chengshui* or "conventional middleman" under the notary system after 1919), in contrast to the *guanzhong* (official middleman).

The division of duties between the sizhong (the xiangdi) and the guanzhong (official middleman) was clear. The former, the real middleman in local sales, was to bring together a buyer and a seller and work out an agreement. The latter was to investigate white deeds, issue official deed forms, stamp the deed drawn up by the xiangdi, and collect deed taxes. The government recognized the xiangdi's role as unofficial middleman in local sales after 1916, allowing him to share a fraction of the deed tax as his fee,

0.75 percent of sale price under the guanzhong system and 0.5 percent under the notary system after 1918 (656.1.967, 1917–19).

MALPRACTICE BY THE GUANZHONG

Because of the entrepreneurial nature of the guanzhong post, malpractice in deed taxation prevailed throughout its short existence. The guanzhong were frequently charged with embezzling fees, not sharing fees with their partners, hiding sales in their reports to the county, writing deeds without using official forms, and entering a sale price lower than the actual one.

To illustrate the abuses by guanzhong, let us first consider an instance in which a guanzhong disputed with his partners. In 1916, Wang Wende and four others pooled 100 yuan to purchase a guanzhong license. The license was in Wang's name. The five agreed to share the fees in proportion to the amount each contributed to the license. In May 1917, however, two partners filed a petition against Wang. According to their charge, Wang pocketed all the fees he had collected without sharing with the others. And he did not use the official forms to write deeds in four sales he had handled. Instead, Wang stamped the unofficial deeds with his own seal, promising the buyers not to pay deed taxes to the government. Wang, in turn, charged the two accusers with not using the official forms in their handling of land sales. The magistrate responded by asking Wang to submit his record of the sales he had handled for court examination and eventually ruled in favor of the accusers. Wang, as a result, paid a fine of 20 yuan (656.1.1100, 1917).

Another widespread form of abuse by guanzhong, was to enter a price on the deed lower than the actual one in exchange for a higher fee. In 1918 a guanzhong named Lei Kexiang accused his partner, Yao Juhai, of receiving a bribe of 7 yuan from a buyer and in turn writing 160,000 wen on the deed, which was only one-fifth of the sale price (656.1.947, 1918). In fact, recording a low price was not only a way to get a high commission, but also a way for the guanzhong to compete for deed-writing opportunities. By regulation, a buyer had the right to select a guanzhong at his own discretion to draft an official deed. The guanzhong had no specific or exclusive jurisdictions. Therefore, they competed with one another by entering lower prices on deeds in order to attract clients.

In 1917, for example, Wei Yuanchang of Dongliangxiang village bought a plot from his fellow villager for 380,000 wen. Three months later, a guanzhong named Li Luoqi from another village let one of Wei's relatives persuade Wei to receive a land deed from Li, and Li promised to write only 200,000 wen on the deed in exchange for a commission of 10,000 wen. At the same time, the seller introduced to Wei another guanzhong named Rong Jinde from yet another village, who promised to write Wei a deed with an even lower price (180,000 wen) and yet insisted on a commission commensurate with the actual sale price (13,680 wen). On July 9, Rong petitioned against Wei, claiming that the buyer refused to use his deed form and pay him a commission. Rong's charge prompted Wei's counterpetition, which brought to light the competition between the two guanzhong. The magistrate, after cross-examination during a court hearing, believed that the two guanzhong "had reduced the price in writing the deed in order to profit themselves" (*jianjia xie qi, feisi wubi*) and ordered Wei to choose another guanzhong to write the actual price on the deed (656.1.749, 1917).

CONFLICTS WITH DEED HOLDERS

The relationship between the guanzhong and deed holders was similar to that between the tax-collecting sheshu and enclave taxpayers. For deed holders in most villages, the guanzhong was merely a profiteering agent, whose only concern was to "detect" white deeds and to extort a "commission" that would flow into his own pocket. Understandably, few were willing to pay an outsider such a commission, for he provided no middleman service at all. Instead, most villagers turned to the local xiangdi for an unofficial deed and evaded deed tax whenever possible. The guanzhong system also offered deed holders openings to evade taxes. As I noted earlier, under this system the buyer had the liberty to choose a guanzhong. Therefore, once their evasion of official land deeds and deed taxes was uncovered by one guanzhong, they would immediately turn to another for a formal deed. Many disputes between the guanzhong and white-deed holders thus arose owing to the latter's evasion.

The reason behind the intense lawsuits between the guanzhong and local people was the same as that which led to the sheshu's frequent disputes with delinquent enclave taxpayers. The guanzhong as an outsider could not count on local community mediation to settle his dispute with local deed holders. His only recourse was to file a plaint. And as an outsider who had no relations (neighborhood, friendship, or kinship) with the delinquent deed holder, he would not hesitate to do so. The relationships between the official middlemen and local communities inevitably worsened, as the following three cases show.

In November 1917, Rong Jinde, the above-mentioned guanzhong, accused five land buyers from different villages of refusing to use his official deed forms despite his repeated promptings. Such delinquent proprietors, Rong complained, would stealthily turn to other guanzhong for a deed upon his petition and then charge him with false accusation. His efforts to investigate untaxed deeds were therefore wasted. The magistrate responded by instructing the ward police officer to look into the matter and to make sure that the accused used Rong's forms and paid him the commission due. Four of the accused paid their fees immediately. The fifth was brought to court and was ordered to pay his fee to Rong within ten days (656.1.749, 1917).

In a similar case, a guanzhong named Shi Xiangquan found that one Yang Qi of Beiqiema village sold his fellow villager a house for 150,000 wen. By regulation, the buyer should have paid him a fee of 5,400 wen and a deed-form fee of 50 wen, and the seller should have paid him a fee of 3,600 wen and a deed-form fee of 50 wen. According to the guanzhong's accusation, both parties refused to pay him despite his promptings. He therefore requested a summons of the two villagers. The guanzhong also submitted with his petition an excerpt from the provincial ordinance, by which a white-deed holder, upon investigation, should be assessed a fine equal to the deed tax due. The magistrate responded by instructing the ward police to prompt the two parties to draw up official deeds. And he closed the case when the police reported that both had purchased the official form from the guanzhong and paid him a commission (656.1.731, 1917).

As the preceding cases indicate, the magistrate seldom applied the penalty to white-deed holders in accordance with official regulations. His leniency in handling these disputes may have further encouraged evasion of deed taxes. Widespread evasions of deed taxes, in turn, offered the guanzhong opportunities to increase their income by uncovering the white deeds. Thus many were accused of nonpayment of deed taxes. On January 16, 1919, for example, a guanzhong by the name of Li Fengbao claimed in his petition that he had found as many as several hundred households that had untaxed deeds. His petition charged twelve persons with nonpayment and illegally receiving commissions (si chou zhongyong) in five sales. During a court session attended by all the charged, the magistrate simply instructed them to pay their taxes due as soon as possible, and exempted them from a punishment "in consideration of the ignorance of the country bumpkins" (xiangyu wuzhi). Two weeks later, however, the guanzhong filed yet another petition, charging the same villagers with persistent nonpayment. This time the magistrate ordered all of the accused at the court hearing to pay their deed taxes within three days at a rate in accordance with the regulation (656.1.1085, 1919).

TENSION WITH LOCAL ELITES

Tension existed not only between the guanzhong and deed holders, but also between the guanzhong and local elites. As guanzhong abuse thrived and their activities became "disturbing" (raomin) to local society, the notables became both envious of the lucrativeness of the guanzhong post and intolerant of the guanzhong's intrusion into local communities. Elite resistance to the guanzhong thus filled the short period of their existence (1916–19).

In a telling case, eight village heads from the southeastern district of the county collectively petitioned against Wang Wende, the same guanzhong who argued with his partners over the apportioning of tax monies. In that case the magistrate found for the partners and assessed Wang a fine of 20 yuan. The eight village heads, dissatisfied with Wang's activities in their villages, filed a petition immediately after the magistrate's ruling, stating that they "would not acknowledge his eligibility as the guanzhong any longer" and requesting his removal. At the same time they nominated Guo Zhaoji, a man they asserted to be "just and well-to-do, and [who] has long had a good standing in the locality." The magistrate, however, avoided making any formal comment on the petition. His ambiguous attitude was also evident in the remark he attached to the file: "unease recurred among the gentry, who all believed [the guanzhong's activities] to be a disturbance" (656.1.1100, 1917).

To fight the infamous guanzhong, some local leaders encouraged their fellow villagers not to pay them fees. This boycott proved to be quite effective in communities where the leaders established their influence. Zhao Mengbi, a member of the Education Promotion Office (EPO; see Chapter 8 for its details) in charge of the southeastern district and head of Nandu village, played a conspicuous role in this regard. On July 24, 1917, three guanzhong of the district filed a petition against Zhao. According to them, "behind the scenes" Zhao had persuaded several buyers not to use their deed forms. "Since the creation of the guanzhong more than one year ago," the plaint went on, "we have made great effort in prompting and handling [deed taxes], but [the collection of deed] taxes and commissions has not been so smooth and fruitful. The reason is nothing other than Zhao Mengbi's mobilization of the gentry to resist. The whole district has been affected [by their resistance]." The magistrate, not wanting to harm his relationship with local elite, made no comment on that plaint. Two months later, one of the guanzhong submitted another petition, complaining that a seller and a buyer in two separate sales refused to use his official deed forms, and they did so at the instigation of Zhao Mengbi, "who is determined to destroy the guanzhong [system]." This time, the magistrate responded merely by instructing the ward police to prompt deed-tax payment (656.1.749, 1917).

Without any interference from the magistrate, Zhao Mengbi grew bolder and employed a ward policeman to distribute flyers to villages in the district, urging the villagers to gather at his office to discuss the dismissal of the guanzhong. And Zhao himself visited neighboring villages to seek support for his action. The guanzhong thus filed a third petition against Zhao and submitted with it a copy of Zhao's flyer. Once again, the petition produced no response from the magistrate (656.1.749, 1917).

Elite opposition exerted considerable pressure on the guanzhong, such that some of them gave up their jobs. A guanzhong named Lei Kexiang, for example, petitioned for resignation in 1918, asserting that he had become dissatisfied with his partners' "various kinds of unlawful activities" in deed taxation, which, according to Lei, had caused "denouncement from all sides and thorough discrediting of his reputation" (*mayan siqi, minyu saodi*). He therefore was "willing to give away his position to just gentry." The magistrate accepted his petition, and instructed the outgoing guanzhong to look for a candidate himself (656.1.947, 1918).

The guanzhong system eventually ended in 1919 because of escalating nationwide elite resistance. Most provincial assemblies proposed to abolish the notorious post for the "disturbance" (*zirao*) it had caused in the countryside. Based on their propositions, the parliament in Beijing passed an act in April 1919 to formally abolish the system. This act was quickly put into force through an ordinance issued by the Beijing government.

The short-lived guanzhong system was indicative of the predicament of the Republic in its course of modern state-making. The fact that the state created the guanzhong position at the supra-village level, rather than turning to the preexisting village governments to tax deeds, reflected the ineffectiveness of the village governments (see Chapters 3 and 7) and the state's inability to penetrate local society. The guanzhong, as it turned out, was merely a profiteering broker between the government and deed holders. After paying a contracted license fee, the guanzhong was allowed to collect deed fees himself and therefore would employ all kinds of malpractice available to maximize his income from this source.

Earlier scholarship has observed the trend in which the state's efforts to increase its tax revenues resulted in the proliferation of entrepreneurial activities at the taxpayers' expense (e.g., Duara 1988). What has been generally overlooked, however, is elite resistance to such profiteering activities. The motivation behind the elite's collective actions, as we have seen in the short history of the guanzhong, was mixed, involving its traditional obligation to protect local communities as well as its desire to take advantage of the lucrative opportunities opened to the guanzhong. At any rate, their opposition effectively held the guanzhong's malpractice in check and successfully ended the ill-favored system.

The Land and Housing Transaction Notary, 1919–1930

In April 1919, the new post of land and housing transaction notary (*tianfang jiaoyi jianzhengren*) was created to replace the guanzhong. By order of the Zhili provincial governor, this new post was to be filled by the village head; if a county had too many villages and the villages heads were not proficient in arithmetic, the magistrate might divide his county into several districts and appoint to each district several notaries, who were to be chosen from the village heads within the district. If a village head was not willing to assume the post, he needed to nominate a deputy to act for him, but the village head was still entrusted with full responsibility.

Clearly, the government intended the village head to be its agent in deed taxation. The village head was created at the beginning of the twentieth century to replace old-style quasi-officials (such as the xiangbao, dibao, or xiangdi) under the baojia system and its local variations. However, his function as government agent was quite weak and inefficient. In Huailu county, the village head only assumed part of the xiangdi's traditional duties in local administration, leaving tax collection, the most important task of the village office, entirely to the xiangdi.

Aware of the possible difficulty of delegating the notary's tasks to the village heads, the provincial government allowed exceptions whereby the magistrate might choose the notaries from the xiangdi, from members of "self-government" associations, or from personnel in charge of local education, depending on the particular situation of the locality. This exceptional arrangement, stressed the governor, would be allowed only when the magistrate explained the reasons, and the village head would still be charged with the duty of investigating white deeds.

As a notary, the village head was saddled with the following tasks: reporting to the county government all land and housing sales in his village; reporting untaxed deeds and unofficial deeds; issuing official deed forms, collecting the deed-form fee, and stamping the deed with the notary's seal; and acting as a witness to land and housing sales.

Unlike the guanzhong, who needed to pay a license fee and a levy every year to secure his position, the notary (the village head in most cases) was merely a government functionary, as was the xiangdi before 1916; he did not need to pay the government for his position, and therefore it was risk-free. Yet unlike the xiangdi before 1916, the village head was privileged to share a portion of the deed tax, which was 1 percent of the sale price, and to receive a subsidy of 50 wen for each copy of the deed he issued. Meanwhile, the village head did not have to be the go-between in local sales and transactions; it remained the xiangdi's task.

Local notables, who had avoided the entrepreneurial, high-risk guanzhong post, now coveted the lucrative yet risk-free post of notary. With greater influence at the supra-village level and more direct connections to the authorities than the village heads, they competed for the notary position with the village heads. As a result, the Huailu magistrate issued an order on June 1, 1919, terminating the village head's role as notary in land and housing sales and instead authorizing the EPO members in the five districts of the county to act as notaries for their respective districts. The village heads, by that order, were only held responsible for investigating untaxed deeds.

Tension inevitably arose between the supra-village elite and the village heads. Zhao Mengbi, the EPO member of the southeastern district, who had waged a war with the guanzhong before 1919, became the notary of his district by the magistrate's new decision and was to handle land and housing sales in all of the forty-odd villages in his district. In December 1919, when the pace of transactions typically increased at the end of the lunar year, Zhao distributed a notice to the villages in his charge, announcing that all those who had bought land and housing should ask him for an official form. This notice caused confusion among the villagers, who hesitated about making a choice between the village head and Zhao to draw up an official deed. At the same time, the village heads had become dissatisfied with the new regulation that nullified their right to issue deed forms and draw fees yet still held them responsible for untaxed deeds.

The conflict between the EPO and village heads reached a peak when over 200 village heads from the five districts of the county filed a collective petition (date not specified) to appeal for their right to hold the position of notary. To support their claim, the petition first quoted the provincial ordinance, which allowed the village head to be the notary. It then pointed out the EPO members' inability to be notaries, for they were busy with school affairs; handling sales would distract them from their proper work. What is more, according to the petition, although the EPO members controlled the notary position on the pretext of raising funds for schools, the proportion of the educational funds derived from the deed tax was as low as 0.5 percent of the sale price. In contrast, the EPO member's share of the deed tax was as high as 1 percent of the sale price. Therefore, the petition went on, those members should have given up their share to augment the proportion of educational funds if they were really devoted to promoting education. In spite of the eloquence of the petition, the magistrate declined the village heads' appeal, quoting another clause of the provincial ordinance, which allowed the people in charge of education to be notaries when needed.

Nevertheless, the EPO members' role as notary was short-lived. The county's Educational Council (*jiaoyu hui*) soon found that those members were all so preoccupied with land and housing sales for their personal gain that few had time to take care of school affairs. In order to avoid the "paralysis of education," the county government ended the EPO members' notary duties in August 1920. In their place, it appointed the five members of the county's newly established Financial Office (*caizheng suo*) as notaries for each of the five districts. The Financial Office was a self-government body composed of local elites (see Chapter 9 for details). It performed the function previously assumed by the County Assembly, such as deciding on new taxes and managing the financial needs of local self-government institutions. Its five "investigators" (*diaochayuan*), who also acted as notaries, existed until

1924, when the Financial Office was abolished and its functions assigned to the reopened County Assembly. After that year, the notaries were elected by the village heads of their respective districts rather than appointed by the magistrate.

Without effective supervision from both above and below, the notaries' abuse of the deed-taxation system became as severe as the guanzhong's. And the tension between this new agent and village heads continued. This is seen in a case in which the village heads of South Second District succeeded in removing an abusive notary named Song Huanwen. In 1924, Song was elected as a notary to take charge of deed taxation in nine villages of the district. According to the testimony of a village head from the district, Song was able to get that position because he was a relative of the head of ward police, who "pressed" the village heads in his district to elect Song. However, Song was too old to attend to his duties; he had to turn over most of them to his son, Song Xinzheng, who, however, was believed too young to handle local transactions. Much confusion thus arose from his writing of deeds. What is more, according to a collective petition from six village heads of the district, submitted on February 27, 1927, Song's son engaged in extortion. For example, he always demanded a deed-form fee higher than the official rate (100 wen per sheet). When a buyer refused to use his form, he would then report the untaxed sale to the ward police, which would result in severe punishment of the buyer. A new owner thus had to purchase his deed form whatever its cost. His writing of deeds, too, was full of errors; for example, he often entered on the deed amounts and prices higher or lower than the actual ones in order to extort higher fees or to show favor to those he protected.

Following this petition, the village heads submitted another four plaints, accusing Song of even more wrongdoing. According to the village heads, Song, when asked for a deed form, would require the buyers to pay him the deed tax directly, and he would then embezzle part of the money by reporting a lesser amount to the government. To augment his income, Song also illegally assessed the buyer an extra amount of deed tax equal to 0.5 percent of the sale price.

The magistrate's responses to these petitions became increasingly unfavorable to Song. His comment on the first petition was merely to let the ward police investigate the matter. On the second petition, he noted: "Song Huanwen has been charged with over-taxing more than once. Wait for a summons and investigation." This apparently encouraged the village heads to take further action against Song. Two of them thus investigated the notary's wrongdoing "day and night" and then reported to the magistrate that Song had taxed one of their fellow villagers 23,415 wen more than she should have paid. The magistrate's comment: "A severe punishment should apply [to

Song] upon verification at the court; no compromise is allowed." Another two village heads reported that their fellow villager Qin Luoyuan had sold 3.8 mu of land in December 1925 for 191.96 yuan and should have paid a deed tax of 23 yuan. Song, however, changed the date of the transaction to 1916, the price to 30 yuan, and the amount of land to 3.4 mu. In that way, the notary illegally entitled himself to a large fee. The magistrate's response was furious: "Song Huanwen's malpractice constitutes a great violation of the state's law."

During the court session held on May 10, in which all six village heads and the notary appeared, the magistrate ruled: "Song Huanwen as the land and housing notary in charge of the nine villages has erred in charging extra commissions for deed forms and in writing deeds with mistakes. With so many wrongdoings, he has clearly violated the regulation." The magistrate therefore demanded that Song pay a fine of 40 yuan in accordance with relevant regulation, and dismissed (*chige*) him from the notary post. At the same time, the magistrate ordered the nine villages to elect a new notary (656.2.983, 1927).

To sum up, deed taxation in late Qing and early Republican Huailu underwent a transition from the state's reliance on the old-style, inefficient xiangdi before 1916 through the guanzhong to the notary system after 1919. It must be stressed that both the guanzhong and the notaries were informal agents existing outside the regular bureaucratic system. Both obtained their positions by purchase or local nomination rather than by the magistrate's formal appointment. Therefore, neither one received a salary from the county government and both made a living only on the fees they drew from their clients or a portion of the deed taxes they collected. Consequently, both treated their activities as a business, and their only concern was to maximize their profits from deed writing and taxation.

Thus the new measures of deed taxation in the 1910s and 1920s were in effect a continuation of the old method of rural control, which was characterized by the government's reliance on local informal agents. Unlike the xiangdi, whose activities were subject to village regulations and community supervision, however, both the guanzhong and the notaries performed their duties as outsiders and were therefore more likely to engage in malfeasance. Conflicts between the profiteering outsiders and local residents persisted throughout the years of their existence. But elite activism also effectively curbed their abuses. The local notables, who competed for opportunities to enrich themselves, also continued to protect local communities in order to maintain their reputations. Their efforts to fight corruption in deed taxation effectively reduced the impact of the guanzhong and notaries' illegal activities on local communities.

The Management of Tax Liabilities

The management of tax liabilities, or more exactly, the transfer of tax duties and the updating of tax rolls, was another field in which the traditional method of governance continued in the early twentieth century. To guarantee the prompt and full payment of land taxes, the imperial states repeatedly enforced the *lijia* system, in addition to the *baojia* system for neighborhood surveillance and criminal control. The lijia, as Chapter 3 has documented, was first introduced during the Ming (1368–1644) and then restored at the beginning of the Qing. Under this system, 110 households were grouped into a *li*, in which the ten households with the largest tax quotas were to serve as the yearly *lizhang* (head of the li) in rotation, and the remaining 100 households were further divided into 10 *jia*. Aside from collecting and delivering taxes for households in his li to the government, the lizhang was required to update adult-male registers, which were needed for collecting head taxes and to record changes in tax liabilities for collecting land taxes. When reestablishing the lijia, early Qing rulers released the lizhang from the burden of tax collection but still held them responsible for compiling adult-male registers. After merging the head tax with the land tax in 1726, the Qing state further ceased the periodic updating of the adult-male registers and abandoned the lijia system. But the lizhang's function in managing tax rolls survived and was shifted to local literate people, who eventually became the professional sheshu (known variably as *lishu, ceshu, tucheng, tushu,* or *tutou*) in charge of the taxpaying households in their respective *she*, an informal geographic area comprising several villages (Cheng Fang 1939: 201–2; Jiang Shijie 1944: 58; Saeki 1965; Kawakatsu 1980; Chen Zhiping 1988: 153). Those who filled the sheshu post included lower degree holders, commoner-landowners, yamen runners, and even the landless (Saeki 1965; Yamamoto 1980).

In south-central Hebei, each county comprised twelve to eighteen she.[8] Huailu county had eighteen she during the Qing and early Republican periods.[9] The size of the she varied from two or three to as many as twenty-four villages. In order to avoid confusion in tax obligations, it was mandated in the early Qing that land sales and tax transfer must be made within the same she. By the nineteenth century, however, inter-she land sales and tax transfer had become quite common, and this practice was believed to have contributed to the disorder in tax liabilities (*Huailu xianzhi* 1985 [1876]: 70).

In early twentieth-century Huailu, each she had one or several sheshu, whose basic duty was to transfer the tax quota incumbent on a given land from the prior landowner to the new proprietor. For each transfer, the sheshu charged a fee of 0.10 yuan per mu of land in the transaction (Li Hongyi 1977 [1934]: 6461). This job allowed the sheshu to keep private books, which recorded details about the taxable land in his charge, including the name of its real owner, as well as its size, location, and tax quota. These books were treated as their personal belongings, which the sheshu used to earn his living, and therefore were never made available to the public. Given this monopoly on tax-liability records, it is no wonder that the sheshu was usually a hereditary position (Wang Yuanbi 1935).

Another task of the sheshu was to compile the tax rolls for tax collection, which were submitted to the magistrate at the beginning of the lunar year and then distributed to individual villages before the collection started (*Huailu xianzhi* 1985 [1876]: 70). The tax rolls were compiled according to the sheshu's personal records of tax liabilities, but listed only the official names of individual taxpayers in his charge and their tax quotas. The names of the taxpayers on the tax roll often remained the same for generations and therefore were in many cases different from the names of the real taxpayers in the sheshu's private records (Cheng Fang 1939: 201–6).

The sheshu's monopoly of the tax records accounted at least in part for the difficulties the county yamen encountered in prompting delinquent tax-payers. Not knowing the real names and locations of the taxpayers, yamen runners (bailiffs after 1900) who were sent out to villages to prompt tax payment often reported back that "the person [with taxes in arrears] was not found" (*cha wu qiren*) (656.3.455, 1931). It is not surprising that the magistrate, in order to reduce tax deficits and improve the periodic evaluation of his performance, was often willing to farm out the duties of tax collection to the sheshu, despite the state's repeated prohibitions during the Qing and Re-public periods, and despite official and elite discourse, which always held this unlawful practice responsible for ills in taxation and extra collection. Before the abolition of the sheshu in 1930, this business prevailed in many counties in Hebei province (Li Hongyi 1977 [1934]: 6459).

In Huailu, however, the xiangdi system effectively kept the sheshu from engaging in tax farming. By local regulations in most villages, it was the xi-angdi's duty to advance taxes for the whole community. The basic task of the sheshu remained to handle tax transfer and compile tax rolls. The only ex-ception was the collection of "enclave" taxes, which the residents of the neighboring counties owed to the Huailu government. Nonpayment of en-clave taxes was quite common, and the county government had great diffi-culty prompting tax payment in the territories outside of its jurisdiction. The sheshu, who knew who and where the real taxpayers were, thus was of-ten held responsible for the fulfillment of enclave taxes in his charge. When tax quotas were not met, the sheshu had to pay the balance due and then collect the monies from delinquent taxpayers (see Chapter 5).

THE SHESHU ABUSES

Given the sheshu's exclusive possession of records on tax liabilities, it is no surprise that attacks on his misdeeds dominated official discourse and elite writings on tax transfer and tax-roll compilation. One of the most notorious techniques was *feisa*, the reduction or elimination of certain households' tax quotas by "spraying" them to other households. Another is *guiji*, the registration of land under a false name so that the real landowner could evade tax duties, or the registration of property under the title of a degree holder in order to allow the landowner to pay taxes at a reduced rate. The third is *huandui*, changing the grade of the registered land in order to raise or lower the tax rate since the tax quotas were set according to the grade of land. These practices, prevalent during the Qing, remained pervasive throughout the country in the Republican decades.[10]

Although it is hard to judge how the operation of the sheshu system in Huailu differed from the situation in the rest of the country, evidence from the Huailu archives does attest to the abuses described above. A common fraud that the sheshu in Huailu practiced in preparing tax rolls was to raise tax quotas. This often occurred with enclave taxes, because the sheshu, who was responsible for fulfilling enclave taxes, could easily pocket the extra amount when delinquent taxpayers reimbursed him for the money he had advanced. Take the lawsuit involving Li Luoxun, a sheshu living in Songcun village, for example. In January 1913, He Min from South Gaojiaying village of neighboring Zhengding county filed a plaint against Li for increasing his tax quota. According to the plaint, He Min used to fulfill a tax of 0.458 tael under the name of "Hejingtang." But Li had added an extra 0.04 tael to his quota, bringing the tax to 0.498 tael. And what was worse, Li had discourteously rejected He Min's request for a correction. To show the correct amount of his tax quota, He Min enclosed in his plaint all his tax receipts from preceding years. The magistrate, at the request of his colleague in the neighboring county, issued a warrant to the sheshu immediately. Li soon asked the county assembly to mediate the dispute and promised to cancel the additional 0.04 tael. The magistrate, however, refused to close the case and insisted that the sheshu submit a petition to explain how he had made this mistake. According to Li's explanation, he, at age 72 and with dim eyesight, had merely made a clerical error when preparing the tax roll (656.1.69, 1913).

In a similar case, the head of Beizai village charged Zhao Jierong, a sheshu from Xiumen village, with imposing extra tax quotas totaling 2.18 tael on a number of taxpayers in his village and at the same time removing 0.383 tael from a plot of enclave land approximately 13 mu in size. The village head claimed that the sheshu had intended to pocket the enclave tax by shifting the tax burden to his villagers (656.3.611, 1932). A third case came from Xiaoyudi village, where a Yang Baini had paid a tax of 0.408 tael under the name of Yang Zongyi for a long time. But a sheshu named Zhao Luomao duplicated Yang's name in the tax roll he compiled in 1930 so that Yang had to pay the tax twice. Upon the victim's accusation, Zhao promised to correct the tax roll the next year. For the current year, he would pay the extra tax burden for Yang out-of-pocket (656.3.431, 1931).

An even more flagrant abuse was adding fictitious taxpayers and tax quotas to tax rolls. According to a joint petition from the village head and xiangdi of Dongxin village submitted on April 26, 1927, the sheshu who prepared the tax roll for their village had removed eight taxpayers from the roll, whose tax quotas totaled 3.33 taels, and at the same time added eleven new taxpayers with tax quotas totaling 0.21 tael. The two accusers were puzzled because the eight persons whose tax quotas were removed had not sold their land and the eleven new taxpayers named did not exist in the village. The magistrate responded by instructing the county office in charge of tax to correct the tax roll. It turned out that the newly added 0.21 tael of land tax quota under the names of eleven unknown taxpayers were "unidentified quotas" (*kongyin*), the tax liabilities left by those who had died or had disappeared without designated successors. The sheshu had "sprayed" (*feisa*) the "unidentified quotas" to all taxpayers in his charge, since he could not identify any specific taxpayers responsible for the tax duties (656.2.992, 1927).[11]

What needs to be discussed here is the actual extent of the sheshu's illegal practice in transferring tax duties and updating tax rolls. It was not impossible for the sheshu to secretly increase the unidentified quotas when spraying them to existing taxpayers, and thereby reduce the tax liabilities of those under his protection. He could even fabricate "extinct households" (*juehu*) or "missing households" (*taohu*), and then reduce or eliminate the tax burdens of those in his favor and shift these burdens onto other taxpayers. However, the actual number of deceased or missing households was small in the local communities; the sheshu could not make up such households or increase their tax quotas without limit. It follows that these types of fraud, though occurring from time to time, could not have been committed regularly by the sheshu, who made a living on tax transfer for life and whose position was usually hereditary. Moreover, since the sheshu did not collect land taxes, fabricating extinct or missing households or increasing and spraying their tax quotas did not directly benefit himself; the sheshu, in other words, would likely engage in such practices only when he was also a tax collector. In Huailu, as well as the neighboring counties of south-central Hebei, however, the sheshu acted as a tax farmer only on the limited number of tax enclaves (*jizhuang di*). Normally, the sheshu was just responsible for tax transfer and tax roll updating; collecting and paying land taxes were the duties of the xiangdi.

It was even more unlikely that the sheshu would increase the tax duties of existing households without a reason or pretext. Under normal conditions, every village or subvillage pai had its own record of individual taxpayers' quotas. The taxpaying household also knew very well how much it owed, for it preserved the tax receipts that it had received upon fulfillment of tax quotas. It was thus almost impossible for the sheshu to deceive the taxpayers and increase their tax duties. He Min, the aforementioned plaintiff from Songcun village, thus stated in his plaint: "how could we tolerate the [sheshu's] adding or deleting [of tax liabilities] since our village has the record of tax quotas as well as the tax receipts for verification?" (656.1.69, 1913). Far from ignorant victims of sheshu abuse, the taxpayers took action to protect themselves once they found out about such fraudulent activities, for the tax liabilities directly affected their livelihood; even a slight increase in their tax quota would become a permanent burden. The sheshu's fraudulence, though inevitable now and then, was not unlimited under this circumstance.

It is in this light that we can understand why the county yamen, especially its Revenue Office (hufang), which was in charge of taxes, did not take over the sheshu's duties to record changes in tax liabilities and to update tax rolls on its own. The ostensible reason was the limited number of the yamen underlings. It was impossible for the yamen clerks, living at the county seat and few in number, to be familiar with everyday land sales and to handle the resulting tax transfers in hundreds of villages. The only official record of tax quotas the government possessed was the "Complete Compendium of Land Taxes and Labor Services" (fuyi quanshu), which was compiled by the imperial court at the beginning of the Qing on the basis of the official records of tax liabilities of late Ming. In the absence of a formal government at the subcounty level, the yamen office had no way to update the tax rolls on its own but had to assign the task to the ages-old sheshu personnel.

A more profound reason the government tolerated the sheshu system was the limited scope of the sheshu's fraud and the fact that the sheshu was able to fulfill his duties under normal conditions. First, those who had sold their land tended to ask the sheshu to transfer their tax duties to the buyer immediately after the transaction; it was unlikely for them to continue paying taxes on property that no longer belonged to them. And the sheshu would not forgo any opportunity to earn a fee for transferring the tax duty. Therefore the sheshu was always able to perform his task in tax transfer without the government's supervision. Second, the sheshu also showed competency in updating the rolls of taxpayers annually for the government. The government allowed the sheshu to survive and to draw a tax-transfer fee precisely on the condition that he submit to the county's Revenue Office an updated list of taxpayers in his she and their tax quotas; it was based on these tax rolls that the office prepared its tax payment notices for individual taxpayers. To preserve their positions and secure their livelihood, the sheshu unfailingly did so every year before the collection period. The fact that the Revenue Office always distributed the notices to individual households right before the collection suggests that the sheshu submitted the updated tax rolls promptly. Despite the critical role of tax transfer and tax roll updating in land taxation, the imperial state did not involve itself in these activities directly. Devolving these functions completely to the informal sheshu in local communities, the county magistrate intervened as an arbitrator only when the community failed to mediate the disputes that took place between the sheshu and his clients. In the magistrate's opinion, letting the sheshu shoulder the duties of tax transfer was preferable to delegating them to yamen clerks and runners, for the sheshu had professional training for the hereditary position and as a member of the local community was less likely to engage in reckless fraudulence than a yamen clerk or runner from above.

This reliance on the informal sheshu remained unchanged in the early twentieth century. Although the state attempted to extend its reach to the countryside through the installation of ward police and village government after 1900, their roles in taxation were limited. The ward police's responsibility was limited to prompting delinquent taxpayers, while the village heads usually served only as the intermediary between the county government and village communities without being involved in taxation. In the absence of any official agencies in charge of tax liabilities, the sheshu post lasted well into the early 1930s, playing an indispensable role in the preparation of tax rolls.

Conclusion

To conclude, let me summarize the county government's changing approaches to land and tax administration in the late imperial and early Republican periods, and discuss their implications for understanding the nature of the traditional methods of government in rural North China before the Guomindang regime.

The county government's traditional method of local administration was to devolve its tasks pertaining to land and tax management to local informal agents, including the xiangdi and the sheshu. These agents played a dual role in local communities: they served the needs of rural inhabitants in land and housing transactions and tax transfer while performing the duties imposed by the county government. More specifically, the xiangdi worked for his fellow villagers as a middleman in their sales of land, housing, and other commodities in exchange for a middleman's fee; meanwhile he also helped the government investigate and tax land deeds. The sheshu, too, transferred tax liabilities for local residents for a fee and updated the tax rolls for the government.

From the government's point of view, delegating its duties to the informal agents in the local communities had obvious advantages. As unofficial personnel, the xiangdi and the sheshu received no salary from the government; instead they drew a fee from their clients for the services they rendered in local transactions and tax transfer. Using the unofficial agents, therefore, cost the government nothing and saved it from having to hire its own agents to carry out those duties. More important, devolving the taxation of land deeds and tax liability transfers to local communities also reduced the possibility of abuse in these activities. As a member of a local community, the xiangdi or the sheshu lived and worked in a social network embedded in the local society. It was inevitable, to be sure, that these people abused their power and sought illegal gains or showed favor to their kinsmen and friends. However, because the same network also put them under the close scrutiny of the whole community, overt fraud was rare and limited.

The disadvantages of this approach were also obvious. Without compensation and sufficient pressure from the government, the xiangdi had no incentive to perform his duties in deed taxation and investigation. As a member of the local community, he was unwilling to do so seriously at the expense of his relations with fellow villagers. Untaxed land deeds thus were widespread because of the xiangdi's dereliction. However, the county government showed no inclination to take over the xiangdi's duties and to tax the unofficial deeds by itself, in large part because the deed tax accounted for only a small fraction of the state's total revenue and its collection did not affect the magistrate's promotion as much as the collection of land taxes. Moreover, all the deed taxes collected had to be remitted to the provincial government during the Qing; collecting deed taxes did not benefit the county government. Nor did the magistrate show interest in taking over the transfer of tax liabilities from the sheshu despite confusion over tax liabilities, for the total land tax quota of the county was fixed; the disorder of tax liabilities was only a matter between the sheshu and individual taxpayers. As long as the sheshu was able to provide a tax roll that produced the total amount, the magistrate showed no interest in reforming the system of tax liability management. When confusions in tax liabilities caused any problems in tax collection, the magistrate always held the sheshu responsible for making up any deficits caused by the disordered tax liabilities.

Not surprisingly, the government's role in the management of land transactions and tax liabilities was very limited. Normally the government dealt with the informal agents (xiangdi or sheshu) rather than individual taxpayers, and it did so only under the ordinance of provincial authorities or when disputes arose between the agents and taxpayers. Most of the time, the magistrate simply tolerated the wide use of untaxed deeds and confusion in the tax records. The county yamen showed interest in taxing land deeds only when it attempted to embezzle the deed taxes by printing and issuing the illegal forms for writing land and housing deeds in substitution for the legal forms issued by the provincial government. Standing between the provincial government and village communities, the magistrate manipulated his prerogatives as an administrator to enlarge his private gain; he did not have to adhere to the policies and regulations of his superiors. Far from a faithful representative of the state, the magistrate employed a practical approach to local governance; he used all available means, formal and informal, to achieve his goals in land taxation and local control.

This approach, while largely feasible before the twentieth century when the government's financial need was relatively stable, became increasingly difficult after 1900 when the state's demand on tax revenues steadily increased. To be sure, the total amount of land tax quotas remained constant throughout the late Qing and early Republican years in Huailu and many other counties in North China; this explains in large part why the sheshu system, which had to do with the land tax only, remained untouched until the coming of the Guomindang regime in 1928. However, to fund a series of modern projects, such as the police system and public schools, the government had to create new taxes and improve the collection of the preexisting taxes, including the deed tax, which was now partly kept by the county government. To do so, the county government could no longer rely on the xiangdi, who was primarily a representative of his own community rather than the government. In the absence of formal government agencies below the county level, the only option available for the county government was to farm out its duties in deed taxation to local merchants in exchange for a fixed contribution or, alternatively, to devolve the tasks to the newly created "land and housing notaries" at the supra-village level and allow them to share a portion of deed taxes. Malpractice boomed in their activities owing to the profiteering nature of their business and lack of constraints from the community. Elite protests against their abuses only confirmed the traditional concern of neo-Confucian writers about the excessive involvement of the government through such intrusive agents in local communities.

The traditional approach to local government, characterized by the incorporation of government functions into local informal institutions, thus encountered a fundamental challenge in the early twentieth century. It became problematic after 1900, when the state's financial needs suddenly increased, which in turn enhanced its reliance on the informal elements. The devolution or farming out of the administrative functions to profiteering agents only resulted in more abuses in local administration, which caused more conflicts in administrative activities and eroded the state's legitimacy. To solve this problem, it was necessary for the state to extend its administrative arms to levels below the county government and put land and tax administration under its direct control. As we will find in Chapters 10 and 11, this was precisely the task that the Guomindang government intended to take on after 1928.

PART TWO

New Changes after 1900

CHAPTER 7

Power, Discourse, and Legitimacy

The Village Head Office in Dispute

As an important aspect of the "New Policy" (*xinzheng*), the late Qing and early Republican governments widely instituted the office of village head (*cunzheng* or *cunzhang*) as its formal agent in local communities to replace the old-style, semiofficial xiangdi after 1900. Previous scholarship on North China villages has explored the organization and operation of village government in the early twentieth century (Li Jinghan 1933; Fei 1939; M. Yang 1945; Gamble 1954, 1963), including its role in taxation and local control (Myers 1970; P. Huang 1985; Duara 1988; Cong 1995) and its involvement in peasant rebellions (Zhang 1957; Prazniak 1999). But little attention has been paid to changes in the shared assumptions of the villagers about community leadership and in the consciousness of village elites that occurred in the course of state intrusion and the restructuring of local power patterns. My primary concern in this chapter, therefore, is how the creation of village government caused a power reconfiguration in the village community, and more important, how this change further affected the peasants' perceptions of village leadership, which in return shaped the strategies of both the notables and the ordinary for their competition over, or struggles against, various forms of power in local society.

Central to these changes was the process by which community members established and accepted the new leadership. To understand this process, we need to distinguish between the power base of village elites and the legitimacy of their power and status. Scholars have identified a wide array of resources or bases on which elites established dominance in village communities, such as lineage strength and landholding (e.g., Beattie 1979; P. Huang 1985), social hierarchies and networks involved in local religious and lineage activities (Duara 1988), roles in tax collection (Pomeranz 1993), control of corporate property (Dennerline 1979–80; Watson 1990), roles as paternalistic patrons in local community (Duara 1990, 1995), monopoly of coercive and military force (X. Zhang 2000), or a combination of these factors (Esherick and Rankin 1990). Obviously, these means and resources, while critical in producing and maintaining one's prestige and status in the community, were far from enough to justify leadership and dominance. To legitimize and perpetuate his dominant status, a person had to strive to act in compliance with the popular image of a desirable community leader. The legitimacy of his leadership, in other words, was based on the wide recognition and acceptance of his authority in the community, which were in turn linked with his adherence to the values and norms of community members.

It is also worth emphasizing that, in the context of state-making and increasing influence from outside in the early twentieth century, the process of legitimization could never be limited to the village community. As a position imposed from outside, the legitimacy of being a village head was closely linked with the government's representation and endorsement of the office; this was especially true when the state itself still more or less maintained its own legitimacy to govern the society, thus remaining influential in the community to varying degrees. To understand the process of legitimization, then, we need to consider both the values and attitudes of local communities and external influences on officeholding.

To illustrate the changing notions of local leadership and their effect on power relations, this chapter focuses on disputes over the village head service in the Republican years. The Huailu archives contain a total of forty-seven files on such disputes.[1] These materials are valuable for several reasons. First of all, the plaints, counterplaints, and statements from those involved in the disputes show how the peasants looked at the newly created office and what their image of a qualified and legitimate village head was. Second, these disputes involved all of the prominent figures in the community, including the village head, gentry members, clan elders, and the xiangdi, as well as government officers from outside who came to the village to conduct investigations. Therefore, we will be able to analyze changes in local power configurations caused by the advent of village government. Third, the magistrate's adjudication of the lawsuits and method of handling administrative disputes reveal his interactive relationship with local society.

These case records are unusual also because they concentrate on the years from 1913 to 1928, a period largely not covered by past scholarship on village politics. A number of studies have addressed local self-government programs in the late Qing and early Republican periods (Kuhn 1975, 1986; Esherick 1976; MacKinnon 1980). However, village government, as an important part of the self-government movement during the 1910s and 1920s, has remained largely unexamined, owing in large part to the general unavailability of published data. The aforementioned studies of North China villages, mostly drawing on data produced through fieldwork, have focused on the period after 1928 under the Guomindang government and / or Japanese occupation. My focus on the early Republican years is intended to fill a gap in the research.

The Village Head Office

Village leadership in the early twentieth century was vested in two distinct yet closely related groups of local elites. One was traditional village notables, many of them eminent gentry members (usually entry-level degree holders, that is, *shengyuan* or *jiansheng*) and clan elders. We may also include in this category agents of the old-style surveillance organizations (baojia or its local variants), such as the xiangdi in Huailu, although these personnel mostly came from ordinary households and seldom qualified as local elites. The other group included those who held new positions that came into existence as a result of the self-government movement in the late Qing and Republican years, such as village heads and schoolmasters. The most prominent among all these local notables, old and new, was no doubt the village head, a position usually filled by the most influential people in the community.

In Huailu, village government came into wide existence during the last years of the Guangxu reign (1875–1908).[2] Candidates for the village head position, according to official regulations, had to have an established reputation in the local community and a minimum level of literacy to hold the office.[3] Clearly, the state expected local notables, who had been assisting the yamen in rural administration through informal channels, to fill the newly created village office. The official method of selecting the village head was a villagewide vote by ballot (*toubiao gongju*). Upon receiving the results of a legitimate election, the magistrate would issue a certificate of appointment to the newly elected village head.[4] The term of office was normally three years. When his tenure expired, the village head usually submitted a request for retirement and returned the certificate of appointment to the magistrate.

Most disputes over village head service, as the case records show, had to do with competition for the office. The post was coveted because the village head controlled all of the village's public funds and therefore his position was lucrative. Disputes over the office thus often occurred as a result of competition for the control of funds, such as "school monies" (*xuekuan*) (see Chapter 8) and the "the xiangdi's monies" (*gensui xiangdi qianwen*) (see Chapter 3). In Xujiazhuang village, for instance, where the xiangdi's monies amounted to 30,900 wen in the mid-1920s, two xiangdi accused their village head in

1926 of attempting to control the funds he should have given them for their advance payment of taxes (656.2.814, 1926).

Whereas the village head position was usually profitable and attractive before the mid-1920s, the situation quickly changed when warfare between warlords in North China intensified and irregular military levies, which were usually imposed directly on the village head rather than the xiangdi, multiplied. Therefore, the village head office became a thankless burden that most people wanted to avoid, and disputes over evasion of village head service increased significantly. Liu Yurui, the vice-head of the aforementioned Xujiazhuang village, for example, was involved in a dispute with the village head, who wanted to quit his job and turn his duties over to the village head. Thus every time a new levy was imposed, the village head submitted a complaint against the vice-head for not cooperating. In June 1926, for example, when the village head was required to provide a saddle and a laborer, he blamed the vice-head for "not sharing the public duties." The next month the village head received another order to provide mules. Once again Liu refused to cooperate, and the head filed yet another complaint. Two months later, the village head was ordered to provide forage. Without assistance from the vice-head, the village head complained that "it is indeed beyond [my] capacities to handle the matter on [my] own." Finally, in the same month, the head returned his certificate of appointment to the magistrate and petitioned for retirement (656.2.814, 1926).

Qualifications for Village Heads

Although it was primarily the material gain or loss relating to village head service that drove villagers to sue each other, the proceedings of the lawsuits often centered on people's qualifications for the position. These qualifications included the incumbent or would-be village head's age and literacy, his personality and social background, his moral standing and ability to handle public matters, and, no less important, how he was selected. I will show that the villagers' view of what constituted a qualified village head was a mixture of their traditional notion of a virtuous community leader and the official vision of a formally elected, capable government officer of proper age. Their changing perceptions of community leadership directly shaped their strategies in dealing with lawsuits.

LITERACY, PERSONALITY, AND AGE

Let us begin with a dispute from Yaojiali, a village of over 180 households, all surnamed Yao. In 1912 the village founded its primary school, using the public fund of the Yao clan. The clan at that time had over 80 mu of public land, generating an annual rent of 40,000 wen, which increased to

611,200 wen in 1915. Most of the rent was used to support the village school. As the fund increased, however, the villagers' competition for the village head office also intensified in order to control the rent income. In 1919, Yao Hanjie, a shengyuan and teacher in the village, initiated a lawsuit against Yao Chengshen, who was 68 and had served as village head for sixteen years and as schoolmaster for eight years. The tension between the prestigious teacher and the powerful village head had a long history, for the teacher had coveted the village head and schoolmaster positions, and the village head in turn had seen the teacher as a constant threat. In his initial plaint, Hanjie accused Chengshen of "hiding school monies" by reporting "less of the revenue and more of the expenditure." Because of this, declared the teacher, the villagers had removed Chengshen from the village head office for his "failure to meet the public's expectations." He then explained Chengshen's disqualification for the posts he had held. The village head, accused the teacher, "is totally illiterate, temperamental, and likes to shout abuses in the street." "Being close to his seventies," the teacher went on, "[the village head] is muddleheaded in handling public business. As a man of hot temper, he has never done things in an attentive and thoughtful manner. He has also called people names in public and oppressed them with his power. Those who have tried to argue with him always have gotten scolded and therefore they are all discontented with him." These shortcomings, together with the village head's tempering with public funds, disqualified him for the village head service, concluded the teacher.

As a privileged shengyuan in the community, the teacher focused his attack on the village head's biggest weakness, his illiteracy. It was unacceptable, the teacher claimed, that "[the village head] does not know a single character yet he is still in charge of the school." In his successive plaints against the village head, the teacher repeatedly claimed that the village head's "lack of minimum literacy" had led to his "contempt for school affairs" and "destruction of the village's education." To remove the village head from his current position, the teacher nominated a new candidate, who, according to the teacher, was "a person with excellent calligraphy," "faithful to villagers, and experienced in community affairs."

The village head well knew his weakness. He acknowledged at the outset of a court hearing that he "did not attend school when [he] was young and therefore [he] does not read anything." In his counterplaint, the village head explained his hot temper as a result of his "forthright and sincere manner in dealing with people." In his defense, the village head emphasized his past good service and his reputation among the villagers. "The village head office," he explained, "can only be filled by those with a villagewide reputation and upright moral standing. Though not talented, I have been doing things impartially and without misconduct for several decades since I became a village head." The teacher's nominee for the village head office, according to the head, was a peddler "who used to push a cart in the streets of Shijiazhuang, selling steamed foods and crying his wares." This person, he asserted, was definitely unqualified for village head service.

Despite their different and even contradictory representations of the village head and village head candidate, it is clear that no one disputed the importance of literacy, good character, and appropriate age as qualifications for village head service. The strategies each took in the dispute highlighted their importance. The teacher, taking full advantage of his gentry status, attacked the village head's illiteracy, bad temper, and old age throughout the litigation. To deal with such a formidable adversary, the village head had to admit his weaknesses from the start while stressing his reputation and good performance.

Illiteracy and old age, while used as disqualifications for village head service, could also be used as good excuses for quitting or evading this office when it became a burden rather than a desired job. Liu Yurui, vice-head of Xujiazhuang, age 63 in 1926, described himself as "old and infirm, thus unable to handle public matters," when petitioning for retirement. At the same time, he recommended Hu Yuancheng as his successor, describing him as a person "from a well-to-do family and of good character, competent in writing, and impartial in handling official business." Hu, nine years older even than Liu and unwilling to take the vice-head office, described himself as "over 70 years old, walking with difficulty, coughing and spitting all the time, unable to read a single character," and thus "unable to take on the vice-head's duties" (656.2.814, 1926). In another instance, Zhang Xiulin, 62, head of Zhangjiazhuang village, petitioned for retirement in 1919 on the grounds that he had become "incompetent [for the office] because of old age" and was "mediocre, stupid, ignorant, and lacking virtues and abilities" (656.1.1158, 1919; similar cases are found in 656.1.70, 1913; 656.1.377, 1915; 656.2.140, 1921; 656.2.569, 1925).

The image of a qualified village head as suggested above did not completely square with either that of a traditional community leader or that of the village head as envisioned by the state. Emphasis on the village head's personality was more of a traditional value than an official requirement. Its origins can be found in Confucian tradition, which advocated the exemplary role of "gentlemen" (*junzi*) in moral indoctrination. In this tradition, a well-cultivated gentry member, who often assumed community leadership, should be genteel and polite in the manner of a junzi when dealing with common people. When the village head office came into existence, the villagers naturally applied their idealized image of a traditional community leader to the new officeholder, expecting him to be moderate and self-restrained with fellow villagers. To have a "hot temper" or to "shout abuses in the street" as village head Yao did was considered a severe defect that would disqualify one for this official service.

While speaking of good character may be seen as a manifestation of traditional values, emphasizing the proper age for village head service was unmistakably a response to state expectations. Old age had long been seen as an asset rather than a liability in community service. The elders were usually among the most respected and influential people in the community, who held positions such as head of intra-village or trans-village associations and clan organizations (Fei 1939, 1953). However, from the viewpoint of the twentieth-century state, such people were not suitable candidates for the village government, for the new officeholders were to shoulder proliferating duties in local administration and taxation that required ample energy. An ideal village head should be a person "in the prime of life, energetic and strong" (*nianli jingzhuang* or *nianli zhengqiang*) (656.1.70, 1913; 656.1.561, 1916). Viewing old age as a disqualification for village service or using it as an excuse for evading this service reflected the villagers' reaction to the state's purpose and was a departure from their traditional values.

MORAL STANDING

Moral standing was another factor that affected eligibility for village head service. The reputation of a village head, like that of a traditional community leader, lay not only in his ability to extend patronage to community members but also in his observance of community norms and the virtues associated with a community leader (Bourdieu 1977: 193–94). An ideal village head should be just and impartial in handling public businesses while moral and beyond reproach in private life. The phrases used most often to describe a candidate's qualifications for the office of village head were "a person of good moral standing" (*renping duanzheng*) (e.g., 656.1.733, 1917), "impartial and gentle" (*zhongzheng heping*) (e.g., 656.1.70, 1913), "upright and selfless" (*zhengzhi wusi*) (e.g., 656.1.377, 1915), and "unselfish in public business" (*bangong wusi*) (e.g., 656.1.1158, 1919). Deviation from community norms would subject the candidate to the villagers' censure and disqualify him for village leadership.

Illicit sex, probably more than anything else, damaged one's community standing. A case in point was a dispute in Dongkun village, in which Zhang Shijun, the village schoolmaster, attempted to remove Zhang Hemian from the village head post because he had had an illicit affair with a "bandit woman." According to his complaint, the village head had attempted to have sex with the woman at the school on a Sunday after the teacher had left for home, leaving the school unattended. They were caught by a student, who picked up a hairpin left by the woman when she fled in haste and returned it to the schoolmaster. Since then, the complaint went on, all of the villagers had learned of this scandal and were determined to remove the village head. The village head denied the accusation. But he admitted later, in his second counterplaint, that he had had sex with the schoolmaster's "unmarried, beautiful" third daughter when he was still in his early twenties. Although he had given the girl "a lot of money and ornaments" as well as "several dozen mu of land" to placate her father, the latter, after marrying out his daughter to an unknown person in a remote village, still "looked for chances in secret to pick a quarrel." To accuse him of having sex with a "bandit woman," explained the village head, was merely a pretext for the schoolmaster to vent his hatred toward him. And it was for the purpose of disproving the school-master's false accusation, said the village head, that he now revealed the true story, "disregarding any sense of shame." Nevertheless, the village head's illicit sex, whether it had been with the bandit woman or the schoolmaster's daughter, was inexcusable in the view of both the community and the magistrate. His removal from office thus became inevitable (656.2.2, 1921).

Indulgence in gambling could similarly damage one's eligibility for village leadership. Du Zhixiang, son of the deceased village head of Daguo village, immediately took his father's position with support from those who had been under their protection. Others, however, were discontented with the Dus' control of village government and accused Du Zhixiang of being addicted to gambling. According to their plaint, Du "used to invite people to gamble in groups" and his only purpose was to "cheat others out of their money and property." While his father had been in office, people "had to keep their resentment to themselves without daring to speak out." Once in 1917, the plaint continued, the police arrested Du when he was gambling in the village. Backed by his father, however, Du beat the policeman and was detained by the police office, facts that could be verified by checking the court files. Du thus was clearly unqualified for the village head position.

To inherit the village head post from his father does not conform to the law, to be sure. Had Du Zhixiang showed good conduct and proved competent in serving the village, all of us would have welcomed his assumption of the office; who would dare to oppose it? Du, however, has long been addicted to gambling and has shamelessly sought personal gain by brazenly doing whatever he wanted to do. If he is allowed to take his father's position, then he would be even more reckless and no one would dare to offend him. Gambling in our village would thrive to a level beyond control. . . .

Despite this eloquent accusation, the magistrate rejected the villagers' plaint (656.2.139, 1921). However, this incident and the preceding case both show the immediate or potential damage that immoral conduct could cause to one's reputation in the community and qualification for village service.

It should be noted that villagers did not resort simply to traditional values or community norms when fighting unqualified leaders. Living in the twen-

tieth century under the penetrating influence of a national discourse on local "self-government," they also turned to official formulations about offices
to justify their claims and accusations. In the dispute from Daguo, the villagers linked their charge against Du with the fate of "self-government" in
their community. "It was just a few months ago," argued the villagers, "that
the president promulgated a decree to implement the village-level self-government program. The future of self-government depends upon the person
in charge. Without a proper person to take charge, there will be no good result. The village head office thus is closely related to the fate of village self-
government. Hence goes the saying, 'things prosper with proper people in
charge and perish without them.'" After charging Du with gambling, the
petitioner further reminded the magistrate that "local self-government directly affects the village's weal and woe, which can be keenly felt by fellow
villagers" (656.2.139, 1921).

To what extent the official language of "self-government" had penetrated
village communities and become part of the villagers' own rhetoric is hard
to judge. Most likely the man who prepared the plaint was an informed person with access to resources on national politics. Nevertheless, this case
shows a new source of legitimization that was now open to villagers for their
fight against unqualified officeholders. Whereas before the twentieth century they had had only traditional values and norms to appeal to, now they
found it convenient and forceful to justify their struggle with vocabularies
readily available from official sources.

THE PATH TO VILLAGE OFFICE

By regulation, the village head had to be chosen in a villagewide election.
The magistrate, as a rule, only appointed candidates who were ostensibly selected through formal elections. In most cases, the villagers did respond to
the state's requirement and reported such an election when asking the magistrate for a formal appointment.[5] Once a dispute over village office service
occurred, whether the disputant had assumed or quit his office through a legitimate procedure could become the focus of arguments.

Thus Hu Yuancheng, a plaintiff from Xujiazhuang village who was unwilling to be a vice-head, charged Liu Yurui, the incumbent vice-head, with
"reporting to the court in secret a fabricated nomination of him as vice-
head candidate without a proper election in compliance with state law." "If
he wants to quit his vice-head position," complained Hu, "Liu should have
observed the official law and invited all villagers to elect a proper person by
ballot to take over his office." In order to prevent Liu from quitting his office and thus shirking his duty to share the burden of military levies imposed
on the village, the village head repeated Hu's charge and accused Liu of a
"false nomination of vice–village head, which was based on merely his per-

sonal, selfish opinion." Like Hu, the village head emphasized the proper procedure to quit public service. "Even if Liu is unwilling to be a vice-head," claimed the village head, "he should remain in office until the expiration of his tenure. Only then could he retire by asking the xiangdi to assemble all of the villagers to elect a candidate in accordance with established regulations."

Liu, however, justified his quitting by claiming that he had observed legal procedures. According to his court testimony, when his (and the village head's) three-year tenure expired in July 1925, the village head wanted to extend his service in order to continue his control of the public funds of the village and therefore delayed the reelection. Liu, after tolerating his overdue service as vice-head for five months, eventually posted a notice informing villagers of a reelection to be held on December 29, 1925. On that day the xiangdi beat a gong to summon the villagers to the village temple, where Liu quit his job and Hu was elected as his successor over the village head's objection. The magistrate accepted Liu's explanation after it was confirmed by both the previous and the current xiangdi (656.2.814, 1926).

Likewise, villagers from Daguo disputed Du's succession to the village head position after the death of his father not only because of Du's addiction to gambling, but also because he was not the person chosen by the villagers. According to their complaint, they had elected a man named Liu, who had "a proper character" and had long held "villagewide reputation." However, asserted the accusers, when vice-head Chen reported the result of their election to the county magistrate for certification, Chen, a protégé of Du, changed the village head—elect's name to Du, thus "perpetrating a fraud, violating the will of the public, and deceiving the magistrate." The magistrate, the petition went on, "[had] appointed the village head merely according to words on the report without thoroughly knowing the real will of the people in the countryside" (656.2.139, 1921). The case record offers no details for us to judge whether the villagers' accusation was true. But the villagers' complaint nevertheless indicates a basic assumption behind their actions: one's assumption of the village head office could be accepted as legitimate only when one had been selected through a villagewide election in accordance with government law.

In other disputes this chapter has examined, those who attempted to remove village heads invariably emphasized that they had done so through legitimate procedures. The teacher from Yaojiali claimed in his initial plaint that the person who was to replace the incumbent village head had been selected through a "villagewide public election" (*hexiang gongju*) (656.1.1099, 1919—20). The schoolmaster from Dongkun village also claimed that to replace the village head, the vice-head of the village had beat the gong around the village to bring the villagers together, and the new village head had been elected by "public discussion of the whole village" (*hecun gongyi*) (656.2.2,

1921). Charging their village head with a variety of misconduct, the xiangdi from Qiejiazhuang asserted that they had ousted the head owing to "public anger" expressed by over 100 households of the village and that they had held a "public election by ballot" (*toubiao gongju*) to find a proper candidate (656.2.23, 1921).

It is difficult to determine if these elections were mere formalities or if they were seriously conducted. In some instances, such as that in Dongkun village, the ward police reported a formal election under its supervision; in others, few participated, as in Xujiazhuang village, where only the two xiangdi, the village head, and the vice-head attended and no one else was interested in the election. Nevertheless, this was the first time in Chinese history that villagers were allowed to select their leader by public election, a development that well preceded the Communists' similar experiments in their rural base areas in the 1930s and 1940s. Regardless of the perfunctory elements involved in the election, one thing is quite obvious from the preceding cases. Once a dispute took place, whether the village head had assumed or resigned office through a legal procedure became a focal point of the dispute. Compliance with the state law became as important as personality and reputation in determining the village head's legitimacy.

To be sure, there were a few instances in which the villagers chose their village head according to a distinct practice instead of the state law. In Nanguo village, for example, there were two descent groups in the 1920s, the Wangs and the Lis. The practice there was for the two groups to alternate in supplying a xiangdi and a village head for the whole village. The Lis' one-year xiangdi term was to be followed by a two-year term as village head, while the Wangs' one-year xiangdi term was to be followed by a two-year term as vice–village head. The head of each descent group then chose from his group the candidates for the xiangdi post and village office according to their landholdings (656.2.1120, 1928). Here official regulations regarding the selection of the village head did not work at all. There was neither a villagewide election of the village head nor a regular reelection every three years as the state prescribed. But this practice should be seen as exceptional. In most villages, as the Huailu archives show, peasants chose their village heads through an election, at least in a perfunctory manner.

It is interesting here to compare the villagers' perception of the selection of the village head with that of the old-style xiangdi. As I have demonstrated in Chapters 3 and 4, villagers in Huailu always chose their xiangdi according to endogenous village regulations (*cungui* or *xianggui*). The regulations stipulated that the heads of all taxpaying households had to serve as the xiangdi by turns regardless of their age, personality, education, or moral standing; there were no specific qualifications for the xiangdi service other than their landholdings or tax liabilities. When disputes arose over this post, villagers invariably appealed to their native regulations to justify their claim to or rejection of the xiangdi post. The state law did not work here at all, for the xiangdi post was primarily a product of local initiatives, and there were no official regulations pertaining to the selection of the xiangdi.

In contrast, state regulations played a prominent role in the selection of village heads. In arguments over the office, villagers referred to state regulations and used terminology they borrowed from official representations. The candidates' age, education, and assumption of the office through a formal election in compliance with state regulations became as important as character and moral conduct in determining their qualification for the post. The villagers' idealized image of a moral, virtuous, and even-tempered village head chosen by a legal election from those of proper age, then, signaled both the continuation of traditional norms and a growing national influence on the peasant communities.

Power Relations

Studies of local politics in late Qing and Republican China have noted many changes in local elites, most noticeably the rise of what Esherick and Rankin call "functional elites" that accompanied commercial growth and military modernization in that period. Unlike the traditional gentry, who enjoyed social prestige and wide influence because of their background as degree holders and their access to the magistrate, the status of the new elites was based on their professional jobs and occupations. As merchants, industrialists, financiers, journalists, and so forth, functional elites were less influential and less legitimate than the old-style gentry (Esherick and Rankin 1990).

In village communities, likewise, scholars have found that in some parts of North China traditional elites withdrew from local governing bodies. Many resigned from the job of village head as their task of collecting the multiplying irregular levies became an increasingly intolerable burden that threatened their relations with fellow villagers, making way for a subsequent rise to leadership of local bullies, who brazenly pursued their own interests at the expense of the community. However, scholars have also argued that before the rise of abusive power holders became a conspicuous phenomenon in the late 1920s and the 1930s, village elites had played a protective role in the community. Chosen from members of the endogenous village council (known as *huishou* or *shoushi*), village heads represented their respective lineage groups and identified themselves primarily with the interests of their communities rather than the state (P. Huang 1985; Duara 1988, 1995; Yang Nianqun 2001). Thus it was continuity rather than change that characterized local politics in the early Republican years.

The following examination of power relations in Huailu villages in the 1910s and 1920s presents a clearer, more accurate, and somewhat different picture of village politics. What occurred in the villages under investigation was a more-or-less discernible transition from the old pattern of power structure characterized by the diffusive influence of traditional elites to a new one in which the duties of officeholders were more clearly delineated and the scope of their influence was more limited. This process cannot be equated with either the continuation of an old power structure under the imposed village government or the disruptive transition from traditional protective leaders to abusive ones.

VILLAGE HEADS

The village head, as noted earlier, handled local administrative affairs together with the xiangdi, and he alone had the power to raise and manage funds for local projects. At the same time, the village head avoided the burdensome task of land-tax collection, thanks to the xiangdi's traditional role in this regard. This had been the case until the mid-1920s, when village heads became primarily responsible for the additional tax burden imposed on the village by a sudden increase in irregular levies and military imposts. Before the mid-1920s, however, the village head post was a desirable one that attracted the prestigious and powerful in the community. Ideally, the village head should be literate and excel in calligraphy and writing, like the degree-holding gentry members who had formerly dominated rural communities where they existed. Moreover, as a community leader, he should be even-tempered and morally beyond reproach, command wide respect from his fellow villagers, and win favor from superior authorities. An ideal village head, then, should possess both traditional, informal influence derived from the prestige and formal authority. One example of such a village head was Du Jusheng of Daguo village, who served his village for over twenty years, from the last years of the Qing until his death in 1921. While in office, Du once received a carved wooden plaque from Magistrate Zeng, which was inscribed with the praise:"On intimate terms with fellow villagers" (qingjin xiangyi). The villagers, too, presented him with a plaque inscribed with the words "Gentle and impartial" (gongzheng heping). After his death, many who had been under his patronage willingly nominated his son as his successor, and they succeeded in obtaining his appointment (656 ?.139, 1921).

In actuality, however, many types of people filled the village head office, as the case records show, including people like Du Jusheng, who won the support of his fellow villagers and praise from the magistrate, and Yao Chengshen, who was illiterate yet had occupied the village office for over sixteen years. At any rate, in most cases the village heads were the most powerful members of their communities. They came to power not necessarily because of their qualifications for the post, but because of their abilities to maintain support from villagers and to gain protection from those in power at higher levels. Thus, when involved in a dispute, the village head often had little difficulty shaping the representation of the dispute to his favor by his own effort or through his supporters in the village.

Yao Chengshen, head of Yaojiali village, for example, was so influential in his community that during his dispute with the village teacher he mobilized as many as forty-eight households, including the xiangdi, to file a joint statement in his support (656.1.1099, 1919–20). The newly appointed village head of Daguo, in another instance, succeeded in defending his position because he had support from the vice-head, the four xiangdi of the village, and graduates of the self-government training school and teachers' training school (*zizhi sheng* and *shifan sheng*), who collected seventy signatures from the villagers in their joint statement of support for the village head (656.2.139, 1921). The village head of Qiejiazhuang, likewise, preserved his office because he had won critical support from a police officer whose investigative report dismissed all charges against him by the villagers (656.2.23, 1921). Each of these instances suggests the likelihood that the village head used his power network to manipulate the litigation and produce the results he desired.

GENTRY ELITES

The village head did not always have the upper hand in such disputes, however. He could find himself in trouble and even lose his job when his opponent was a member of the local gentry elite. During imperial times, degree-holding gentry dominated rural communities where they had actively assisted the government in local administration, using their influence in and outside the community (Chang 1955). After 1900, when the state instituted village government, it expected the village elites, whether traditional degree holders or graduates of new-style schools, to fill the village head posts. While in many cases the literati did join the village government, in others, the village head positions fell into the hands of the most powerful individuals in the community, who were not necessarily members of the rural literati as the state intended. Often the only positions left to the village gentry were as schoolteachers and schoolmasters. Sometimes, a powerful person seized the positions of both village head and schoolmaster, even though he was as illiterate as Yao Chengshen of Yaojiali village. Tension between village heads and teachers or schoolmasters thus was inevitable. In principle, the latter should have limited their business to the school. In practice, village gentry often extended their influence beyond schools and interfered in public affairs of the community, which were now the sphere of the village head. This was understandable, given traditional gentry leadership in the community and their remaining influence and prestige. However, their presence threatened and challenged the village heads, and tensions between the two often broke out into open and fierce conflicts.

Once again consider Yao Hanjie, the teacher of Yaojiali village, as an example. As the only degree holder in his village, Hanjie was entrusted with preserving and updating the genealogy and household register of the Yao clan. He also managed the clan's 70-plus mu of charity land, which was divided into fifteen pieces and leased to clan members for a rent just one-tenth of the market rate. Thus in the clan's annual meeting held on the lunar New Year, Yao Hanjie always announced the names of the fifteen households that were given the opportunity to lease the land and then brought with him the register to visit individual households for signing the lease. When the village founded its school in 1912, Yao became a teacher. To qualify himself for this position, Hanjie even attended a teacher-training school for half a year in his forties.

Given his gentry background, his position as a schoolteacher, and his eagerness to control the school monies, tension was inevitable between Hanjie and the village head. When the head refused to reimburse him for expenses he had incurred in ordering a gate for the school, Hanjie became even more resentful and determined to remove the village head from his position. The first action Hanjie took was to press the village head to make a public accounting of the school funds. After several promptings, Hanjie warned the village head on February 1, 1919, that he would be allowed fifteen days to square and publicize the account. If the village head failed to meet the deadline, warned Hanjie, he would assemble the villagers to elect a new village head. When the village head failed to respond, Hanjie eventually gathered some villagers to change the village head. In his report to the magistrate requesting a formal appointment of the new candidate, Hanjie gathered eighty-eight signatures from villagers who supported him. To remove Chengshen from his schoolmaster post, Hanjie repeatedly accused him of embezzling school funds, which eventually forced the village head to post the accounts publicly.

Hanjie, though, had his own vulnerabilities. Since 1904, when the village government was established in Yaojiali, the teacher had lost his dominating influence in village life despite his gentry background, for it was now the village head who handled the administrative affairs of the village. Therefore, if Hanjie sought to intervene outside the scope of his own duty, he would face accusations of "intervention in business beyond his concern" (ganyu waishi) from his opponent. The magistrate also responded similarly to the teacher's plaints, warning him twice that his "interference in the public business of the village" (ganyu cungong) deserved "severe censure" (yanchi) or "special censure" (techi) (656.1.1099, 1919–20).

Another example was Zhang Shijun, schoolmaster of Dongkun village. Like Yao Hanjie, he was an influential figure in his community and had long controlled the village school fund. According to village head Zhang Henian, every time he had to make a decision about village business, he would invite Shijun for consultation. Although the village head had been discontented with Shijun's possible fraud regarding the school fund, his conflict with the schoolmaster did not break out until 1921, when they argued over a candidate for the vice-head post, which had been vacant for many years. The village head recommended a man named Yang for this position. His rationale was that Yang had served as a low-ranking officer in the army earlier, and when a band of defeated soldiers had passed by the village in the fall of 1920, the experienced Yang, who had just returned home, ably helped the village head deal with the soldiers and peacefully sent them off. The schoolmaster, however, opposed the village head's nomination and insisted on putting his nephew in the vice-head position. Inevitably, he was accused of the same things Hanjie had been charged with. The village head blamed the schoolmaster for his "interference in village affairs." "[Zhang Shijun as a schoolmaster] should have limited his concerns to the school," declared the village head. "Village matters have nothing to do with him," he continued, "even if he is asked to join the discussion [of village affairs], the schoolmaster should merely chime in with others in support of the public projects. In no case should he speak out straightforwardly in violation of the public will. To put his own man [into the vacant vice-head post], Zhang Shijun indeed transgressed the rules and went beyond his bounds [yuli fanfen]" (656.2.2, 1921).

These two cases are suggestive of the village gentry's situation in the early twentieth century, when their social status and educational background still allowed them a degree of influence among the villagers, which could not be ignored or underestimated by any party involved in a dispute. When litigating with the village head, their remaining influence could win support from some villagers. But it was also true that institutional changes, in particular the creation of village government, had greatly narrowed the scope of gentry influence. Many of their original local administrative functions were transferred to the formally appointed village government, which was not necessarily in their hands. As a result, the village gentry found a significant change in both the villagers' and the government's view of the role of the literati. Whereas during the imperial times it was acceptable for the literati to sponsor and take care of projects pertaining to community welfare, now any action that went beyond the range of their proper duties would be deemed a transgression, for which they would be blamed by enemies within the community and officially reprimanded from above. Given the rapidly shrinking sphere of community influence, it is no accident that the village gentry could not prevail against village heads who had accumulated their strength by both formal and informal power networks.

THE XIANGDI

When disputes over the village head office occurred, the xiangdi often appeared as a critical courtroom witness. Sometimes he also acted as a representative of fellow villagers and submitted his statement to the magistrate to confirm or deny the litigants' accusations or counter-accusations. Needless to say, his words were important in shaping the magistrate's adjudication.

Unlike the village head office, which was usually in the hands of the most powerful in the community, however, the xiangdi was most often an ordinary villager, for the annual xiangdi service was furnished by all taxpaying households in rotation. It was therefore difficult for him to take an independent stance when involved in disputes over the village head. More often than not, his attitude was shaped by the powerful in his community. This means that on most occasions the xiangdi allied with and spoke for the village head. We thus find, in the dispute from Daguo village over Du Zhixiang's succeeding his deceased father as village head, all four of the xiangdi from that village followed their vice-head to support Du in spite of many villagers' accusation that they had fabricated the election results (656.2.139, 1921). The two xiangdi of Yaojiali village, too, spoke for their village head throughout his litigation with the teacher. They supported the village head in both their statement and the court hearing, claiming that Yao as a village head had been cautious in handling public business and as a schoolmaster had done nothing wrong (656.1.1099, 1919–20). Zhang Henian, the head of Dongkun village, also got two xiangdi of his village to speak for him during his litigation with the schoolmaster. In their statement, the two xiangdi justified the village head's nomination of a vice-head candidate and blamed the schoolmaster for misusing school funds in exactly the manner the village head had done earlier (656.2.2, 1921).

We must keep in mind that the relationship between the xiangdi, an ordinary villager, and the village head was actually reciprocal in nature. The xiangdi spoke for the village head, usually in exchange for protection or benefits from the head. If the village head interfered with their interests, however, the xiangdi would turn their backs on him. This is best seen in the dispute from Xujiazhuang village as mentioned earlier. The village had a public fund of 30,900 wen, which the xiangdi could use to advance taxes and was kept in the hands of the village head. According to a joint plaint from the previous and the current xiangdi, in spite of their repeated requests the village head had refused to make the money available when it was needed. What was worse, after the xiangdi had advanced the taxes for the whole village, the village head collected what was due from individual households and refused to return the money to the xiangdi. Finally, when the village head refused to pay the customary stipend of 8,000 wen to each of them, the two xiangdi's resentment culminated in their joint plaint that accused the village head of his "misconduct and improper behaviors" (656.2.814, 1926).

Likewise, when the village head and schoolmaster of Qiejiazhuang roused widespread discontent among the villagers in 1921 by pocketing money gained from selling the village's willow trees, a xiangdi named Hong Aicheng organized many villagers to assemble in the village temple twice to demand a clear explanation from the village head about his use of school funds. When the village head remained unresponsive, the xiangdi gathered the villagers a third time to elect a new village head and schoolmaster. Although their attempt to change the village head failed because of the magistrate's refusal to certify their election, this case nevertheless indicates the potential influence of the xiangdi in his community, especially when he was backed by a group of villagers opposed to the village head's abuse of power (656.2.23, 1921).

CLAN HEADS

Given the strong lineage ties in the region, one would expect clan heads to have equally strong influence in their communities. However, the role of the clan head was often less prominent than that of the village head, especially when compared with that of their counterparts in certain areas of South China (Ye Xian'en and Tan Dihua 1985; Chen Zhiping 1988; Katayama 1982a, 1982b). In disputes over xiangdi service, few clan leaders demonstrated great power. This is also true of disputes over the office of village head. Yao Luojun, head of the Yao clan, for instance, had traditionally kept in his hands the clan funds derived from leased clan land. However, because of the disrepute he gained from "embezzling clan funds," the villagers deprived him of the right in 1915 and allowed the village head to take over his task. The clan head was obviously unhappy with the village head's control of clan funds. Thus when the teacher argued with the village head over the control of school funds and filed a plaint against the village head's fraudulent conduct, he listed the clan head as a witness. However, when summoned to a court hearing, the 73-year-old clan head, afraid of offending the village head, claimed that he had never joined the accusation against the village head and that the teacher had used his name in the plaint without his permission. He further asserted that the village head "has been prudent in public business and has never pocketed school funds" (656.1.1099, 1919–20). The clan head, as this case shows, was obviously a lesser figure than the village head, a person of real strength in the community.

The clan head may have failed to exert as much power as his position implied because it was based merely on seniority in the clan. The head was not necessarily the wealthiest or the most powerful in the community, and the public resources available to him were limited. The public land in Yaojiali, for example, was just 80-odd mu, which accounted for only a small fraction of the total landholdings of clan members.[6] After the management of clan funds was handed over to the village head, the clan head lost all control of clan resources. Thus while he might still command respect from some clan members, the clan head was in no case as influential as the village head.

To sum up, changes in power configurations in early twentieth-century Huailu villages were obvious in the course of institutional expansion in local administration. For village elites who had traditionally exerted diffuse influence through informal means, the establishment of village government offered opportunities to formalize their power. Many of them thus filled the village head office. However, the impact of state intrusion on the rural elites was complex. In many instances, the village head office came under the control of the powerful in the village, who were not necessarily among those with the literacy or gentry background the state desired. An inevitable result under such circumstances was the waning influence of traditional community leaders, including the gentry elites, the clan heads, and the xiangdi, and a transition from traditional, informal village leadership centered on the literate and/or the prestigious to formal leadership by those of real strength but less prestige in the community.

A corresponding change was visible in the discursive context in which village leadership functioned. The gentry elites, while remaining influential in certain aspects of village life, were expected to limit their actions to what their positions permitted. This was especially true when they fell into conflicts with other power contenders. Those who intervened in community affairs in the traditional manner would risk being attacked for overstepping their bounds. The village head, too, was no longer as prestigious as village leaders in the old days. He could be easily challenged if he failed to behave in line with the villagers' expectations and the government's demands on its local officials. The traditional assumption that village leaders had wide influence over all aspects of community life yielded to a new consensus on the division of duty among officeholders, a notion that became increasingly familiar to bureaucrats in twentieth-century China.

Dispute Resolution

Let us turn our attention from the changes within the community to the relationship between the village and external authorities, especially the county magistrate, who was arguably the representative of the state in local society during imperial times and whose administrative role remained largely unchanged in the early Republican years. In comparison with the situation before 1900, conflicts between the government and local society in the early twentieth century were epidemic. As the tax burden escalated and abuse of local officials became rampant, tension mounted steadily between the villages and county government, which was responsible for collecting taxes and remitting them to the treasuries at higher levels. Although peasant protests, riots, rebellions, and participation in revolutions in different areas were not uncommon during the late Qing and Republican years, these collective actions should not lead us to assume a sharp distinction and confrontation between the state and village society. After all, armed resistance became a conspicuous phenomenon in many places only after the late 1920s, when the irregular levies imposed on villages became intolerable. There were also localities where the pressure of state penetration had not yet reached a level sufficient to cause villagewide or trans-village resistance in the late 1920s or even later. We thus need to consider other forms of village-state relations.

The following examination of the county magistrate's role in the resolution of village head disputes aims to shed light on a more complicated relationship between the county magistrate and village communities in their efforts to establish and maintain the legitimacy of village government. This is a relationship in which their mutual accommodation and interdependence were more evident than their confrontation and conflicts. Just like the villagers who embraced official regulations on village offices while adhering to their traditional standards for community leaders, the county magistrate did not merely insist on official standards for selecting the village head. As a practical administrator, he often took into consideration the traditional values of community leadership and acted more as a mediator than an adjudicator in handling the disputes.

THE MAGISTRATE'S ADJUDICATION

This is evident in most of the examples examined earlier. Let us first take up the lawsuit from Yaojiali village. After both sides in the dispute had dragged out their litigation, ignoring the magistrate's repeated instruction to "cease the quarrel," Magistrate Cheng held a court hearing on June 7, 1919. He insisted that officeholders meet the official qualifications for the office of village head, chiding the village head for "lacking self-knowledge": "Yao Chengshen claimed that he himself has never attended school and does not read a single word. After serving as village head for so many years, he still refuses to retire, though he is close to his seventies." He then blamed the teacher who had allegedly removed Chengshen from the village head position for interfering with village business. At the same time, the magistrate upheld the traditional value of community harmony. "It is improper," the magistrate rebuked Yao Hanjie, "to gather a number of people and start a litigation over such a trivial matter."

From the magistrate's point of view, what Yao had done was contrary to the traditional image of virtuous gentry avoiding litigation and devoting themselves to the promotion of community peace and harmony. Rather than making a clear-cut ruling, the magistrate's solution was to instruct both parties to reach a compromise and cease the litigation: "All of the Yaos belong to the same clan. I hereby allow this matter to be concluded in peace. Both parties should cease fighting each other and avoid causing further trouble in the future." The teacher, however, refused to accept a compromise, claiming that "the magistrate's method of harmonizing the clan was perfect and well-intentioned. Yet it does not necessarily square with the state codes regarding law enforcement and promotion of education." Despite the magistrate's intention to bring about a "peaceful ending" (*heping liaojie*), the teacher submitted a total of eight plaints against the village head. In response, the magistrate branded him a "litigation instigator" (*suosong zhi ren*) and finally threatened to terminate his job as a teacher if he persisted in litigation (656.1.1099, 1919–20). Clearly, the magistrate's approach was to combine the state's requirements for age and education with old values of compromise and community harmony.

The magistrate used the same approach to deal with the dispute from Dongkun village, in which the schoolmaster attempted to remove the village head from office on the pretext of the village head's scandalous behavior, while the village head accused the schoolmaster of "tampering with village business." The magistrate, after hearing courtroom testimony from both parties, decided to remove both from their posts. His rationale: "Village head Zhang Henian is too shameless, and principal Zhang Shijun oversteps his bounds. Both lost qualification for their respective posts." The magistrate, in fact, did not make any effort to investigate whether their accusations were true. Nor could he find any well-defined provisions from state law to ground his ruling. However, by reproaching and removing both from their positions, the magistrate successfully forestalled further evolution of the dispute (656.2.2, 1921).

There are practical reasons why the magistrate insisted on compromise in his handling of the disputes. Unlike civil disputes over land, debt, inheritance, old-age support, or marriage, in which the magistrate could get to the facts through investigations, court hearings, and examinations of documentation, it was difficult for him to judge a given person's eligibility for the village head service, in particular his moral conduct and reputation among his fellow villagers. And it was even more difficult to know whether the person had assumed office legitimately, for the magistrate generally accepted and endorsed a nomination as reported by village representatives, no matter whether the nominee was legally elected, nominated by a few, or emerged from an "election" that had been fabricated by the reporter. For these reasons, the magistrate tended to act as a mediator when disputes over the village head office were brought to him. His approach was to forestall the further development of the dispute and to press both parties to accept a compromise by blaming or punishing both in a similar manner regardless of the truth behind the dispute.

In fact, not only did the magistrate find it difficult to make a clear-cut ruling, but on certain occasions he even failed to use consistent principles to guide his handling of the disputes. Take the village head's age, for example. In general, to be sure, a candidate had to be of proper age to qualify for the office. And he could be allowed to retire when he was too old. Thus, when the 48-year-old Kong Fancheng, head of Kongjiazhuang, petitioned for retirement in 1916, magistrate Zeng declined on the ground that Kong was still "in the prime of life and therefore should continue [his service]" (656.1.561, 1916). But when 65-year-old Yao Chengshen from Yaojiali attempted to continue his control of the village head post in 1919, magistrate Cheng rebuked him for "lacking self-knowledge," as noted above. However, seven years later, when the village head office became an unwelcome burden in the war years and when 72-year-old Hu Yuancheng from Xujiazhuang village asked to retire, Magistrate Zhang persuaded him to stay in office, claiming that Hu's seniority and experience would help the village deal with the hard times (656.2.814, 1926). Likewise, the magistrate also declined a request for retirement from the 70-year-old Bai Shulin, head and schoolmaster of Xiaobi village, asserting that as a "practiced hand" (*sushou*) the village head should stay in office so that the villagers could rely on his experience (656.2.140, 1921). The overriding concern of the magistrate was to end the disputes or prevent them from further complication and thereby ensure the normal functioning of the village government, no matter how old the candidate was or whether he was qualified for the village head position.

These stories show that the magistrate did not consistently impose official standards on the villagers. Wherever possible, the magistrate would devolve resolution of the dispute to the local community, as was evident in his preference for compromise and community mediation over formal adjudication in accordance with state formulations. An ostensible reason for this approach is that he wished to dispose of lawsuits expediently, a tactic that more or less bespoke the government's limited reach in the countryside. However, we must also bear in mind that the state had never intended to include the village government in its formal bureaucracy. As a cornerstone of the self-government program, the village head was designated a formal intermediary between the county authority and local society, replacing the informal xiangdi position inherited from imperial times. Formally elected by the villagers and officially appointed by the magistrate, the village head was supposed to act on behalf of higher authorities before the villagers and on behalf of the villagers before the magistrate. To make the village government fully functioning, therefore, the magistrate had to consider and even yield to the villagers' opinions at the expense of official standards. From the magistrate's point of view, such an interdependent and mutually supportive relationship with the local community was indispensable in maintaining the normal and smooth operation of the village government.

Nevertheless, reliance on community mediation could in no way guarantee that the disputes would be resolved in compliance with either state stipulations or community expectations. It often left the resolution to the working of local power relations. Given the self-interest of local power holders and the patron-client network in which they were involved, abuse and manipulation were inevitable. This was true even when the magistrate insisted on official standards in the selection of the village head. Before electing or changing a village head, according to the proper procedure reasserted by the magistrate, the villagers had to obtain authorization from the magistrate. And the magistrate would endorse the result of an election upon receipt of a report from the village representative—that is, the incumbent xiangdi, no matter whether there was manipulation or abuse during the process. Thus when the villagers from Daguo disputed the magistrate's appointment of Du Zhixiang as their new village head, asserting that Du was not the person they had actually elected, the magistrate declined their request on the ground that his appointment had been made in accordance with the joint report from the vice-head and the xiangdi of the village, who had asserted that Du had been "nominated in public by the just people of the village." The magistrate replied to the discontented villagers that it was therefore "unnecessary to issue an authorization for another election of the village head" (656.2.139, 1921).

The magistrate could also reject the villagers' nomination if they had made it without obtaining his authorization, even if they had good reasons. Thus when the villagers of Qiejiazhuang petitioned the magistrate to certify their newly elected village head after they had removed the old village head from office because of embezzlement, the magistrate's reaction was predictable. He commented on the petition: "It is improper in particular to have an election without first filing your accusations against the village head and without my authorization. This election thus should be deemed invalid" (656.2.23, 1921).

Together, these cases show the dilemma the magistrate faced in his handling of village head disputes. By accommodating popular values and relying on community mediation, he could dispose of cases expediently and make the village office more acceptable and more legitimate from the villagers' point of view. However, this approach also left the resolution of the disputes largely to the operation of local power relations, which was inevitably accompanied by abuses of power that in turn jeopardized the legitimacy of the village head office. This was even true when the magistrate adhered to offi-

cial standards, for he normally based his decisions on what had been reported to him through a formal procedure, regardless of the machinations
and manipulation behind the report or the election.

THE ROLE OF SUPRA-VILLAGE AGENTS

To further understand the relationship between the magistrate and village
communities, we have to examine the role of two important agencies at the
supra-village level, namely the police office (*jingcha suo*) and the Education
Promotion Office (*quanxue suo*). Huailu county had eight policing wards
(*jingqu*) in the late Qing and early Republican years, and each ward had a
branch of the police office with a patrol officer (*xunguan*) as its head. The
ward police's duties were not limited to local security. In addition to assisting the magistrate in civil and criminal justice, its tasks covered taxation and
local administration, such as bringing a delinquent xiangdi to the county
court for a hearing and supervising the election of the village head. Before
the Guomindang government formally instituted the ward government in
1928, the ward police functioned as the intermediate government between
the village and the county yamen. In his handling of disputes over village
head service, the magistrate often delegated to the ward police the task of
investigating disputes and then made his decision according to what the
ward police had reported. In such cases, the ward police played a critical role
in shaping the result of the disputes.

This is evident in the dispute between the xiangdi and village head of
Qiejiazhuang. After receiving a plaint from the xiangdi, who charged the village head with five instances of wrongdoing, the magistrate instructed the
police to investigate and verify the accusations. The police soon submitted a
report that excused the village head from all blame. A few days later, the magistrate received another plaint from four "representatives of famine victims"
(*zaimin daibiao*) of the same village, who accused the village head of, among
other things, receiving famine relief grain and copper coins three times using
the fabricated name of "Zhao Luoxiang." In the same plaint, they also
charged the vice-head with receiving 126 wen in copper cash and six catties
and twelve taels of wheat using the fabricated name of "Hong Shengxiang."
They further charged both the head and vice-head with embezzling forty-
two catties of relief grain that remained after initial distribution. "It is for the
poor that the relief should have been used," the plaint went on; "the village
heads, both from well-to-do families, went so far as to fabricate names and
seize the food from the poor. . . . [T]his is as if eating our flesh with a heart
as cruel as a wolf. We the poor cannot tolerate any more. . . . "

The magistrate once again asked the police to verify their accusations.
The police officer quickly submitted a report speaking for the village heads.
According to the report, Zhao Luoxiang was not a fabricated name, but a

refugee from the county seat, who had been in real poverty when visiting the village. The village head thus had included Zhao in his report of famine victims. Hong Shengxiang, according to the report, was the styled-name (*zi*) of the vice-head, who had used his zi to receive the relief grain in order to support his poverty-stricken family. The remaining relief grain had been sold to support the xiangdi's traveling expenses for tax delivery (656.2.23, 1921).

Such exculpation for the head and vice-head was far from convincing. To include a visitor in the victims' list was dubious from the villagers' view. They also doubted the vice-head's stated reason for using his zi instead of his proper name to receive relief grain. The police officer, when arriving at the village to investigate, was invariably first received by the village head. Thus it was not impossible that the village head had made every effort to please and win favor from the officer. Rather than reflecting the truth of the dispute, the police report was more likely a product of collusion between the officer and the village head.

In the dispute from Xujiazhuang village in which village head Lu accused vice-head Liu of a fabricated nomination of Hu as his successor, the police report proved to be false. The police officer, speaking for the village head, claimed in his report that "all of the village head's accusations [against Hu] are true." In fact, however, Liu did arrange a formal nomination of Hu in which both the previous and incumbent xiangdi attended. And the village head himself later admitted during a court session that Hu had been nominated as the vice-head, but refused to take up his post (656.2.814, 1926).

The education promotion officers' performance was no better than that of the police officers in carrying out the magistrate's instructions. The Education Promotion Office was headed by a director (*quanxue suozhang*). Under the director were eight education promotion officials (*quanxue yuan*), each installed in a "route" (*lu*, corresponding to the policing ward). This office handled all affairs pertaining to public schools, including the construction of school buildings, the selection and appointment of schoolmasters and teachers, and the supervision of school funds (see Chapter 8 for details). Thus when a dispute occurred between the village head and the schoolmaster or a teacher, the magistrate invariably instructed the office to investigate the dispute. He then made a decision according to the officer's report. Like the police officer, however, the *quanxueyuan* was unable to extricate himself from local networks. Although his report was often ostensibly impartial, the officer had no difficulty showing his support of one or the other side through subtle wording and suggestions.

Consider, once again, the dispute from Yaojiali village. The education promotion official who was instructed to investigate the case turned out to be the most influential person in this lawsuit. To win his favor, the village head made every effort to please the official, including creating a fictive kinship with him by letting his grandson call the official *ganfu* (fictive father). Not surprisingly, to clear village head Yao Chengshen of the accusation by teacher Yao Hanjie that he was unqualified for the office, the official described Chengshen in his report to the magistrate as "a person of extremely moderate character, who has never shown a hot temper." He skillfully admitted that the village head "is fond of teasing and bantering and therefore cannot avoid scolding mingled with laughing [*xiaoma*], which, however, should not be equated with cursing in rage [*numa*]." He also added that "the village head, though with only limited literacy, can always get assistance from his nephew when he is in need of writing" (656.1.1099, 1919–20).

To defend Chengshen, the education promotion official further described the village as a closed, conservative community, where "all villagers were hostile to school education" and no one had been willing to fill the schoolmaster post because of inadequate funds ten years earlier. It was the village head's "single, consistent effort," he asserted, that had made possible the survival of the school. Resentment toward the village head arose because he had sponsored the construction of a schoolhouse that used funds from the Yao clan, he further explained: "If Yao Chengshen has conducted any kind of malpractice, then no one can protect him from reproach and dismissal. However, if he just made a few mistakes, or if he just wasted a small sum of money, then his position [as the village head] should probably be maintained in the light of his contribution in the past."

To prevent further attack from the teacher, the official persuaded the illiterate village head to resign his post as schoolmaster and nominate a successor. The village head followed his instruction and this way preserved his job. The teacher, aware of the education promotion official's unusual relationship with the village head from the outset of the dispute, charged the officer with "pursuing personal gain at the cost of impartiality" (*xunsi haigong*) because, as the "fictive father" of the village head's grandson, he had merely gone to the village head's house to fabricate his report of investigation instead of checking the village head's school account in the presence of honest people. From the teacher's view, those who served the Education Promotion Office were not necessarily "moral and impartial people" (*duanfang zhi shi*) (656.1.1099, 1919–20).

The ward police and Education Promotion Office, as these cases have revealed, were the nexus at which local power intersected with county authority. Operating at the intermediate level between the village and the county seat, they had direct contact with village communities and thus were more likely to get involved in, and even became part of, the local power network. When carrying out the magistrate's instructions, they were very unlikely to be unaffected by the influence of the powerful in local society. Thus, far from acting as the new agents of the magistrate in local communities, these intermediate authorities tended to function as a buffer between the magistrate and village notables at best, and as a tool for the latter to abuse their power at worst.

Altogether, the foregoing discussion reveals how the village office functioned in a network of patron-client ties in and outside the community. Within the community, the village head was a patron to his protégés and a competitor to other power contenders who had their own followers. Abuse of power and manipulation of power relations thus were unavoidable in rivalries and conflicts. Beyond the community, a network existed between local notables and official agents at the supra-village level, in which the village notables sought protections from those above them, whose misrepresentation and abuse of power again became unavoidable. As a result, there always existed a tension between the power holders' needs for legitimization and the exercise of their power in personal networks that often undermined their legitimacy.

Given the complexity of power relations in rural communities, we may wonder if the abuse of village heads had gone so far as to result in a crisis of legitimacy in the 1910s and 1920s. My answer to this question is generally no. There was a strong consensus on local leadership among the villagers, including both the powerful and the powerless, that emphasized the village head's moral standing and conformity with state regulations. The magistrate, too, invariably emphasized the village head's uprightness and abilities in performing his duties. Situated in this discursive context, the village head would find it difficult to ignore the public opinion of the villagers. The villagers had no difficulty using weapons available from traditional conceptions of community leadership or official formulations of village government to combat abuses of power,

Therefore, to preserve his position, a village head had to avoid overt abuses in violation of the public will, and when the community faced intrusions from outside, he had to speak in the name of the whole village and protect local interests in order to maintain and reproduce his prestige. This is why the village heads in Huailu county actively engaged in collective actions against tax escalation and wrongdoings by supra-village tax agents in the 1910s and 1920s, and even continued to be protectors in the investigation of unregistered land in the 1930s (see Chapters 6, 9, and 11). Under normal circumstances, however, the village head maintained and reproduced his domination by extending his protection to favored villagers in exchange for their support, while avoiding attacks from those outside his patronage or minimizing damage from their attacks by keeping his profiteering activities covert. The village head was thus a complex figure: he was neither a state agent acting on the will of the government, as the latter had envisioned, nor an ideal representative acting in the interests of the entire community.

Conclusion

This chapter has focused on changes in the shared values and mentalities pertaining to the holding and exercise of power in peasant communities, and on the consequent adjustments in the strategies of legitimization, competition, and operation of village leadership. I have identified the two most salient changes in this regard. One has to do with the legitimization of officeholding. What justified the holding or renunciation of the newly created village head office was not merely the traditional values embedded in village communities that stressed the reputation and personalities of the leaders. Equally important were the new ideas introduced from outside, which emphasized the officeholder's abilities, appropriate age, and, most important, the legitimacy of his election to the office. The other has to do with the functioning of local leadership. While old assumptions about the pervasive influence of the privileged in community life remained alive, equally powerful was the state-imposed idea about functional differentiation among village offices. Village communities in the 1910s and 1920s did not merely perpetuate the old power structure under an imposed, nominal village government, as scholars have tended to assume. There were in fact profound changes in both administrative institutions and village discourse on local leadership.

It is in this context of changing perceptions of community leaders and of mutual penetration between the official representation and popular notions of village leadership that various forms of local power operated, competed, and struggled for dominance. The village notables, including both old-style elites and newly created officials, had to translate into consciousness both indigenous and externally imposed assumptions about their roles when interacting with the community. It was on the basis of the internalized ideas about village leadership that power contenders formulated their representations and shaped their strategies of mutual rivalry. Those who ignored either popular notions or state-imposed standards of officeholding would find themselves vulnerable to attack from their competitors. Abuses and misdeeds by the power holders, though inevitable in a pervasive network of patronage, were never unlimited in this circumstance. The rampant abuse of power and the consequent breakdown of village communities, a phenomenon well observed in previous scholarship on North China villages, did not yet prevail in Huailu during the early Republican years, when the stable and cohesive villages in the core area still accommodated the less disruptive penetration of the state.

CHAPTER 8

Cooperation and Conflict over Village Schools

Another New Policy program that affected most villages in early twentieth-century Huailu was the founding of primary schools. The teaching methods and curriculum in the new-style schools, according to county officials and local elites, were much superior to those in traditional tutor schools, or *sishu*. By regulation, a primary school should provide courses in moral cultivation (*xiushen*), written Chinese language, arithmetic, handicrafts, painting, music, and gymnastics, as well as farming for male students or sewing for females.[1] This curricular diversity contrasted sharply with the dull, rote learning of Confucian texts in the traditional sishu. The new schools, in their opinion, were not merely an effective tool to improve literacy, but also a means to "popularize education" (*puji jiaoyu*), to spread modern knowledge, and to improve the quality of the people; all these were deemed critical to the survival and strengthening of the Chinese nation under the threat of imperialism.

The educational reform involved three parties: the county magistrate, who was responsible for urging and supervising the establishment of schools, and whose performance in educational affairs was directly linked with his promotion or demotion; local elites, including village leaders responsible for funding the school and county-level gentry members who served as intermediaries between the magistrate and villagers in coordinating educational affairs; and ordinary villagers who shouldered the bulk of the financial burden and constituted the main body of beneficiaries of this new program.

The Huailu county government's archives pertaining to this reform, especially files on disputes over the creation, funding, and staffing of primary schools and educational agencies, permit here a close examination of the activities of all participants in the educational reform. What interests us is how the cooperative tradition in local communities influenced the villagers' participation in founding and maintaining the schools, and to what extent the implementation of the new program changed the way the government interacted with the villagers individually and collectively in the context of modernization and reform in the early twentieth century.

The School as a "Self-Governing" Project

The founding of new-style primary schools as a nationwide phenomenon began in 1904 when the Qing government promulgated a series of regulations to govern the movement (Xuebu 1904). By the design of the late Qing and early Republican governments, every county should establish at least two or three schools at the county seat and one in every large market town. These "official" (guanli) schools would receive full support from the government and charge no tuition from students. Meanwhile, every village of 200 households or more should create a "public" (gongli) primary school for children age 6 through 13 or 14.[2] And the village or neighboring villages were responsible for the costs of construction and maintenance of the school as well as the salaries of its staff. In addition, the government encouraged individuals to found "private" (sili) schools as a supplement to the official and public ones.

To promote primary schools in local society, the early Republican state emphasized the role of local communities. According to its interpretation, the educational reform in the late Qing had produced little effect because the government had relied heavily on the single effort of the county magistrate, who perfunctorily founded only one or two schools at the county seat. Few people had showed interest in the schools; they saw them merely as a means for the magistrate to preserve his position or for the few gentry managers in charge of the school to make profits. Consequently, most schools were found in cities and towns; they were scarcely seen in rural and remote areas (Xuebu 1904: 293; Xuebu 1909: 544; Jiaoyubu 1914: 231).

A fundamental solution to this problem, in the view of the new Republican government, was to promote "self-governing education" (zizhi de jiaoyu) in place of the traditional "government-sponsored education" (guanzhi de jiaoyu). In other words, the success of the educational reform lay in the active participation of local communities; it was the community that should assume the responsibility of funding and maintaining the schools. The government should limit its role to "supervising and encouraging" their activities. The purpose of this new formulation about educational reform was of course to move the burden of financing new-style schools from the government to local communities. To justify this shift of burden, however, the government turned to "statism" (guojia zhuyi), a political discourse that had prevailed among the intellectuals in the late nineteenth and early twen-

TABLE 11

Primary Schools in Huailu County, 1904–1917

Year	Schools Founded	Total Number of Schools
1904	1	1
1906	8	9
1907	10	19
1908	11	30
1909	8	38
1910	14	52
1911	14	66
1912	5	71
1913	27	98
1914	12	110
1917	39	149

SOURCE: Huailu archive file 656.1.308, 1914.

tieth centuries. An official statement, announced in the "Plan for Educational Consolidation" by the Republican government in December 1914, is revealing:

Teaching children has long been a task of parents and elder brothers. So why does the state have to intervene and hold local communities responsible for it? The reason is that since the day when statism prevailed, the strength of the state has been determined by the strength of the people. The state has always treated children who have received education as elements of the nation, whose talent and morality are to be fully developed in order to enhance domestic order and resist foreign humiliation. If there is one individual left uneducated, the state would lose the utility of one person. Therefore, the implementation of statism can only be sought in public education rather than the old-style private schools. And public education does not have to rely on the revenue of the government; it should always be shouldered by local communities. A country is made of different localities, therefore the country's projects are also made possible by the joint efforts of both the government and the people. Since the people accept education as the most critical matter to the fate of the state, how can local communities ignore it? The local society has the inescapable responsibility for funding local education. (Jiaoyubu 1914: 230)

The primary purpose of the new schools, from the government's point of view, was to train people for promoting the interests of the state rather than to benefit their local communities. Whether to found a school thus was not a decision for the local people; establishing a school was compulsory and subject to intervention by the state. The government thus held local communities responsible for financing the schools and village elites for creating and managing them, while its own role was to supervise the activities of the elites.

The first new-style school in Huailu county was founded in February 1904. As an "official school," it was located at the county seat and fully funded by the county government. Two years later, eight public schools were created in local villages. The number of primary schools steadily increased in the ensuing years and numbered 110 by 1914 and 149 by 1917. The total number of primary schools in Huailu county hovered around 150 in the 1920s (see Table 11). Three were official schools run by the county government (*guanli*); six were private schools; and the rest were public schools. Together, these schools enrolled 5,515 students in 1917, of which 5,399 were males and 316 were females.

The official agency in charge of the schools at the county level was the Education Promotion Office (*quanxue suo*, hereafter EPO). The office had a director (*quanxue suozhang*, or *quanxue zongdong*), who was nominated by the county magistrate from local gentry members and appointed by the education commissioner (*tixueshi*) of the provincial government (Xuebu 1910: 284). In early Republican Huailu, a group of prominent members of local gentry elected the director from three candidates. Under the director were five office members (*quanxueyuan*), each in charge of one of the five school districts in Huailu county for a term of three years. The office's duties were to persuade and prompt local villages to set up schools, and to monitor the activities of schoolteachers and students.

Each village school had a schoolmaster (*xuedong*). Ideally chosen from the literate among local dwellers through a villagewide election, the schoolmaster was responsible for managing school funds that he had received from the village head or the xiangdi, appointing a teacher for the school on an annual basis, and maintaining the daily operation of the school. Depending on the financial situation of the community, the schoolmaster either received a salary for his job or simply worked as a volunteer. Given the power he had, however, the schoolmaster was usually a prestigious and educated person who, together with the village head and sometimes the xiangdi, dominated the community.

Financing the School

To establish a school, a village head faced two basic tasks: to locate or construct a building to house the school and to find financial sources to support it. The 1914 report of primary schools in Huailu shows that 40 percent of them (44 schools) were housed in temples of local communities, including temples for Taoists (such as Laojun's Hall, the Jade Emperor's temple, or the Three Officials temple), for Buddhists (such as Guanyin's Hall, the Immeasurables' nunnery), and for popular cults (such as Guandi temple and the Dragon King's temple). These religious buildings were used for public schools because they had been usually treated as the properties of local communities, which according to an ordinance of the early Republican government were among the first to be appropriated for educational purposes (Jiaoyubu 1914: 232). Alternatively, the villagers sited the school in a vacant house of the community. Forty-two schools (38 percent) were thus accommodated. Where neither a temple nor a vacant house was available, the village head had to use his own office building as the site of the public school. Eighteen villages (16 percent) turned to this solution. The villagers only rarely constructed a new building for the school (three villages did so) or used a clan temple (just two). Only one village used its preexisting *yixue* (community-run free sishu) as the site of its new school. No matter how the school was housed, it was mainly the duty of the local community to finance and maintain the school. The government's support was limited to providing irregular stipends to schoolteachers, which ranged from 3,600 wen to 14,400 wen (approximately 3 to 12 yuan) per semester for each teacher in the early 1910s (656.1.149, 1913; 656.1.308, 1914).

VOLUNTARY COOPERATION IN FINANCING THE SCHOOL

An even more challenging task for village heads was to raise enough money to support the school. The main expenses of a school were salaries for one or two teachers, which ranged from 50 or 60 yuan to over 70 or 80 yuan a year, and miscellaneous expenses between 20 and 40 yuan. In addition to the limited stipend from the county government, a village head had three means of funding the school. The first was "public funds" (*gongkuan*) of the village, which came mostly from selling village properties or collecting rents from corporate land of the community. Some villages used their ample public funds as the only source of support for the school. For example, Dongxuying village and Yuancun village provided 170 yuan and 200 yuan, respectively, in school funds. Most schools, however, could obtain only 20 to 40 or 50 yuan from their villages' public funds. Some schools received no public money at all.

An alternative and more common method was to let individual households contribute a certain amount of money to the school according to the size of land they owned (this contribution was thus called *dijuan* or *mujuan*) or according to the amount of their land tax quota (thus called *paijuan*). The third source was tuition from participating students. Table 12 indicates the

TABLE 12

Primary School Tuition in Huailu, 1914

Tuition	Number of Schools		Percent of Schools
(yuan per student)	Public	Private	
0	40	0	36.36
0.01–0.49	20	0	18.18
0.50–0.99	23	0	20.90
1.00–1.99	10	0	9.09
2.00–2.99	4	2	5.45
3.00–3.99	4	2	5.45
4.00–4.99	1	2	2.73
5.00–9.99	0	2	1.82
Total	102	8	100.00

SOURCE: Huailu archive file 656.1.308, 1914.

collection of tuition in Huailu villages in 1914.

As the table shows, forty village schools (or over 36 percent of all primary schools in Huailu) did not charge tuition. Most of the schools that collected tuition charged less than 0.99 yuan. Only ten schools (9 percent) charged students between 1.00 yuan and 1.99 yuan. Schools that charged 2.00 yuan or more were either private schools or public schools with only a few students.

What interests us here is how a school determined its tuition rate and what it implied about the cooperative nature of the school. The primary school, as a collective undertaking of the whole village, was supposed to make education affordable for all members of the community. According to the late Qing and early Republican governments, public schools should be free to all school-age children in villages; this was what made a public school different from private ones or traditional sishu. The 1912 and 1915 regulations of the Ministry of Education allowed tuition collection only when it was deemed necessary under special circumstances and only when it was approved by the county magistrate. In practice, however, such government regulations had little effect on local communities; and the wording of the regulations made it possible for local schools to collect tuition on a variety of pretexts. Therefore, whether to collect tuition and how much to collect were in effect matters left to the village communities. By and large, the villagers had two choices in regard to the collection of tuition.

First, the community could decide not to collect tuition at all and just rely on its public funds or contributions from its members. This meant that all village households would share the cost of funding the school, regardless of whether they had school-age children. This is how most of the forty primary schools that did not collect tuition operated. Consider the public school at Songcun village, for example. In 1914 it had a total revenue of 140 yuan, of which 120 yuan was obtained as *mujuan* (levy on the land), and 20 yuan came from the village's public funds. In Loudi village, school funding of 100 yuan came completely from mujuan. Yuancun village chose to use 200 yuan from its public funds as the sole source of support for its school. In all of these instances, the burden of school funding was collectively shared by all members of the community in the form of a contribution according to the amount of land or tax, or public funds, or a combination of both. Even households with no children in school were required to contribute.

Second, the community could charge tuition to supplement public funds and contributions. This was a solution where the public funds or villagers' contributions were insufficient to cover the school's costs. By this solution, part of the burden of supporting the school was shifted from the community as a whole to individual households that had children attending school and directly benefited from the school. Depending on the availability of public funds and the willingness of the community to support the school, the tuition rate varied from village to village. A community was willing to support the school only when most members had children in school and hence became its beneficiaries. The reverse was true where just a few households had schoolchildren. This was exactly the situation in Xiguan village, where only eleven students attended school. With only 30 yuan from public funds and without any contributions from the community, each student had to pay 3.64 yuan a year. In Hengshan village, for another example, there were only twelve students in the school. The community contributed only 40 yuan plus 18 yuan from public funds. Each student thus had to pay a tuition as high as 4.33 yuan (656.1.308, 1914). It should be noted, however, that such villages were the exception. Most schools, as shown in Table 12, charged tuition of less than 1 yuan, and the total tuition collected was a small fraction of their total revenue.

There also existed communities that received no public funds and with villagers unwilling to support a school. Obviously, under these circumstances, no village school could be founded or survive without administrative pressure from outside. Many village schools thus failed around 1912 when disorder prevailed in rural North China in the wake of the Revolution of 1911.

Thus, there were two preconditions for establishing and maintaining a public school. First, most community members had to be willing to cooperate and share the cost of school founding. Second, where they were unwilling to do so, government pressure had to be present in order to force the villagers to pay school contributions. It is surprising in this light that 36 percent of the public schools in Huailu villages collected no tuition, and another 39 percent of the schools limited their tuition to less than 1 yuan. In other words, the burden of funding the primary school was completely or mainly shouldered by the village community as a whole rather than merely by the households with schoolchildren. Government interference alone could not explain this phenomenon, for official regulations did not strictly prohibit the collection of tuition or limit the rate of tuition. There are two likely explanations for the fact that most schools collected no tuition or set it at a minimal level.

First, a long tradition of cooperation among the villagers in Huailu enabled them to cooperate in founding the schools. Villagers in Huailu had cooperated under the xiangdi system, which offered them a variety of benefits. The benefits of the new school were equally perceivable. Where no tuition was collected, the villagers' only cost to send children to school was their contributions to school funds. The 1914 survey of all schools in Huailu county shows that the total amount of such contributions to a school ranged from 50 or 60 yuan to 80 or 90 yuan. Only a few schools collected as little as 30 yuan or as much as 120 yuan. Contributions averaged 75 yuan per school. Given that every 1.3 villages in Huailu county shared one primary school, and that each village had 190 households on the average (see Chapter 3 for explanations), then each household only shared 0.30 yuan in school contributions. This was only 6 to 15 percent of the cost of sishu education. Where villagers had to pay tuition (and let us take 1 yuan as the average amount of the tuition) in addition to contributions based on landholding or tax liabilities, the total cost of school education was only 26 percent or at most 65 percent of the cost of sishu education. The collective good produced by cooperation in funding the school was obvious.

Second, the relatively high land-yield made school education affordable to most farming households. The net income from farming in Huailu villages ranged from 18 yuan to 36 yuan per household in the 1910s.[3] If the land/tax-based contribution, which averaged at 0.30 yuan, was the only obligation of villagers in funding a school, then it just cost each household 0.83 percent to 1.67 percent of its net income from farming. If, in addition to school contributions, a household had to pay a tuition (again let us take 1 yuan as the average rate), then the total cost of schooling was 3.61 percent to 7.22 percent of its net farm income. All these suggest that the villagers' burden in supporting the school was well within the range of their financial capacities.

It is thus my proposition that primary schools mushroomed in early Republican Huailu not only because of government promotion and pressure, but also owing to the villagers' voluntary cooperation. They participated in the program out of their "rational calculation" of the obvious benefits of schooling against the cost they shared. And their cooperative traditions in tax payment made it much easier for them to embrace this new form of cooperation.

PEASANT RESISTANCE

Still, new-style schools encountered some resistance. A villager might have refused to cooperate in funding the school for two primary reasons: if he did not benefit from the school, or if only a few in the village would benefit; and if the tuition were too high. In Nanwei village, for example, the villagers had paid for years a total of 30 yuan according to their land-tax quotas as contributions to the school of twenty-seven students by 1914. In March of that year, however, a villager named Ma Shuangquan assembled a crowd and proposed that the burden of school funding be imposed only on households who had students and that the old method of collecting contributions from all households be discontinued. This move, according to the EPO's report to the magistrate, had caused the delay of the school's new term. When the school eventually opened in early March under the mediation of his uncle, Ma surprisingly broke into the classroom and removed desks and benches from the school, thus causing the closing of the school and the return of the teacher to his home place. To punish Ma, the EPO suggested that the magistrate issue him a summons; otherwise, the director argued, the troubles of the school would be endless. Under the threat of the magistrate's court hearing, Ma finally returned the furniture to the school through a third party's mediation. The school reopened after the teacher came back (656.1.152, 1913).

A similar dispute occurred in Nanzhai village, where the school had only seven students in 1914. To support the school, however, all landowners of the community had to contribute a total of 50 yuan, as well as allocate 18 yuan from the village's public funds to the school (656.1.308, 1914). There may have been even fewer students in the village in 1912 when a dispute broke out between a group of villagers led by Liu Shuangde and Feng Luogong on one side, and the village head and xiangdi on the other. According to the EPO's report, Liu and Feng had gathered "a bunch of rascals" and forced the village head and the xiangdi to dissolve the school and send the teacher back to his home village. So reckless had been Liu and his followers, the report continued, that they had even intimidated and insulted an EPO official who came to the village for a mediation at the invitation of the village's schoolmaster. And Lu was allowed to leave the village only when he promised to convert the school to a private sishu and to keep the public funds of the village intact (656.1.33, 1912).

Villagers may also have refused to pay tuition if it was exceptionally high. A pertinent case here was a dispute in Xilonggui village, where the primary school had only fourteen students in 1914, but its budget, mostly for the salaries of its two teachers, amounted to 88 yuan. Although the village provided 58 yuan from public funds to cover most of the expenses, the fourteen students' parents had to pay a total of 30 yuan to meet the budget. This meant that each student had to pay tuition of 2.14 yuan or 3,000 wen of copper cash. For villager Wang Shenxiu, the tuition for 1913 was such a burden that he was unable to pay up even after he returned from a court hearing where he had promised to clear the debt immediately. The village head and the xiangdi thus filed another plaint on March 15, 1914, to accuse Wang of persistent refusal. To ask the magistrate for another hearing, they claimed that the villagers had reached a consensus: if the village leaders failed to force the debtor to pay the tuition by filing a petition, then the villagers would shut down the school. However, the dissolution of the school, the plaint continued, would cause the magistrate's punishment of the village leaders. So they had no option but to petition for another court session. Six days later, both the petitioners and the accused appeared in court. This time the magistrate decided that Wang should pay not only the 3,000 wen that he had owed for the previous year but also the same amount for the current year. To enforce his ruling, the magistrate ordered that Wang be detained until a guarantor paid all of the 6,000 wen in tuition for him (656.1.298, 1914).

It is worth noting that although some disputes occurred, most villagers did not resist the collective funding of primary schools. Disputes were likely to occur only when the tuition was exorbitant or when the beneficiaries of the collectively funded school were relatively few. Violent resistance never occurred in Huailu villages throughout the late Qing and early Republican years. By and large, the villagers adopted a cooperative attitude toward educational reform, and they did so voluntarily because of the perceived collective good it brought to them.

The Discursive Context: The School Versus the Sishu

Despite the alleged superiority of new-style schools, the early Republican government did not intend to completely abolish the traditional *sishu*. Quite the contrary, it encouraged the reform of the sishu by updating its curriculum and teaching methods and only prohibited those that refused to change (Jiaoyu bu 1914: 236). In actuality, however, those responsible for founding new schools, including local elites and officials, often insisted that the schools and the sishu were incompatible, for they competed with each other for students and local resources. In their opinion, new schools would prosper only when the sishu were strictly forbidden. The magistrate, too, adopted a practical attitude. He unequivocally supported the schools when they were in conflict with the sishu, for the smooth founding of the schools was critical to his periodic performance evaluation.

Thus, when An Luohong, the richest person in Beigucheng village, opened a private sishu in 1912 and attracted three students from the local school, he soon came under the attack of the school's teacher, Feng Shaowen, who charged An with "undermining the school and enriching himself with the sishu." In his petition to the magistrate, Feng requested "severe punishment" of An in order to let the students who had switched to the sishu come back immediately and to prevent his current students from leaving. Otherwise, the teacher argued, his school was bound to break down; and "once this happens to one village, other villages will follow suit. All schools will be destroyed overnight." The teacher's petition led to mediation by an EPO official who eventually persuaded An to send back the three students to Feng's school (656.1.36, 1912).

Likewise, Yao Mengrong, head and schoolmaster of Shijiazhuang village, accused two fellow villagers, both named Yin, of "destroying the school," for the two Yins had set up a sishu and even hired a shengyuan degree holder as its teacher in July 1914. In his complaint, Yao described himself as an active supporter of the school, who had successfully dissolved five or six sishu and merged all of them into his school. The reason that the two Yins had refused to close their sishu and join the school, Yao continued, was that they had used it to make profits, for they had collected over 100,000 wen in tuition and paid the teacher only 30,000 wen, pocketing most of the money. Yao then requested an immediate dissolution of the sishu. His reasoning: "Shijiazhuang is a pivot of the railroad network where passersby are clustered. If the school in Shijiazhuang runs poorly, other villages will lose their confidence. The school of Shijiazhuang does play a significant part in this regard." Therefore, Yao concluded that if the Yins' sishu were allowed, then school education in all neighboring villages would be undermined. The EPO, too, described the Yins' sishu as a "threat to the school" and repeated the village head's charge in its report to the magistrate. To avoid a court interrogation, the two Yins finally made a concession upon receiving a summons from the magistrate. The case record ends there without details about their compromise (656.1.309, 1914).

It should be noted that the accusers' real purpose in the above two cases had more to do with their self-interest than with their asserted commitment to promoting public schools. In the first case, the teacher sued An not only because An's sishu took away a number of students from his school, but more important, this incident affected the school's tuition income. Similarly, in the second case, the village head probably sued the Yins when he failed to merge the sishu because he had been envious of the large sum of tuition that the sishu had collected. Material gain, rather than anything else, motivated them to take action against the sishu.

However, these disputes did involve conflicts between different perceptions of the sishu. For the wealthy An, opening a sishu was a perfect way to show off his wealth and to enhance his status in the community. For the Yins, hiring a degree holder as the teacher only made their sishu more reputable and creditable. From the teacher and the village head's point of view, however, the sishu was both a threat to their incomes and a challenge to the school itself, for it shattered the confidence of ordinary villagers in the newly created school, which was still so exotic to them. It was no wonder that village head Yao "repeatedly instructed" his fellow villagers "how the instruction methods in the school benefit students and how the sishu, without any reform, is futile in teaching the children." For the school supporters, producing a consensus among the village members on the superiority of new schools to the sishu was critical for the survival and prosperity of the schools.

This discourse on new-style schools could not have prevailed without support from government officials, especially the EPO members and the magistrate. The role of the government in producing a favorable public opinion of schools is demonstrated by the Kong Xianlin case in 1917. The restoration of the last Qing emperor to the throne in 1917 under the patronage of warlord Zhang Xun led to a brief moment when sishu defenders staged a counterattack against the new schools. The Society of Confucian Teachings (Kongjiaohui), an organization headquartered at Qufu, hometown of Confucius in Shandong province, thus sent its members to neighboring provinces to propagandize against the new schools in favor of the sishu. One of them, named Kong Xianlin, a man in his forties and an alleged descendant of Confucius, arrived in Huailu county in April 1917. He first appeared at the storytelling site of a marketplace in Shijiazhuang village. Standing under two Kongjiaohui banners and waving a small flag, Kong made frequent speeches to crowds surrounding him. According to Magistrate Zeng's report to the provincial governor, Kong told the audience that no teachers in new-style schools were prestigious degree holders (*jugong* and *shengyuan*); neither did they teach the four Confucian classics; what was discussed in class was only the age and beauty of girls. Kong further told people that the students, learning nothing from schools, managed to graduate only by bribing the teachers. Kong's public speeches caused much turmoil in Shijiazhuang and neighboring villages. To persuade Kong to cease his attacks, the EPO argued with him that new-style schools did include the study of Confucian classics, which were taught by a new method that only made the classics easier to understand than the traditional method of rote recitation used in the sishu. Kong responded by moving to neighboring villages, where his public speech caused even greater "confusion and panic" among the parents of students.

The magistrate avoided taking any administrative measures against Kong at first, considering his unusual background. Later, with support from the provincial governor, who denounced Kong's speeches as "wildly arrogant and presumptuous," Magistrate Zeng issued an order to all police offices and EPO officers, instructing them to "compel" (*leling*) Kong to leave the county. Kong quickly fled. To pacify the populace and reduce the damage of Kong's activities, Zeng distributed a poster to all primary schools in his county, which was written in verse and read as follows:

> Rumors have recently been circulating
> To attack the "New Policy" and schools,
> Saying there are no longer Confucian teachings
> And students only read foreign books.
> Such absurd words only confuse the mind of villagers and kids.
> Chanting without understanding the text in the old sishu
> Proves no match to the effective instruction in the new schools
> Where each word is explained in every lesson
> And Confucian texts remain in use.
> Learning abacus and arithmetic makes transactions accurate
> And detailed records of expenditures and revenues possible.
> Practicing gymnastics, moreover, strengthens physical health.
> If you are still in doubt,
> Just distinguish between the superior and the inferior.
> So pay heed to this earnest exhortation
> And never readily believe in the nonsensical words;
> Anyone who uses rumors to disturb the people
> Will be sent to his native place under escort. (656.1.828, 1917)

The role of the county government, as this case shows, was not just limited to urging and supervising gentry members and village leaders to found local schools. Also important for the magistrate was convincing people that the sishu, as an outdated institution, was no longer a desirable and legitimate means of teaching and learning, for it had lost the government's endorsement. And as he made clear in the poster, since the sishu had actually functioned to "undermine the school" (*pohuai xuexiao*), it was even *illegal*. The new-style school, he argued, was a better substitution for the sishu not only because it was promoted by the government, but also because it was far better than the sishu in "popularizing education" (*puji jiaoyu*). Using his status as the most authoritative and powerful person in the locality, the magistrate worked with the gentry to forge a shared assumption about the legitimacy and supremacy of the school in relation to the sishu. This new consensus, in their opinion, was indispensable for the smooth progress of educational reform.

"Borrowing the Government's Power"

The role of village heads in founding a school, as seen earlier, was critical. In addition to providing classrooms, selecting a schoolmaster, and hiring teachers, the most important task of the village head, together with the xiangdi, was to raise money for the school. Most village heads in Huailu county were indeed active in all these activities, for they saw their role in founding the school as not only an effective means to enhance their status as community leaders but also an opportunity that could enrich themselves. In some villages, though, the EPO found that the biggest resistance came precisely from the village head rather than from the sishu or ordinary villagers. Liang Zhi'an, director of the office, identified in his report to the magistrate in May 1912 a number of reasons behind the village heads' reluctance to reopen schools after the "military incident" (the 1911 Revolution). According to Liang, his EPO officials had failed to meet the village heads and the xiangdi when they visited three neighboring villages south of the county seat, for they had hidden themselves or refused to acknowledge their identities. When eventually identified, the village heads would use the difficulty of raising contributions from villagers as an excuse for failure to reopen the school. However, the director pointed out that the village leaders should already have enough money, raised from the rent of temple land. He thus surmised that the village heads had embezzled the public funds. In Beihu village, the report mentioned, the village head had refused to reopen the school because "all of the students have left the school." Again Liang found that this was merely an excuse, for all of the students had entered a sishu of the xiangdi. He reasoned that the village head had most likely colluded with the xiangdi to profit from the sishu by closing the school. The desire for personal gain might well be an important factor in the village heads' unwillingness to restart the school.

Popular resistance was another excuse used quite often by the village heads. The head of Taitou village, for example, asserted that all of his villagers, including "over a hundred adult males" and "several tens of elders," had opposed the reopening of the primary school when discussing the matter during a gathering. When asked why they opposed it, the villagers referred to several larger villages that had never founded a school and to villages that had abandoned their schools without a reason, yet had never seen an EPO official urging them to reopen. The village head thus claimed that he had been unable to collect school funds, for "it was dangerous to incur public wrath." And he warned against the use of administrative enforcement, which had been applied in the previous year to a villager, named Wu Kuliang, who had broken into the school, disbanded the class, and forced the teacher to leave the village. To punish Wu, the magistrate had detained him in prison for several days until the school reopened. However, the village head argued, Wu had acted only on the basis of his personal opinion. Now, the whole village rallied against the school. If the EPO attempted to suppress the masses by asking the magistrate to detain the xiangdi, an agent of the community, then the public anger would turn into violence, for "any barbaric action imposed on them will necessarily incur their barbaric reaction." The village head therefore suggested that the delay of school and a return to peaceful order were preferable to a hasty reopening and a break with the government. He would not reopen the school until the neighboring villages did so (656.1.46, 1912).

Despite village head Dong's warning, the EPO listed Beihu village as one of the six villages where resistance was believed particularly strong. In his report to the magistrate, director Liang insisted that their resistance could not be resolved without "borrowing the government's power." He suggested that the magistrate first summon the heads of the six villages to the court and instruct them to open the school, and then call in the xiangdi of thirty-three villages, including the aforementioned six villages that had not yet reopened their schools. In the meantime, the EPO would also send its officials to individual villages to "urge and persuade" (cuiquan) the opening of schools. To do this, in the director's opinion, would be in line with the principle of "government supervision and gentry persuasion" (guandu shenquan) (656. 1.46, 1912).

The magistrate acted accordingly. He summoned the heads of the six villages on May 20. On June 2, he summoned the xiangdi of seven villages. Two days later, sixteen more xiangdi were brought to court. The next day, another ten xiangdi were summoned. The results were immediate. Almost all the villages quickly reopened their schools. Some of the villages reported to the magistrate just a few days after they received the summons that they had either scheduled a reopening date by the consensus of most villagers or invited a teacher to restart the class. Even the village head of Taitou village, who had threatened the EPO with violent action from his community, reported to the magistrate on May 30 that, because of his persuasion, the "agitation has gradually calmed down"; and the villagers had all agreed to reopen the school and to use Guanyin's Hall as classroom. The only exception was Beihu village, whose head remained inactive after the court hearing (656.1.46, 1912). The magistrate thus summoned that village head again on June 8. Five months later, the EPO found that the village head had still taken no action, on the pretext that there were no children to attend the school. The village head thus was summoned to the court for a third time, where he was compelled to accept the magistrate's instruction to "open the school immediately" (656.1.44, 1912).

To summon the village head or the xiangdi to the court for an on-the-spot instruction, as shown above, was indeed intimidating to most village leaders but not completely effective. Some village heads, after returning home, simply forgot the instruction or merely reopened the school for a moment and then took no further action to maintain it. The magistrate thus had to summon the village heads in groups time and again to account for the shutdown of their schools (656.1.293, 1914). To make his intervention more effective, the magistrate had to take measures more radical than merely a court hearing, as seen in the case of Huozhai and Shijing villages in 1915. According to a complaint from the director of the EPO, now Wu Donglin, these two villages had delayed again and again the creation of a primary school, despite several "persuasions and urgings." Both villages had taken a wait-and-see attitude and remained inactive even after their neighboring villages opened their schools. The director thus suggested that the magistrate summon the heads of the two villages and set up a deadline for the opening of their schools, while the office would send its officials to the villages for "diligent persuasion": "Only when the two sides [the magistrate and the EPO] act together, then could the goal be easily achieved." In other words, the office's one-sided persuasion would not work without the administrative pressure from the magistrate. As the director expected, the two village heads were brought to the court on April 23, where the magistrate allowed them ten days to set up the school. And the village heads submitted a pledge to guarantee the establishment of the school by the time limit before they left the court. The head of Huozhai village fulfilled his obligation by May 3. However, the head of Shijing village failed. He thus was brought to the court again on May 8, where the magistrate took him into custody and would not permit a release on bail until the village had a definite plan to open the school. Two days later, three guarantors from Shijing village submitted a pledge to promise that the school be set up within fifteen days. The magistrate thus released the village head on bail and warned that the guarantors would be held responsible if the school was not established by the deadline (656.1.490, 1915).

The magistrate's involvement was not limited to urging the founding of schools, but also extended to such affairs as the construction of school buildings and even the appointment of teachers. After a tour in the countryside in March 1914, Magistrate Zeng sent an order to the village heads and the xiangdi of four separate villages. In his view, the schools in these villages had been created and then abandoned repeatedly since their founding ten years earlier. The main reason for their short-lived history was that these schools had no fixed sites. He thus required the village leaders to discuss this matter with the gentry and elders of their communities immediately and to finish the construction of school buildings within two months: "The building must be spacious, and the sports ground must be able to accommodate numerous people, to make possible the expansion of schooling in the future." Any village leaders who hesitated in this regard, warned the magistrate, would be summoned for proper punishment. To ensure that the village leader complied with his order, the magistrate instructed the EPO officials to urge and supervise the construction of schools in their charge. The head of Shanxiayi village soon replied to the magistrate that, after a public discussion with the gentry and elders of his village, they had decided to purchase a complex of thirteen rooms as the site of the primary school, which was priced at 500,000 wen of copper cash. The village had paid the owner half the price in cash. And the school would be opened as soon as the repair work on the building was done (656.1.301, 1914).

Problems with the appointment of a proper teacher could also delay the opening of a school. Some villages sent the teacher back to his home place when the term was over and did not invite him to return for the next term, thus causing the shutdown of the school. To such problems, the magistrate's response was invariable. He would first allow the village to nominate a teacher on its own for the EPO's approval. If the village failed to find a teacher by itself or delayed the nomination, the county government would directly appoint a teacher to the village in accordance with the official regulations on schoolteachers (656.1.301, 1914).

These cases indicate the critical role of the county government in dealing with local resistance to new-style schools. To be sure, in most communities the elites were active in founding the schools for both the alleged purpose of "popularizing education" and enlarging their personal gain. Ordinary villagers, too, joined the program voluntarily for the perceived collective benefits of school education. However, resistance from village heads or villagers did exist in some villages for the reasons outlined above. And the number of these villages rose to thirty-three (16 percent of all villages in Huailu) in 1912, when the fall of the Qing caused local disorder and loosened government control. As the EPO admitted, its own power of persuasion and supervision alone was far from enough to get those villages to reopen their schools. It had to rely on the government and its "barbaric action" to overcome local resistance and push forward the educational reform.

Competition among the Powerful

The founding of primary schools, albeit a burden for many village heads, did provide county and village elites an opportunity to promote their influence in local communities. Those who assumed positions in the Education Promotion Office and local schools saw their appointments as a recognition and reconfirmation of their standing in society. Material gain was also important to the school enthusiasts, for the positions allowed them to receive stipends and salaries from the government and the village, and to control resources in connection with schools. Competition among the elites thus took place over issues ranging from the appointment and compensation of the Education Promotion Office personnel to the location, funding, and staffing of local schools. To fully understand the motivations behind their competitions and the strategies they employed in the conflicts, let us first consider a dispute over the EPO personnel.

THE EDUCATION PROMOTION OFFICE RESHUFFLED

The Education Promotion Office in Huailu county was founded in 1906. Its director, Liang Zhi'an, held the *juren* degree (graduate of provincial-level examinations) and supervised five office members (*quanxueyuan*); the latter in turn were responsible for educational affairs in their respective school districts. Because of his unusual degree and his position as EPO head, Liang was recognized as an undisputed leader of the gentry circle in Huailu county. The funding for his EPO came exclusively from the owners of coal mines (*meijuan*) of the county, who were also the biggest source of local New Policy projects and were under the control of Zhang Shicai, president of the county's Chamber of Commerce. Zhang had no degree or formal education. Yet his wealth and wide connections had enabled him to become a member of the Provincial Assembly. Because of their different social backgrounds and their status as accepted leaders in the gentry and merchant circles respectively, Liang and Zhang had long despised each other. Zhang's long-term control of New Policy funds and Liang's constant complaints against him only made their relationship worse. Eventually, a battle broke out between the two in July 1912, when Zhang led a group of county-level notables in filing a petition to remove Liang from the EPO position. Zhang blamed Liang for the "deterioration and abandonment" of many schools and for appointing only his protégés as schoolteachers. None of these failures, however, was substantial. To accentuate his accusation, however, Zhang labeled Liang a "shameless" person who had received salaries for doing nothing and a "corrupt, old-style gentry member, who does not understand what education is and yet opposes anything that is new to his conservative mind." In return, Liang accused Zhang of controlling the coal mine contributions and refusing to release them to the EPO for fully six months, which had almost caused the standstill of the educational system in the county. In support of Liang, several schoolteachers filed individual petitions that attacked Zhang as a man who was alien to "the academic circle" and a "true native tyrant" who had once been put in custody for "abducting a woman" years earlier.

The magistrate delegated the task of investigating the dispute to the county's deliberative assemblies (*yishihui* and *canshihui*). In their report to the magistrate, the assemblies verified and reconfirmed all of Liang's accusations against Zhang, concluding that "Zhang's monopoly of coal contributions remained as usual, which has put all of the New Policy programs in jeopardy. . . . If this personal control [of the coal contributions] is tolerated and no measure is taken immediately, the overall situation [of the county] is doomed to deteriorate." Despite the assemblies' report so favorable to Liang, the education commissioner of Zhili province decided to replace the EPO director of Huailu simply on the ground of Zhang's accusations, an action that indicated his unusual connections with Zhang. Again the Huailu magistrate turned to the assemblies to select another director for the EPO. The assemblies delayed for fully six weeks to show their objection to the education commissioner's decision and the possible interference with the election process by those "outside the educational circle." Eventually, on September 3, 1912, the "qualified gentry members" of the county gathered in the hall of the county assemblies and elected Wu Donglin as the new EPO director; he won thirty-three of the thirty-seven votes.

The fight over the EPO director was only the first in a wave of conflicts among the elites. The next was to replace the five EPO members. In September 1912, Feng Yuhua, a member of the county assembly from Nanguyi village, led an elite group of twelve to submit a petition requesting the reelection of EPO members. According to their complaint, all these members had been in office for almost three years, much longer than the two-year term stipulated in a resolution of 1910. And the EPO members had done nothing to earn their salaries; this dereliction had accounted for the disbanding of dozens of village schools and the failure of any students to graduate from primary school in the past five or six years. In response, the new director asked each school district to nominate two candidates for the position of EPO member. On November 5, 1912, the Education Council of the county elected five EPO members from the ten candidates. Three of them were former EPO members, including Lu Quanhe from the southern district where Feng came from. Feng himself, however, was not nominated. Disappointed, Feng once again led a group of twenty-six individuals to accuse the three elected members of bribing or colluding with voters to win the election. The magistrate declined their request for a reelection (656.1.37, 1912).

The reasons for these disputes varied. One focus of the disputes was the reputation and creditability of EPO officials. To expel Liang and his personnel from office, Zhang and his supporters attacked them as "dishonest," "shameless," "derelict," and "corrupt." And Liang requested the magistrate's thorough investigation of the dispute precisely for the reason of "saving face before fellow villagers." Concern with material benefits was another focus of their disputes. Both Zhang and Feng attacked their respective enemies, Liang and the five EPO members, as being interested only in receiving salaries rather than in their duties. Ironically, the new EPO director refused to take his job until the magistrate increased his salary from the original 180,000 wen to 312,000 wen, an action indicating his own preoccupation with material gain rather than with promoting education.

Struggle for personal fame and fortune was nothing unusual for the elites who competed over local leadership. What was new in this case were the strategies they employed. Both sides in these disputes assumed the importance of primary schools and the critical role of the EPO in promoting education. Understandably, while Zhang accused Liang of being uninterested in education, Liang attacked Zhang's control of the coal mine contributions as an action that undermined the schools. Situated in a discursive context in which modern education was exalted as fundamental to national strengthening, both sides found it expedient and forceful to defend themselves and attack each other using the new language and vocabularies of statist discourse.

The use of an election to select the EPO personnel provided the elites another new means of pursuing their rivalries. To the extent that they were able to determine the result of the election by their votes and that the magistrate had to routinely endorse the result rather than appoint the personnel he preferred, the elites indeed had greater autonomy than ever before. The influence of those who won the elections also had more legitimacy than before. However, the working of traditional power relations among the elites ultimately determined the results of their competition. Zhang successfully removed Liang from the EPO director's position primarily because he had received patronage from the provincial education commissioner, whose personal decision took precedence over the County Assemblies' collective will. Meanwhile, Feng failed to secure an EPO member's position not because his charges against the three former officers were groundless, but because his opponents had more social resources, which allowed them to survive the election and keep their original positions.

PRIVATE SCHOOLS FOR GIRLS

The government, while imposing on village heads the mandatory task of creating public schools, also encouraged individuals in local society to establish private schools. Several private schools were established in Huailu county during the 1910s, some of which were exclusively for girls. These girls' schools were necessary because most public school students were boys; few parents were willing to let their daughters mingle with boys all day in a public school or to receive education at all if their economic situations did not permit. Thus private schools for girls became an option for better-off parents who wanted their daughters to have minimum literacy. Some leading members of local communities also treated the founding of girls' schools as a way to promote their influence and to receive government recognition of their leading role in the community. Besides, a private school could bring them benefits in the form of tuition and stipends from the county government; these were particularly attractive if the costs of running a private school were minimal.

Wu Donglin, who succeeded Liang as the EPO director, thus created a primary school for girls in Tumen, his home village, in 1915, that admitted more than twenty students in its first year. Wu justified the creation of this school with official rhetoric. "The girls' school," he said, "was the basis of modern family-based education and also the foundation of national education. Therefore, the establishment of this kind of school can no longer be delayed." Because of his repeated propounding of this idea to his fellow villagers, Wu continued, the school had been able to attract a considerable number of girls. The magistrate's favorable response to Wu's report was predictable. He praised Wu's action as a "pioneering effort to change the general mood of society and to lay out the foundation of family-based education," and Wu, in his opinion, was "indeed enthusiastic in promoting education and thus worth commendation."

To run the school, however, Wu had to find stable sources of funding. As Wu reported to the magistrate, this school, "temporarily" located in his own house, was established upon the proposal of the head and the schoolmaster of the village. To fund the school, Wu Donglin himself donated 20 yuan, so did his two brothers, Wu Molin, who was principal of the village's public school and also an acting manager of this private school, and Wu Guilin, who was a teacher in the girls' school. In addition to these donations, the school would rely on the public funds of the village. Wu did not make clear whether this school belonged to the village or the Wu brothers. To minimize objections from within the community, Wu assured his fellow villagers that the Wu brothers were solely responsible for funding the school; if their donations were inadequate, they would supplement them with tuition from students, and no burden would be placed on the community. In actuality, however, as the EPO reported several years later, the Wu brothers' financial contribution to the school was very small, even during the initial few years, and then they stopped donating altogether. The school's funds then came from three sources: the public funds of the village, student tuition, and stipends from the county government that amounted to 50,000 wen a year, all of which fell under the control of the Wu brothers. Accordingly, the nature of the school changed from "semiprivate, semipublic," as the EPO termed it, to completely public.

Following the example of Tumen village, seven other villages created their own schools for girls, drawing on public funds or private donations. Two public girls' schools opened in Nantongye village in March 1918 and in

Zhentou village in October 1919, enrolling fifteen and sixteen students respectively. The Tian family of Hengshan village, in another instance, created a private school for girls in June 1918, using the funds of the Tians and student tuition. In Shijiazhuang village, eight villagers voluntarily funded a school for twenty-five girls.

Once a school was created, it was always the EPO director's duty to report its founding to the magistrate for official approval and recognition. The director, Wu Donglin, invariably praised the founders' enthusiasm and described those schools as "precious buds" that should be protected when "the atmosphere of the society is about to change." Once the school was approved, the founders would submit a petition to the county government, requesting an official stipend, which was normally 50,000 wen for each school.

Competition among the powerful in the village to control the girls' school and its funds was inevitable. In Tumen village, for example, the village head, Gu Lianchang, had long been unhappy with the Wu brothers' conversion of the girls' school from private to public. Gu thus submitted a plaint against Wu Donglin in 1922, after Wu lost his EPO director's position and his brother Guilin, who taught at the girls' school, died. According to Gu, the Wu brothers' real purpose in running the girls' school was "to use the public for private gain" (jiagong jisi). All villagers, Gu argued, had treated that school as the Wus' private school. And every year the Wu brothers pocketed the 50,000 wen stipend from the county government. He thus requested that the Wu family resume the burden of funding the school. However, the village head's petition failed to persuade the magistrate. The latter found from the new EPO director's report that the girls who attended the school were not just from the Wu families; several Gu families had sent their daughters to that school for six or seven years, since its founding. It was thus justifiable, in the magistrate's opinion, to use the public funds of the village to subsidize the girls' school (656.1.487, 1915–22).

However, not all girls' schools, whether public or private, were profitable. Once the county government terminated its stipends, as it did in 1922, or once the number of students decreased, the school would have difficulty continuing without support from the village. The private girls' school of Hengshan village, for example, petitioned to close in April 1922, when its enrollment fell from the original ten to just three students (656.1.487, 1915–22). Unlike initiating a new school, which always received the government's encouragement, closing a school ran counter to the purposes of the New Policy. Predictably, the magistrate declined all such petitions and instructed the petitioners to prevent the school's disbandment by all efforts. From the magistrate's point of view, approving the closing of a school was not only discursively incorrect, but also counter to his public image as a leading figure in local modernizing projects.

THE SCHOOLMASTER VERSUS VILLAGE ADMINISTRATORS

Within a village, conflicts sometimes took place between the schoolmaster and the village head or the xiangdi over school matters. According to regulations, the village head normally collected school monies from individual households. In some villages, the xiangdi assumed the task in the village head's place. The schoolmaster had the right to receive the school monies from the village head or the xiangdi and to use them for school purposes at his own discretion. He also had the right to annually nominate a teacher for the EPO's approval. Inevitably, conflict would arise when the schoolmaster and the village head (or the xiangdi) disagreed on the use of school monies and the appointment of teachers.

To illustrate this kind of dispute, consider the following two cases. The first comes from Yudi village in 1912. This village created a school in 1906, which after only a few years enrolled more than seventy. The funds of the school were ample, from four sources: a special public fund totaling 300,000 wen, which was generated by selling the trees of the village temple; over 60,000 wen in annual rent from the temple land; contributions from landowners according to acreage; and tuition from the students. All of this money was under the disposition of schoolmaster Li, who had a purchased entry-level degree (zengsheng) and had controlled the position since the founding of the school. Village head Zhao was jealous and resentful of Li and attempted to remove him from office by eliminating the schoolmaster's salary, which had been 25,000 wen a year. Li brought the dispute to court, charging Zhao with "benefiting himself at the expense of others," for the village head had changed the collection method from one based on land acreage to one based on land-tax quota and thereby himself avoided contributing to the school, for he paid no taxes on his 100-odd mu of banner land (see Chapter 11 on banner land). The schoolmaster believed the elimination of his salary was unfair also because the village head had given over 50,000 wen to the three village xiangdi to subsidize a feast for more than thirty villagers who had helped them recollect their prepaid taxes. This subsidy, in Li's opinion, was completely wasteful. In its investigative report to the magistrate, the EPO sided with the schoolmaster, remarking that the village head's evasion of a school contribution was unjustified and that the schoolmaster's salary was much more necessary than the xiangdi's subsidy. As a result of the EPO's mediation, the village head continued to pay the schoolmaster, but his salary was reduced to 15,000 wen (656.1.35, 1912).

Another dispute occurred in Zhandao village in 1918. Its school had thirty-seven students, and most of its funds came from villagers' contributions. The xiangdi collected the school contributions of 27,200 wen from individual taxpayers, of which 80,000 wen was to be paid to the teacher, Liu, as his salary. According to Liu's complaint, however, he received only 52,500 wen from the schoolmaster for the prior year (1917), and was still owed 27,500 wen. The schoolmaster, Wang, in turn blamed the xiangdi for controlling the remaining 70,000-odd wen in school contributions. The xiangdi justified his retaining of the school funds with two explanations. First, the schoolmaster had failed to balance the school account, which implied his "improper handling of school affairs." Second, the village had suffered severe flooding in the previous year that had made many villagers unable to make their contributions to the school. The xiangdi, together with the village head and the vice-head, thus had allegedly advanced the payment for those villagers in order to prevent the shutdown of the school, and they had not yet recollected the advanced monies. The magistrate responded by asking both the schoolmaster and the xiangdi to clear up their accounts. It turned out that the xiangdi had over 70,000 wen in school funds still in his hands. However, he refused to hand over the money to the schoolmaster and further shouted curses about the school, "scaring off" all the students, according to the teacher's complaint. The magistrate put the xiangdi in custody and did not release him until two guarantors promised the full payment of the teacher's salary on behalf of the xiangdi (656.1.1012, 1918).

The appointment of schoolteachers was another focus of disputes between schoolmasters and village administrators. In Shuangmiao village, for example, schoolmaster Li decided at the end of 1916 to reappoint Zhang, from a neighboring village, as the local school's teacher for the coming year, given Zhang's satisfactory performance in the current year. The EPO immediately approved this appointment. Both the village head and the xiangdi, however, had intended to nominate Jiang, a native villager and recent graduate of a teachers' school, as the teacher. To justify this nomination, they described Jiang as a well-trained scholar of modest temperament, while attacking the current teacher as a person who had abandoned his teaching duties and indulged in gambling, prostitution, and opium smoking. With their support, Jiang broke into the school and assumed the teacher's position when the new semester started in February 1917. When the EPO discovered that all of the accusations against Zhang were groundless, however, they forced Jiang to quit his job. So frustrated were the village head and the xiangdi that a few days later they beat up the schoolmaster on the pretext that the schoolmaster's repair of the school, which was located in the Guandi Temple, had damaged the deity's statue. The dispute did not end until the village head and the xiangdi made a formal apology to the schoolmaster on the magistrate's order (656.1.817, 1917).

In a similar dispute from Shijiazhuang village, the schoolmaster appointed Shi, a native villager, as the teacher for the 1913 academic year, despite four xiangdi's insistence on retaining current teacher Hong. According to the schoolmaster, Hong's dereliction had caused the decrease of students in the previous year, while Shi had successfully attracted more than forty students since taking the job. The four xiangdi, who collected the school monies, asserted that they would not release them to the schoolmaster unless Hong resumed his position. However, the EPO upbraided their claim as "inappropriate and absurd." The xiangdi eventually gave up their insistence after receiving a summons from the magistrate (656.1.155, 1913).

All of these disputes show that conflicts among the village notables intensified after the establishment of village schools, owing to their competition for the control of school funds and appointment of teachers. The village head and the xiangdi obviously had an upper hand in such disputes, for they collected the funds directly from the villagers and thus could force the schoolmaster to concede by delaying the collection of school monies, or delaying the release of the funds to the schoolmaster. But the schoolmaster had his own advantage in such disputes; he often had support from the EPO, and the EPO's report directly shaped the magistrate's opinion. The founding of primary schools thus was both a burden for the village elites and at the same time an opportunity for self-aggrandizement.

BETWEEN THE ANCESTRAL TEMPLE AND DRAGON KING'S HALL

Competition for financial and social resources of the school took place not only between powerful individuals, but also between dominant descent groups of a community. Nanguyi, for example, was a multi-surname village consisting of five subvillage *pai* units. The public life of the community centered on its Dragon King's Hall (*Longwang tang*), whose land generated a rent of over 200,000 wen in copper cash for the village. These public funds allowed the village to create a primary school in 1908, without contributions from individual households. The total revenue of the school amounted to 108 yuan or 151,200 wen in 1914 (656.1.308, 1914), which equaled the total net income of a 72-mu dry farm or a 36-mu irrigated farm. Partly because of its abundant funding, the school had ranked first for several years among all the public schools in the county.

From its inception, however, the school had been controlled by the Fengs, the largest lineage group in the village. The Fengs used their ancestral hall to house the school and filled its teacher and schoolmaster positions. And most of the school's students were also from their clan. The most influential Feng was Feng Yuhua, a graduate of Zhili Provincial Normal School and member of both the Assembly and the Education Council of Huailu county, who had played an important role in the 1914 dispute over the EPO positions. In competition with the Fengs were the Zhangs, another large descent group in the community, whose leader, Zhang Qingyun, controlled the village head office. Their rivalry over the control of the school began at its founding. In the Zhangs' opinion, placing the school in the Fengs' ancestral temple made it essentially the Fengs' private school. Using the schoolteacher's adultery with a woman at the ancestral temple as the reason, village head Zhang eventually relocated the school to the Dragon King's Hall and appointed an outsider as its teacher in 1910. But the Fengs, counting on Feng Yuhua's county-level connections, quickly moved the school back to their ancestral temple and appointed a new teacher, Feng Fuli. These actions soon obtained the magistrate's approval (656.1.161, 1913).

The Zhangs revived the battle in early 1914, when the Fengs' schoolmaster failed to balance and publicize the school account for the prior year, which implied the possible abuse of school funds. Village head Zhang thus discharged both the schoolmaster and the Fengs' teacher from their posts and again moved the school to the Dragon King's Hall. In their place, the village head himself filled the schoolmaster's position and appointed Zhang Hongmo, his nephew, as the teacher. Feng Yuhua fought back by filing a petition to the magistrate that accented the new teacher's disqualifications. To prevent further complication of the dispute, the magistrate decided that the litigants from both families be prohibited from interfering with school affairs for one year. Instead he charged the xiangdi-in-chief (*zong xiangdi*) of the village with managing the school and appointed Xin Shizheng, an outsider, as the teacher.

The village head's struggle continued. He first tried to prevent the xiangdi-in-chief from inviting the teacher to the school, asserting that anyone who brought the teacher to the village would be responsible for supporting him. Later, when the teacher eventually arrived, the village head, who possessed the key to the school, refused to open the door and hand over the account book and school monies to the xiangdi-in-chief. The xiangdi-in-chief, again a Feng, thus accused the village head of noncooperation and of embezzling over 20,000 wen in school funds. During a subsequent court session, the magistrate accepted the village head's assertion that he had used up all of the school funds and, at the suggestion of four assistant xiangdi of the village, allowed the village to establish two public schools, including the original school at the Dragon King's Hall (the "Northern School") and the new one, the "Southern School," to be located in a house of the Zhangs. According to an agreement between the Fengs and the Zhangs, which was reached under the mediation of the EPO, the Northern School was to be headed by Feng Yuhua, and the Southern School by Zhang Hongmo. The agreement further provided that each of the two schools would receive 40,000 wen from the village's public funds.

This agreement, however, did not end the war between the two lineages. Village head Zhang soon discovered that Feng Yuhua, now principal of the Northern School, had again moved the school from the Dragon King's Hall to the Fengs' ancestral temple. He filed a petition saying that he was no longer able to collect school monies from the villagers because people treated that school as the Fengs' private property and were unwilling to pay school contributions. In a counterattack, Feng Yuhua complained to the magistrate that the Zhangs had not established the Southern School at all; they merely used the school's name to share the village's school funds. Once the Zhangs obtained their share, said Feng, the Zhangs would fabricate expenses and embezzle them all.

The magistrate responded by instructing the EPO to conduct an investigation. To the magistrate's surprise, in just a few days, four "representatives" of Nanguyi village submitted a petition saying that the years-long litigation between the Fengs and the Zhangs over the school had aroused "public indignation" among the villagers, who had consequently ousted all those in charge of the village and the school. In their place, the villagers had elected a Yang as the village head, a Wang as the vice–village head, and another Wang as the schoolmaster. Furthermore, they had decided to merge the two schools into one, to be located once again at the Dragon King's Hall. Skeptical of this unexpected result, the magistrate ordered the EPO to conduct another investigation, and he soon endorsed the petition after the EPO verified the results (656.1.312, 1914).

Throughout the litigation, the two families focused their disputes on the location of the school. From a purely economic point of view, keeping the school at the ancestral temple of the Fengs did not bring to them any material benefits, for they received no subsidies from the village for using their corporate property; instead they had done some repair work to the temple at their own expense to accommodate the students. But siting the school at their ancestral temple did have important symbolic meaning for them. The Fengs, with financial support from their 200-odd mu of corporate land, had produced most of the literary individuals and students in the community. This had enabled the Fengs to fill all the positions of the school when it was first created. Locating the school at their ancestral temple only strengthened their influence in school matters and enhanced the status of the Fengs as the leading lineage in the community, which in return validated their control of the schoolmaster and teacher positions. The Dragon King's Hall, on the other hand, was a public place of the whole village, where the village head had the greatest influence, for he was not only the leader of the community, but also responsible for maintaining the temple and collecting rent from the temple land. Obviously, moving the school to the temple would weaken the influence, or the symbolic capital, of the Fengs and at the same time enhance the influence of the village head on school affairs.

These intentions, however, never surfaced in their petitions and counterpetitions. Instead, each side only argued how inappropriate the Fengs' ancestral temple or the village's Dragon King's Temple was for housing the students. In the village head's opinion, the Fengs' ancestral temple could not be used as a school building because the Fengs used the temple to collect rent from their corporate land, to lend their corporate funds (which mounted to as much as 2,000,000 wen), and to collect debts. With customers "coming and going all the time," the business in the temple was a big disturbance to students. In response to the village head's accusation, the Fengs argued in their counterpetition that the Dragon King's Temple could never be used as a school either, for the hall was filled with statues of deities and dragons, where women burned incense and farmers prayed for rainfall. To place the students in such an environment would not only distract them, but also cause them to grow a "superstitious mind" (*mixin zhi naojin*). And the front yard of the hall could not be used as a playground, for it was narrow and at the center of the yard stood a stone furnace for burning incense and a tablet of crossing dragons. Furthermore, the noisy business of the neighboring tea-house was also a big source of disturbance to the students.

Despite their different views on the suitability of the ancestral hall or the Dragon King's Temple as school sites, both the Fengs and the Zhangs agreed that the school was of the utmost importance as a tool for public education and that it should have priority in community affairs; this agreement provided them a common ground for argument. From the Zhangs' point of view, the Fengs' relocation of the school to their ancestral temple and hence the enrollment of students mostly from the Fengs were tantamount to "destroying the popularization of education." "When the state ordered all villages to build a school," argued the Zhangs, "its purpose was to ensure that even the poor in the village were able to send their children to the school. Therefore, the educational duties are to be shouldered by the whole community; this is an accepted principle in both China and the world." The Fengs' actions thus were nothing less than "monopolizing the power of education" (*bachi jiaoquan*) and undermining the New Policy.

The Fengs, too, focused their counterattack on the Zhangs' "destruction" of the school. According to their accusation, the village head had sabotaged the school in two ways. It had agitated illiterate peasants without children in school by saying that the school only benefited the households with students; it was unfair to use the public funds of the whole village for the school. Meanwhile, the village head had told the parents with schoolchildren that the school was to be abolished and that the traditional civil service exam (*kekao*) was to be revived. Moreover, according to the Fengs' plaint, since assuming the schoolmaster's position, Zhang Qingyun had taught the students only "old knowledge" (*jiuxue*), using the *Three-Character Classic* and the *Hundred Surnames* as textbooks. His resistance to the "new knowledge" (*xinxue*), which was essential for learning, was more evidence of the village head's "destruction of the public school."

This dispute, then, did not just repeat an old-fashioned battle between two dominant families for fame and fortune; it incorporated a national discourse on modernization and educational reform into the public debate among village elites. This discourse offered shared assumptions and a new language with which to legitimize their own claims and attack those of the other side.

Conclusion

The results of the campaign for founding primary schools in Huailu villages were impressive. During a short period from 1904 to 1917, nearly 150 schools enrolling 5,400 students were created to serve 200-odd villages. An entirely new educational system, based on communal cooperation and open to all community members, thus took shape in the countryside of Huailu county. Not only the educational system was transformed, but also popular perceptions of education. It was widely accepted, at least in public debate, that the school as a tool of teaching and learning was superior to the traditional sishu and that founding and maintaining the school was among the top priorities in community affairs. It is no wonder that when a dispute erupted in connection with the school, the disputants invariably legitimized their own claims by appealing to the central importance of the school in the "popularization of education." This notion about the superiority of school education was not limited to the powerful, but was also accepted, willingly or unwillingly, by ordinary villagers. Not surprisingly, no popular resistance took place in Huailu villages against housing schools in local temples and ancestral halls, which had been so important and sacred for most villagers in their spiritual lives.

To what extent could the success of the educational reform be attributed to the government's intervention and the elite's initiatives, which represented the traditional method of local administration, or to a new way of governance emerging from the joint endeavors of the government, the gentry elite, and village society? To answer this question, a brief summary of the respective roles of the government, the elites, and the populace is in order.

The county magistrate's role was critical in founding the schools. It was under his threat of punishment that many unwilling village heads started the construction or reconstruction of a local school. Without the government's compulsory measures, the creation of a countywide school system during a short span of time would have been impossible. The magistrate was able to wield such influence not only because he had the traditional power that was mandated to his position, but also because of a "modern" statist discourse that presumed an interfering government and a "society" that was obliged to modernize its education system for the purpose of national strengthening. To mobilize local support and facilitate the educational reform, the state did allow local elites greater autonomy through their control of the New Policy agencies such as the EPO and County Assemblies. However, the magistrate's own authority had never been lessened; instead he continued to exercise his power in a traditional manner, including issuing mandatory orders, summoning derelict village heads or xiangdi, and holding them in custody until bail or a solution was provided. To the extent that the magistrate had extensively interfered with local educational affairs, which had traditionally been the realm of the gentry elites, the magistrate's power became even more pervasive after 1900 than ever before.

Village elites' reaction to the school varied. While some village heads and xiangdi treated it as a burden because of their duty to raise the school monies, most elites saw it as an opportunity to pursue personal gain and actively participated in founding the school. Unlike their predecessors in the nineteenth century and earlier, who had exercised their influence informally, the rural elites in the early twentieth century controlled the EPO posts as well as the village government and the village school through a formal election, and they all served for a fixed term in accordance with official regulations. Consequently, the rural elites found greater room than before to establish their dominance in rural society and, at the same time, were subject to constant challenges from their competitors. Such competition, while motivated by their traditional pursuit of personal fame and fortune, was fashioned in the language of official discourse in support of educational reform. All of these factors suggest that in the context of local modernization in the early twentieth century, the influence of local elites was not only more formalized but also discursively more legitimized than ever before.

The considerable success of the educational reform in the villages, however, should not be seen as merely a result of the joint efforts of the county magistrate and local elites. Ordinary villagers, too, participated in founding village schools. In fact, their cooperation was probably more important than anything else in the smooth establishment and operation of primary schools in most Huailu villages. Their cooperation cannot be simply interpreted as a result of the peasants' traditional submission to government authorities. Nor should it be seen as a sign of their embrace of statist ideas on educational reform. To be sure, the magistrate, the EPO officials, and village elites all endeavored to indoctrinate the villagers with new ideas about modern education through oral persuasion, written instructions, and even the use of compulsory measures. But the effectiveness of this propaganda should not be overestimated. The main reason for their voluntary participation lay in the fact that they benefited from the reform, because most schools set their tuition rates very low or did not collect tuition at all. Equally important was the fact that the peasants had a long tradition of cooperation in dealing with the state's needs for local control and taxation, which had shown them the collective good of such communal cooperation.

Therefore, when the burden of contributing to the school monies was limited to an acceptable level *and* when the school-age children of most households in the community benefited from the cooperation, the peasants would likely choose to cooperate in funding the school. They refused to co-operate only when the school benefited only a few and the burden imposed on the whole community became intolerable. But this situation was quite rare; once the number of students decreased, the tuition rate would increase to lessen the burden on the community and shift much of it onto the bene ficiaries. The peasants participated in the reform primarily because it made sense to them.

To sum up, the magistrate, the elites, and the peasants each played a dis-tinct role in founding the new schools. The magistrate relied mainly on his traditional power and old methods of administration to promote modern education in his villages, and his actions proved to be indispensable in over-coming local resistance to the reform. The elites cooperated with the mag-istrate in the reform for traditional reasons: primarily to further their per-sonal and family interests. This motivation drove them to compete with each other for control of the school and, at the same time, to form shared as-sumptions in favor of modern education. Finally, the villagers' cooperation in school founding was not so much a result of the government's pressure or the elites' persuasion as a new way to pursue the collective good that they had been familiar with for generations. The basic means and motives that made the booming village schools possible, in the final analysis, remained largely the traditional ones that had worked effectively before the twentieth century in governing the rural communities. These factors provided the platform on which the new schools came into being and grew steadily in the early twentieth century.

CHAPTER 9

Elite Activism

It has been well observed that North China, a dry-farming region of predominantly owner-cultivators, produced many fewer degree holders, or gentry elites, during the imperial times than the prosperous, rice-growing Yangzi and southeastern regions (Chang 1955; Hsiao 1960: 316; Esherick and Rankin 1990: 21–22). It was also true that the imperial state, in order to put taxpaying farmers under its control, had a stronger presence in rural North China than in the southern areas, where most farmers, as landless tenants, owed no taxes to the government, and the latter in turn dealt with them only indirectly through absentee landlords (P. Huang 1990: 154). These facts, however, should not lead us to conclude that the elites in rural North China were weak and politically insignificant. As we have seen in the previous two chapters, the elites in Huailu county were quite active in the early twentieth century; they responded to the New Policy fruitfully and controlled self-government organs at both the county and village levels. This chapter discusses their activities in response to land taxation, focusing on their resistance to tax increases in Huailu county and Hebei (then Zhili) province in the 1910s and 1920s.

The advent of the self-government projects, such as the police force, new schools, and other institutions at the county and village levels, brought to local elites not only unprecedented opportunities but also a greater tax burden (see Chapter 2). As the largest landowners, the elites suffered from tax increases much more than ordinary landowners. Tensions between the state and the elites thus mounted steadily over time. I show in this chapter how the elites' use of legitimate and peaceful means—that is, their participation in formal political processes and negotiation with state authorities—repeatedly foiled the state's attempts to raise taxes. This approach contrasted sharply with the collective violence against taxation commonly found in the peripheral areas of North China.

The elites under examination included those who assumed leadership in village communities and those who were able to gain access to and influence the county government. The village elites, as seen in the preceding chapters, normally built their leading status in the community on their lineage strength, personal networks, material wealth, and social reputation. Some of them were literate and even held an entry-level degree (*shengyuan*). The advent of self-government programs at the village level after 1900 further allowed them to play an active part in the creation of village governments and primary schools. The urban elites, most of whom lived in the county seat and market towns, had much greater influence than their rural counterparts. Many possessed a shengyuan degree, having passed the county-level exam, or a *zengsheng/jiansheng* degree by purchase, and therefore earned direct access to the county magistrate during the imperial times. After the abolition of the civil service examination in 1905, however, an increasing number of students received modern educations in foreign countries (primarily Japan), domestic Western-style schools, and local self-government training institutions, and they gradually came to dominate the urban elites in the 1910s and 1920s, known contemporarily as the "new gentry." When the self-government movement was introduced in the 1900s and revived in the early 1920s, the urban elites naturally assumed leadership of the county-level self-government agencies, such as the County Assemblies, police office, the Education Promotion Office (EPO), and chambers of commerce.[1]

The term *state* is often ill-defined and has elusive meanings. The county magistrate, located at the bottom of the formal bureaucracy under the Qing and the early Republic and in direct touch with local people, supposedly represented the central government in local society. Therefore, it has been often taken for granted that the magistrate was an agent of the state at the local level, acting on the will of state authorities above him. I demonstrate in this chapter, however, that the magistrate was more than just a representative of the state. Throughout the late imperial period, the magistrate, short of formal administrative arms below the county level, had to rely on the cooperation of the elites to carry out orders from above. As a practical administrator, the magistrate could not act just as a bureaucrat, answering only to provincial authorities. He had to take into account the views of rural notables. This circumstance remained largely unchanged in the early twentieth century when the local gentry members, old and new, controlled the self-government organs and thus were even more forceful in articulating and advancing their interests. The magistrate had to act as a buffer between the demanding provincial authorities and the assertive elites.

What was at work in local politics thus was a triangular interactive relationship among the provincial authorities, the magistrate, and the gentry elites. The state in this context meant primarily provincial authorities, who interacted with the magistrate directly. It also included the central government during the late Qing period and the Yuan Shikai regime from 1912 to early 1916, when Zhili province was under its effective control. During the ensuing years from 1916 to 1928, however, Zhili was only intermittently subject to the influence of the Beijing government, when it changed hands frequently among warlords. Therefore, for those warlord years, the term *state* more often referred to the provincial government than to the nominal central government in Beijing.

This chapter examines three of the most conspicuous events in elite activities in early twentieth-century Huailu: the mobilization of village- and county-level elites against the labor service (*chaiyao*) surtax from 1906 through 1915; their resistance to the levy for postwar rehabilitation (*shanhou liangjuan*) between 1920 and 1921; and the struggle against the "special military levy" in the last two years of the warlord government.

The Reduction of the Chaiyao, 1906–1915

The elites' disputes with the government during the late Qing and early Republican years focused on the chaiyao, which was the only surtax in Huailu before 1915. The origin of the chaiyao may be traced back to the eighteenth century, when the *dingyi* (the poll tax on male adults) was widely merged with the *diliang* (land tax) throughout the country and no longer collected separately (Wei Guangqi 2000b). Since the land tax was a fixed statutory quota and could not be touched by the magistrate, the local government had to create a nonstatutory surtax, known widely as chaiyao, to cover its expenditures. The method of chaiyao collection varied in different counties. It might be assessed according to either the land tax quota or the actual amount of land, and the taxpayer could be either individual households or a village (656.1.243, 1915). The amount of the chaiyao also varied from county to county and from year to year, since a magistrate usually decided the collection rate on the basis of the current year's harvest rather than on the actual fiscal needs of his administration. During the self-government years at the beginning of the twentieth century, the chaiyao, together with deed taxes, became the major funding sources for the modernizing measures undertaken in most counties. Most of the chaiyao monies, however, were believed to be embezzled by the magistrate and yamen functionaries (*Yuanshi xianzhi* 1931, xingzheng: 18). It is no wonder therefore that local elites started their efforts to limit the chaiyao as soon as the self-government movement came into being at county seats.

As a preliminary step, the reform-minded local literati in south-central Zhili (Hebei) counties widely set up the Chaiyao Investigation Office (*chaiyao diaocha suo*) in 1906, for they believed that "self-government starts with the eradication of entrenched local ills" (*Jingxian zhi* 1932, 4: 1). To regularize the collection and use of the chaiyao, some counties organized the Chaiyao Bureau (*chaiyao chu*), which was composed of gentry-managers (*shendong*). The purpose of the bureau was to manage and decide the allocation of the chaiyao. In Yuanshi county, for example, the chaiyao was limited to 3,975,803 wen, 24 percent of which (956,400 wen) was to be used as the self-government fund; another 24 percent as the police fund; and the rest, 52 percent, for government administrative expenses (*Yuanshi xianzhi* 1931, xingzheng: 18).

After 1910, the elites in Zhili counties widely participated in local politics through the newly created County Assemblies (including the *yishihui* or deliberative assembly and the *canshihui* or executive council).[2] By regulation, the yishihui consisted of ten elected members in counties with 150,000 people or fewer and was to "discuss and decide all matters of the county." For counties with larger populations, one member would be added for each additional 30,000 people. The canshihui was to "execute all the decisions passed by the yishihui" and to have four members with the magistrate as their head. Half of the members were elected by the yishihui and half appointed by the magistrate (Qian Shifu 1984). Many of them had a gentry background. In Yuanshi county, for example, the chair and vice-chair of the first yishihui (elected in 1910) as well as the four members of the first canshihui were all low-level degree holders (shengyuan) (*Yuanshi xianzhi* 1931, xingzheng: 30). The state tolerated and even encouraged the creation of the assemblies and other self-government agencies because the elites' political participation both enhanced the state's legitimacy and enabled its initiatives to finance local modernization programs.

Contrary to the state's purposes, however, the elites often used the self-government organizations as a legitimate forum in which to articulate their concerns and to aggrandize their own interests. The reduction of the chaiyao soon became the focus of disputes between the County Assemblies and magistrates. As a result, government administrative expenses dropped to 30 percent of the chaiyao in most counties in Zhili province, while the self-government fund grew to as much as 70 percent. In some counties, the chaiyao was completely wiped out.[3] In Huailu, the County Assembly decided in 1912 that the chaiyao should be reduced by 66 percent (from 17,700,000 wen to 6,000,000 wen) and be used exclusively for the county's administrative expenses. Funds for self-government projects in Huailu came mostly from deed taxes rather than the chaiyao. To avoid additional expenses for taxpayers and to close the loopholes used by yamen functionaries, the assembly further decided that the chaiyao should be collected together with the land tax. The next year (1913) when the magistrate was changed, the

Huailu assembly, following the example of neighboring Jingxing county, further requested the complete elimination of the chaiyao. The new magistrate refused to comply on the grounds that the chaiyao was the major source of administrative fees (656.1.243, 1915).

The bargaining between the elites and the magistrate over the reduction of the chaiyao was full of tension. In Huailu, "mutual accusations between the magistrate and the gentry" (*guanshen hukong*) prevailed throughout the process. In Xiong county, northeast of Huailu, the conflict went so far that the magistrate even accused the assembly members of being "rebellious partisans" (*liedang*) and forced all of them to leave (*Xiongxian xinzhi* 1929, 3: 44). On February 3, 1914, the Beijing government under Yuan Shikai finally ordered both the Provincial and County Assemblies disbanded, on the pretext that those assemblies "monopolized finance, resisted levies and taxes, intervened in lawsuits, and obstructed administration" (Lai Xinxia 1983: 119).

Immediately after the dissolution of the self-government bodies, the Zhili provincial government decided to restore the chaiyao to its former level. In most counties, however, the chaiyao was restored to only 60–70 percent of its original figure. The Huailu magistrate, surnamed Zeng, invited local gentry (*difang shenshi*) to discuss the recovery of the chaiyao several times in early 1914. Each time, however, the elite resisted on the ground that the "county people have not yet recovered from the soldiers' riots after the restoration [the Revolution of 1911] and are now further burdened with new taxes and government bonds. Recovering the chaiyao will exceed the people's capability." Realizing that "the chaiyao could not be recovered at one stroke" because of gentry resistance, the magistrate agreed to collect the chaiyao at the current rate (6,000,000 wen for the whole county) and to delay its recovery to the coming year (1915). In his report to the provincial government, the magistrate justified his postponement by stressing the importance of elite cooperation. "In the past two years [since assuming his post]," said the magistrate, "my relationship with most gentry members has been blended with good feelings and understanding. Cooperation is possible only when mutual trust is established. They [the elite] are presumably willing to share the hardship of the time. It seems that I am now not so tied up [by the resistance of local elites] as I was at the beginning of my office."

One year later, in April 1915, Magistrate Zeng decided to collect the chaiyao at 0.40 yuan per tael of land tax, which would be 9,230 yuan or 11,810,000 wen in total. In the magistrate's opinion, this figure was merely two-thirds of the original chaiyao and was much lower than the collection rate of the chaiyao in neighboring Jingxing county (0.50 yuan per tael of the land tax). Shortly after the announcement of the collection, however, leaders from sixteen villages under his jurisdiction, headed by a Li Qifeng, submitted a petition to reduce the chaiyao. They complained that their crops had been devastated by locusts and heavy rain in the past year and that their tax burden had already been aggravated by the change from the silver tael system to the yuan system (see Chapter 2) and the newly imposed water-work levy. The increased chaiyao together with the existing imposts would make the tax burden spiral up to 2.93 yuan per tael, an amount beyond the villagers' ability to bear.

Magistrate Zeng replied in a sympathetic manner. He noted that he was "aware of the misfortune of the people" and had "left some leeway by de-laying the recovery of the chaiyao to the current year in spite of the repeated orders from above and by restoring the chaiyao to just two-thirds of its full level." Nevertheless, the magistrate agreed that his people were "overbur-dened." He therefore promised to reduce the chaiyao to 0.20 yuan per tael, pending the governor's approval. The magistrate's reduction was soon ap-proved by the provincial government (656.1.243, 1915). The chaiyao in Huailu then stayed at 0.20 yuan per tael throughout the remaining Repub-lican years.

The Dispute over the Shanhou Liangjuan, 1920–1921

The dissolution of the County Assemblies in 1914 did not put gentry ac-tivism to an end. Before the self-government bodies were revived in 1923, the elites demonstrated their strength through both their representative body at the provincial level and the elite-controlled financial agencies at the county seat. The Zhili Provincial Assembly (*sheng yihui*) was first convened in the heyday of the self-government movement at the end of the Qing dy-nasty and then dispersed by President Yuan Shikai in 1914 together with the National Congress and County Assemblies. In June 1918, following the elec-tion of the second National Congress, the Zhili Provincial Assembly was re-opened, with most of its members elected from the counties. By regulation, the governor had to consult the assembly about any decision he had made before it was put in force. And the assembly had the right to advise the gov-ernor to change or abandon a decision.

At the county level, the Financial Office (*caizheng suo*) was widely estab-lished after 1920 under the order of the Zhili governor to perform functions previously assumed by the County Assembly (Wei Guangqi 1998a, 1998b). The core of this office was the financial board of directors (*caizheng dongshi hui*). The directors were nominated by local notables, with each ward pro-viding one director, and were granted the right to decide the creation of new levies and to manage local finance. The government set up this agency because it needed the cooperation of local elites in expanding its revenue and legitimizing new taxes.

To the disappointment of the bureaucrats, however, the elite agencies at both the provincial and the county level acted only in their own interest. They endorsed the government's measures only when the latter would benefit them, such as creating the militia fee (*baoweituan fei*), which was urgently needed by the county notables to organize local militia in face of the rampant banditry in the 1910s and 1920s. However, when the new levies ran counter to their own interests, they did not hesitate to resist. Two events, the struggles against the "after-war rehabilitation levy" (*shanhou liangjuan*) in 1921 and the "special military levy" (*junshi tejuan*) in 1927–28, are good examples of elite resistance.

The preparation for the imposition of the shanhou liangjuan went through several steps. Restoring the chaiyao to its full level was, as it turned out later, actually the first step taken by the provincial government to put the largest nonstatutory local revenue fund under its control. The next step was to investigate the details of the chaiyao in each county. In March 1916, the very beginning of Yuan Shikai's short-lived imperial regime, the Zhili Financial Department issued an order to each county, asking the magistrate to report the names of the chaiyao, together with its collection rate, actual uses, and method of collection. The same step was repeated in 1919. But instead of asking each county to report its chaiyao, this time the Financial Department sent out its own agents to the counties to check local government files. An agent then needed to report back to the department in conjunction with the magistrate. The result of the investigation was reasonably satisfactory to the department, judging by the report submitted by the agent to Huailu, which offered the required information about the chaiyao in Huailu as it actually was (656.1.243, 1915–19).

With the biggest surtax restored in most counties (though not to its previous level) and its details made clear, the provincial government was in a position to take it over. In August 1920, Cao Rui, the Zhili governor, announced the abolition of the chaiyao and the imposition of the shanhou liangjuan in its place. The reason for this new levy, according to the governor, was that the provincial government faced a big budget deficit in the current year. "Nevertheless," explained Governor Cao, "all the administrative and military expenses have to be allocated on schedule each month. Without an immediate measure to make up [the deficit], the administration will come to a standstill and public order will be hard to maintain" (656.1.1232, 1920–22).

By that order, the liangjuan would be assessed at a rate of 0.30 yuan per yuan of the main tax and be collected together with the main tax. All the liangjuan should be remitted to the province instead of being kept by the county government, as the chaiyao had been. The governor promised to allot a portion of the liangjuan to subsidize the county's administrative expenses as well as funds for self-government institutions like schools and the police system, which used to depend upon the chaiyao. The county government's loss of income thus was minimized, for all its revenues from the chaiyao could now be made up by the new liangjuan.

For taxpayers, however, the liangjuan meant a substantial increase in their burden. In Huailu, for example, the chaiyao used to be 0.20 yuan per tael of land tax. The liangjuan now was as high as 0.69 yuan per tael (2.30 yuan x 0.30 yuan), which would bring the total tax burden to 3.53 yuan per tael, a 16 percent increase over the immediately preceding years.

Such an increase in the tax burden could not take effect without the co operation of local elites. Realizing the difficulties in imposing the liangjuan, Governor Cao urged his magistrates to invite "local gentry" (*difang shishen*) as well as village heads to the county seat, and "to persuade and instruct them conscientiously in order to make them aware of the righteousness of the matter." To arouse the magistrate's enthusiasm in collecting the liangjuan, the governor claimed it to be the most important item in the annual evaluation of the magistrate's performance (*kaocheng*) (656.1.1232, 1920–22).

Before he encountered reactions from below, however, the governor soon gave up his decision in face of the worsening drought on the North China Plain. On August 28, just two weeks after his announcement of the liangjuan, Governor Cao instructed all the magistrates to delay its imposition to the next year and to collect the chaiyao as usual.

The drought persisted into 1921, and there was no sign of improvement by March, when the tax collection of the "first harvest" period (*shangmang*) began. The governor thus had to delay the collection of the liangjuan to the "second harvest" (*xiamang*) of that year. Five months later, Governor Cao, foreseeing a good harvest in the coming season, finally announced the collection of the liangjuan. The Huailu magistrate accordingly distributed notices to each village on September 5, which required the villagers to pay the liangjuan together with the main tax (2.99 yuan per tael in total, in addition to the police fee and receipt fee).

The imposition of the liangjuan, however, encountered unexpected resistance from local elites, who believed that the new tax would be used for the military and not for the good of the local people. The governor thus had to issue a notice on September 21 to explain the purpose of the liangjuan. The new tax, according to the governor, was to be used exclusively for grain reserves to deal with droughts and floods as well as for local self-government. This explanation, however, did not convince the elites, in part because it differed from his earlier explanation, and also because the tax monies were to be remitted to the province and would be out of the reach of both the magistrate and the elite-managed agencies. Two months later, Governor Cao found that the local people's "misunderstanding" and their resistance were as strong as ever. He thus had to make a concession on November 8. "Since misunderstandings arise," claimed the governor, "the liangjuan monies need not be remitted to the provincial treasury. I would charge the magistrate and local gentry of each county with the full responsibility for it. The money must be managed properly and prudently. Random misappropriation is strictly prohibited" (656.1.1232, 1920–22).

The governor's attempt to enlarge the province's revenue thus was aborted. Two weeks later, the Zhili Provincial Assembly further advised the governor to postpone the imposition of the liangjuan and to levy the chaiyao as usual. After recounting the sufferings of the local people in the preceding years, the assembly complained: "To add to the tax burden with one-third of the main tax will do harm, rather than bring benefit, to the people, and therefore will run counter to the original intention of the government in imposing the liangjuan." Governor Cao accepted the request and issued an order immediately to stop the collection of the liangjuan. All the liangjuan that had been paid would be counted as part of the land tax for the coming year (656.1.1232, 1920–22).

Resistance to the "Special Military Levy," 1927–1928

The County Assemblies (yi/canshihui) were widely reopened in Zhili in 1924, with their duties and organizations exactly the same as before. The canshihui, as the executive body of the assembly, further took over the duties of the former Financial Office, which was immediately abolished when the canshihui was recreated. What had changed was the background of its members. Unlike the first assemblies twelve years earlier, in which old-style gentry members (lower-degree holders) dominated, the new assemblies became the fortresses of the so-called new-style gentry (xinshi shenshi). In Yuanshi county, for example, both the chair and the vice-chair of the yishihui were educated at modern institutions (the normal school and police school, respectively). Two of the four canshihui members were normal school or law school graduates and the remaining two traditional shengyuan. This difference in their backgrounds was indicative of changes in the composition of local elites in the early twentieth century, when the development of modern education in the 1910s and 1920s gave rise to a new generation of elites in local society.

Although the backgrounds of the elite changed, their concern with local interests remained the same. The following statement made by the Huailu assembly and council suggests their identity with local interests: "We colleagues at the assembly are all residents of Huailu. We are all involved in the public matters of our villages. And we all have the tasks of supplying military levies and advancing tax monies . . . " (656.2.1120, 1928). In counties where the chaiyao was restored after 1914, the assemblies continued their efforts to reduce it. In Yuanshi county, for example, the County Assembly successfully abolished the chaiyao by bargaining with the magistrate (*Yuanshi xianzhi* 1931, xingzheng: 32). By the late 1920s, as warfare among the competing northern warlords intensified, the taxpayers' burden in financing the military had skyrocketed, causing the County Assemblies to pay more attention to local interests. When discussing the creation of new levies, they insisted on compensating villagers who had advanced monies for fodder and grain. The assembly of Nanpi county, for example, decided in early 1928 to collect a provisional levy (*mujuan*) of 0.10 yuan per mu in order to repay local people who had advanced monies for military needs (*Nanpi xianzhi* 1932, 6: 2). Some assemblies even refused to cooperate when the military demands went beyond the taxpayers' ability to pay. This was the case in Huailu when the government attempted to collect the special military levy in 1927.

In 1926 the Beijing government under the control of the northeastern warlord, Zhang Zuolin, decided to collect in advance for the first time the following year's land tax (656.2.852, 1926). In 1927 the warlord government repeated the advance collection of the next year's (1928) taxes, since the current year's taxes had been collected in the preceding year. To augment the rapidly expanding expenses, the warlord further decided to impose the "anti-Reds military special contribution" (*taochi junshi tejuan*). This new levy, equaling the main tax (2.30 yuan per tael of land tax), encountered wide resistance in Zhili province. As a result, many magistrates stopped collecting the levy (Li Dian and Li Ming 1986: 134). In Huailu, Magistrate Liu collected only 7,881 yuan by July 25, 1927, when the Shanxi warlord faction, headed by Yan Xishan, defeated the northeastern army and captured the county seat. The new magistrate, a certain Xiong, announced the suspension of the new levy immediately upon assuming office (656.2.1002, 1927).

The Shanxi troop's occupation of Huailu lasted more than eight months, in which Magistrate Xiong collected in advance 36,088 yuan or two-thirds of the next year's (1928) taxes. The northeastern warlord faction retook the county on April 3, 1928. Magistrate Liu, who returned to his office, soon received an order from the governor to collect the next year's land tax and the current year's military levy, as well the remaining land tax for the current year, which should have been collected the previous year. The three taxes, totaling 6.90 yuan per tael, together with the current year's chaiyao and police fee, would bring the total tax burden to 7.50 yuan per tael. On April 1 the governor decreed that the collection of the next year's land tax and the current year's military levy must be finished within sixty days.

Local taxpayers became increasingly intolerant of the exorbitant burden. Many village heads came to the county seat to claim exemption from the requirement that all taxes were to be collected in advance. On April 9, the

County Assembly submitted a letter to the magistrate, requesting him to forward its petition to the governor. The petition insisted on an exemption from the following year's (1929) land taxes and the current year's military levy and requested only the collection of the remaining land taxes for the current year. To justify its requests, the County Assembly stressed the heavy losses suffered by the county residents. During the Shanxi warlord's occupation, said the petition, the Huailu people were forced to supply food, fodder, and carts at a cost of 100,000 yuan. For villages located within the battle areas, the military service levy assessed on each household was as high as 100 yuan per tael of land tax. Furniture, clothes, quilts, and farm animals had been requisitioned. Most houses were thus emptied: "Judging by the current situation, it is hard to tell if the people can recover from the suffering in two or three years. If the taxes are to be collected in full and no leniency is shown, people will be forced to leave home and wander about" (656.2.1118, 1928).

In his letter of April 10 to the governor, Magistrate Liu agreed that the assembly's account of local suffering tallied with what he had witnessed. One week later, he further reported to the governor that he had decided to collect just the remaining one-third of the current year's land taxes (the other two-thirds had been collected in advance in the prior year) and not to collect the next year's land taxes and military levy as demanded. The magistrate warned that collecting even the remaining taxes for the current year would be difficult, for the county had just been recaptured and fighting had just ceased. "The warfare lasted for over eight months," the magistrate contended, "the people who survived become destitute and scattered about. As a consequence of the war, farmland lies in waste, and houses are ruined. Misery and suffering greet the eyes everywhere. . . . Although military supplies need to be prepared, people's livelihood should also be considered" (656.2.1118, 1928).

Nevertheless, the financial department of the province declined the petition on April 26 and reasserted that all the demands must be fulfilled by the deadline. The Huailu County Assembly thus had to file yet another petition on May 1. Located between two main railways (Beijing–Hankou and Taiyuan–Zhengding), said the petition, Huailu had suffered war casualties much more severe than any other county's. Therefore it again requested a partial exemption of the taxes. Endorsing the second petition, Magistrate Liu insisted in his letter to the department that he would not start the advance collection of the next year's (1929) land taxes and military levy until the remaining taxes for the current year were cleared. Likewise, the magistrate stressed the war casualties in his county and the fact that the county's citizens were still burdened with the ceaseless demand for military supplies.

Meanwhile, many petitions from individual villages reached the county government, requesting relief and a delay in the tax collection. Without exception, these petitions justified their claims by referring to the crop failure caused by the drought, the exorbitant cost of military supplies, and the plundering by defeated soldiers and bandits.

The governor again rejected the petition on May 3. Two days later, the financial department urged Magistrate Liu to start the collection of the next year's taxes simply by reproaching the magistrate:

It is now close to the deadline. . . . All other counties have complied with the order and remitted 60 or 70 and 80 percent of the demanded taxes to date. Some counties reported that they would soon fulfill the complete quota. This county is the only exception. The magistrate repeatedly requested the exemption and delay [of tax collection] on the pretext of war casualties and banditry. Each time the request was declined immediately. Nevertheless, the magistrate has not yet reported the start of collection. This neglect of imperative duty is downright misbehavior. No further delay is tolerable at this moment when military supplies are extremely urgent. I order this magistrate to start the collection right now and remit it in full in accordance with the preceding orders. If the magistrate hesitates on any pretext and disrupts the military supplies, the department shall in no way bear the blame for him and can only ask the governor that he be properly punished. (656.2.1118, 1928)

Magistrate Liu disregarded the order. A few weeks later he was removed from his post. The new magistrate announced the collection of the remaining tax for the current year on May 29. With elite opposition as strong as ever, he was not able to collect the following year's taxes either. The collection of the incoming year's taxes started as late as July 12, when the county was already in the hands of the Nanjing Guomindang government and the County Assembly had been disbanded. Nevertheless, the county was successfully exempted from paying the special military levy because of Magistrate Liu's repeated postponement under the pressure of local elites.

State-Elite Relations in Perspective

Elite resistance in Huailu was fruitful; it effectively curbed tax escalation in the early Republican years. The tax burden would have been 16 percent higher than it actually was in 1914 without the elite struggle against the full recovery of the chaiyao. With the cancellation of the liangjuan in 1921, taxpayers in Huailu further avoided paying 16 percent more to the government. Finally, the tax burden would have doubled in 1928 had the liangjuan and the military levy been collected that year.

The elites' actions to reduce, nullify, and delay government imposts suggest the complexity of state-elite relations in south-central Hebei, a core area of North China. By and large, this area witnessed both a relatively strong presence of the state and the active involvement of rural elites in local politics in the early twentieth century. As an economic center and hence an important source of tax revenue, the government had channeled its influence to the villages through the xiangdi post before 1900 and the village government as well as the supra-village police force after 1900. The elites, too, enhanced their influence after 1900 through their control of self-government organs, a development that marked a departure in their relationship with the government from the imperial times when the elites participated in local administration mainly through informal channels.

URBAN ELITES VERSUS RURAL ELITES

Elite activism in Huailu was characterized by the coalition between urban elites who controlled the provincial and county assemblies and rural elites who joined their actions as local leaders. To be sure, occasionally the two strata of elites conflicted with each other, such as when they competed for the land and housing notary position, which they saw as an opportunity for financial gain. However, once the state attempted to impose a new tax, the two elite groups worked together to fight the increased burden. The elites spoke for taxpayers, for as large landholders they felt the increased tax burden more than anyone else in rural society. Moreover, defending the interest of the local populace was also the most effective way to maintain their prestige and reconfirm their leadership.

The warlord government had to yield to elite resistance from time to time when its administrative arms did not yet reach beyond the county level and its control of rural society was still based on the cooperation of local elites. It did not become notoriously rapacious in tax exaction until its final years (1926 through 1928), when military rivalries intensified among warlords and their demands on local resources skyrocketed, causing unprecedented tension between the government and taxpayers. By and large, it is safe to say that the government and local elites in Huailu were able to maintain a conciliatory and cooperative relationship during the 1910s and 1920s.

PROVINCIAL AUTHORITIES VERSUS COUNTY MAGISTRATES

The responses of government authorities to elite activism varied. Rather than treating the county and provincial bureaucrats as a monolithic entity representing an abstract "state," this chapter has brought to light the changing attitudes and strategies of individual officials, including the county magistrate and his superiors (the provincial governor and his financial department), in dealing with local elites. The magistrate's attitudes differed significantly from the provincial authorities'. Unlike the latter, who often imposed their will on the magistrate regardless of the practicability of their measures and opposition from below, the magistrate, traditionally the lowest-ranking bureaucrat in direct touch with the people, had to listen to the opinions of rural elites, whose support was indispensable for maintaining local order. And unlike the state, which might disband or summon the elite-controlled assemblies at will, the magistrate had never been able to completely do away with the rural elites. This was even true under the dictatorship of Yuan when the assemblies were abolished; to win consent from the elites, the magistrate nevertheless instituted the Financial Office to replace the County Assembly.

The magistrate's dilemma was obvious: as a bureaucrat answering to superior authorities, he had to carry out their ordinances; however, as a practical administrator, he also needed to listen to community leaders. When a demand from above was obviously impractical, the magistrate often sided with the local society, speaking on behalf of the elites and taxpayers. It is no wonder that from the provincial governor's point of view the main obstacle to carrying out his orders was not the elites but the magistrate himself. Clearly, the provincial governor rather than the magistrate represented the interests of the state under this circumstance. To understand village-state relations in the early Republican years, we then need to think of a three-way relationship among the provincial governor, the county magistrate, and local elites at both the county and village levels.

A COMPARISON

The coalition between the county- and village-level elites, the convergence of interests between the protective elites and taxpaying communities, and the conciliatory relationship between the county magistrate and rural elites as a whole contrasted sharply with the situation in the peripheral areas of the North China Plain. In Laiyang county of Shandong province, for example, the villagers, unable to cooperate to pay taxes on their own, left their communities open to tax-farming. The elite at the county seat, predominantly rich merchants, sought to enrich themselves at the expense of villagers by contracting with the county yamen to collect the land tax. To maximize their gains, the tax farmers imposed additional surcharges and manipulated the exchange rate between the silver dollars used in tax assessment and the copper cash used in actual tax payment. In the face of a predatory county elite who were allied with the county magistrate, local communities had no way to vent their grievance or to bargain with the state, but resorted to collective violence under the leadership of village elites, primarily headmen of the village and the supra-village units called *she* (Prazniak 1999: 45–91). In Huailu, by contrast, the county elite safeguarded local communities, for most of them had rural origins and their interests coincided with those of taxpayers, and communal cooperation in taxation also prevented the county elite from engaging in tax-farming, thus eliminating a divisive conflict of interest. Unlike in the peripheral area, where conflicts took place mainly between the rural taxpayers and the county magistrate, which led the state to act as a mediator, the core area witnessed a confrontation between the province and rural elites, in which the magistrate acted as a mediator and buffer between the two.

To conclude, elite activism in the core area of North China showed the state's predicament in the course of its intrusion into the countryside in the 1910s and 1920s. Without effective reach below the county level, the state had to rely on gentry elites to mobilize local resources, just as the imperial state had done. To win their support, it had to incorporate the elites into the formal process of local administration through the creation of self-government organs, which, however, only offered them a legitimate means to enhance their influence. To get rid of this problem, the state had to make two breakthroughs: it had to extend its reach down to the village level and at the same time terminate the role of rural elites as an intermediary between the county government and the village. This is exactly what the Guomindang attempted to do after 1928. The next chapter explores how the new regime embarked on these two undertakings.

CHAPTER 10

Village Reorganization

Hebei province came under the Nationalist (Guomindang) government after 1928. Unlike the imperial and early Republican states, which had relied on gentry elites as intermediaries between the county government and village society, the Nationalists intended to build a more direct relationship with villagers by circumventing the elites and weakening their presence in the countryside. To integrate the villages into a nationwide administrative system, the new regime reorganized the natural communities into artificial *xiang* and imposed new systems and regulations in place of endogenous institutions. Meanwhile, the Nationalists also attempted to popularize their policies and instill their ideology into the villagers' consciousness. In comparison with the late Qing and early Republican states, the Guomindang government was indeed audacious and revolutionary in attempting to bring "state-making" down to the villages.

Hebei was among the five provinces where the Guomindang started the administrative reform. Huailu county, located at the center of south-central Hebei, bore the brunt of the administrative reform in the early 1930s. This chapter first analyzes the Guomindang government's schemes for transforming the rural society and then discusses the implementation of the new systems in Huailu villages. In the last section, I focus on the reorganization in two communities in order to scrutinize changes and continuity in village politics in the 1930s.

Purposes of the Guomindang State

The Republican governments in the 1910s and 1920s relied mainly on local elites to mobilize rural resources in their efforts to "modernize" the state and village communities. The result, however, was more often than not a stronger and more organized elite resistance to state penetration through formal channels. The institution of village government after 1900, for example, in fact offered the local leaders a legal means of articulating and protecting their interests. It was in their capacity as village heads that the notables mobilized to oppose the increased tax burden and abuses in taxation. At the county level, an active group of elites took advantage of the newly created self-government bodies to promote their influence in local politics and to defend their interests and those of the communities they represented.

One purpose of the local administrative restructuring, therefore, was to weaken the influence of rural elites and to enhance the Guomindang state's influence in the countryside. From its early days, the Guomindang force had adopted an anti-gentry policy and targeted abusive rural elites as "evil gentry" in its propaganda. According to the Act of Punishment of *Tuhao Lieshen* (local tyrants and evil gentry) enacted by the Nationalist government on July 28, 1928, the *tuhao lieshen* were those who "dictate local community"; who "bully and wound the common people"; who "bully the widowed and force them to remarry"; who "charge exorbitant interest on loans"; who "instigate and manipulate litigation and cheat litigants of their money"; who "gather mobs and interfere with local public affairs"; and who "control local public organs and embezzle public funds to enrich themselves" (Guomin zhengfu 1928). The Guomindang party's propaganda attacked tuhao lieshen using the same language. The "Opinion" section of *Difang zizhi quanshu* (A complete compendium of local self-government), a political pamphlet, describes tuhao lieshen as the "biggest barrier to local self-government":

They [tuhao lieshen] acted arbitrarily in local communities and victimized the people [*wuduan xiangqu, yurou xiangmin*]. . . . Counting on their wealth and influence, they tyrannically abused their power. They duped the ordinary and the weak, and sucked off their flesh and blood to satisfy their desire. They bought land in large amounts and lent money at high interest rates, thus dominating the economic activities of the people. Moreover, they took advantage of people's submission to family ties and their insularity, and bought support from the ruffians to bully the people. Their influence was so unparalleled that ordinary people could never offend them. They turned local officials into their puppets, and the latter in turn treated them as their falcons and hounds to exploit the people in collusion with each other. (*Difang zizhi quanshu*: 331–32)

To be sure, the gentry elite as a whole were not under attack, but only the tyrannical and abusive elements usually found among the rural lower-level elites (see Kuhn 1975). However, it was difficult to separate the rest of the gentry elites from those under official attack, for all elite members had been involved to some degree in the activities mentioned above. Thus, although the target was tuhao lieshen, the campaign in effect curbed all elite activism. This was especially true in the early 1930s, when the Guomindang government revived the anti-gentry policy in order to prevent the powerful tuhao lieshen from monopolizing the newly created county and ward governments (Peng 1998).

In Huailu, the Guomindang forces took action against local elites shortly after their occupation of the county. They disseminated propaganda to promote their anti-gentry ideologies and policies. The streets of the county seat and local villages were full of posters with slogans such as "Eradicate Local Tyrants and Evil Gentry!" (656.2.992, 1927–31). To squelch elite activities, the Guomindang party in Huailu quickly dissolved the County Assembly, which had been a stronghold of local community leaders. Although the County Reorganization Act (xian zuzhi fa) promised to create a similar organ called a county council (caiyihui), the Guomindang state never put it into effect (Kong Qingtai 1998: 437). Instead, the new government created the County Administrative Council (xianzheng huiyi) to assume the county council's duties. The administrative council consisted of the county head, his secretaries, and the heads of individual offices and bureaus of the county government.[1] The county head, as chair of the council, actually controlled it, for all members of the council were his subordinates, whom he had nominated for provincial approval of their appointments (Kong Qingtai 1998: 433–34). The reorganization of the county government thus only tightened the county head's personal control of the decision-making process and eliminated organized activities of local elites.

Aside from consolidating the state's control of county-level politics, another purpose of the reorganization was to channel the state's influence down to the village by imposing on the village a nationwide, formal administrative system in place of the traditional, informal institutions and the inefficient, unreliable village government that had come into being after 1900. According to the County Reorganization Act and the Xiang and Zhen Self-Government Implementation Act (xiangzhen zizhi shixing fa), both promulgated by the Guomindang government in 1929 and revised in 1930, villages with more than 100 households were to make up an administrative xiang (market towns with over 100 households were to become a zhen). Villages with fewer than 100 households were to be combined to form a xiang. The xiang was further divided into several subunits, called lü, composed of twenty-five households each. Under the lü was the five-household group called a lin (Guomin zhengfu 1930).

The xiang government (xiang gongsuo) was headed by the xiangzhang and the vice-xiangzhang, who were chosen through an annual election to serve the xiang for a term of one year. To be a xiangzhang candidate, one had to have passed the civil service examination; served the government; taught in an elementary school; graduated from a middle school; received self-government training; or successfully managed local welfare as reported to, and verified by, the county government (*Difang zizhi quanshu*: 1–18). Obviously, only a small number of people were able to meet one of these qualifications in rural communities, where most villagers remained illiterate in the 1930s. The reorganization thus reopened the door for local notables to dominate local politics. Nevertheless, to prevent the rise of abusive notables, the Act of Xiang-level Self-Government Implementation deprived those who had been labeled tuhao lieshen citizenship in the xiang and the right to run for office.

The Reorganization Act also allowed all adult males and females 20 years of age or older to attend the assembly of the xiang citizenry (*xiangmin dahui*), which was to be held twice a year to elect or recall the xiangzhang; to create or revise the self-government regulations of the xiang; and to discuss and examine the budget and final accounting of the xiang government; as well as matters delegated by superior authorities or proposed by the xiang government. It was also up to the assembly to annually select five to seven members to form a supervisory committee (*jiancha weiyuanhui*) of the xiang, whose duties were to oversee the revenue and budget of the xiang and to uncover and report to superiors any wrongdoing by the xiang government (*Difang zizhi quanshu*: 18–26). In addition, all adult males between the ages of 18 and 35 were required to join the local militia of the xiang, called *baoweituan*. Headed by the xiangzhang, the job of the baoweituan was to protect the xiang from bandits; to search for and arrest bandits and thieves; and to prohibit banned items. Finally, to prevent the tuhao lieshen from manipulating litigation, each xiang was ordered to create a "dispute mediation society" of five to seven people, again to be elected by the *xiangmin dahui*, who would mediate disputes "according to human feelings and based on conscience" (*Difang zizhi quanshu*: 38–39).

The "self-government" in the Guomindang state's design contrasted sharply with the traditional methods of governance in the imperial and early Republican periods. Unlike the preceding regimes, which had taken advantage of endogenous practices and relied on both kinship groups and the informal leadership of rural elites in local administration, the new state after 1930 treated all these elements as obstacles to the cause of self-government. Not only were the "local tyrants and evil elites," who were inextricably linked with the rural elites, ranked as the primary enemy of the new regime in its political discourse, but traditional notions and institutions in connection with the family and the village community also came under the attack of its propaganda. For example, the notion of family loyalty (*jiazu guannian*), according to Guomindang activists, was "fatal to the self-government movement" for two reasons. First, it prevented people of different clans from developing mutual trust, thus causing them to seek protection from bureaucrats and inevitably becoming the victims of their abuse and exploitation. Second, this notion prevented people from developing an awareness of China as a nation, thus making the whole society like "a sheet of sand" (*yipan sansa*).

Even more harmful than family loyalty, according to the nationalist propagandists, was the parochialism (*buluo sixiang*) that resulted from the "insularity of village society, the lack of convenient transportation, and the backwardness of agricultural economy." The propagandists argued that parochialism conflicted with self-government because it turned peasants into extremely conservative individuals, who were "concerned only with themselves, not interested in communicating with one another, and resistant to any ideas and reforms from outside." They observed that while tuhao lieshen and other forms of feudal systems could be wiped out by military and political forces, the same means could not be used to deal with backward notions. This task would await the growth of Guomindang's "democratic forces" to fight the "feudal remnants." As they claimed, "self government, after all, will not grow safely without completely eliminating the foul atmosphere caused by the old ideas" (*Difang zizhi quanshu*: 328–31).

The reorganization thus is best seen as part of the larger endeavor of the Guomindang state that involved two distinct yet inseparable goals. One was the making of a modern state with a nationwide administrative system reaching all the way down to the village and households to replace old systems based on local institutions and endogenous forces. The new self-government, though it relied on the participation of all village citizens, was imposed by the state. In the words of the Nationalist activists, "It is the government that organizes the self-government groups, and gives them the right of government" (*Difang zizhi quanshu*: 33). And the xiang government, located at the lowest level, was seen as an integral part of the larger system of administration. Thus, "if the xiang is well run, then the xian is well run; if the xian is well run, then the province is well run; and if the province is well run, then the whole country is well run. The state, the province, the county, and the xiang, all these should be linked together to make an integrated nation. The administration should be based on a systematic system. It should no longer be disorganized and out of check [*sanman wuji*]" (*Difang zizhi quanshu*: 34). Clearly, what the Guomindang attempted to achieve here was the making of a modern state that reached the bottom of society.

The second goal was to indoctrinate the rural populace with nationalist ideas and transform them from members dependent on their communities or clans into individuals in an integrated society and citizens of a modern state, a task that the Nationalists had tried in the cities (Tsin 1999). Only when the peasants did away with parochial notions tied to the family or community and wholeheartedly embraced nationalist ideas could they judge things according to national standards rather than native rules and values. It was through this process that the Guomindang state expected to transform

214 Village Reorganization

the country from a "sheet of sand" to an integrated society and thereby create its own legitimacy among the citizens. For the Nationalist state-makers, the transformation of the consciousness and awareness of the people, or "nation-building" as social scientists would call it, was as important as the transformation of the administrative framework, or "state-making" itself.

These reorganization schemes were no doubt idealistic in nature. But the Guomindang state-makers were not just idealists. They were practical when putting their agenda into action. Consider the qualifications required of xiangzhang candidates, as stipulated in the County Reorganization Act. They were so restrictive that few villagers could meet them. Therefore, the Xiang Organization Guidelines (*xiangzhi zuzhi yaoze*) revised them to require only the following three qualifications: (1) to be sincere, honest, and just, with a minimal level of literacy; (2) to have no addictions; and (3) to have no criminal record (*Difang zizhi quanshu*: 36). Another example is the *xiangmin dahui*. According to the Nationalist state's design, "Everyone in the Republic has the right of political participation. The *xiangmin dahui* is therefore to promote people's interest in politics and to prepare them for democracy. All residents of the xiang at the age of 20 and above are required to attend the *xiangmin huiyi*." However, they realized that most villagers were first members of their family rather than individual citizens. Later, therefore, the rule was amended to allow one member of each household to attend, if the custom of the village so demanded (Kong Qingtai 1998: 437).

Despite these compromises, the purpose of the Guomindang state was clear. It was to fundamentally change rural governance from a system based on elite leadership and endogenous institutions to one based on state-imposed institutions, and to change the view of legitimacy from one based on popular notions and local practices to the one based on nationwide standards and formal, legal principles. To what extent were these new systems put into effect, and how did they affect power relations in the community and the everyday lives of villagers? The following examination of the implementation of the Reorganization Act in Huailu is intended to offer some answers to this question.

The Reorganization in Huailu

The Reorganization Acts took effect in Huailu in 1930. Eight ward governments (*qu gongsuo*) were set up on the basis of the prior policing wards (*jingqu*). The 211 natural villages of the county were organized as 182 xiang (the seven market towns were expanded to 12 zhen) (Hebei sheng minzheng ting 1933) and later increased to 204 xiang (*Hebei tongzhi gao*: 2889). Therefore, most of the xiang remained identical to the natural villages. It is no wonder that in many communities the xiangzhang (head of the xiang) was treated as village head and was still called cunzhang (see, e.g., 656.3.436, 1931; 656.3.911, 1934). As the new xiangzhang office came into being, the xiangdi and village head positions disappeared altogether.

It is noteworthy, however, that while the xiangzhang displaced village heads after 1930, in some villages the xiangdi did not disappear immediately. Instead, the xiangdi coexisted with the xiangzhang, and the division of duties between the two was just like that between the xiangdi and village head before 1930. The xiangdi was still responsible for advancing tax monies for the community, while the xiangzhang acted as an administrative functionary between the government and the village. However, this coexistence of the xiangdi with the xiangzhang was nonetheless exceptional, occurring mainly in 1931 when the xiangzhang system was enforced.[2]

Each xiang was further divided into a number of lü, which consisted of twenty-five households by regulation. Huailu had a total of 2,352 lü, averaging 11 lü per xiang or zhen. And each lü had an average of 25.4 households (the county had 59,726 households in total), which were further divided into a number of subgroups called lin. Each lü had an average of 5 lin (the county had 11,661 lin in total), and each lin had an average of 5.1 households (*Hebei tongzhi gao*: 2889, 2900). There were two types of lü in Huailu villages, those newly created and those originating from the former pai. (As I explained in Chapter 3, before 1930 some large villages in Huailu consisted of a number of pai, and each pai comprised 20 to 50 households. The xiangdi in these villages had existed at the subvillage pai level instead of the village level.) The new lü unit was very close to the pai in size and thus was most likely formed on the basis of the preexisting pai units.

THE SELECTION OF THE XIANGZHANG

The practice of xiangzhang selection in Huailu deviated significantly from the official regulations. Although the Reorganization Act required that the xiangzhang be selected through an election from those with proper qualifications, in many villages the taxpaying households continued to serve as the xiangzhang in annual rotation, just as they had done previously under the xiangdi system (656.3.436, 1931). An incumbent xiangzhang was thus often called *xiannian xiangzhang* (xiangzhang for the current year) or *xiannian cunzhang* (village head for the current year), and the outgoing xiangzhang *qunian xiangzhang* (xiangzhang of the last year) (see, e.g., 656.3.911, 1934; 656.3.912, 1934). Where the head of the lü (*lüzhang*) undertook the tasks previously assumed by the xiangdi at the pai level, taxpayers within the lü took turns furnishing the lüzhang service annually. This lü leader thus was likewise called *xiannian lüzhang* (lüzhang for the current year) (656.3.1100, 1936). The continuation of such practices in Huailu was no accident, given the fact that most xiang units remained identical to natural villages and the sub-xiang units (lü) identical to the prior pai. Old village regulations thus survived and dictated the selection of the xiangzhang and the way he acted.

To be sure, there was no lack of instances in which the xiangzhang was chosen through a formal election in line with official regulations rather than through annual rotation. This was the case where the xiang covered more than one village, and old regulations of individual villages regarding the xiangdi selection could not be applied to the selection of the new xiangzhang. It was also common for villagers to elect a xiangzhang where the xiang comprised a single large village of multiple pai before 1930. The burden of the advance payment of taxes was imposed on the lüzhang instead of the xiangzhang. The xiangzhang position here was equal to the previous position of village head. People of the village elected their xiangzhang exactly the way they had elected the village head, while those within the lü rotated to serve as the lüzhang.

DUTIES OF THE XIANGZHANG

The Guomindang state intended the xiangzhang office not only to be filled by village elites but also to take on the functions previously performed by the notables. By regulation, the xiangzhang's duties included: household registration; land investigation; construction and repair of roads, bridges, and other public projects; educational and cultural matters; local security; sports and health; water work; cooperative organizations; improvement of customs; and so forth (Cheng Maoxing 1936). The state thus assigned to the xiangzhang two basic roles: as a government agent at the lowest level to carry out official duties, and as a community leader to sponsor public projects and promote local welfare as village elites had done before.

The actual functions of the xiangzhang office in Huailu departed remarkably from the state's design. The most important task of the xiangzhang, as will be shown shortly, was to advance tax monies for villagers in his charge, a job that the Reorganization Act did not prescribe at all.[3] According to official regulations, taxpayers had to deliver tax monies to the government in person. Prompting tax payment was the duty of local police. Because the xiangzhang did the same work as the former xiangdi in taxation, the new officeholder was simply equated with the xiangdi in some villages (656.3.911, 1934; 656.3.912, 1934).

Like the xiangdi, the xiangzhang in Huailu shouldered some government duties, such as the management of tax liabilities (discussed in this chapter) and the investigation of the unregistered "black land" (discussed in Chapter 11). Suffice it here to say that the xiangzhang was strikingly inefficient in performing those official duties, just as the xiangdi had been before 1930. In reporting black land, for example, the xiangzhang usually listed only a nominal amount of unregistered land in his village. His lack of literacy and professional skills also resulted in the xiangzhang's inability to manage tax liabil-ities, which eventually led to the government's transferal of this task from the xiangzhang to supra-village ward personnel. The county head was soon to find that the xiangzhang was as disappointing as the bygone xiangdi and vil-lage head when performing official duties.

This is not to say, however, that the 1930 reorganization had no impact on rural society. One conspicuous change in village politics was the withdrawal of local elites from the formal xiang government in many localities. Unlike the village office before 1930, which had been controlled by rural notables, the new xiangzhang office was usually filled by ordinary taxpayers in rota-tion. Without formal positions in the xiang government, community leaders found it difficult to extend their influence beyond the boundary of the vil-lage. Chapters 6 and 9 explained how the village heads mobilized themselves throughout the county to resist tax increases and fight against abusive offi-cial notaries. Such trans-village elite mobilizations disappeared altogether af-ter 1930, because the elites could no longer act in official capacities to rep-resent local communities. Although the tax burden rose quickly after 1930, there were no signs of trans-village, organized elite resistance.

The Xiangzhang and Tax Collection

In tax collection, old practices continued in Huailu after 1930. Tax payment in most villages remained a collective undertaking governed by preexisting village regulations. By such regulations, it was up to the xiangzhang, in place of the xiangdi, to pay the taxes in advance for households in his charge. If the xiangzhang failed to meet the tax quotas of his xiang by the deadline, he would be detained until the deficit was cleared (e.g., 656.3.911, 1934). At the end of the lunar year, the incumbent xiangzhang (or lüzhang) would make a "general accounting" (suan dazhang) to allocate the tax monies he had ad-vanced to individual households for reimbursement. The xiangzhang would then hand over his job to the incoming xiangzhang.[4]

Like the xiangdi, the xiangzhang was allowed by village regulations to draw fees as a middleman in local transactions in order to offset his tax payment ex-penses. This integral part of the xiangdi system now continued to bolster the xiangzhang system (656.3.435, 1931; 656.3.912, 1934; 656.3.1100, 1936).

Occasionally, village regulations were adjusted to conform to the new ad-ministrative structure under the xiangzhang system. People called such reg-ulations xianggui (xiang regulations) rather than cungui (village regulations). Some xiang regulations required the lüzhang to join the xiangzhang to ad-vance taxes. To illustrate this circumstance, consider the following statement by the xiangzhang of Zhangying village in his petition against a delinquent fellow villager on December 22, 1933:

Every year in our village, it is the duty of both the xiangzhang and the lüzhang to advance the land tax and the chaiyao [a surcharge] during the collection period in order to avoid tax delinquency. Then an accurate accounting is made in order to collect the advanced monies from individual taxpaying households. This is the xiang regulation and has been in force without violation for the past several years. (656.3.772, 1933)

While old practices survived after 1930, the relationship between the xiangzhang and his villagers was not as smooth as that between the xiangdi and the villagers in the past. Disputes over tax payment increased greatly in the 1930s. As shown in Chapter 5, nonrepayment of advanced taxes was rare before 1930; only one such instance was found in the Huailu archives between 1912 and 1930. In contrast, I found twelve instances of nonrepayment between 1931 and 1936. Mediated tax disputes that did not go to court could be even more numerous. This suggested villagers' increasing failure to repay the xiangzhang after 1931.

The reasons for nonrepayment varied. Most of the tax disputes, however, could be attributed to the rapidly rising tax burden after 1930. As a direct result of the 1930 reorganization and the creation of local governments at the xiang (village) and ward (supra-village) levels, three new fees (the ward office fee, the construction fee, and the educational fee) were created in 1930, totaling 0.85 yuan per tael of the land tax quota, a 30 percent increase over the original tax burden. The next year a self-government fee of 0.60 yuan per tael was added. The four new fees amounted to 1.45 yuan per tael, bringing the total tax burden to 4.66 yuan per tael of the tax quota or 0.17 yuan per mu (see details in Chapter 2). Although this burden accounted for only 2 to 5 percent of the gross farm income, for peasants living at the subsistence level, this sharp increase could well go beyond their ability to pay.

The following two examples illustrate the circumstances in which villagers failed to reimburse the xiangzhang. On February 10, 1931, Sun Fengyi, the xiangzhang of Yuecun village, filed a plaint to charge a woman named Shi with nonpayment of more than 20 yuan in taxes he had advanced for her. In response, the county head sent out a bailiff to prompt Shi to pay off the tax in arrears. According to the bailiff's report, Shi had no cash in hand and was looking for someone to buy her land, promising to repay the xiangzhang as soon as she sold it (656.3.436, 1931). The delinquent taxpayer was obviously in a dire situation. In another instance, Cui Dengxian, the incumbent xiangzhang of Zhangying village, submitted a petition together with a lüzhang of his village on December 22, 1933, to accuse a fellow villager named Fan Rongtai of failing to repay more than 10 yuan in advanced monies. The county head responded by issuing a warrant. The accused soon negotiated with the xiangzhang through a mediator and paid part of the debt. The two petitioners agreed on a grace period for the delinquent villager to pay off the rest (656.3.772, 1933). This arrangement indicated that the tax burden was too high for the accused to fulfill immediately.

Tax delinquents may have had other grounds for nonpayment as well. Li Changsheng from Hengshan village, for example, refused to repay his lüzhang, named Yang Xiqun, a tax of as little as 0.50 yuan in 1936, because Yang, when acting as a middleman for Li's elder brother's wife, had not sold the land to Li but to an outsider. From Li's point of view, the lüzhang had violated the custom of the locality that accorded the seller's family members or kinsmen the priority to buy land. Although the lüzhang's breach of custom made Li feel justified in not repaying his taxes, in the county head's opinion Li's action was unfounded. He rebuked Li: "Your elder brother's wife's sale of land has nothing to do with this case involving you. He [Yang] as the lüzhang had advanced monies for you. How could you not pay him back?" Afraid of possible punishment, Li promised to repay the lüzhang after going home (656.3.1100, 1936).

A similar dispute occurred in Shenhou village in 1934. A villager named Tian Yuchun refused to reimburse his xiangzhang a tax of 6.18 yuan because the latter, when acting as a middleman, had attempted to sell conditionally two mu of the corporate land of the Tians to people outside his lineage, although Tian then successfully prevented the sale (656.3.912, 1934).

In the same village, a dispute between the incumbent xiangzhang and two fellow villagers was brought to court in 1936. One of the two delinquent taxpayers claimed that he refused to repay the xiangzhang because the latter had borrowed money from him and had not yet returned it. However, he failed to provide proof of his moneylending during the court session. The other claimed that he still owed his taxes because the xiangzhang accepted only silver dollars and had refused the paper notes that he had offered. The county head repudiated all these pretexts and released the two after they pledged to repay the xiangzhang in three days (656.3.1100, 1936).

As always, there were also a few villagers locally known as "native ruffians" (tugun), who showed little respect for community norms and regulations and refused to reimburse the xiangzhang for any reason. One Ren Zaobao of Beima village was thus accused by the xiangzhang of "tugun-like deeds," for Ren had "stubbornly refused to repay" him a tax of about 7 yuan at the end of the lunar year, when all others had paid off their shares. The xiangzhang's petition resulted in the county head's immediate summons to Ren, who soon paid back the xiangzhang after community mediation (656.3.434, 1931). Likewise, Li Tianyong, the xiangzhang of Nantongye village, filed a plaint on January 10, 1934, against three fellow villagers for non-repayment of advanced monies totaling over 34 yuan, in spite of his "repeated collections." The dispute was mediated after the county head issued a notice to investigate the case (656.3.910, 1934). These examples all demonstrate that, while old village regulations on tax collection continued to work after 1930, they were less binding than before. This new tendency, compounded with the increased tax burden, explains the greater number of tax disputes.[5]

However, we should be cautious in evaluating the effectiveness of village regulations in Huailu after 1930. As seen in the resolution of these disputes, both community mediators and the county heads respected the local regulations. The fact that only twelve formally filed suits over nonpayment are found in the Huailu archives between 1931 and 1936 suggests the limited extent of violations against local regulations on tax payment. And all those accused eventually paid back the tax-advancing xiangzhang. With these regulations at work after 1930, most Huailu villages continued to be solidary communities, and their cooperative practices in taxation remained largely untouched despite the imposed reorganization of local administration. The Guomindang state, though successful in replacing the informal and endogenous xiangdi system with the formal, nationwide xiangzhang office, had to tolerate such practices when they still proved effective in satisfying its need for tax extraction.

"Land-Tax Consolidation"

The recording and transfer of tax liabilities, as shown in Chapter 6, had long been the business of the *sheshu*, a quasi-official clerk living in the countryside and responsible for approximately a dozen villages. Owing to frequent transactions of land, the inconsistency of taxpayers' registered names with their real names, and possible fraud by the sheshu, confusion over tax liabilities was commonplace throughout the country, which made it very difficult for the government to collect taxes, especially from delinquent taxpayers. The disordered tax rolls also accounted in large part for the uneven distribution of the tax burden. It was observed that large landowners were usually favored with light tax duties while small households were overburdened (Li Hongyi 1977 [1934]: 6555–64). The extreme ends of the uneven tax burden were illustrated by two phrases often found in contemporary discourse on land taxation: *you di wu liang* (the landed were free of taxes) and *you liang wu di* (the landless were burdened with taxes). The large landholders' evasion of taxes and small landowners' inability to pay their unduly heavy taxes combined to account for the government's tax deficits.

The Guomindang government was aware of the inequality of tax burdens and its financial consequences. As the financial department of Hebei province observed in 1931:

In every county of this province, tax rolls are confused and malpractice is entrenched. People usually do not bother with tax transfers. The names of taxpaying households on the tax rolls thus are often different from the names of the current owners. As a result, clerks and runners are able to embezzle taxes and tamper with tax rolls, perpetrating whatever abuses they wish. Because of the accumulated ills, investigation becomes even more difficult. Tax revenue has been shrinking over time. (656.3.449, 1931–34)

To maximize its tax revenue, the Guomindang government made great efforts to update the management of tax liabilities, focusing on the abolition of the old sheshu post and the devolution of its duties to the newly created xiangzhang office. From 1928 to 1930, it tried several measures to eradicate the ills associated with the sheshu without abandoning the post. The financial department of Hebei province repeatedly instructed the counties in its jurisdiction to correct the registered names of taxpaying households on tax rolls and to investigate and tax unregistered "black land" (see Chapter 11). But as the department admitted, these measures had few results in most counties (656.3.449, 1931–34). The sheshu system continued during the first few years of Guomindang rule.

A change took place in 1931 when the central government abolished the *lijin*, a transit tax that had been an important source of revenue for most provincial governments. To make up the loss resulting from this change, it became even more urgent for the Hebei provincial government to put tax administration in order. Shortly after the cancellation of the lijin, the provincial government abolished the sheshu system in 1931 and instructed all of its counties to set up a Land-Tax Clearing Office (*tianfu qingli chu*) to guide tax reform. It even sent out an examiner to each county to supervise the reform.

In Huailu county, the Land-Tax Clearing Office was created in November 1932 (656.3.449, 1931–34). In each xiang (identical to a village in most instances) a Land-Tax Consolidation Committee (*liangzu zhengli weiyuanhui*) was also set up on the county head's instruction. The committee was headed by the xiangzhang to take on the sheshu's duties. By the organizational regulations of the committee, the xiangzhang had three basic tasks in this regard: taxing the unregistered land, handling tax transfers, and updating tax rolls. Land buyers, as the provincial government required, had to have the tax quotas incumbent on the land transferred to their names within six months after the writing of land deeds. The xiangzhang who handled the transfer would assess a fee of 0.15 yuan per mu of land. Above the villages was a "standing committee" at the ward level to guide and supervise the xiangzhang's work. This standing committee was composed of two to four "directors," who were required to be "from well-to-do families, of good repute, and acquainted with land tax" (656.3.449, 1931–34).

By shifting the task of tax administration from the old-fashioned sheshu at the supra-village level to the xiangzhang at the village level, the government hoped to prevent all of the fraudulent practices embedded in this field.

To be sure, having the xiangzhang serve as the state agent in tax administration had certain advantages. As a member of the village community he could in theory perform all of the duties the state assigned to him. He was able to make the "registered names" on the tax rolls consistent with real owners because he knew who was responsible for which tax quotas on the tax rolls; he was able to transfer tax liabilities because he was aware of the land sales occurring in the village; and he was able to uncover black land because he knew who cultivated which pieces of land. Also, his performance could be closely supervised by his fellow villagers. Under normal conditions, the xiangzhang would find no loophole to engage in the frauds at which the sheshu had been so adept, such as adding or deleting taxpayers and increasing or reducing their tax quotas. Villagers in a community were fully informed of each other's tax quotas and the names under which they fulfilled them.

But the defects of the new system were as obvious as its advantages. Handling tax transfers and compiling tax rolls required a minimum level of literacy and a degree of professional skill. Although the state expected those who filled the xiangzhang posts to be educated local elites, most xiangzhang in Huailu villages were simple peasants who were illiterate.[6] At the same time, the annual rotation of the xiangzhang office also made it impossible for the officeholder to accumulate the experience or skills to perform his tasks. Thus, delegating the sheshu's duties to the xiangzhang ran the risk of paralyzing tax administration and making the recording and payment of tax liabilities even more chaotic. It was not inconceivable that the xiangzhang would transfer tax liabilities informally and avoid reporting the transfer to the county government in order to embezzle the transfer fee (see, e.g., 656.3.911, 1934).

So this new system did little to forestall the fraudulent behavior that occurred when the sheshu was in charge. Take Zhang Youlin, the xiangzhang of Dengcun village. In 1932 he duplicated the names of three taxpayers in his village and their tax quotas, which totaled 2.318 taels (equal to 9.96 yuan), in the tax roll of his village. The tax roll was then submitted to the county for official authentication and sent back to the village for tax collection. The xiangzhang's duplication caused the three fellow villagers to pay their taxes twice. According to the accusation from the three, all named Xu, the xiangzhang "had long borne resentment toward the Xu families." The plaint went on to charge that "by repeating the three names and hence obliging us to pay additional taxes, he harmed us in a covert manner." Their accusation was proven to be true on investigation, and the magistrate agreed to delete their duplicated names from the next year's roll (656.3.603, 1932).

The xiangzhang's inability to fulfill his duties in tax administration eventually led the county government to assign the daily handling of tax liabilities to the ward government in August 1933. According to a resolution passed by the County Administrative Council, the xiangzhang's task of tax transferring would be taken over by the newly created Transfer Office (*guoge chu*) of the ward government. This office was composed of five members of the "transfer committee," who were selected by the ward head from "those within the ward who were good at accounting and finance and had good conduct." Taxpayers involved in land sales were required to visit this office to have their tax liabilities transferred. To encourage tax transfer, the fee was reduced from 0.15 yuan to 0.10 yuan per mu (656.3.449, 1931–34).

There is no documentation to show how the Transfer Offices at the ward level operated after August 1933. It is unlikely, however, that the new regime was able to eradicate fraudulent practices, given the short-lived operation of this office (1933–37) and the fact that the Guomindang government did not embark on a thorough land investigation to straighten out the disordered tax rolls.

Effects on Village Politics

To assess the effects of the reorganization in village society, including both the visible changes in village institutions and the invisible and subtle changes in the consciousness of the villagers, I focus here on two disputes. One took place between two neighboring villages over the right to collect taxes, and the other between two officeholders of the same village over the control of local finance. They illustrate how the new system operated in rural society and to what extent the state penetrated the villages at both the institutional and discursive levels.

FANCUN AND TANCUN VILLAGES

Fancun and Tancun, both located in the seventh ward, were two settlements about half a mile apart but shared the same tax roll. Fancun thus was called the "front pai" and Tancun the "back pai." Before the 1930s, each had had a village head and a school. In 1931 the two communities also became two separate administrative xiang, each with its own xiangzhang. Since the miscellaneous levies (*zapai*), such as those for the mandatory supply of carts, horses, mules, laborers, and straw, were usually imposed on the village as a whole, rather than on individual taxpayers, each village had to fulfill its respective duties. In March 1930, for example, both villages were ordered to provide 500 catties of straw to a troop. The xiangzhang of each village, who was responsible for supplying the materials or manpower, then allocated the burden of the zapai at the end of the lunar year to individual households according to their tax liabilities.

Of course, the more taxpayers there were, the lighter would be the burden shared by individual taxpayers. To prevent an increase in the shared tax burden, Tancun village created a regulation in 1924 demanding that any household, when selling a piece of land, had to retain the tax liability imposed on the plot in the village. In other words, even a buyer outside the village had to share the tax burden owed by the village where his property was located (*zuodi xingcai*).

In 1928, three villagers from Fancun bought a total of over 70 mu of land from Tancun village and, in line with the aforementioned regulation, their deeds specified that "the lot is sold on the condition of zuodi xingcai, and therefore the buyer is responsible for sharing the zapai of the seller's pai." This was unfair, however, from Fancun villagers' point of view, for they could not allocate the zapai to the newly obtained land that belonged to their fellow villagers. To end this situation, it was necessary to first separate Fancun from the tax roll it had shared with Tancun. The reorganization of villages into administrative xiang in 1930 offered them a good opportunity to do so. Thus Xu Xizhen, a 61-year-old school principal (formerly a shengyuan degree holder) and also the de facto leader of Fancun village, submitted a petition together with its xiangzhang to the county head in March 1930, requesting the separation of the two villages. The county head rejected the request, reasoning that the reorganization did not necessarily mean splitting the tax obligation of a preexisting unit in two. Xu followed with another petition, revealing the conflict between the two villages over the tax responsibility of the 70-odd mu of land that had been sold to Fancun villagers. The county head thus instructed the head of the seventh ward to conduct an investigation. The ward head soon submitted a report that verified the facts Xu had included in his petition and endorsed his request. In the meantime, Xu filed in a third petition, repeating his request. On this the county head ruled: "Since the two villages can no longer cooperate, owing to their different views, which would cause much obstruction to village administration, their separation is hereby granted in order to resolve the dispute" (656.3.230, 1930).

But the splitting of their shared tax roll did not resolve the problem, for Tancun still held the tax liability of the land sold to Fancun. It was the advent of the land-tax consolidation campaign in 1931 that offered Fancun villagers a perfect opportunity to transfer the disputed tax duty from Tancun. Shortly after its founding, the Land-Tax Consolidation Committee of Huailu county made a resolution, which was announced in the meeting of all the xiangzhang in the seventh ward. According to that resolution, "When the land of village A is sold to village B, its tax liability is also transferred to village B, and vice versa. To be fair and consistent, the tax liability of a lot must always go with its buyer's place [*liang sui di zou*]." The xiangzhang of Fancun village thus immediately transferred the taxes of the three lots from

Tancun to Fancun and listed them under the name of their respective owners. Tancun, however, soon took back the taxes from Fancun, insisting on the
validity of its own regulations and the terms specified in the land deeds. In a
court hearing held on March 6, 1932, the two xiangzhang from their respective villages adhered to their earlier positions; so the county head instructed
both parties to consult the county's Land-Tax Consolidation Committee
and the seventh ward's Mediation Committee for a proper solution. In their
joint report, the two committees remarked that "liang sui di zou" as an official resolution had been announced to all villages; "Fancun's transfer thus
was well founded and Tancun's rejection was downright wrong." To conform to the countywide policy, the committee members ordered Fancun to
transfer the taxes of the three lots from Tancun to its own tax roll, and as a
compromise, they also ordered Fancun to pay Tancun 40 yuan to cover their
expenses in the lawsuit. Both villages, however, rejected this mediation and
continued submitting petitions and counterpetitions to the county head. To
break the deadlock, the county head brought the dispute to the forty-fifth
meeting of the County Administrative Council, which, according to the
Reorganization Act, was the supreme decision-making body of a county.
The council endorsed the two committees' decision on the transfer of the
disputed taxes to Fancun as well as Fancun's payment of 40 yuan to Tancun
(656.3.608, 1932).

   This case is interesting because it shows not only the working of the new
policy on tax transfer, but more important, the degree of state penetration of
village society. Several new organs were involved in handling the dispute. At
the supra-village ward level, the ward head, a salaried official to assist the
county head in local administration, played a critical part in the separation of
the two villages in 1930; it was on his recommendation that the county head
eventually accepted Xu's petition for separation. The ward's Mediation
Committee, composed of five local notables, was also important in mediating the dispute in 1932. At the county level, the Administrative Council
played a decisive role in the final settlement of the dispute. All of these new
organs came into being with the 1930 reorganization to formalize the state
apparatus.

   From the county head's point of view, the ward head as a regular bureaucrat was more reliable than an unsalaried yamen runner in the imperial era
or an undersalaried ward policeman before the 1930s. And the collaborative
five-member Mediation Committee was also more effective and trustwor-
thy than individually assertive elites in community mediation. The Administrative Council, comparable to the County Assemblies in the early Republican years, was directly responsible to the county head who nominated
them, whereas the County Assemblies' members had been elected from the
local society. All these developments did not always mean that the state had

a greater presence in rural society, for the informal connections of the ward agencies with the local society, as shown in the next example, might be as strong as their formal relations with the county head. But the relationship between the county head and the village was indeed more institutionalized and formalized, a development that had already started in the 1900s and proceeded steadily in the early 1930s.

What shaped the results of a dispute were not only the newly created administrative organs, but also the strategies used by the disputants, which in turn reflected their changing perception of the legitimacy of social institutions and actions. The strategy of Mr. Xu, a representative of Fancun village, was to adhere to the resolution of the Land-Tax Consolidation Committee. In his representation, that resolution was a "countywide agreement" (*quanxian gongyi*), whereas Tancun village's regulation on tax liability was merely a "privately created regulation" (*sili tiaoyue*); and his claim was in compliance with the resolution, whereas Tancun's action was to "oppose the public agreement" (*fankang gongyi*) by "counting on its private regulation" (*yizhang siyue*). To enhance his argument, Xu borrowed vocabulary from the national discourse on imperialism and likened the relationship between the two villages to that between a world power (*qiangquan*) and a weak and small nation, and Tancun's regulation to an "unequal treaty" (*bupingdeng tiaoyue*). Tancun's refusal to transfer taxes to Fancun, in Xu's interpretation, was to "bully the weak and small," and to let his village's land share Tancun's zapai was to "turn Fancun into a permanent slave of Tancun." He thus asked the county head to accept his claim in order "to support the weak and to suppress the powerful." So eloquent was Xu's argument that the county head had to agree with him, commenting that Tancun's "private regulation" (*siyue*) was not allowed as a tool to obstruct the implementation of the Consolidation Committee's resolution.

To fight Xu, the xiangzhang of Tancun village emphasized the relative invalidity of the Consolidation Committee's resolution in view of the *legal* validity of its own regulation on tax transfer. As he put it, "the Land-Tax Consolidation Committee is not a legislative organ. So how could its resolution completely eliminate all the customs that have been effectively observed in the past? Furthermore, this committee's resolution has no specific date of enforcement. According to the nonretroactive principle of law, all things that occurred before the announcement of the resolution are not subject to its binding power. Therefore, it is difficult to abide by this resolution." He further argued that the claim of Fancun village was unjustified, for the resolution that supported it was "completely ungrounded in a legal sense," while its retention of the taxes of the three lots sold to Fancun had been agreed on by both the sellers and the buyers, as evidenced by the land deeds. "Since [these arrangements] are clearly stated in the deeds," the xiangzhang continued, "they should be honored by both parties, and legally they should be valid for good." And "since all contracts and deeds are protected by law, they can never be invalidated by the resolution of the committee." The xiangzhang's argument thus was equally compelling; small wonder that the county head concurred that the xiangzhang's words "sound reasonable" (*yanzhi chengli*) while insisting on a settlement of the dispute by mediation.

In spite of their contrasting views, the two parties did have something in common in the way they each represented the case: both backed their claims with official regulations or the purportedly formal, legal principles that had been novel to village residents, rather than the shared assumptions or moral principles embedded in the village community. For Mr. Xu, the supremacy of official regulations over local institutions was plain enough, because the former was made by the government on the basis of public agreement and the latter was merely a private product of the local community. Any action based on "private regulations" thus was illegitimate and superseded by official regulations. But the xiangzhang of Tancun village did not justify his claim by adhering to the importance of the regulation of his own village per se; instead he argued that the immobility of the taxes of the lots sold to Fancun was clearly stated on the land deeds signed by both parties in the transaction, and that the deeds as legal documents were protected by law.

These arguments are signs of the villagers' changing perceptions of the meaning of legitimacy. Before the 1930s, disputes over the land tax had centered on the observance or breach of village regulations. The villagers legitimized their actions by primarily turning to local regulations or moral principles rather than external systems or legal principles. In fact, not only did the villagers attach great importance to their own regulations, but the county government also accepted local institutions in place of official systems in its handling of the disputes. What prevailed in this dispute, however, was no longer the taken-for-granted supremacy of endogenous institutions, but legal, formal principles or institutions imposed from outside.

Some other techniques used by Mr. Xu, who prevailed throughout the dispute, were also suggestive of this change. The deeds that specified the immobility of the tax liabilities of the lots sold to Fancun village were actually unofficial "white deeds." Such white deeds, as discussed in Chapter 6, were quite common in the rural society, for land sellers and buyers usually just turned to a middleman (mostly the xiangdi in Huailu) to negotiate a price and draw up a deed that detailed the terms agreed on by both parties. To enhance the legal validity of the transaction, however, they might also visit the county yamen to pay a tax and obtain an official, stamped "red deed." The buyers of Fancun village had both versions of the deeds. Thus, to support his claim, the representative of Tan village requested that Xu provide the white deeds; otherwise he would not allow Fancun to take away the disputed land

228 Village Reorganization

taxes. Xu, however, just displayed to the court the standard red deed, which contained no specifications on tax liability, and claimed that the white deeds were all missing. He knew that only the red deeds were acceptable to the court; the white deeds were not only unfavorable to him but also legally invalid.

To justify his claim, the xiangzhang of Tancun argued that the land in dispute was sold to Fancun at a low price of merely 102 yuan per mu precisely on the condition that its taxes were to be kept in his village; the price would have been 130 yuan per mu if it had been sold out together with its tax liability. It is not unlikely that there was indeed such an arrangement in Fancun village, for the local residents had a strong incentive to keep the tax liabilities from being taken out of the community. To compensate the loss to the buyer's village, the seller might give a discount to the buyer. This, however, was possible only when the community was strong and cohesive enough to impose effective pressure on the seller that forced him to sacrifice his self-interest for the collective good of the community. An implicit assumption behind the asserted arrangement was the moral obligation of village members to communal norms and the production of collective good. Xu, however, denied this assertion, using a different reasoning: "Preserving the tax quotas benefits the whole village, and reducing the price produces a loss to the seller alone. The seller sold his land because he was in need of money. So how could he reduce the price at the loss of himself to benefit the whole village?" Xu's argument here was based on his presumption that human beings are self-interested individuals concerned more about personal gain rather than collective goods, an idea not unfamiliar to proponents of the "rational choice" thesis.

These strategies allowed Xu to eventually win the lawsuit. We may interpret this result as a preponderance of externally imposed, official institutions over endogenous institutions, a prevalence of legal, official actions over popular yet illegal ones, and even a triumph of "rational" reasoning over moralistic assumptions. The villagers, as this case shows, did begin to embrace legal principles or official systems in place of old values and local practices for legitimizing their actions, especially when they were involved in lawsuits and had to effectively communicate with the county head, who was unequivocally in favor of official principles and formulations. But village institutions and popular practices did not become obsolete and unimportant in the 1930s. Quite the contrary, the county head showed his respect for the claims of Tancun village from the outset of the dispute and insisted on mediation rather than a straightforward adjudication in line with the resolution of the Consolidation Committee. The mediators, while accepting Xu's request on the basis of the official resolution, did not totally ignore the request from Tancun, as seen in their arrangement of Fancun's payment to it. We thus find from this case both an unmistakable departure from the traditional way of legitimization and the waning yet still visible validity of informal, local practices.

SHANGZHUANG VILLAGE

Shangzhuang, located in the fourth ward of the county, was a large multi-surname community of over 400 households. It had one xiangzhang, two vice-xiangzhang (or xiangfu), and fourteen lüzhang. In January 1934 a dispute over the control of village finance took place between Yang Lianyun, xiangzhang of the village, and Lu Guanguang, a vice-xiangzhang and school principal who initiated the lawsuit. The dispute broke out at the end of the lunar year, when the xiangzhang was to announce the public account of the village and to allocate the balance left over from the prior year to individual households. On January 17, Yang invited Lu as well as three members of the supervisory committee of the village and some lüzhang to the school in order to approve the account report and finalize the allocation plan. Lu, who had long been dissatisfied with Yang's control of the account, insisted that the xiangzhang clarify all details and provide all receipts. Especially in dispute were the following three items: (1) a meal stipend of 2.90 yuan for a vice-xiangzhang and two lüzhang who had traveled to the county seat to pay off tax arrears in order to free Yang from custody; (2) a meal stipend of 0.48 yuan for three villagers who had used their own carts to transport coal for the superior government; and (3) a meal stipend of 1.00 yuan for the xiangzhang who had attended the meeting of the county's education board. The two village leaders quarreled when Lu refused to endorse the three expenses. So furious was Lu that he grabbed the account book and ripped out some pages. A lawsuit became inevitable.

To get an upper hand in the litigation, Lu took the first step and filed a plaint the next day. In his plaint, Lu charged Yang with pocketing the public funds and being responsible for the discrepancy between the revenues and expenditures in the village account. The xiangzhang, according to Lu, "controlled the public account of the village by himself alone." Because of his "malpractice and fraudulence" (*xunsi wubi*), their relationship had deteriorated to that "between charcoal fire and ice."

As a counterattack, Yang submitted the torn account book to the county head and requested a summons in order to have Lu punished. The county head instructed the ward government to conduct an investigation and handle the dispute. In a few days, Yang, together with another vice-xiangzhang and three supervisory committee members as well as fourteen lüzhang of the village, submitted another plaint, in which they described Lu as a "native tyrant" (*tuhao*), whose destruction of the account book had made it impossible for them to square the account and for the fourteen lüzhang of the village to collect the public expenses from individual households without an allocation schedule.

The ward head's attitude disappointed Yang. When inquiring about his possible actions, the ward head, named Guo Shuhua, merely told Yang to "wait for his investigation and handling." A few days later, Guo sent Lu a private letter to "invite" him to the ward office "for a chat." In that note, Guo merely used his styled-name at the end of the letter and addressed Lu as "Mr. Lu Guanguang." These acts demonstrated his close relationship with Lu. Using his effective network in the village, Yang acquired the letter and submitted it to the county head as evidence of the ward head's protection of Lu. "Because of his private relationship with Lu Guanguang," argued Yang, "the ward head has suspended the case and thus deliberately persecuted [me]." A few days later, the ward head submitted a report to the county head, claiming that he had summoned the two disputants to his office, where he conducted a patient mediation; both had made a concession and were willing to end the lawsuit. The county head accordingly disposed of the case and instructed the ward head to return the account book to Yang (656.3.911, 1934).

The effects of the 1930 reorganization were obvious in Shangzhuang village. Here both the xiangzhang and vice xiangzhang were annually elected by villagers. The xiangzhang, who was in charge of village administration, publicized the revenues and expenditures of the village government at the end of the year as the Reorganization Act required. The supervisory committee's members were involved in the clearing of the account. The lüzhang, as subordinates to the xiangzhang, were held responsible for assisting the xiangzhang and collecting the allocated dues to individual households in their own lü. When the dispute took place, the ward head also played a role as an intermediary authority between the county head and the village. These facts indicate that the reorganization of 1930 was not just a perfunctory formality to Shangzhuang village, but did result in the restructuring of local systems.

It should be noted, however, that the same reorganization might also have allowed old power patterns to continue in a new form during the Guomindang era. Lu Guanguang, for example, was able to be a vice-xiangzhang precisely because he had support from his descent group, which was one of the two largest descent groups in the community. According to Yang's accusation, Lu "bribed" members of his descent group to vote for him during an election held at the end of 1932. Whether this was true or not, support from the Lus was certainly a critical factor in his assumption of the post. Another source of Lu's strength was his position as school principal in the village. As the most educated person in the community, Lu was literally more qualified than the rest in the village to check and supervise the account that had been managed by the xiangzhang. Tensions between the principal and the xiangzhang thus were inevitable over that matter. Even more important for Lu, however, was his relationship with the ward head. As a member of the literati with wide connections outside the village, Lu was able to build a friendship with the ward head, and the latter in return relied on the cooperation of local elites during his term of office. Clearly, it was a combination of these traditional factors that encouraged Lu to be aggressive and arrogant in dealing with the xiangzhang over the financial matter.

Yang, in contrast, came from a relatively small lineage of the village. Yet most of the villagers had supported his election as xiangzhang. In his consecutive plaints against Lu, the xiangzhang was always able to obtain signatures from the other vice-xiangzhang, the three supervisory committee members, and even all the luzhang. This indicates that Yang maintained his influence mainly by his popularity, rather than the support of his own clan. His reputation in the community allowed him to firmly control the position through the annual reelection and even defy the authority of the ward head, as seen in this case. Because of his influence in the community, the xiangzhang's relationship with the school principal was very different from what we found in Fancun village in the previous case. In Fancun, the xiangzhang was changed annually. And Mr. Xu, the school principal, was so powerful that he dominated the community and turned all the xiangzhang into his puppets. In contrast, the popularity of Yang allowed him to control the village government and challenge the principal. The relationship between the xiangzhang and school principal here thus was quite similar to that between the village head and the schoolmaster in many villages during the 1910s and 1920s (see Chapter 7).

Although the sources of power and the relationship between the powerful figures in the village remained largely unchanged in the 1930s, they did use new strategies. Like the disputants in the previous case, the litigants borrowed from the Nationalists a new language and legal methods. The political discourse of the Nationalists had two targets: imperialism in international relations and tyrants (tuhao lieshen) in domestic politics. Whereas Mr. Xu in the previous case likened Tancun to an imperialist power in the intervillage dispute, here Mr. Yang labeled Lu as a "native tyrant" in intravillage politics. In his representation, Lu was a typical native tyrant: "Counting on his close relations with the ward head, this native bully has been reckless in the community. Give him an inch and he'll take an ell. So arbitrary in the locality and oppressive to the people was he that the villagers were simply terror-stricken upon hearing his name. They were all forced to keep their resentment to themselves." For Yang, depicting Lu as a native tyrant and portraying him as the enemy of the Nationalist revolution was no doubt the most eloquent way to make his claim legitimate and forceful.[7]

Another strategy used by Yang was to turn to legal regulations. Destroying the account book, from villagers' traditional point of view, might be just a trivial matter of the community, or at most a transgression that deserved public denouncement. In this dispute, however, Yang treated it as a violation of state law that was subject to prosecution. He cited article 144 of the Republican penal code and insisted that destruction of the public account book was a felony. This kind of crime, Yang argued, subjected the perpetrator to punishment "by the law of both China and foreign countries." Not only did Lu violate the law, even the ward head, according to Yang, was "in infraction of the law" for merely inviting Lu to the ward office "in his personal name" for a "secret talk," rather than in his official capacity. Clearly, Yang was no longer using local regulations or a communal sense of right and wrong to fight his opponent, but externally imposed legal standards that were supposed to be more legitimate in justifying his claim.

To Yang's disappointment, however, the county head did not adjudicate the lawsuit in accordance with the penal code. Instead, he insisted on mediation by the ward head from the outset. As it turned out, this old approach to administrative disputes left enough room for the working of local power relations, and Lu indeed survived Yang's vigorous attacks, thanks to his friendship with the ward head.

Conclusion

Huailu county in the early 1930s can be seen as a microcosm of the nationwide reorganization of the local administrative system under the Nationalist government.

Changes took place at two levels. At the institutional level, the changes were most obvious in the administrative system. Within the village, the centuries-old xiangdi position disappeared, and the more recent office of village head was abolished. In their stead were the xiangzhang, the lüzhang, and the supervisory committee. These new personnel performed their duties more or less in a manner prescribed by state regulations. The way the villagers chose these personnel also changed in some communities. Whereas before 1930 the villagers rotated to serve as xiangdi in line with native regulations, now they elected the xiangzhang and lüzhang by vote in compliance with official regulations. Where the old practice of annual rotation among the villagers continued in selecting the xiangzhang, the rural elites had to withdraw from the formal political arena, as did the county elites after the dissolution of the deliberative bodies. Consequently, elite activism, so conspicuous during the late Qing and early Republican periods, largely vanished after 1930; this was exactly what the Guomindang government intended. Therefore, the reorganization was not merely a superficial phenomenon but an effective process that reached local society and brought the state's influence deeper into the villages.

More profound was the change in the way people perceived what was legitimate and articulated their concerns. Traditionally, the villagers had tended to adhere to local regulations indigenous to their communities when involved in disputes. And very often they defended their stance by accentuating a shared assumption about the supremacy of village regulations in local society. This situation began to change in the first three decades of the twentieth century when New Policy programs were widely implemented in Huailu villages, exposing local inhabitants to formal institutions imposed nationally. Their acceptance of the supremacy of legal codes and legal principles in public debate during the 1930s is evidence that the state systems and discourses slowly yet steadily penetrated rural communities.

Nevertheless, the reorganization did not fundamentally transform the village communities. In many localities, the xiang remained the original village, and the xiangzhang were no different from the traditional xiangdi, for in many places they were chosen in the same way and performed the same duties as their predecessors. Many of them were just ordinary villagers, who were illiterate and unable to perform the duties ordered by the government. Reflecting this reality, the Huailu county head had to shift the xiangzhang's tax management tasks to the ward office, an action that bespoke the inability of the state apparatus to intrude into the villages.

With the village communities largely unchanged, the power relations that had dominated rural society survived in the 1930s. Village elites continued their traditional leadership in local communities. Where the villagers rotated to serve as the xiangzhang, the elite may have stepped back from the forefront but continued their influence on village politics through informal channels, as we saw in Fancun village. While the xiangzhang position of that village changed hands every year, its influential de facto leader Mr. Xu successfully led the village through the three-year struggle for separation from Tancun village. Where the village selected the xiangzhang through a formal election, the elites only enhanced their influence among the villagers, as Mr. Yang of Shangzhuang village exemplified. Thus although the reorganization brought many changes to the village, preexisting power relations largely continued to determine the results of village politics.

CHAPTER 11

Uncovering "Black Land"

From the 1880s to the 1930s, the late Qing and Republican states launched successive campaigns to uncover the so-called black land (*heidi*), landholdings hidden from official cadastres and therefore exempt from taxation. However, these efforts produced few results before the 1930s because of the general indifference of both local elites and the county magistrate. After 1930 the Guomindang state reorganized the local administrative system to enhance its presence in rural society. Eager to expand its tax base, the new regime revived the battle against black land. This chapter addresses how the approaches of the Guomindang state differed from those of its predecessors in dealing with black land, and how effective its new strategies were in uncovering the illegal holdings. Again, my emphasis is on the issue of state penetration into village society and the resulting changes in village governance during the Guomindang era.

The Origins of Black Land

Black land was widespread in early twentieth-century Hebei. The Provincial Department of Civil Administration (*mingzheng ting*) estimated in 1932 that only 86,508,000 mu (or 84 percent) of the 103,432,000 mu of cultivated land in the province were registered and taxed. Between 1927 and 1933, land that was taxed averaged only 74 percent of the taxable land or 62 percent of the cultivated land (Li Hongyi 1977 [1934]: 6325, 6411). In other words, land that evaded tax liabilities accounted for as much as 38 percent of all the cultivated land.

During the late Qing period, most black land in this province originated from the "banner land" (*qidi*), land that was enclosed and occupied by the Manchu rulers at the beginning of the Qing dynasty. The "bannermen" (*qiren*) who cultivated this land owed no taxes to the government but instead paid rent to the Board of Inner Affairs (*neiwufu*) of the imperial court through an agent called *zhuangtou* (Tie Nan 1994; Huang Fengxin 1998; Wei Qingyuan 2001). By the late nineteenth century, however, many bannermen had sold their land to non-bannermen outright or conditionally as their living conditions deteriorated. The new owners paid no rent to the neiwufu or tax to the government. Black land of this origin increased to as much as 8,000,000 mu by the late 1880s, which accounted for about 53 percent of the original amount of the banner land in Zhili (15,000,000 mu) (655.1.834, 1889; Yang Xuechen 1963; Myers 1970: 217–19).

Another common reason for the rise of black land, as Li Hongyi observed in 1934, were constant natural disasters and wars in this province, during which many landowners died or fled, often to Northeast China. When they came back after many years, the government had already lost track of the landowners as well as the taxpayers. Much cultivated land was thus left untaxed (Li Hongyi 1977 [1934]: 6520). This explanation, while holding true for the province as a whole, does not apply to south-central Hebei as much as to the northeastern area. As described in Chapter 2, Huailu county and the surrounding region were endowed with a relatively secure ecology. They enjoyed peace for long periods during the Qing and the Republic and suffered successive wars only in the late 1920s, when the northern warlords competed for control of this strategically important place and then combated the Guomindang's Northern Expedition (1926–28).

Also accounting for the large amount of black land were villages' different customs on the transfer of tax liabilities after land sales. It was common for a land buyer, regardless of where he lived, to pay its tax duties to the village where the land was located. This was called *zuodi xingchai* (literally, "stationary land yet mobile taxes"). This custom was important for the land-selling village, because it obliged the land-buying outsider to share the tax burden, especially miscellaneous levies, incumbent on the whole village (see Chapter 10). Other villages stipulated, however, that "the tax goes with the land" (*liang sui di zou*); that is, the land buyer just needed to pay the tax on the land to his own village and owed no obligations to the village where the land was located. These local variations in the rules of tax transfer inevitably caused confusion and opened loopholes for land buyers to evade tax duties. Disputes thus often erupted between different villages over the transfer of tax liabilities because of their different practices (656.3.230, 1930; 656.3.608, 1932). In fact, whatever the practice, the government had a hard time keeping track of the tax liabilities on land when it changed hands several times.

Official efforts to uncover black land can be traced back to the late nineteenth century. In 1888 the Zhili (Hebei) financial commissioner, a certain Song, set up a General Bureau of Land-Tax Rectification (*qingfu zongju*) in his yamen to supervise land investigation in counties under his jurisdiction. Beginning in December 1888, the bureau allowed people to register their illegal holdings within a year and to start paying tax thereafter; in exchange, the bureau exempted all the taxes owed on the black land. It also held baojia leaders responsible for supervising and prompting the black land holders to register their hidden land. After the one-year period, it would allow the baozhang as well as local residents (*dilin*), village leaders (*cunzhang*), gentry members (*shenjin*), and the elderly (*qidong*) to report the black land to the government. For every 100 mu of black land, the reporter would receive a reward of 4 taels (655.1.838, 1889). How this effort actually worked is unclear because of the lack of documentation. But the fact that black land remained a big concern of the state in the early twentieth century suggests its limited result.

In fact, black land possibly became even more pervasive in Zhili after the fall of the Qing. The Republican government attempted to tax the banner land but soon found that many of the zhuangtou, who collected rent from the bannermen for the imperial court, had fled during the 1911 Revolution, and their records of the banner land and the names of the Manchu rent payers were missing. It thus became even more difficult for the government to uncover the actual banner land cultivators. As a result, most of the banner land became black land (*Zhili quansheng caizheng shuomingshu* 1915: 23).

A fundamental solution to the problem of black land, as many commentators of the Republican period observed, was a thorough nationwide land survey and a land register compiled on the basis of the survey (see, e.g., Yao Shusheng 1936). But it was widely agreed that this project entailed huge inputs of manpower and material resources, which could hardly be furnished under current circumstances. As a temporary measure, then, the government encouraged people to register their hidden holdings, a strategy that had been tried by the Qing rulers. The Republican state made a series of efforts toward this end during Yuan Shikai's presidency (1912–16), the warlord period (1916–28), and the Guomindang regime (1928–37).

Black Land Investigations, 1914–1915

The investigation of black land in Zhili was initiated in 1914 by Li Liangmo, magistrate of Cangxian county (about 130 miles east of Huailu). Li allowed black land owners to report to their yamen the amount and fertility of their illegal holdings between July 1 and September 30, 1914, in order to be assigned a tax quota. He promised to waive the past taxes on the hidden land. After that period, any black land, once uncovered, would be confiscated (656.1.237, 1914). The provincial Financial Department (*caizheng ting*) endorsed Magistrate Li's method, holding it to be "easy and feasible." On August 4, 1914, it instructed all magistrates in the province to investigate black land by using Magistrate Li's method (656.1.237, 1914).

Several months later, however, the provincial government found that few magistrates had done so. In his report to the Financial Department, the Huailu magistrate denied the existence of any black land in his county. He asserted, "Huailu has long been able to meet its tax quota in full. There is no household with a tax deficit. Nor is there cultivated land that evaded taxation" (656.1.237, 1914). It was true that Huailu, like many other counties in south-central Hebei, had paid taxes in full in most years (see Chapter 2). But this does not mean that there was no land that evaded taxation; black land in Huailu was in fact plentiful. The assertion that the county had a record of full tax payment was just a pretext for the Huailu yamen to shirk its duties in black land investigation.

Unsatisfied with the magistrates' reaction, the Zhili Financial Department reasserted the prior ordinance on January 11, 1915. Following the example of Cangxian county, the department allowed a three-month period beginning from January 1, 1915, during which people were to register their black land. The tax assessed on the black land would be collected beginning in the first collection season of 1915. Likewise, the department promised to waive all the past taxes due on the black land while warning that it would confiscate any black land uncovered after the deadline. Informers who reported black land would be rewarded with 40 percent of it, and the rest would be taken over by the government (656.1.360, 1915).

Again the response of black land holders fell short of expectations. The department complained in late 1915 that although the magistrates had submitted reports of uncovered black land "one after another," the amounts were always "negligible." In his report to the department, Magistrate Zeng of Huailu county stated, "no one has come and reported [black land]," although he had disseminated as many as 250 notices to villages in the county. In fact, the magistrate did nothing other than post the official notices (656.1.360, 1915).

The magistrates showed no enthusiasm for the drive for two reasons. First, they saw few potential benefits. By regulation, all of the land taxes (diliang, or main tax, as well as various surtaxes on the land) had to be remitted to the provincial treasury. The county yamen relied mainly on deed taxes and miscellaneous commercial taxes, and had no share in the land taxes, except a chaiyao, which was equal to about 8.7 percent of the main tax. Uncovering the black land, in fact, would only increase each magistrate's burden: he would be responsible for fulfilling more tax quotas resulting from an enlarged tax base. Second, the magistrates had to maintain a smooth relationship with local gentry, upon whom they had relied in taxation and local administration. As Li Hongyi pointed out in the early 1930s, the gentry elite were always those who possessed the largest black landholdings in Hebei province (Li Hongyi 1977 [1934]: 6520–21; 6556–64). Uncovering the black land would inevitably infringe upon their interests and put the magistrate's local support in jeopardy.

Aside from his unwillingness to investigate black land, the magistrate also lacked any efficient agents at the village level to perform the duties he delegated. Although village governments were widely instituted after 1900 and were expected to act as the state's agents at the bottom of society, the village heads, chosen from among villagers, necessarily identified themselves with local interests more than with the state. It was no wonder that the provincial government did not let them play any substantial role in land investigation. Nor could the magistrate count on the villagers to accuse each other of illegal holdings. Although a reward of 40 percent of the black land could be a real incentive to report black land, few were willing to inform on their fellow villagers. The villages in 1910s Huailu, after all, remained tight-knit communities in which local social ties, such as kinship, friendship, neighborhood, and patron–client relations, predominated. The inability of the state to penetrate village communities was, therefore, a fundamental reason for the failure of the land investigation.

The Land Survey, 1915–1916

The central government in Beijing under Yuan Shikai (1859–1916) launched a nationwide land survey in 1914. President Yuan was able to do so because he had taken firm control of the government after defeating the revolutionaries in South China. By late 1915, Yuan had reached the peak of his influence and was in a position to restore dynastic rule with himself as the emperor. To meet its mounting demand for tax revenue, the Yuan regime was determined to embark on a nationwide land survey that had been deemed impractical before.

To guide the land survey in Zhili, the provincial Financial Department enacted the Zhili Land Survey Regulation on October 28, 1915. Accordingly, each county set up a Land Survey Office (qingcha dimu shiwusuo) to take charge of the matter. According to the regulation, the county was to be divided into thirty to fifty districts for the purpose of the land survey. Within each district, the persons responsible for surveying the land would be two dongshi or directors chosen from the "just gentry." Their duties were to make "detailed and accurate survey of all kinds of land, including those cultivated and uncultivated, owned by the government, the public, private parties, or temples." The survey thus was not limited to black land or holdings that were unregistered and untaxed, but also included "land that is untaxed but has either an official deed [red deed] or an unofficial deed [white deed]," "land that has been assessed a tax quota but has not yet paid taxes," and "land whose tax quota is not commensurate to its size." The survey was to start on December 1, 1915 (656.1.369, 1916).

To win support from local gentry, the regulation demanded that, before launching the land survey, the magistrate should first invite "urban and rural gentry" (*chengxiang shenshi*) to the county seat to "discuss, explain, and seek advice [from them]." Then the county would be divided into districts and the dongshi nominated: "The point is to make sure that a strong consensus is reached throughout the county in order to facilitate the endeavor" (656.1.369, 1916). The government's method here was no different from its traditional approach to rural administration, characterized by its reliance on the cooperation of local elites.

Most magistrates in Zhili treated this ambitious plan perfunctorily. In the view of Magistrate Zeng of Huailu county, although the survey might help him handle disputes over land ownership due to the lack or confusion of land deeds, it was largely irrelevant to his county because Huailu, asserted the magistrate in his report to the Zhili Financial Department, met its tax quota in full every year and had no tax deficit. To respond to the department's ordinance, however, he nevertheless set up a Land Survey Office in his yamen on December 1, 1915, simply by appointing the head of the First Section, which had been in charge of land taxes, and two clerks from that section to positions in the office.

On December 4, Magistrate Zeng further issued a notice requiring "the urban and rural gentry" to come to the yamen to discuss how the land survey would be conducted (656.1.369, 1916). Although the magistrate addressed the notice to the gentry as a whole in compliance with the provincial regulation, in fact he just let the yamen runners send the notice to village heads. It should be noted that the term "urban and rural gentry" was ambiguous. The gentry consisted of two groups: those residing in county seats and market towns and those in village communities, notably the village heads and schoolmasters. The magistrates had long relied on the urban gentry in local administration during imperial times. The rural elites, in contrast, were believed to be "scattered and out of control" (*sanman wuji*) (656.1.1105, 1919–21). By sending the notice only to the unmanageable village heads rather than the urban gentry upon whom the magistrate had long relied, the magistrate indicated his lack of real interest in the land survey.

The Huailu magistrate's correspondence with his colleagues in the neighboring counties also showed that they had taken few concrete actions five months after the start of the survey. The magistrate of Luancheng county, southeast of Huailu, allegedly planned a three-step schedule for the survey. The first step was to let village heads survey the land in their own villages. This was to be followed by a further investigation by the dongshi of the district. It was to conclude with a spot check by members of the Land Survey Office of the county. The magistrate of Yuanshi county, south of Huailu, claimed that he had selected the Number 1 District of his county as the "model district" and had visited this district in person in order to supervise the dongshi's work (656.1.369, 1916).

But few magistrates took real steps to complete the land survey despite repeated urging by the provincial authorities. On March 27, 1916, the Zhili Financial Department observed: "Although every county has reported in detail its start [of the survey] one after another in the past several months, this department's inquiry shows that the populace has been hesitating because of insufficient instructions and that the magistrates have been delaying on the pretext of the inactiveness of neighboring counties" (656.1.369, 1916). Eventually, on April 30, 1916, the Zhili Financial Department, on the instruction of the central government, announced the "postponement" of the land survey in the province.

A summary of the survey costs in Huailu showed that the yamen had spent only 188 yuan. Its expenses included the purchase of 200 copies of official regulations regarding the survey and official forms for land registration; the travel expenses for the bailiff to deliver notices to the dongshi, and the making of fifty wooden sticks for land measurement (656.1.369, 1916). In other words, Magistrate Zeng had only done some preparatory work; he had not yet started the land survey in his county by the time of its suspension.

The immediate reason the survey was aborted, as the head of Baoding Circuit observed, was the people's loss of confidence in the government (renxin dongyao) resulting from the rebellion of southwestern provinces against Yuan's new dynasty (656.1.369, 1916). Although Yuan abandoned the throne and reassumed the presidency in March 1916, the rebellion spread quickly in South China. Consequently, the government's concern with the land survey yielded to the more pressing task of suppressing the rebels.

Local resistance was another reason the land survey failed. President Yuan complained on April 7, 1916, that, "where the land is measured, there are always people who gather a crowd and make trouble (juzong zishi)" (656.1.369, 1916). The resistance was widespread because black land as well as land that was untaxed or undertaxed existed almost everywhere, and those who owned the most black land were invariably the rich and powerful. Li Hongyi observed on the basis of a survey produced by Nankai University in 1932 that "the more land the farmer possesses, the less acreage he has registered, and hence the more taxes he evades" (Li Hongyi 1977 [1934]: 6562). Needless to say, it was also these people who controlled most of the village governments and, ironically, whom the government relied upon in land surveys.[1] Not surprisingly, the survey encountered strong resistance from local society and was eventually abandoned.

The Warlord Government, 1921–1922

China entered an era of warlordism after the fall of Yuan Shikai. While a national government ruled in Beijing, regional warlords dominated different provinces and fought with each other to enlarge or protect their holdings. Zhili (Hebei) was home to the warlords of the so-called Zhili Clique headed by Cao Kun (1862–1938), who also controlled the Beijing government beginning in July 1920. To meet its expanding military expenditures, the provincial government under the Zhili Clique made repeated efforts to investigate untaxed land.

On February 23, 1921, the Zhili Economic Department (*shiye ting*) ordered its magistrates to "investigate in detail the acreage and location of barren mountains and wasteland" in their respective counties and to report to the department within fifteen days. The purpose of this investigation, according to its explanation, was to "reclaim the waste areas in order to augment the provincial revenues and to provide relief for people who suffered constant droughts and floods" (656.2.8, 1921).

The magistrate of Huailu county, named Cheng, delegated that task to the police offices of the five wards in his jurisdiction and required them to report the results to the yamen within ten days. In the following three weeks, the police offices reported back one after another, claiming that they had either sent policemen to villages to investigate or had instructed the village heads to do the job. Without exception, these reports all asserted that "there is neither barren mountain nor wasteland" in their respective wards (656.2.8, 1921). In fact, as a prefectural official complained, both the magistrate and the ward police had "treated it [the investigation] as a mere formality" (*shi wei juwen*), for it was practically impossible for them to carry out the task in a short period, given the limited number of policemen and their unfamiliarity with landholdings in individual villages (656.2.8, 1921).

As an alternative, the provincial government instructed the magistrates on March 5, 1921, to order their Education Promotion Offices, instead of the ward police, to report the barren mountains and wasteland "within twenty days." The five EPO members in Huailu submitted a joint report to Magistrate Cheng on March 27, claiming that there was no wasteland in the county. However, unlike the earlier reports from the ward police, which denied the existence of any wasteland in Huailu, this report listed in detail the barren mountains in individual wards. These mountains, according to the report, were "owned either by individual villagers or by villages collectively" and "were suitable for foresting only" (656.2.8, 1921).

The warlord government was of course not interested in such barren mountains. What it was really interested in was land that had been reclaimed but remained untaxed under the guise of "wasteland." The EPO members failed to report the wasteland not because it did not exist, but for other reasons. First, the EPO members, five in all, were too few in number to investigate black land in the more than 200 villages in the county. Furthermore, these members were the most prominent of rural elites who likely owned varying amounts of "wasteland." They could hardly be expected to report these untaxed holdings to the government at a cost to themselves or at the risk of offending those who dominated local society.

In desperate need of more taxes, however, the Zhili Financial Department tried in 1922 the same sort of black land investigation that the Yuan regime had attempted six years earlier. As before, the department instructed every county to set a period of self-registration for owners of black land. According to its ordinance, black land uncovered after that period would be confiscated, and 30 percent of the land value would be awarded to the person who reported it. To stimulate the magistrates' interest in this matter, the department allowed the county yamen to share equally with the provincial government the rest of the confiscated black land.

But again the magistrates did not act; they knew full well that none of the existing subcounty personnel, be they the village heads, the gentry, or the ward police and EPO officials, were reliable enough to be entrusted with the task of black land investigation. Unlike the Guomindang government in the 1930s, the warlord regime after Yuan took no measures to further its control over rural society. Most magistrates thus continued to treat black land investigation as a formality. In Hauilu county, Magistrate Cheng let his yamen post official notices regarding this investigation on the wall gates of the county seat and in market towns in the county, but not in individual villages. Predictably, no one responded to the notice and registered the black land on their own or informed against the black land of others (656.2.151, 1922).

Black Land Investigations after 1930

The Hebei provincial government under the Guomindang regime after 1928 faced still greater urgency to increase its tax revenue to meet the escalating expenditure of the expanded state apparatus. Its financial situation became even worse after January 1931, when the central government in Nanjing abolished the transit tax (lijin), an important source of income for provincial treasuries. To make up its budget deficit, the provincial government took firm steps to eliminate black land.

In May 1930 it required all counties in the province to set up an Official Property Office (guanchanju) to take charge of black land investigations. Unlike the short-lived Land Survey Office in 1915, which was established by the magistrate and staffed by yamen clerks, this office, parallel to the county government, was established by the Head Office of Official Properties (guanchan *zongchu*) of the province and was responsible directly to the general office rather than the magistrate. During its first three years of existence, the county office insisted that black land holders register their holdings by paying the full market price of the black land (656.3.780, 1933).[2] This exorbitant fee in effect prevented black land holders from doing so.

The situation did not change until March 1933, when the provincial head office launched a new campaign. It allowed black land holders to register their land between March 1 and October 31, 1933. This eight-month period was further divided into four phases, each comprising two months. During the first phase, those who registered their black land were allowed to pay a fee of 1 yuan per mu (0.5 yuan for wasteland). For each of the following phases, the fee would be 1 yuan more than in the prior phase. Thus the later the black land was registered, the higher the cost would be. In this way, the office intended to urge people to register their illegal holdings as early as possible. The office also encouraged "village heads as well as all other kinds of people" to "inform against" (*jubao*) the black land during the eight months and promised to pay informers an "informing fee." But it did not specify how much the fee would be. After the eight-month period, warned the office, the government would confiscate and auction any black land it uncovered. People who reported the black land after the eight months would have first priority to buy the land.

During the first two months, however, not as many black land holders registered their black land as the provincial office had expected. On May 26, it had to delay the deadline of the first phase by two months, to June 30, 1933. And the following three phases were postponed accordingly. When the end of the second phase arrived, the provincial office further announced that, beginning immediately, each phase would be extended by two to four months. The end of the second phase thus was extended to October 31, 1933, after many county offices complained that people who had survived the successive wars were financially unable to register their illegal land by the original deadline. By the end of October 1933, though, the provincial office again received many petitions from county offices for yet another extension of the second phase on the same pretext. Once again, the office agreed and extended the second phase to the end of 1933. But it stipulated that each of the following two phases would still be four months long.

Unlike the magistrates in the 1910s and 1920s who denied that black land existed in Huailu, the Official Property Office of Huailu county, which was equal to the county government, admitted that "there are large quantities of official properties as well as waste- and black land [in this county]." But it took no real measures during the first few months of the campaign (starting in March 1933), except for circulating official notices regarding this drive to villages. It was not until July 19, 1933, that the office convened all of the newly appointed xiangzhang of all villages at the county seat, where Mr. Wu, director of the office, instructed them to report the waste- and black land in their respective villages. He further required the xiangzhang to "explain in detail [to their fellow villagers] the necessity and benefits of registering the land" and to "ensure that the villagers report the land conscientiously."

In September 1933, the Official Property Office together with the county head further issued a notice to prompt black land registration. Four months later, that is, at the beginning of the third phase, the two authorities issued yet another joint notice, written in the vernacular, observing that while black land holders "have been vying with each other" to come to the office for registration, there were still people who "have been hesitating and stalling." In fact, both self-registration and reporting of black land became rare in 1934. The campaign was concluded in August 1934.

Unlike the preceding land investigations, which had produced few results, the new effort under the Guomindang government achieved a measure of success. Take the First Ward of Huailu county, for example, on which we have complete data. A total of 528 mu of black land was uncovered in this ward, of which 95 mu (18 percent) were reported by the xiangzhang, 123 mu (23 percent) were registered by black land holders themselves, and the rest (59 percent) reported by the official informers.[3] It should be noted that the First Ward was a relatively small one among the eight wards of Huailu county. Its land-tax quota (1,987 taels) accounted for only 9.54 percent of the county's quota (20,838 taels in 1931) (656.3.431, 1931). If the black land investigations in other wards did not depart too far from what we have seen in the First Ward, then the total black land uncovered in the county should be no less than 5,000 mu, which was equal to 0.7 percent of the total cultivated land in this county. The actual amount of black land in Huailu was no doubt much larger than what was uncovered, given the fact that the total amount of the black land in the province accounted for as much as 16 percent of cultivated land (according to the conservative official estimate cited at the beginning of this chapter). Also, the concealment and underreporting of black land by its holders, as well as the xiangzhang and informers, were not uncommon during the investigation period.[4]

To see how this campaign unfolded concretely in Huailu, I focus on the following three aspects: the black land holders' self-registration of black land, the xiangzhang's reporting of black land, and the reporting of black land by ward informers.

SELF-REGISTRATION OF BLACK LAND

In spite of the low registration fee set for the initial phase, black land holders in Huailu adopted a wait-and-see attitude during the first two months and few visited the Official Property Office. Sporadic registration occurred in late May 1933, when the initial phase was first extended. But the amount of reported black land was often very small, ranging from half a mu to 3 mu per holder.

Disappointed, the office took two measures in July 1933. It summoned all xiangzhang in the county to the yamen on July 19, urging them to report the black land in their own villages. At the same time, it also required every ward to appoint a few official informers to investigate and report black land in the ward.

As a result, self-registration of black land increased notably beginning in August 1933. But the size of registered illegal holdings remained small in most cases, usually less than 5 mu per holder. Few large black land holders registered their land voluntarily. They did so only when their fellow villagers were accused of illegal holdings and when it became impossible for them to hide their black land any longer. In Dongzhuang village, for example, two villagers were accused of having 2 mu and 25 mu of black land, respectively, on July 23. The next day, a Wang Erbai from this village reported to the Official Property Office black land as large as 25 mu. On July 27 another three villagers in the same village were accused of having 12 mu, 6 mu, and 7 mu of black land, respectively. Five days later, two other villagers, Wang Xi'ai and Zhang Jingming, reported their black land of 22 mu and 25 mu, respectively. In Shijing village Li Mengxue reported his 10.5 mu of black land on August 7, following an accusation that five households in his village possessed a total of 11 mu of black land. In Gujiayu village, Gu Xingong registered his 12–mu of black land as late as January 6, 1934, when the investigation had entered the third phase. He did so most likely because he feared the possible revelation and subsequent confiscation of his land after the end of the period. But large black land holders as honest as Gu were few. Many of them made efforts to hide their black land and reported just a few mu in order to get through the campaign.

XIANGZHANG'S REPORT OF BLACK LAND

According to a report from the xiangzhang of Donghushenpu village, Xue Qingxian, he held a "village assembly" (xiangmin dahui) on the night of July 20, 1933, immediately after the magistrate's "face-to-face instruction" to the xiangzhang at the county seat. At that villagers' meeting, the xiangzhang asked the lüzhang (head of the twenty-five-household group) and linzhang (head of the five-household group) in his village to "persuade [the villagers] household by household to conscientiously report [their black land]." In just three days, these lüzhang submitted to him a list of black land in their respective groups. On the basis of these lists, the xiangzhang submitted a report of black land in his village to the Official Property Office on July 24, 1933,

TABLE 13

Black Land Reported and Unreported by the Xiangzhang in the First Ward, Huailu County, 1933

| Village Name | Black Land Reported | | | | Black Land Unreported | |
	No. of descent groups	Holders	Total size (mu)	Per holder (mu)	Holders	Total size (mu)
Anxia	2	9	20.5	2.28	—	—
Donghushenpu	1	6	6.5	1.08	—	—
Dongzhuang	4	10	5.6	0.56	4	95
Duanzhuang	1	8	4.0	0.50	1	4
Gujiayu	1	4	6.7	1.68	—	—
Huangyan	1	7	18.0	2.57	1	30
Xixuezhuang	1	9	5.0	0.56	1	7
Xiyangzhuang	1	9	5.0	0.56	1	5
Xuejiazhuang	1	7	10.0	1.11	—	—
Zhandao	4	12	13.7	1.14	1	12.7
Average		8	9.5	1.17	—	—

SOURCE: Huailu archive file 656.3.780, 1933.
NOTE: "—" means data are unavailable.

which listed only six households with black land totaling 6.5 mu (see Table 13 for details).

The actual process of the xiangzhang's reporting of black land was far more complicated than what Mr. Xue described above. Villages on the early twentieth-century south-central Hebei plain remained overwhelmingly kinship communities, many comprising a single lineage or only a few descent groups. The xiangzhang, as an ordinary member of the group, could hardly report the black land honestly to the government at the expense of his relationships with fellow villagers and his status in the kin group. Needless to say, it was extremely difficult for the xiangzhang to determine whose black land and how much was to be reported. This work inevitably involved intense negotiations and bargaining between villagers or his kinsmen. The difficulties that the xiangzhang encountered in carrying out this task might explain why the majority of them failed to submit a report to the Official Property Office. In the First Ward, for example, only ten of the twenty-eight xiangzhang filed a report. As Table 13 indicates, seven of the ten villages were lineage groups; all of the black land holders as well as the xiangzhang in each of those villages shared the same surname. One village (Anxia) consisted of two descent groups, and the remaining two had four and six descent groups, respectively. The predominance of kinship ties in these communities was obvious. Table 13 also shows that an average of eight black land holders were reported per village. Given that each village had an average of 180 households (Jiang Taixin 1991), the reported black land holders accounted for only 4 to 5 percent of all households in the village.

What is striking is the nominal amount of black land reported by the xiangzhang: an average of only 1.17 mu per household. In Duanzhuang village, for example, the xiangzhang reported eight black land holders, each having a negligible 0.5 mu of black land. Likewise, eight households in Xixuezhuang village were reported to each have 0.5 mu of black land, too; the ninth had 1 mu. The xiangzhang of Xiyangzhuang village reported exactly the same case. In general, the black land reported by the xiangzhang varied from 0.5 mu to 3 mu.[5] This range would have been acceptable to most black land holders, and the registration fee (from 0.25 yuan to 1.50 yuan) was also tolerable. For the xiangzhang, reporting black land on a larger scale could have placed a substantial burden on his fellow villagers and would inevitably have hurt his relationships with the holders.

The black land that the xiangzhang hid from his report could have been substantial. Wang Xi'ai of Dongzhuang village, for example, was reported to have only 0.5 mu of black land. Later it was found that he had as much as 22 mu of black land. Table 13 lists the unreported black land uncovered by the ward informers during the later phases or registered by illegal holders themselves to avoid confiscation after the deadline. The average amount of unreported black land was 17 mu per holder, or almost fifteen times the size reported by the xiangzhang. The actual holdings of black land in these villages was likely higher than what was uncovered. As will be seen shortly, the ward informers who investigated black land holders also engaged in fraud; they often collaborated with the xiangzhang to hide the illegal holdings for personal gain.

The way the xiangzhang reported black land in his village suggested strong resistance among village communities to state policies in the campaign. The xiangzhang office was far from functioning as the full agent of the state. Entrenched in the local community network, the xiangzhang had to first consider the interests of his fellow villagers, or more accurately, members of his descent group and neighbors. In fact, as described in Chapter 8, the xiangzhang in most cases was merely an average villager. His report reflected the result of negotiations and compromises among the black land holders in the village, and the village elite often played a decisive role in this process. At any rate, with the village structure untouched, the state could hardly expect from the campaign the desired results by relying on an agent chosen from within the community.

Although the Official Property Office encouraged "all kinds of people" to report the black land to it, ordinary villagers seldom informed on their fellow villagers, since doing so would alienate them from the rest of the community. The Huailu archives contain reports on only two who did so. One was from Huangyan village, where Wang Wanling accused Liu Ruihong and Liu Huanni of having 25 mu and 24 mu of black land, respectively. The other came from Qiejiazhuang village, where Wang Xijiu reported a total of 14 mu of black land owned by four fellow villagers of different surnames.

Community resistance to the black land investigations caused the Official Property Office to assign one or two official informers to each ward. No documentation exists to explain the backgrounds of these ward informers. Unlike the xiangzhang, who was unwilling to inform on his fellow villagers, the ward informer often appeared as an outsider to many villages in the ward. Therefore, he could be much less scrupulous than a native xiangzhang about reporting the black land. My statistics on the uncovered black land in the First Ward of Huailu county between May 25, 1933, and January 9, 1934, show that the ward informers contributed the most to the black land investigations (310 mu, or 59 percent, of the total 528 mu of uncovered land).

To the informers' reports of black land of less than 10 mu the Official Property Office usually responded with a notice to the illegal holder, asking him to pay the fee due and register his land. For black land larger than this amount, the office would send out a clerk to the village for an on-the-spot investigation or summon the illegal holder to the office to verify the report. When registering the black land, the holder as a rule was required to submit a pledge claiming that this plot under registration involved no disputes with others. The xiangzhang, by regulation, also had to authenticate the document. Sometimes, when numerous black land holders in a single village were reported by the informer, the office would simply ask the xiangzhang to pay the fees and submit a pledge on behalf of his villagers.

These measures, however, did not prevent the ward informers from abusing their power. This is clear from the informers' reports of black land and the illegal holders' pledges. The Huailu archives contain a complete collection of these two kinds of documents from the First Ward (656.3.780, 1933), which often show striking disparities between what the informers reported and what the villagers pledged. Often the informer either exaggerated or underreported the illegal holdings. Let us first consider his possible underreporting.

Earlier I described the xiangzhang's underreporting of black land. Surprisingly, the ward informers sometimes reported exactly the same landholdings that the xiangzhang reported. This was true in Donghushenpu, Gujiayu, and Anxia, where both the informers and the xiangzhang reported black land as small as 1.08 mu, 1.68 mu, and 2.28 mu per holder, respectively. These reports, as discussed earlier, did not reflect the actual size of black land in these villages. Most likely, the informers had colluded with the xiangzhang to underreport it in exchange for personal gain. This was possible because the informers were underpaid. The official regulation stipulated that the ward informer was a "voluntary officer" (yiwu zhi) and was to be rewarded with only a "meal stipend" (shanfei) during his working period. Thus it was necessary for him to make a living in other ways.

It is no wonder therefore that many informers exaggerated the size of black land in their reports. In an extreme case, a person named Bi Chengqun of Lijiazhuang village was accused of having as much as 303 mu of black land on August 15, 1933, by Liu Youwu, informer of the First Ward. The Official Property Office summoned Bi immediately. It was soon made clear through court inquiry and on-the-spot investigation that Bi had only 16 mu of black land. Another person of the same village, Liang Yinfu, was accused of having 75 mu of black land. Liang, however, denied having any black land at all at the hearing on August 27, 1933. Likewise, a Liu Fu from Shanhou village was charged with having 72 mu of black land. After Liu denied the charge in court, the clerk sent to investigate determined that he had only 15 mu of black land.

Other instances involved exaggerated reports of relatively small holdings. Liu Xunxin of Shijing village, for example, was charged with having 5 mu of black land. In the court session held on August 10, 1933, Liu insisted that he had only 2 mu. He then submitted a pledge, vowing that, if his words were proven untrue, he would be willing to see his land confiscated. Five days later, an investigator reported back and confirmed Liu's assertion. A second case was from Xixuezhuang village, where Xue Lianzhuang was accused of having 7 mu of illegal holdings. It turned out that he had just 4 mu of black land.

Obviously, these victims had failed to pay the ward informers to underreport or had been left outside their patronage. Informers exaggerated also because they needed to report as much as possible in order to receive the government's good evaluation of, and stipends for, their work, and they were in effect exempt from any punishment for making false accusations despite the Official Property Office's warnings.

Conclusion

Two factors account in large part for the early Republican state's repeated frustrations in conducting land investigations before 1928: the failure of the state to penetrate village communities and elite resistance. The government lacked any effective agents at the subcounty level to carry out its policies. The magistrate could not entrust village governments with black land investigations in 1914–15. Nor could he expect the ward police or the EPO members to be helpful. And certainly the magistrate could not depend on local elites in land investigations, for they were often the largest black land owners. Thus the county yamen took a wait-and-see attitude toward land investigation until the state "suspended" the program.

What success the Guomindang government enjoyed in the early 1930s was due to its enhanced control of local society. To effectively carry out its programs in black land investigation, the Guomindang state fully employed the subcounty administrative network that it had created. The reorganization of peasant communities into the xiang, lin, and lü groups made possible a vigorous campaign that mobilized the villagers to an unprecedented degree. As a result, some of the black land holders registered their land voluntarily. Adding to the state's strength was its creation of the Official Property Office at the county level, which was parallel to the county head and was intended to circumvent the impassive county yamen. No less important was the Official Property Office's use of ward informers against black land holders: as outsiders to most villages, the informer was not reluctant to report on black land. In addition, the government launched an unprecedented propaganda campaign to mobilize the people. All of these efforts enabled the new regime to uncover more illegal holdings than any of its predecessors and suggest the Guomindang state's deeper reach in the local society.

However, the weakness of the Guomindang state's approach was equally evident. The unpaid ward informers proved to be as dishonest as traditional yamen clerks, who at once protected those under their patronage and victimized those outside their networks. Likewise, the newly created xiangzhang office turned out to be as unreliable as the former village government. Its perfunctory performance of its official duties and its protection of local black land holders offset the state's purpose of land investigation. Despite the stronger presence of the government at the local level, the villages in Huailu remained strong and cohesive after the state tried in vain to dissolve traditional community ties by reorganizing the natural villages into administrative xiang.

CHAPTER 12

Conclusion

One challenge that frequently confronts researchers of rural China is how to distinguish between regional patterns and national trends in peasant life. Although local conditions varied widely in the vast territory, village practices in different parts of imperial and Republican China did show some commonalities: the enforcement of baojia and lijia systems in early Qing; the government's reliance upon gentry elites in social control; and the "state-making" of the early twentieth century that led to deeper penetration of the state apparatus into rural society and an escalating tax burden, to mention only a few. It is thus possible to arrive at some national-level generalizations about changes in local governance, especially when we focus on the imposed systems and the flow of state power from the top down. However, when attention is paid to actual practices in rural communities, we find a wide array of variations embedded in local ecological and social settings. Therefore, a solid grasp of village practices and regional differences is necessary to develop a reliable picture of local administration in rural China as a whole.

This study has focused on Huailu county in south-central Hebei, a core area of the North China macroregion. In many respects, village communities in this region existed in circumstances between those of their counterparts in the disaster-prone, low-yield peripheral areas of North China and those in the rice-growing, prosperous regions of South China. Irrigated land in south-central Hebei, while more prevalent than in northeastern Hebei, was not as widespread as in South China, where networks of canals had been developed to channel river and lake water. Likewise, the diversified cropping pattern in south-central Hebei allowed a level of land fertility higher than in the ecologically insecure, dry-farming northeastern Hebei. Yet it was undoubtedly much lower than in South China, the home of intensive wet rice and cash crop cultivation.

In social composition, lineage organizations were more pronounced in south-central Hebei than in the northeastern region, where most villages were multi-surname communities. Yet they were much less predominant than in South China, especially the Canton delta, where clan organizations virtually substituted for village institutions (Liu Zhiwei 1997). Rural elites in south-central Hebei, too, were much more active than those in the northeastern area. However, living in communities of mainly owner-cultivators, they were not yet as powerful as their counterparts in the highly differentiated Lower Yangzi region. The latter dominated local society through rent exploitation and self-government institutions they sponsored in the late Qing and early Republican years (Bernhardt 1992: 119–24, 161–88; Xiao Tian 1997: 223–41).[1]

The advantages of studying the villages in Huailu are twofold. First, the inner workings of the peasant society, including its cooperative institutions, community identities, shared assumptions, and established practices were more visible and more clearly articulated in the strong communities in the core area than in the weak communities in peripheral areas. At the same time, unlike the communities of mainly tenants in South China, where the villagers paid no taxes and thus had few contacts with the government, the vast majority of villagers in Huailu as landowners and taxpayers dealt with the government frequently in activities pertaining to taxation. A close examination of these activities permits a better understanding of government involvement in local governance and the working relationship between state and village.

The Peasant Community Revisited

What made a peasant community was a set of endogenous practices and institutions that brought individuals together for collective purposes, and shared assumptions and norms that defined their relationships. Central to the village norms and peasant values was reciprocity, the mutual obligations and rights of community members. This was evident in local regulations (*cungui*) pertaining to the annual rotation of xiangdi service, tax collection and payment, and sales of land and housing in Huailu villages. All these arrangements sought to achieve a balance of duties and privileges between those who offered a service and those who received it. No less important was a survival ethic, as evidenced in the arrangement in many villages that linked one's contribution to the collective goods with landholding, thus producing a "redistributive effect" in favor of the poor, who were often exempted from the public burden. So important were these norms in village life that when a dispute took place among the villagers, they unfailingly appealed to relevant cungui to justify their claims and to correct their rivals' misdeeds.

This does not mean, however, that the villagers were merely moral citizens committed to communal norms and regulations. Material gains were no less important than collective obligations in shaping their social behaviors. This was true for the villagers both as a group and as individuals. As a collective, they formed and maintained cooperative arrangements precisely because those arrangements benefited them more than systems imposed from outside. As individuals, most villagers observed the cungui and fulfilled their roles in the collective undertaking, for they knew that the smooth working of the cooperative institution was critical to the well-being of both the community as a whole and themselves as individuals. However, it was not unusual for them to avoid burdensome duties or to compete for lucrative public service positions, as shown in my examination of disputes pertaining to xiangdi selection, tax payment, the village head position, and school contributions.

Nevertheless, deviations from collective norms in Huailu villages were never so severe as to cause the breakdown of communal cooperation, as proponents of "rational peasant" theory would assume (Popkin 1979: 31). On the contrary, cooperative arrangements had existed in local communities for centuries and remained effective until the 1930s. The key to the durability and effectiveness of cooperation in Huailu villages lay in the informal and invisible social constraints imposed on individual villagers. A person in such villages was first a member of the community, who had to fulfill his communal commitments and engage in the existing social networks and power relations. The peasant's perceived and actual security of subsistence could not do away with these social ties and obligations. Those who failed to fulfill their duties inevitably confronted social sanctions, in the form of cursing, gossip, ridicule, and open denunciation. It was thus unwise for the villager to breach established rules in pursuit of personal goals, for doing so could jeopardize his reputation in the community. Those who attempted to evade their duties had to disguise their intentions.

The powerful and prestigious in the community, such as the village head, clan elders, and schoolmasters, were even more constrained by the cungui and collective sanctions, for their leadership was based on their prestige among the villagers. And their prestige was in turn linked with their ability to maintain the working of village institutions that promoted public goods. When the institutions were threatened or interrupted, the community leaders were expected to be among the first to safeguard their operation. However, just like ordinary villagers, the village elites were motivated by private interest as well. It was not uncommon for them to abuse their influence for self-aggrandizement or the patronage of others. But a powerful villager well knew that his reputation rested upon his conformity with, and defense of, village institutions. It was unimaginable for him to openly violate them; he had to make sure that any breach of established rules would not affect his standing in the community. After all, the ordinary citizens, the poor and the weak in the community, were not completely powerless. Their shared values, public opinions, and appeal to cungui offered them an effective means of social sanctioning, which could curtail the influence of the reputable. It follows that in addition to the visible power based on official positions, status, and wealth, we must take into account the invisible power derived from community norms and assumptions shared by all members, including both the "powerful" and the "powerless." This invisible power, which constrained the powerful while offering the weak a weapon with which to defend themselves, was no less important than the visible one in the peasants' everyday lives.[2]

Two sets of factors interacted to shape the villagers' choices and actions: individual imperatives and group dispositions. The imperatives and possibilities unique to the individual were defined by his role in the production of collective goods, its implications for his private gain, and his position in the social network, power structure, and property relations. All these functioned as "the instantaneous sum of the stimuli" to trigger his motives and actions (Bourdieu 1977: 78). Durable dispositions, the "habitus" of a group or community, resulted from the internalization of the objective conditions common to all members of the community. Varying from group to group, these conditions included the social, geographic, and kinship ties that brought the actors together, the felt need to cooperate in order to produce the desired collective goods, and rules that regulated their interaction and cooperation. In other words, the homogeneity of the objective conditions produced the homogeneous dispositions that shaped the perceptions, attitudes, and expressions of the villagers, evident in unanimously accepted assumptions about the supremacy of the rules that guided their interactions, a public attitude that linked the fulfillment of one's roles in the group with one's status and reputation among the members, and the shared experiences and memories of group members in cooperative activities.

Obviously, we cannot fully understand the diverse strategies of the village members simply in terms of their moral commitment to group objectives or their desire for material gain based on rational calculation. We should instead view their deliberations and actions as the result of the interaction between the durable habitus of the community and their individual changing circumstances. The persistence of cooperative institutions in Huailu villages, in this light, lay not so much in the villagers' internalized obligation to those institutions as in the homogeneity and stability of the objective conditions that produced and reproduced the dispositions to constrain the individuals.

The peasant community, therefore, was a social space, or a "field," in which the villagers formed their perceptions and choices as individuals and group members on the basis of shared assumptions and conditions of existence. This field, often coinciding with a natural village, a neighborhood, or a descent group, was not so much a group of people brought together by their territorial or blood ties as a situation in which they interacted to pursue collective goods and define their specific roles by shared rules and meanings. Thus, although the individuals had different resources and roles, the same institutions, dispositions, and structure of interests and rights enabled them to form opinions and decisions that were readily apprehensible to each other.

To illuminate this conception of the peasant community as a field, a comparison with other characterizations of village society is in order. The first is the concept of the "natural village." In many communities of Huailu, the scope of voluntary cooperation coincided with the boundary of the village; therefore the dwellers developed "*village* regulations" (*cungui*) to govern their collective activities. In such cases, the community was indeed identical to a natural village. But a community was not always a natural village. It was not uncommon in this county for inhabitants of a subvillage neighborhood (*pai*), which was usually a single descent group or a branch of a large clan, to form a cooperative group and have their own regulations (*paigui*). Understandably, they identified themselves more with the pai than with the village. In other cases, the taxpayers of two neighboring hamlets formed a single cooperative entity and their activities were subject to the same local regulation (*xianggui*). The community thus went beyond their respective hamlets. It is quite clear, then, that a peasant community, while often identical to a natural village, could be either a subvillage group, or a supra-village neighborhood. Fundamental to all of these communities, however, were the reciprocal arrangements that allowed their members to express their identities, to build consensus, to perform mutual obligations, and to disagree when their purposes and interests conflicted. It was on the same basis that the villagers formed a discourse that conditioned and shaped their strategies of survival and offered them the means to protect or reproduce their material and symbolic capital in cooperation and in conflict.[3]

It must be stressed that proposing this concept of village society is not to equate the peasant communities in south-central Hebei with "corporate village communities" (*kyodotai*), a term used by some Japanese scholars. The kyodotai idea, when first introduced in the 1930s, was intended to meet the political purpose of the Japanese militarist state. For Japanese researchers, kyodotai embodied the Asiatic ideals of cooperation and community that had survived the intrusion of Western capitalism; they could serve as the basis for the Great East Asian Coprosperity Sphere that the Japanese militarists had envisioned (P. Huang 1985: 28; Duara 1988: 209). As an alternative to individualistic societies of the West, this idea also denoted a harmonious community without competition and conflict. In fact, south-central Hebei villages, despite their high degree of collectivity and solidarity, were full of tensions and conflicts. These conflicts happened between people of the same lineage or separate descent groups, between power contenders, and between outsiders and local residents. The villages in south-central Hebei, in the final analysis, were a peasant universe encompassing at once extensive cooperation and intense competition. The kyodotai idea, though ostensibly connected with a political tradition common to East Asian countries under the historical influence of Confucian culture that emphasized social harmony, does not contribute to understanding the realities of village communities in imperial and Republican China.

Also at issue is the relationship of the community I have focused on in this study to the "standard marketing area" that has been used widely in previous studies of rural China.[4] This study has benefited from G. William Skinner's concept of macroregion and the inherent core-periphery analysis. But the concept of marketing areas, key to his analysis of rural China, is not as valid in describing the social patterns revealed here. The peasants in south-central Hebei were no doubt involved in a regional marketing system as a result of their wide growing of cotton and their reliance on handicraft production for extra income. Their activities in this area certainly surpassed those of their counterparts in the peripheral northeastern Hebei, where the cultivation of commercial crops was very limited. However, the close links with external markets did not necessarily erode the solidarity of their communities. And the integration of local communities with the larger marketing area had not yet produced social ties that overshadowed the peasants' identity with the local community. In fact, the peasants marketed their products primarily to augment family incomes. The consequence of this commercialization was to perpetuate rather than transform the traditional pattern of rural economy that combined farming with family-based handicraft industry, and subsequently to stabilize rather than undermine the traditional community.[5] Therefore, the standard marketing area, a concept that Skinner derives primarily from his observance of peasant activities on the Chengdu plain in southwestern China, is not as useful in understanding governing activities in the peasant community in the core area of North China as it is in interpreting trans-village social and economic activities.

Rural Governance and the Chinese State

Significant efforts have been made to build a sophisticated framework for understanding the Chinese state. Philip Kuhn, for example, interprets the Qing state as a bureaucratic monarchy. Basing his idea on Max Weber's explication of patrimonialism and bureaucracy, Kuhn disputes the received wisdom since Max Weber that has juxtaposed arbitrary power under patrimonialism with routine authority under bureaucracy and presumed a universal tendency of rationalization in which autocrats yield to bureaucrats.[6] Kuhn argues that these two seemingly contradictory forms of power actually lived side by side in the Chinese system. The monarch of the Qing court relied on written codes to regulate his bureaucratic servants and at the same time maintained a distinctive position that enabled his arbitrary exercise of extra-bureaucratic power. He thus dubbed the Chinese state a "bureaucratic monarchy," characterized by the simultaneous coexistence of an autocratic monarchy with its routinized bureaucracy (Kuhn 1990).

Philip Huang (1996) shifts attention from the imperial power to the county magistrate's adjudication of civil disputes. He argues that Weber's thesis of patrimonial bureaucracy is valid in interpreting not only the imperial state but also the operation of the county magistracy. After a thorough investigation of numerous legal cases, Huang concludes that in adjudicating civil disputes, the magistrate acted as both a bureaucrat adhering to standard rules and routine procedures and a morally superior "father-mother official" who relied on informal mediation, and whose power was supposed to be as total as the emperor's. These distinctive characteristics of Qing local government, Huang suggests, may be seen as "products of patrimonial bureaucracy" (P. Huang 1996: 229–34).

Although these interpretations have transcended the old images of despotism, the received wisdom on the Chinese state remains largely limited to its bureaucratic structure and practice at and above the county level. This study has focused instead on informal institutions in villages. What characterized local administration, as in Huailu, was the predominance of endogenous arrangements that assumed day-to-day administrative duties rather than confrontations between the government and village society. The delegation of government functions to local communities was seen in almost every aspect of land taxation that we have examined. In tax collection, for example, the magistrate relied on the xiangdi, a local agent chosen from among the villagers to advance taxes on their behalf. In land administration, the yamen used the same person to write land deeds, prompt the payment of deed taxes, and investigate unofficial deeds. In the management of tax liabilities, the government used the unofficial sheshu to transfer tax duties after land transactions and to update tax rolls. In the investigation of unregistered and untaxed "black land," likewise, the magistrate counted on black land owners' voluntary registration and gentry elites' sponsorship of campaigns against the black land.

An obvious reason behind the government's limited involvement in local governance and its conferring of administrative responsibilities to local communities was the rulers' distrust of local officials and their underlings. It was widely accepted among the ruling elite that the government's interference with local administration, no matter how well-intended it appeared to be, would result in unchecked malfeasance and corruption, for local officials invariably used their power to distort policies for personal gain. Rather than benefiting the people, the government's involvement often became a source of disturbance to local communities. *Wuwei* (effortless action or laissez faire) thus became a political tenet for all Chinese emperors aspiring to be benevolent rulers (Fei 1999 [1946–47]: 336–37). Neo-Confucian scholars since the Song dynasty, too, ardently argued against government intervention in day-to-day governance. In the opinion of Zhu Xi (1130–1200), a leading neo-Confucian master, the best form of local governance was communal cooperation based on the voluntary participation of community members. This cooperation, Zhu Xi believed, cultivated mutuality, reciprocity, and mutual assistance among local residents. It was therefore the most effective and durable method of local administration, embodying the Confucian ideal of "fusion of public and private interests" (*gongsi yiti*) and was preferable to government coercion and control from above.[7]

From the ruling elite's point of view, the dual goals of local governance— to promote the public good and to satisfy the state's need to collect taxes and exercise social control—were not necessarily in conflict with each other. The Confucian political ethic, as reasserted in the writings of neo-Confucian scholars, likened the relationship between the monarch and the people to that between parents and their children. A wise ruler should take care of the livelihood of his childlike people (*zimin*), governing them by virtues and moral teachings rather than administrative means and punishment. "To nourish the people," in the words of Zhu Xi, was a "fundamental" principle in financing and taxation. And the people in return were supposed to serve the ruler with loyalty, fulfilling their obligations in tax payment and labor services just as they had served their parents (Zhang Liwen 2001). Not surprisingly, as neo-Confucian teachings became the orthodoxy in late imperial China, the tenet of "benevolent government" (*renzhi*) came to dominate the official discourse on local governance, exerting tremendous influence on the consciousness and policies of the imperial administrators (Chen Zenghui 2000; Zhang Xingjiu 2000; Liu Chuanguang 2001).

It is in this cultural context of governance that the administrative practices in Huailu villages can be properly perceived. The xiangdi's advance payment of taxes for community members and the latter's obligation to repay the xiangdi and compensate him for serving as a middleman were precisely the sort of voluntary cooperation advocated by neo-Confucian scholars, for such reciprocal arrangements helped promote public well-being and guarantee the government's tax revenue, and also led to many fewer problems than government-imposed systems. Likewise, the county yamen used local agents instead of its own clerks to handle tax transfer and update tax rolls because they were familiar with the actual landholdings in their neighborhood and able to perform their duties. And because they were also subject to the constraints and scrutiny of local communities, they were less likely to engage in excessive wrongdoing than an outsider. Similarly, the magistrate relied on the xiangdi, rather than his own runners or tax farmers, to investigate unofficial deeds in his communities despite his derelictions, for the outsiders' involvement would result in rampant abuses and fraud, which in turn would incur protests from local communities. Finally, the rulers preferred to rely on landowners to voluntarily register their illegal holdings rather than to involve government underlings in the process, again for fear that those personnel were impossible to control. From the ruling elite's point of view, the risk of arousing social turmoil and threats to the legitimacy of a benevolent government far outweighed the limited amount of extra tax income that might be generated by newly taxed land.

It must be emphasized, however, that although the state's delegation of government functions to local society was a universal phenomenon in China before the twentieth century, the actual practices of governance took different forms in different localities as their ecological and social conditions varied. In fact, as we have seen in Huailu villages, different methods existed side by side even in the same county. To fulfill their duties in tax collection and local control, the magistrates, as the lowest-level appointees of the imperial bureaucracy, saw no need to impose the official systems (baojia and lijia) on local communities as long as the local unofficial institutions worked effectively. The magistrates in Huailu invariably acknowledged, respected, and endorsed cungui or xianggui in their handling of lawsuits over xiangdi service or tax collection, despite their deviation from the statutory ones, and at the same time tolerated or turned to the illegal tax-farming business where cooperative arrangements did not exist, such as the collection of taxes on enclaves outside the peasant community and in village communities that were too weak to cooperate in tax payment.[8]

Thus village-state relations in China before the twentieth century cannot be viewed simply in terms of a dichotomous opposition between state and society. Except where gentry elites and/or lineage organizations were so strong as to resist government influences or so weak as to allow the intrusion of extortionate agents, in most parts of rural China, as in the villages in Huailu, informal agents and institutions of local communities routinely carried out administrative functions delegated by the government in the absence of salaried bureaucrats below the county level, and the government did not intervene until disputes arose within the community that threatened the normal functioning of local institutions. Everyday governance in most parts of rural China thus can be characterized as a form of "substantive government," to accentuate the blurring of the distinction between the government and village communities in rural administration, and to distinguish that process from the formalistic administrative system based on systematic codes and a formal hierarchy of personnel, which dominated the Chinese bureaucracy at and above the county level.

To further understand the nature of substantive government, we need to ponder at this point why the Chinese state remained content with its limited reach into local society, and why it did not manage to prevent the possible growth of localism that was believed fatal to imperial regimes in history (M. Mann 1988: 1–31).

I propose that Confucian teachings on benevolent government and concerns about the misdeeds of local officials were not the only reasons behind the government's minimal involvement in local administration. Equally important in shaping the pattern of local governance were the financial needs of the Chinese state, which had to do with its geopolitical setting. Unlike the extremely fragmented Europe in the late-medieval and early-modern periods, when the European monarchs had to expand and maintain a military force as large as possible in order to survive international warfare (Finer 1975; Ardant 1975), China had long since been under a unified empire that had established its cultural, diplomatic, and even military supremacy over the surrounding tributary states. Although the Ming and early Qing dynasties did face frequent threats from the Mongol tribes, in most times the Chinese empire enjoyed peace, prosperity, and superiority over the neighboring peoples. In the meantime, the enormous taxpaying population and the vast taxable territory constituted a tax base so huge that it was unimaginable in Europe. Thus, setting the tax rate at a very low level by European standards would generate enough revenue to support the state apparatus under normal conditions. This vast tax base in turn allowed the Chinese rulers to pursue the "light tax" (qingyao bofu) policy that epitomized "benevolent government" in Confucian political tradition. Obviously, it was China's status as a unified empire and its huge tax source, more than anything else, that explained its low rates of taxes on land, which varied from 2 to 4 percent of land yield in the Qing empire as a whole.

Moreover, unlike the European monarchs in the early-modern period, whose power was greatly offset by rivaling regional lords and autonomous self-governing organs that restricted their rights in taxation (Tilly 1975; Braun 1975), the Chinese political structure was highly centralized, and the imperial court theoretically had absolute control over the bureaucracy down to the county level. Below the county yamen, the ruler had support from gentry elites who identified themselves with the monarch under the influence of Confucian doctrines, as seen in their stipulation and implementation of community covenants that placed tax payment as one of their priorities.

Although the involvement of evil gentry in tax evasion and hidden land was a chronic headache for local administrators, the Chinese ruler had never felt a threat to or restriction of his power from any social groups comparable to that faced by his counterparts in Europe. Therefore, unlike a European monarch who had to combat various forms of localism in the course of taxation and centralization, the Chinese rulers, endowed with tax revenue large enough to support the government in times of peace, felt no need to do so. In fact, so big was the tax base in high-Qing China that it generated more income than it actually needed. Many times the tax surplus allowed the Qing rulers to announce a universal suspension of land taxes throughout the empire (Hu Chunfan 1984; He Ping 1998: 14–26). Tax riots, so rampant and perennial in early-modern European countries, did not become a major challenge for the Chinese rulers until the early twentieth century, when tax surcharges proliferated. The Qing state's decision in 1712 to permanently freeze the head tax quota, a policy that was faithfully observed for the rest of its history, is understandable only in this context.[9] We may then understand why the Chinese rulers were so reluctant to widen the tax base using such means as uncovering black land and taxing land deeds, for these measures often harmed local communities and ran counter to the tenets of benevolent government; and their benefits were insignificant when compared to the readily available tax income that was already sufficient.

So what are the implications of substantive government in local society for understanding the Chinese state? Preexisting theories of the Chinese state do not work perfectly here, be they oriental despotism, patrimonial bureaucracy, or bureaucratic monarchy, for they deal only with the state apparatus itself, including its formal and informal elements at and above the county level, and overlook the actual practices at the village level. To appreciate the nature and functioning of local practices and their importance in the structure of the Chinese state, Michael Mann's concept of "infrastructural power" is useful in this context.

By "infrastructural power," Mann means the ability of the state to penetrate civil society by collecting taxes and information, carrying out the government's directives, and coordinating economic activities. Infrastructural power, according to Mann, contrasts with the "despotic power" exercised by ruling elites over various social groups, which was autonomous and even unlimited because the rulers did not need to consult the ruled. Mann further observes that while despotic power was strong in the histories of many societies, infrastructural power was relatively weak; the reverse is true of modern Western society, where strong infrastructural power has coexisted with despotic power (Mann 1984, 1986).

As for imperial China, we may grossly classify its regular bureaucratic system as one of despotic power, and the informal agents at the village and supra-village level who carried out the duties in tax collection and local control as wielding infrastructural power. From Mann's view, those who held the infrastructural power were of course part of the formal bureaucracy; he does not mention that infrastructural power in imperial China was far from formalized and institutionalized, and was never part of the formal bureaucracy. However, informal infrastructural power was no less important than formal despotic power in the everyday operation of the Chinese administrative system. The Chinese state thus can be best described as a combination of despotism, found in the highly centralized and standardized bureaucratic system at and above the county level, and a laissez-faire tradition in the decentralized, informal institutions in local governance (see also H. Li 2003b).

In sum, the state's reliance on informal institutions in village governance, a pattern of local administration moralized in neo-Confucian discourse and evidenced in varying forms in Huailu county, was not as much a result of the incomplete centralization of the Chinese state or local resistance against state intrusion as the traditional wisdom on the Chinese state has assumed; rather, it was embedded in the geopolitical settings of the Chinese empire and the neo-Confucian teachings on minimal and benevolent government. In the final analysis, what characterizes the village-state relationship in late imperial China was more interdependence than paired opposition.

Continuity and Change in the Twentieth Century

Huailu county witnessed many administrative changes in the early twentieth century. Before the advent of the Guomindang government in 1928, the state had taken measures to absorb rural elites into the formal political process and thereby enlarge its basis of legitimacy, among them the creation of deliberative assemblies and offices in charge of police, education, and finance at the county level, as well as the village head office and primary schools at the local level. These reforms, however, did not effectively extend the government's administrative arm to the village; more often than not the county magistrate had to rely on informal agents and gentry elites, rather than the village head, to carry out his orders, a method that had characterized imperial control of local society before the twentieth century. This method, to be sure, worked well when the land tax remained a fixed quota for the whole county and when the old-style informal agents such as the xiangdi and sheshu were able to fulfill their duties in collecting and administering the fixed land taxes.

What became problematic for the government after 1900 was not the collection of the fixed land taxes; instead it struggled to maximize its income by investigating untaxed black land, imposing surcharges and irregular levies, and taxing land deeds in order to support the newly created self-government projects. It was in these areas that the state found its old methods of control increasingly ineffective. Allowing the xiangdi to retain his role in deed taxation, for example, was tantamount to tolerating the existence of illegal deeds; but farming out the duties of deed taxation to entrepreneurial brokers only resulted in widespread protests from local communities. Letting the elites control the village government and the county assemblies only offered them a legal means of articulating their interests and of opposing the imposition of new taxes. In the investigation of black land, likewise, the government found that the gentry elites were equally unreliable, for they were the largest owners of black land.

In fact, not only were the unofficial agents and the local elites unreliable in carrying out the government's mandates, even the county magistrate himself became a dubious agent of the state when the tax burden increased and elite cooperation remained indispensable for his administration. Unable to break with the landed elites, the magistrate had to compromise between the pressure from above for tax increases and resistance from local elites.

All of these circumstances complicated the predicament of the state when it attempted to increase its tax revenue without reaching further into local society. Several breakthroughs thus took place after 1928 when the villages in south-central Hebei came under the Nationalist (Guomindang) government. The first was the Nationalists' efforts to weaken the gentry elite in local politics. To that end, the new regime abolished the county assemblies and other elite-controlled self-government agencies at the county level as well as the office of village head. Consequently, elite mobilization as a conspicuous phenomenon in the late Qing and early Republican years completely disappeared after 1928. The second was the successful installation of the ward government at the supra-village level and the formally elected xiang government at the local level. The third was the elimination of informal local agents in local control and land taxation, such as the xiangdi and the sheshu, and the shifting of their duties to newly appointed government personnel at the ward and xiangdi levels.

Thus did the Guomindang government depart from the traditional approach of local control and show its determination to penetrate the rural society. Although the implementation of these reforms varied from village to village, the administrative reorganization did indeed enhance the government's tax collection abilities. Without organized resistance from local notables, the government successfully increased its revenues through the "consolidation" of tax liabilities and the collection of many new taxes. The heightened presence of state authorities in village communities also allowed the government to uncover more black land than it had in the past. "State-making" in the rural society, or the creation of a nationwide system under the control of a central government in place of informal local practices, no doubt progressed throughout the late Qing, the early Republican, and the Guomindang periods.

State-making not only brought conspicuous changes to local institutions, but also exposed villagers to new ideas, values, and assumptions that reshaped the way they perceived the externally imposed institutions and articulated their interests. The installation of village government, for example, was accompanied by the introduction of new notions about its legitimacy, such as a formal election of the village head, the requirement that candidates meet age and other qualifications, and the assumption that self-government was linked to the strength and prosperity of the Chinese nation as a whole. These contrasted sharply with their traditional assumptions about informal village leadership, which emphasized one's seniority and prestige. The creation of primary schools, likewise, brought about a new idea that linked primary education with the survival of the nation in the age of imperialism. The school was supposedly not only superior to the old-style private school (sishu), but also critical for ridding the villagers of superstition and improving the quality of the citizenry. Backed by the government and embraced by the elites, these new notions began to influence the villagers' representations of their concerns, especially in lawsuits.

However, the continuity of old institutions and assumptions in the Huailu villages after 1900 was as obvious as the institutional and discursive changes discussed above. Despite the administrative reforms, the peasant communities remained untouched throughout the late Qing and Republican years. Not surprisingly, preexisting social relations, norms, and values continued to shape village leadership. Thus, although the village heads and after 1930 the xiangzhang differed from the traditional community leaders in many ways, they remained first of all representatives of their own communities rather than agents of the state. As we saw in the investigation of black land, for example, the xiangzhang turned out to be as loyal as the former xiangdi and village head to his community, when state policies ran counter to local interests. As a protector of village members, he reported to the government only a token amount of illegal land, although its actual size could be as large as several hundred mu in some villages.

All of these changes and continuities, I suggest, should be seen as phenomena characteristic of the political process in North China villages, which underwent a transition from traditional governance based on local informal institutions and indigenous values to a new way of governance based on national formal systems and discourses. More often than not both the powerful and the ordinary combined the old and the local with the new and the official in their public exchanges and representations. The villagers, for example, did not just insist on community norms and values; they also embraced the imposed concepts on new village offices and primary schools when they realized that those new institutions and ideas could advance their interests and enhance the legitimacy of their claims. The county magistrate, likewise, at once adhered to official regulations in his handling of disputes over the xiangdi service and the village head office, and honored village regulations pertaining to the selection of the xiangdi and popular notions about the qualifications of community leaders. In other words, the government did not just impose its institutions on the village, but also tried to have them legitimized within the community.

Consequently, both official political discourse and popular notions informed the public exchanges among the bureaucrats, local elites, and ordinary villagers. State-making in early twentieth-century China was not just a process in which the new institutions and official discourse superseded local practices and assumptions. It also involved their coexistence and complementary interaction in shaping the local process of legitimization.

It is worth emphasizing that the consequences of state-making varied in different ecological and societal settings. The mutual accommodation between state and village as a pattern of transition to modernity in local governance prevailed mainly in core areas where a strong state was coupled with tight-knit communities. More specifically, the government was able to penetrate the rural society by installing national institutions and disseminating its political discourse to rural elites and the populace because it was itself still stable and accepted as legitimate by local dwellers. And the rural communities were able to reshape the processes of state penetration for their own purposes because they remained cohesive and with their inner workings largely intact. This mutual participation and interpenetration allowed the imposed institutions and notions to grow slowly yet legitimately in the matrix of local informal traditions. It minimized the disruptive impacts of the transition from traditional governance to its modern form in the peasant society and prevented crises of legitimacy for both the state and local powerholders. In contrast, in ecologically unstable localities the increasing pressure of state penetration, especially the multiplying special levies, ate away at traditional protective leadership and gave rise to the tyranny of local bullies and the breakdown of peasant communities, a process that Duara characterizes as "state involution" (1988).

Finally, a few words on local control after 1949. Dramatic changes have taken place in rural China since the victory of the Communist Revolution. The land reform and agricultural collectivization that followed fundamentally weakened kinship ties and wiped out the power structure and property relations that had predominated in peasant communities. At the same time, the transformation of villages into collectives permitted the state's unprecedented penetration of rural social, economic, and political lives. Local institutions and peasant values, which had become interwoven with external systems and notions, lost their foundation amid the unchallenged predominance of state-imposed, nationwide organizations and revolutionary propaganda. Instead, political propaganda came to shape public exchanges between government officials and local dwellers. Community norms, indigenous regulations, and shared assumptions, which had been part and parcel of the open discussions in the early twentieth century, retreated into the villagers' private discourse.

Decollectivization in the 1980s gradually freed the farmers from the state's total control and set in motion a new wave of self-government in the rural communities. Once again, the villages are expected to elect their own leaders, to fund local schools and other public welfare programs on their own, and to shoulder the proliferating fees and taxes imposed from above. In the wake of the state's looser control, traditional institutions, such as kinship organizations and informal associations, have revived and even dominate in many localities (Tang Jun 2001). The waning influence of the government in turn encourages local officials to tolerate and even seek support from traditional resources in local communities for administrative purposes. The mutual engagement between the official and the local, whether in the manner expected by the state or not, once again has come to shape the local process of governance. The century-long transition from the old pattern of rural governance is still in progress, moving toward a destination that has yet to be redefined and reoriented.

Notes

Chapter 1

1. These are official figures from the year 1819 (Hsiao 1960: 5). It should be noted that some yamens also had a "county assistant" (*xiancheng*) and a "chief bookkeeper" (*zhubu*) to assist the magistrate in various administrative tasks and an "inspector" (*xuanjiansi*) in charge of local policing. Although these posts were not widely instituted in nineteenth-century China, they did belong to the regular bureaucracy (Liu Ziyang 1988).

2. Recent studies of the Chinese government at different levels have examined the mechanisms whereby the monarch interacted with high-ranking bureaucrats to keep the officialdom in discipline and at work (Kuhn 1990; Li and Du 1993; Brandauer and Huang 1994; Zhang Fentian 2000; Wu Si 2002), and depicted the organization and functioning, especially judicial administration, of the county office (Wanyan 1994; P. Huang 1996, 2001; Wang Zhenzhong 1997; Reed 2000).

3. As Martin Yang observed in his study of Taitou village, Shandong province, "local affairs have always been dominated by the village aristocracy, the clan heads and the official leaders. Individual villagers, or individual families, have never taken an active role in initiating, discussing, or making plans. By and large, the people have been ignorant, docile, and timid as regards public affairs" (Yang 1945: 241). Kungchuan Hsiao made a similar comment on the character of Chinese peasants: "Villagers, being long accustomed to despotic rule and very largely illiterate, displayed a decidedly passive mentality. They were usually more anxious to avoid personal troubles than to promote general well-being. Moreover, they seldom knew economic prosperity. Many of them lived from hand to mouth and had thus neither the means nor leisure to be interested in community affairs" (Hsiao 1960: 264). Marxist historians in China shared essentially the same view about the Chinese peasantry. As a class-in-itself, we are told, the peasants lacked class consciousness and solidarity. Their petty producer status and fragmented existence led them to political passivity and reaction. Therefore, their social existence was no different from Marx's image of French peasantry as "a sack of potatoes" (Marx 1951). They became politically active only after they were enlightened and mobilized by revolutionary force from outside, thus becoming a class-for-itself.

4. According to G. William Skinner's definition, a core area generally has a higher density of population and a higher proportion of arable land than the periphery. The land in the former is more fertile than in the latter. The proportion of irrigated acreage in the core is generally greater than in the periphery. And, finally, the local economies of core areas are more commercialized than those of peripheral areas (Skinner 1977: 283).

5. These macroregions include North China, Northwest China, Lower Yangzi, Middle Yangzi, Upper Yangzi, Southeast Coast, Lingnan, and Yun-Gui.

6. For recent discussions of the validity and problems of this concept, see Cao Shuji 2001 and Cartier 2002.

7. Aside from North China, the focus of this study, past scholarship has also covered Northwest China (Schran 1976; Keating 1997), Lower Yangzi (P. Huang 1990; Bernhardt 1992), Middle Yangzi (Perdue 1987; Averill 1987 and 1990; J. Chen 1992), and Upper Yangzi (Kapp 1973; Endicott 1988).

8. What has been in dispute is the status of Western Shandong or, to a larger extent, the Hebei-Henan-Shandong border area (or the so-called Huang-Yun) in the North China macroregion. This area was traditionally treated as part of the core of North China, as Skinner indicated in his original study. Recent scholarship, however, has emphasized the vast contrasts between the northern and southern parts of this area. Scholars generally agree that the northern part of this area, or more exactly northwestern Shandong, was a poor agricultural region with extremely low yields. It shared with most of the North China plain a similar insecurity of natural environment, low stratification of peasantry, weak rural elites, and an open community with a high rate of migration. Southwest Shandong or the southern part of Huang-Yun region, in contrast, was favored with higher land fertility and a more prosperous economy, which in turn supported strong landlordism and tight-knit communities based on personal ties between the landed patrons and their clients. However, like the Northwest, this area was also vulnerable to natural disasters because of flooding along the Yellow River. As a border area with the weakest government control and the sparsest gentry presence, it was further plagued with endemic banditry. Esherick thus treats this area, together with the rest of Southern Shandong, as a periphery of the Lower Yangzi macroregion, where the Grand Canal connected South Shandong cities with a commercial network centered on the Lower Yangzi cities (Esherick 1987: 5–28). Pomeranz, however, adheres to Skinner's original classification and treated his Huang-Yun as a *historical* core region of the North China macroregion because of the area's high population density and high yields per acre. But he quickly points out that as a result of the decline of the canal and the growing importance of coastal trade and railroads in the modern era, most of Huang-Yun was transformed into part of the periphery, which he believed to be the largest displacement of any macroregion's core (Pomeranz 1993: 2–11).

9. In addition, there are also over 300 *juan* of mainly cadastres and daily records of tax collection of the early- and mid-Qing period, some of which have been studied by Chinese scholars (Jiang Taixin 1991; Shi Zhihong 1984; Pan Jie and Tang Shiru 1984). Because of this unusually complete collection, the "old regime" archives of Huailu county were first preserved in Beijing Municipal Archive and then moved

to Hebei Provincial Archive, rather than kept by Huailu County Archive (now Luquan Municipal Archive) itself, as most county archives normally do.

10. See, for example, Hsiao 1960; Ch'ü 1962; Fu 1993; and Andrew and Rapp 2000. The Chinese historians who embraced the notion of "Asiatic mode of production" tended to describe the traditional Chinese state as a form of despotism intrinsic to the stagnant Asiatic society (Wu Ze 1993; Gu Zhun 1982, 1999). The more "orthodox" Marxist historians on the other hand characterized the Chinese state as a centralized bureaucracy inimical to the emerging "democratic" ideas in the last phase of the "feudal" society in Chinese history (Hou Wailu 1979; Hu Rulei 1979).

11. Philip Kuhn pointed out this possibility as early as the 1970s, noting that administrators in imperial China tended to rely on local social organs as the basis for their control in order to produce the desired results, as indicated in the fact that the baojia unit was usually based on a natural village rather than a group of 100 households as the state designed. The employment of local indigenous social organs, Kuhn suggested, produced the characteristic ambiguity of sub-county administrative systems, in which the principles of control and autonomy were not entirely separable. However, without solid evidence to support this hypothesis, Kuhn quickly pointed out that the idea about a mutually supportive relationship between state control and local autonomy, found in the minds of Qing bureaucrats and literati, did not work at all in actuality because of the obvious weaknesses of the bureaucratic system, such as the rule of avoidance, which prevented the magistrate from developing interests in improving the welfare of local society (Kuhn 1975).

12. Max Weber's interpretation of the Chinese legal system is suggestive to my conception of substantive governance. Weber describes the administrative system in imperial China as basically anti-formalist and of patriarchal character. Chinese rulers under this system tended to seek "substantive justice rather than formal law" (Weber 1951: 101–2). Weber's assertion is not valid for the formal bureaucracy of the Chinese empire. The actual practice of civil justice at the county level, as we know now, was also largely based on legal codes and far from arbitrary (P. Huang 1996). However, the imperial rulers stipulated no concrete codes to regulate sub-county administration, which was based largely on established practices or initiatives from either the administrator or local society. As a result, local governance remained largely substantive rather than formalistic throughout the imperial and early republican periods.

13. Clearly, the grounds on which the administrative cases were resolved differed greatly from ordinary civil cases. For civil disputes, the magistrate based his rulings primarily on the legal code, while community mediators usually took into account state law, the sense of right and wrong, as well as local power relations when working out a solution (P. Huang 1996: chapters 3 and 4). In the settlement of administrative cases, however, "village regulations" rather than legal statutes were at work.

14. In addition to Scott 1976, a number of studies employ the moral economy approach, including Polanyi 1957; Thompson 1963, 1971; Wolf 1969; and Taylor 1976, 1982. The rational-choice theory is elaborated in Downs 1957; Schultz 1964; Olson 1965; Popkin 1979; Hechter 1983, 1987, and 1990. For a full discussion of the implications of both frameworks for understanding Chinese peasants, see Little 1989, 1998.

15. Bourdieu thus put it, " . . . practices cannot be directly deduced either from the objective conditions, defined as the instantaneous sum of the stimuli which may appear to have directly triggered them, or from the conditions which produced the durable principles of their production. These practices can be accounted for only by relating the objective structures defining the social conditions of the production of the habitus which engendered them to the conditions in which this habitus is operating, that is, to the conjuncture which, short of a radical transformation, represents a particular state of this structure" (1977: 78).

16. To depart from the concept of narrow economic rationality characterized by utility maximization, recent theoretical endeavors have suggested some insightful frameworks to interpret patterns of human behavior and enduring social arrangements. The most noteworthy among them are "context-bound rationality" (Nee 1998: 10–11) and "broadened practical rationality" (Little 1998: 92–94).

Chapter 2

1. Today south-central Hebei remains the "granary" of the province. With only 33 percent of the cultivated land in the province, this area produced 45 percent of the province's grain output and 69 percent of its marketed grains in the 1980s. In contrast, the lowland areas had fully 60 percent of the province's cultivated land yet produced just 25 percent of its output (Xie Feng 1990: 604).

2. See Table 4 for a list of the twenty-four counties in south-central Hebei.

3. The Land Council (*tudi weiyuanhui*) of the Nationalist government estimated in 1937 that 71.35 percent of rural households were owner-cultivators, 10.95 percent were part-tenants, 9.89 percent were tenants and laborers, and the rest landlords (Tudi weiyuanhui 1937: 34). Sun Benwen, on the basis of different surveys, observed in 1943 that 64 percent of rural households in the North China Plain (including those in Hebei, Shanxi, Henan, and Shandong) were owner-cultivators, 19 percent part-tenants, and the rest landless (Sun Benwen 1943: 61). For further discussions of land distribution in North China, see Li Sanmou and Cao Jianqiang 2001; Xu Hao 1999; and Zhang Peiguo 1998, 2000.

4. Conventionally, northeastern Hebei covers twenty counties north and east of the Beijing–Tianjing railroad. See Table 4 for a list of these counties and Map 2 for their locations.

5. The annual temperature in the south-central region is 12.2 to 13.7°C, which is 2–6°C higher than in the northeast. The gap in their temperatures in January is even bigger: -4.5°C to -2.5°C in south-central Hebei and -17°C to -6°C in the northeast. Likewise, the frost-free period in south-central Hebei is as long as 200 to 220 days, whereas it lasts for only 100 to 194 days in the northeast (HBSZ 1993, 3: 440, 450, and 456).

6. These data as well as all data on northeastern Hebei are based on statistics for the twenty counties in the area. Data on south-central Hebei are based on statistics of the twenty-four counties surrounding Shijiazhuang (see Map 2). These data come primarily from three sources: Zhang Xingyi 1933, which contains statistics on land, population, and cropping in individual counties in the province; Li Hongyi 1977

[1934], which has data on land taxation; and Mantetsu surveys, which offer details on villages.

7. For a general discussion of the geographic distribution of different cropping patterns in the North China plain during the Qing, see Zheng Qidong 1992 and Cong Hanxiang 1992.

8. In the mountainous area of northeastern Hebei, where the weather is cold, peasants normally grew one crop (sorghum or maize) a year. In the hilly lands and piedmont plain areas south of Yanshan Mountain, this pattern was coupled with the three-crops-every-two-years method. This rotation system had two patterns. In one, peasants planted maize in the spring and harvested in the fall. Wheat followed and was harvested the next summer. The wheat was followed by sorghum, to be harvested in the fall, leaving the land fallow until the next spring for maize. In the other pattern, peasants planted sorghum (or millet), wheat, and soybean in sequence in two years. The three-crops-every-two-years method was more widespread in south-central Hebei. Here the peasants grew millet, wheat, and soybeans in sequence, or alternatively, cotton, millet, and wheat. Equally prevalent in this area, however, was two-crops-a-year, especially in the Shijiazhuang region, where people planted maize immediately after the harvest of winter wheat (therefore called summer maize). The maize was harvested in the fall and was then followed by wheat (HBSZ 1995, 16: 133–34, 273–76).

9. For a detailed discussion of farm yields under the different rotation systems in south-central and northern Hebei regions, see Huaiyin Li 2000, chap. 2. It should be noted that in addition to farming income, the peasants in south-central Hebei also engaged in nonagricultural activities that contributed to their total income by nearly 30 percent (Hou Jianxin 2001b).

10. By the official conversion rate, one tael equaled 1.5 yuan or 4,023 wen (656.1.243, 1915; 656.1.1223, 1920; see beginning of the References Cited section for an explanation of these numbers citing the Huailu archives).

11. Total land acreage in Huailu was 669,600 mu in 1913 (656.1.103, 1913).

12. According to the Huailu county government's answers to the Zhili provincial government's survey in 1913, the cultivating expense (including costs of seeds, seedlings, fertilizers, and fodder, expenses in ploughing, weeding, crop-watching, mid-ploughing, and all other related costs) was 4 yuan per mu for irrigated land and 2 yuan per mu for dry land. The cultivator's net income after deducting all of these expenses was 3 yuan per mu from irrigated land and 1.5 yuan per mu from dry land (656.1.103, 1913).

13. The average tax rate in 130 counties of Hebei province was 0.172 yuan per mu (Li Hongyi 1977 [1934]: 6382–93). Note that this rate is lower than Buck's estimation for the North China plain as a whole (he calls it the "inter wheat-kaoliang area"). According to Buck, the "main tax" in this area increased to 0.93 yuan per acre or 0.153 yuan per mu in 1932, and the "surtax" (or surtaxes here) was 0.75 yuan per acre or 0.123 yuan per mu (Buck 1937: 324). The main tax and surtax thus combined to 0.276 yuan per mu. However, land tax in North China was in general much lower than in the south. The tax rate in most southern counties of Jiangsu province, for example, was already as high as over 0.60 or 0.70 yuan per mu in 1912 and rose to over

1.00 yuan by 1934 (Bernhardt 1992: 210).

14. Recent studies have stressed the moderate nature of land tax in early twentieth-century China. Thomas Rawski, for example, argues that land taxes together with public spending accounted for less than 10 percent of total agricultural output during the prewar decades (1912–36), and the tax burden did not exceed 5 to 6 yuan per head. Furthermore, in the government's tax revenues, land taxes accounted for only a small proportion; the government relied more and more on revenues from nonagricultural taxes on industry, transport, and commerce. He therefore concludes that "warlords proved incapable of wresting more than a small fraction of economic output from producers and consumers" (Rawski 1989: 19–20; see also Faure 1989 for similar comments).

15. Jerome Chen, for example, writes, "[T]he surtaxes were resorted to by the warlords along the lower reaches of the Yangtze—in Kiangsu 147 kinds, in Chekiang 73 kinds, and in Hupei and Kiangsi 61 kinds. In these provinces the surtaxes exceeded land tax proper by 26 times in Kiangsu, 3.8 in Chekiang, 86 times in Hupei, and 9.5 times in Kiangsi. This was the state of affairs before 1934, five years after the founding of the Nanking government" (J. Chen 1969: 31). Similar views of exorbitant taxation in Republican China are found in other studies (Chen Han-seng 1933, 1936; Eastman 1974; Gilin 1967; Sheridan 1966; Tawney 1932; Young 1965, 1971).

Chapter 3

1. Kung-chuan Hsiao made a similar appraisal of the baojia (Hsiao 1960: 82–83).

2. After the abolition of the lijia system in the early eighteenth century, these lizhang personnel survived and retained their original duties of recording changes in tax liability and updating tax rolls. Some of them continued their illegal baoshou business in spite of the government's prohibition.

3. In some parts of Huailu county people called the xiangdi a "xiangzhang" as well. In fact, as some archival records of disputes over the xiangdi service indicate, the two names were interchangeable and might refer to the same person. The term xiangzhang appeared very often in villagers' plaints, while xiangdi was the standard term in official documents.

4. According to the 1876 edition of Huailu Xianzhi, there were 197 villages in the county in the late Qing period. The total population of this county at the time when the gazetteer was compiled was 176,741. If each household had an average of 4.86 members (Jiang Taixin 1991), there would have been 36,366 households. Each village thus had about 184 households or a population of 897 on average. In fact, however, the size of a natural village ranged from several dozen to over 700 households. The village number increased to 211 by the late 1920s because of changes in administrative divisions, which grouped them into eight police wards (jingqu). These villages were further organized into 182 xiang in 1931 under the County Reorganization Act promulgated by the Nationalist government in 1929. Above the xiang were 8 wards (qu) (Hebei sheng Minzhengting 1933).

5. The number of pai in a village ranged from two to fourteen, with an average of four or five. Each pai contained twenty to fifty households. The subdivision of pai

tended to exist in villages having a large number of households. The biggest village I found was Shanxiayi village, which had over 700 households and consisted of eleven pai (656.1.1065, 1918; 656.2.967, 1927).

6. A joint statement by three xiangdi from their respective villages (Nanxinzhuang, Duanzhuang, and Gujiayu) in 1927 best illustrates this arrangement in tax payment: "Our villages are all located over ten li south of the county seat. . . . Every year when the two periods for land tax collection [spring and autumn] begin, the taxpaying households always pay taxes by themselves in accordance with old regulations. That means the individual households in our villages have to deliver their taxes to the collecting stations on their own, and they each are responsible for their respective tax dues. The xiangdi was only responsible for beating the gong and prompting them to pay; he does not advance the taxes on their behalf. This has always been the case and has never been disordered" (656.2.992, 1927).

7. The xiangdi fund was 40,000 wen in Yaoli village (656.1.1099, 1919); 30,900 wen in Xujiazhuang village (656.2.814, 1926); and 30,000-odd wen in Nangucheng village (656.2.27, 1921). The conversion rate of silver-dollar yuan to copper-cash wen was 1:1,500 in 1921 and 1:3,881 in 1926.

8. Land rented in Huailu in the 1910s and 1920s for between 3,000 and 4,000 wen per mu (656.1.1099, 1919). If the rent of the reserved land averaged 3,500 wen per mu, the xiangdi in Nanzhuang could receive a rent of 35,000 wen, which was just about the amount of the xiangdi fund in other villages.

9. Take Xujiazhuang village, for example. Although this village had a public fund amounting to 30,900 wen, the incumbent xiangdi made advance payments totaling 101,651 wen in 1925, which was more than three times the fund (656.2.814, 1926).

10. Because the length of the measuring stick varied from village to village, disputes arose when a transaction occurred between parties from different villages. In 1912, for example, a xiangdi of Xilonggui village sued a buyer from the neighboring Nanlonggui village who insisted on using the stick of his village (which was shorter than the other village's) to measure the land. After the village head and the ward police failed to mediate the dispute, the magistrate sent out a runner to measure the land with an official stick of the county government and finally settled the dispute (656.1.16, 1912).

11. The Qing state intended this quasi-official to be responsible for "the management of tax payment, disputes over land and house, the clarification of lawsuit plaints, the handling of thieves and cases involving the killing of a person." When there was labor service, it is also his duty to supply implements and to convene and control the laborers (Huangchao wenxian tongkao 21, "zhiyikao" 1).

12. I disagree with Prasenjit Duara here, who treats the xiangbao system in Baodi as a cooperative arrangement (Duara 1988: 52).

13. Wang Fuming (1995) shows that the xiangbao system had already lost its original function and given way to tax-farming even before 1900. "In all the files available," the author observes, "few cases are found in which the xiangbao directly received the tax roll from the government and prompted tax payment. It appears that the xiangbao was mainly assisting the shushou or yamen runners to hasten the tax payment" (Wang Fuming 1995: 37). What was in practice thus was most likely the tax

farming business under the old framework of the xiangbao system, a phenomenon confirmed by other studies (see especially Li Hongyi 1977 [1934]).

Chapter 4

1. On average, the villagers brought to court only two disputes over the service per year, with at most three or four cases a year (see Table 8). This incidence is quite close to that of the "administrative cases" (involving the appointment and duties of the xiangbao or paitou, the counterparts of the xiangdi) in late nineteenth-century Baodi county, east of Beijing. The average number of administrative cases in Baodi was 2.15 per year between 1861 and 1881 (see P. Huang 1996: table 19). Note that the population of this county was slightly higher than that of Huailu. In 1932, the population was 312,282 in Baodi and 276,592 in Huailu (Li Hongyi 1977 [1934]: 6548–51). However, it is disproportionally lower than the number of civil lawsuits an average county court would receive in the Republican period (100–200 new lawsuits per year) (see P. Huang 1996: table 19).

2. Similar statements are found in 656.1.554, 1916; 656.2.967, 1927; 656.2.1120, 1928.

3. In all of the thirty-four recorded disputes over xiangdi service, fifteen case files (43 percent) contain just a single plaint with the magistrate's initial comment. Another eight (24 percent) include a report from either the policeman or the village head on the result of mediation under the magistrate's instruction. The remaining eleven cases (33 percent) are complete lawsuits, including petitions and counterpetitions from the disputants as well as records of court sessions. By and large these disputes evinced the patterns identified by Philip Huang in his study of Qing civil justice. His study shows that, of those disputes evolving into lawsuits, a large portion were settled through what he calls the "semiformal" method characterized by intense interactions between the court and the litigants and their would-be mediators; only a small number were resolved through formal court sessions (P. Huang 1996).

4. The xiangyue, by the Qing state's design, was the person to take charge of ideological indoctrination in his community. In most places, however, this personnel was merged with the baojia system and no longer existed in the nineteenth century. The survival of the xiangyue in Shanxiayi village was just one of the few exceptions.

5. As Pierre Bourdieu pointed out, a leader in precapitalist society maintained his authority by conforming to collective norms. In such a system, "the 'great' are those who can least afford to take liberties with the official norms, and . . . the price to be paid for their outstanding value is outstanding conformity to the values of the group, the source of all symbolic value. . . . The system is such that the dominant agents have a vested interest in virtue; they can accumulate political power only by paying a personal price, and not simply by redistributing their goods and money; they must have the 'virtues' of their power because the only basis of their power is 'virtue'" (Bourdieu 1977: 193–94).

Chapter 5

1. As an exception, in 1926, when the war between the allied northern warlords headed by Wu Peifu and the northwestern warlord Feng Yuxiang intensified and military expenses skyrocketed, the Huailu government ordered all its taxpayers to pay their taxes by the fifteenth day of the eighth month, or two months earlier than the normal deadline, and started the advance collection of the next year's land tax immediately on the next day.

2. Written in a standard format, the notice mandated that "the gentry and people of the county as well as the xiangdi and taxpaying households" (*heyi shenmin bing xiangdi huahu rendeng*) go to the tax-collecting station (*lianggui*) promptly and pay taxes in full, regardless of the fact that in most of the county it was the xiangdi who paid in advance all the taxes for his village or his sub-village pai. Changes took place as late as in 1925, when the notice was further distributed to individual villages and was addressed directly to "all the xiangdi within the county" (*heyi xiangdi*). In that notice, the magistrate requested the xiangdi to "represent" his own village and to pay the taxes incumbent on his village (656.1.366, 1915–26).

3. Aside from the bailiff, a clerk (*shuji*) of the tax-collecting station could also petition against the delinquent xiangdi. For example, Lu Duowen, the shuji of Station C (*bingzi gui*), filed a petition on July 24, 1917 (two months after the deadline of the first collection period) against Xu Shuren, the xiangdi of Liangzheng village, who owed land tax of 36.688 yuan and a police fee of 18,426 wen. The shuji claimed that he had sent a bailiff to collect the debt several times, but the xiangdi had not yet paid. Therefore he asked for a summons of that xiangdi (656.1.750, 1917).

4. The miscellaneous charges mentioned earlier in this chapter, such as the melting fee and the administration fee, were attached to the land tax and were not separate surtaxes.

5. Public funds existed mostly in communities of a single descent group, where a piece of "public land" was reserved to generate sufficient rent to meet the tax quota of the whole lineage (see, e.g., 656.2.27, 1921). In most communities, however, the xiangdi had to borrow money to meet the tax quota and had to pay the interest from his own pocket.

6. Qiao Yongfang, the xiangdi of Nanqiema village, for example, complained in his petition to the magistrate that when he prompted the taxpaying households in his village to fulfill their duties, "all resisted" (*ju shi kangwei*). He thus had to advance the taxes for all those who failed to pay by the deadline. A Qiao Luohe, who owed him a total of 13.1 yuan, repaid him just 4 yuan and refused to pay the balance. The magistrate thus sent a policeman to the village, urging the delinquent taxpayer to clear his debt. A week later, the policeman reported that Qiao Luohe had done so (656.1.1091, 1919). In December 1924, for another example, a xiangdi named Wang Zhan from Nanguan village charged three of his fellow villagers with not paying a balance of 10.52 yuan. Again the magistrate responded by sending a policeman to the village, and the delinquent taxpayers repaid the xiangdi the balance immediately (656.2.438, 1924).

7. The same method of dispute settlement was used in most civil cases during the late imperial period (P. Huang 1996).

8. Unlike ordinary taxable land, enclaves both inside and outside Huailu county had been exempted from paying the nonstatutory chaiyao during imperial times. It was only in 1916, when the chaiyao (which was drastically reduced or completely canceled during the first years of the Republic) was restored in most counties in Hebei province, that the enclave owners were required to pay the chaiyao (656.1.243, 1916).

9. The tax quotas of these outside enclaves owned by Huailu residents mounted to 599 taels, among which were 291 taels taxed by Zhengding county, 40 taels by Luancheng county, 119 taels by Yuansi county, 17 taels by Jingxing county, 10 taels by Pingshan county, and 120 taels incumbent on lands owned by temples (656.1.243, 1916).

10. For example, in February 1918, Han Shijie, the above-mentioned sheshu of Luancheng county, charged as many as twenty-three households of Tunli village with "refusing to pay taxes" despite his "repeated promptings." The magistrate immediately issued a summons to all the accused. The policeman who sent the summons soon came back with a report that all the villagers accused had delivered their taxes to Luancheng county. Attached to his report were the receipts the taxpayers received and a petition from the xiangdi of that village to close the case (656.1.909, 1918).

11. One Su Kuan from Xuying village, for instance, was summoned to Huailu court on January 7, 1917, because of his failure to repay Han Shijie, the sheshu of the neighboring Luancheng county, 0.07 tael Han had advanced for him. Su was later released on bail, after pledging to go to the seat of Luancheng county to deliver his tax payment within ten days (656.1.637, 1916). In a similar case, a bailiff from the neighboring Zhengding county charged Wang Yuyou of Xiaoma village with refusing to pay him 0.0286 tael of tax he had advanced. Wang was soon summoned to Huailu yamen. His excuse for not reimbursing the bailiff, as he testified during the courtroom investigation, was that his plot had recently been purchased by a railway company and his tax liability had not yet been transferred. The magistrate nevertheless ordered Wang to deliver the tax incumbent on the plot to the court before his liability was formally transferred (656.2.270, 1923).

12. A sheshu of Luancheng county named Liu Liu, for example, filed a plaint in July 1915 against the xiangdi of Jiacun village in Huailu county. According to Liu Liu, he had advanced the taxes for a household in that village. When he brought the receipt to the village and asked the xiangdi to prompt the villager's repayment, the xiangdi "firmly refused to take care of [his request]" (*ying bu guanli*). Liu Liu therefore petitioned for a summons of the xiangdi in order to get his money back. The Huailu magistrate immediately summoned the accused xiangdi at the request of his colleague in Luancheng county (656.1.400, 1915).

13. As usual, Liu handed over the tax roll to Han at the beginning of the collection period in 1916. He then visited the village several times, urging the xiangdi to prompt his fellow villagers to pay the taxes due. According to Liu's charge, Han repeatedly refused the sheshu, alleging that his fellow villagers would not deliver the taxes until they saw the official notice from the magistrate of Luancheng county. Without the xiangdi's assistance, the sheshu failed to collect the taxes and submitted

a petition to his own county yamen against the xiangdi. At the neighboring county's request, the Huailu magistrate summoned Han to court. During the court session held on May 20, the xiangdi claimed that he had just prompted his villagers to go to Luancheng county to deliver taxes. The magistrate nevertheless detained the xiangdi and was to send him under escort to the neighboring county for further proceedings. A week later, however, Han informed the magistrate that all households in his village had made their payments to Luancheng county and submitted all of the receipts with his petition. The magistrate sent a letter to his colleague in Luancheng county, asking him to verify that the villagers had paid all their taxes. Without the Luancheng magistrate's prompt reply, the xiangdi was detained in the county seat until June 13, when the village head from Nanqiema village provided bail to have him released (656.1.607, 1916).

14. Likewise, most xiangdi who were accused of noncooperation were tax-prompting xiangdi, for they felt no obligation to help the sheshu collect taxes in the absence of related village regulation. Disputes involving tax-advancing xiangdi, in contrast, were few, for local regulation required them to repay the sheshu for their fellow villagers. There are just two cases available in Huailu archives that document disputes with the tax-advancing xiangdi over enclave taxes. The xiangdi who was charged with refusing to repay the advanced taxes for his villagers quickly went to the neighboring county and paid off all the taxes due under the magistrate's instruction (656.1.1248, 1920; 656.1.1214, 1920).

Chapter 6

1. The deed tax quota for Huailu county was set at 2,980 taels after 1902, which was the amount of deed tax actually collected in that year in Huailu.

2. During imperial times, however, the deed tax was required to be remitted to the provincial treasury in full (*jingzheng jingjie*) (*Hubu zeli*, 10: Tianfu 4).

3. The statutory rate of the deed tax was 3 percent of the sales value of the property during the Qing (*Hubu zeli*, 10: Tianfu 4). By the nineteenth century, it had been increased to 4 percent, of which three-fourths was to be remitted to the provincial government and the rest to be kept by the county yamen as administrative fees. This rate did not change until 1900, when it was reduced to 3.3 percent of the sales value; the proportion remitted to the province remained the same, while the administrative fees dropped to 0.3 percent of the sale price. To finance new-style schools, the deed tax was increased by 1.65 percent of the sales value in 1905, bringing the deed tax to 4.95 percent of the sales value. The deed tax increased to 6 percent of the sales value after 1916 under the *guanzhong* (official middleman) system. It was divided among the provincial government (1 percent), self government bodies (2 percent), county government (0.75 percent), the guanzhong (1.5 percent as his "commission"), and the *sizhong* or unofficial middleman (0.75 percent as his "commission"). This apportioning was changed slightly after 1919 under the *jianzhengren* (official notary) system: 1.5 percent went to the provincial government, 2 percent to self-government bodies, 0.7 percent to county government, 1 percent to the notary as his commission, 0.3 percent to schools and public welfare, and 0.5 to the *chengshuo*

or unofficial middleman as his commission (655.1.876, 1904; 655.1.884, 1905; 656.1.967, 1917–19).

4. White deeds often became a source of dispute between the old owner and the new owner when the former claimed ownership over the property he had sold. The latter often found himself in an unfavorable position in such disputes, for the white deed remained invalid in the government's opinion (see P. Huang 1996).

5. The official deed papers were printed with serial numbers and affiliated with deed tabs (*qiwei*). The stubs of the deed tabs (*qigen*) were to be filled out with the names and addresses of both the seller and the buyer. And the price of the property and the amount of deed tax paid were to be written on the perforation that separated the deed tab and its stub. That way the provincial commissioner hoped to forestall the county yamen's embezzlement of deed taxes and its practice of tampering with deed tabs (*datou xiao wei*, literally, "big head and small tail," a phrase used to refer to the yamen clerks' practice of entering on the deed tab a price less than the value of the property listed on the deed).

6. The number went from 1,600 copies in 1888 to 1,300 copies in 1895; 1,000 copies in 1902; 900 copies in 1906; and 700 copies in 1907 (655.1.835, 1884 through 655.1.880, 1907).

7. I found only one case: the xiangdi of Beiganzi village accused one Feng Tonghe of his village of using a white deed instead of an official deed form and of not paying deed tax. In court, the magistrate blamed the accused for failing to pay deed tax and for tampering with the price in his deed. But he nevertheless exempted him from paying a fine, which would have been half the price of his new property, and merely ordered him to pay the deed tax and to submit a pledge that he would do so in a timely fashion (655.1.829, 1885).

8. There were twelve she in Lingshou and Luancheng counties (*Lingshou xianzhi* 1874, 1:16; *Luancheng xianzhi* 1872, 2:4) and fourteen she in Jingxing county (*Jingxing xianzhi* 1875, 9: 43).

9. Huailu county had fourteen li in the early Ming; their number had increased to eighteen li by the sixteenth century. The eighteen she of the early Qing were identical with the eighteen li of the Ming (*Huailu xianzhi* 1990 [1522–66]: 539–40).

10. For further discussion of illegal practices in the management of tax liabilities, see Xu Yushui 1934; Wang Yuanbi 1935; Yao Shusheng 1936; Chen Dengyuan 1938: 180–81; Hsiao 1960: 107; Saeki 1965; Yamamoto 1980; Chen Zhenhan 1989: 292.

11. The sheshu's fraud in compiling the tax rolls was no doubt the chief reason for confusion over tax liabilities. But the evasion of tax duties by taxpayers also contributed to the chaotic situation in tax management. The sheshu, though he lived in a village and had direct contacts with villagers, was unable to oversee land transactions in as many as a dozen or more villages in his charge, thus leaving opportunities for landowners to evade their tax obligations. One Zhang Fuxiang of Nanhaishan village, for example, had bought 50-odd mu of land in 1915 and avoided taking over the tax quota (1.32 taels) affiliated with it. The xiangdi, Hu Jiyun, who was responsible for any payment in arrears, thus had paid the tax out-of-pocket and brought his dispute with the buyer to court. On the magistrate's instruction, Zhang pledged to have this tax liability transferred to his name and to repay the monies the xiangdi had

advanced for him (656.1.966, 1918). Tax liabilities might be even more complicated if the land changed hands several times without its tax liability being transferred as well. One Su Jinxiang of East Xuying village was thus petitioned by a fellow villager, Su Kegang, because he had bought from the petitioner an 8 mu plot of land without transferring the tax quota to his name and had further sold the land to yet another villager who again did not transfer the tax quota (656.3.435, 1931).

Chapter 7

1. The length of these files varies. Most include just a few pages, usually covering a plaint and the magistrate's comment, sometimes also a counterplaint and an investigation report. They are used here for general discussions of the commencement of the village government, the reasons for disputes, and the election of the village head. The bulk of my discussion, however, focuses on a few disputes about which there are detailed records. These cases reveal the complexity of power relations in the peasant communities and the villagers' opinions of local leaders.

2. Wang Fuming (1995) suggests that village heads were installed in Baodi in the Xuantong years (1909–11). Records from Huailu indicate that it happened earlier. A village head from Yudi village, when petitioning for retirement in 1913, asserted that he had served as village head since Guangxu 33 (1907) (656.1.70, 1913). Another village head from Xiaobi village claimed in 1921 in his petition for retirement that "it has been over a dozen years . . . since I was elected by fellow villagers as the village head" (656.2.140, 1921). And in Yaojiali village the village head stated in 1919 that he "had served as village head for fifteen or sixteen years" (656.1.1099, 1919–20). The village head of Daguo claimed in 1921 that he had been the officeholder for over twenty years (656.2.139, 1921).

3. According to a resolution passed by the Huailu county preparatory council in 1922, the village head had to "have long held a good reputation among fellow villagers, and be familiar with office work" (*sufu xiangwang, bangong shuxi*). This preference for village notables remained unchanged in the early 1930s, when the Guomindang government replaced the village head with the xiangzhang. To be a xiangzhang candidate, according to the newly implemented local government reorganization act, one had to have accomplished at least one of the following: passed the civil service examination; served the government; taught elementary school or graduated from a middle school; received self-government training; or successfully managed local welfare as reported to, and verified by, the county government (Cheng Maoxing 1936: 258–75). Clearly, the state attempted to absorb local elites into the xiang government, for few simple villagers could meet these specifications.

4. The following (656.2.814, 1926) is an example of such a certificate of appointment:

> *Huailu County Government Certificate of Appointment*
> This is to appoint Liu Yurui as the vice–village head of Xuzhuang Village.
> September 16, the eleventh year of the Republic of China
> (Seal of Huailu County)
> Magistrate Cheng Wenmou

5. In Huailu, the villagers reportedly chose their village heads through a vil-lagewide election. See, e.g., 656.1.70, 1913; 656.1.377, 1915; 656.2.814, 1926; 656.1.561, 1906; 656.2.2, 1921. In 1921, for example, in order to have the village head and deputy head's vacancies filled in Dongkun village, the magistrate instructed the ward police to order the village "to elect an appropriate person to take over [the office]." Consequently, the ward police notified the xiangdi of the village that the election would be held on the eighth day of the first month. "At nine o'clock in that morn-ing, Yao Guicai, the head of the ward police [xunzhang], along with a policeman, came to the village, and helped Zhang Shizhe, the xiangdi, assemble the villagers by beating the gong. When the villagers were all gathered in the village school, every-one received a ballot and voted. The ballot box was opened at 2:00 p.m. Hou Jixing won the most votes and became the village head. . . . " (656.2.2, 1921).

6. In contrast, in South China, especially the Canton delta, clan land accounted for 40 to even 80 percent of all village land, which resulted in the immense power of the clan organ and clan leader (Ye Xian'en and Tan Dihua 1985).

Chapter 8

1. Where teaching conditions were poor, the 1912 regulation of the Ministry of Education allowed schools to omit three courses: handicrafts, painting, and music (Qu 1991: 653). The 1915 regulations eliminated farming skills for male students but added classics study for all students, which however was immediately abolished after the death of Yuan Shikai (Qu 1991: 779, 810). The curriculum of primary schools in late Qing, as the 1904 regulation demanded, included moral cultivation, classics study, written Chinese language, arithmetic, history, geography, science, and gymnas-tics (Qu 1991: 293). To simplify the curriculum, the Ministry of Education recom-mended in 1909 merging history, geography, and science into the texts of written Chinese language (Xuebu 1909: 544).

2. The Regulations on Lower Primary Schools of 1904 promulgated that during the first five years from 1904 to 1908 a lower primary school of a single grade or multiple grades was to be created for every 400 households of neighboring villages. In the next five years, the number of the schools should be doubled to have one for every 200 households. The final goal was to have one school in every village of 100 households and over so that all school-age children could attend a school within the distance of half a li. A new education plan announced by the Education Ministry of the Beijing government required villages of over 500 households to create a lower primary school with multiple grades, and those between 500 and 200 households to create a single-grade school; those with fewer than 200 households had to join to-gether to found a school. The Zhili provincial authority required that one public school be established for every village with 60 taels of land tax or more, and villages with less than 60 taels band together to build a school (656.2.23, 1921). In Huailu county, each village had an average of 110 taels (the county had 221 villages and a to-tal of 23,160 taels of land taxes in the early 1920s). This means that most villages had to establish a school.

3. The average landholding in Huailu in the 1910s was about 12 mu. The net in-

come from farming was 3 yuan per mu from irrigated land and 1.5 yuan per mu from land farm (656.1.103, 1913).

Chapter 9

1. My examination of the dispute over the EPO directorship in the preceding chapter provides a good example of the changing backgrounds of the county elites. Whereas Liang Zhi'an, who headed the EPO in 1906, was a juren degree holder (a graduate of the provincial exam), his successor, Wu Donglin, took over the EPO in 1912 as a graduate of a three-year normal school who had served as the principal of the government-funded (guanli) primary school at the county seat (656.1.37, 1912).

2. Local gazetteers provide details about the creation and activities of the county assemblies (Jingxian zhi 1932, 4: 2; Yanshan xianzhi 1916, 10: 6; Nanpi xianzhi 1932, 5: 4–5; Xiongxian xinzhi 1929, 3: 44; Wen'an xianzhi 1922, 12: 35–36; Pinggu xianzhi 1934, 2b: 12; Yuansi xianzhi 1931, xingzheng: 30; Jinghai xianzhi 1934, 12: 2; Daming xianzhi 1934, 4: 1).

3. Examples are Yanshan county (Yanshan xinzhi 1916: 434) and Jingxing county (656.1.243, 1915).

Chapter 10

1. The head of the county government was called xianzhang, or county head, after 1928, rather than zhishi, or magistrate, as used during the early Republican years.

2. In Nanqiema village, for example, a xiangdi named Han Luozao, who described himself as a "poor man" with the duty of "answering to the yamen above and dealing with the taxpaying households below" (shang cheng gongmen, xia ying huahu), accused a fellow villager of not repaying the tax monies the xiangdi had paid for him in advance. The dispute evolved into a court hearing in which the county head instructed the two disputants to make clear the debt the accused owed to the xiangdi before any rulings were rendered. The xiangzhang, claiming himself to be a friend of both parties and unwilling to see a protracted lawsuit between the two, mediated the dispute and asked the delinquent taxpayer to pay his debt (656.3.458, 1931).

3. There were exceptions. Where the lü was created on the basis of the preexisting pai, the lüzhang (head of the lü) assumed exactly the same duties as the previous xiangdi of the pai. Here the lüzhang, instead of the xiangzhang, undertook the duty to advance tax monies for households of his unit and at the same time could earn fees as middleman from transactions occurring in his lü (656.3.1100, 1936). Although the xiangzhang was held responsible by the county government for any tax shortages occurring in his xiang, it was the lüzhang's task to advance taxes. The xiangzhang's duties thus were much lighter than those of the lüzhang. The xiangzhang position under this arrangement was attractive. To seize the deputy xiangzhang office, Lu Guanguang of Shangzhuang village, for example, had to bribe his kinsmen to vote for him (656.3.911, 1934).

4. There were still some villages where the xiangzhang was merely responsible for prompting his villagers to pay their taxes on time and was not required to advance

their taxes during the collection period (the same responsibilities as the "tax-prompting xiangdi" discussed in Chapter 6). However, he did need to make good on any tax shortage caused by the nonpayment of his villagers after the deadline (656.3.458, 1931).

5. Disputes between the xiangzhang and villagers were even more likely to occur in villages where no communal regulations existed to oblige the xiangzhang to advance taxes for villagers during the collection period. The xiangzhang did so only after the deadline for delinquent taxpayers in his charge, just as the tax-prompting xiangdi did before 1930. To avoid making good on any tax shortages out-of-pocket, the xiangzhang would urge the taxpayers to pay the taxes due before the deadline. Tensions between the xiangzhang and the taxpayers thus were exceptionally keen, just as they were in villages under the tax-prompting xiangdi before 1930. Those with real power would most likely ignore the xiangzhang's prompting efforts during the collection period, resulting in the xiangzhang's legal actions against the powerful. A rich villager named Wu Qingrui of Xiwulizhuang, for example, was accused by his xiangzhang of refusing to pay surcharges on a 12 mu piece of land Wu had newly bought conditionally. Wu, owner of over 100 mu of land, was powerful enough to mobilize as many as fifteen kinsmen to petition against the "false accusation" against him. The xiangzhang was intimidated into retracting his original accusation as a "pure misunderstanding," despite the fact that Wu actually cultivated the land in dispute. Wu was able to deny his tax liabilities on the land simply because he had avoided any formal paperwork for the newly owned land (656.3.1102, 1936). In another case, a villager named Han Binglin, who was a graduate of the Beiyang Law and Administrative School and had served as a military officer, owned as much as 300 mu of land. He was also charged with nonpayment of 150 yuan in taxes the xiangzhang had advanced for him. Han had to pay off his debt to the xiangzhang within five days following the county head's ruling (656.3.458, 1931).

6. No data on the literacy of Huailu residents is currently available. However, a statistic from neighboring Dingxian county is suggestive. A field survey conducted in the early 1930s indicated that "some 80 percent of the population over six years of age were illiterate" and that "[a]pproximately one-third of the males over six years of age were literate but only about 3 percent of the females" (Gamble 1954: 185).

7. An earlier lawsuit that involved Lu Guanguang added strength to Yang's depiction of Lu as a local tyrant. According to the Education Promotion Office's accusation in 1915, Lu's father had retired from the position of teacher in the village but still kept at home a clock that belonged to the school. To take it back, Zhao Mengbi, an EPO officer, visited Lu's home at the request of the schoolmaster and was badly beaten by Lu Guanguang, who was then 24 years old. The magistrate was furious upon receipt of the plaint; he branded Lu a "barbaric son" of the derelict former teacher and ordered during the following court hearing that Lu be detained for his two unforgivable crimes: illegal possession of the school's clock and beating and wounding the EPO officer. Later Lu was released when he paid a fine of 30 yuan (656.1.492, 1915).

Chapter 11

1. Ethnographic data show that the village heads often owned the most land in villages (see P. Huang 1985: tables 13.2 and 13.3).

2. This single file contains more than 300 pages of documents regarding black land investigations in 1933–34. All of the following discussion is based on this file.

3. These figures are arrived at from statistics in the three kinds of documents from the First Ward of the county: the black land cultivators' self registration, the xiangzhang's report, and the ward directors' reports, respectively (656.3.780, 1933).

4. Nevertheless, the above description of land investigations in Huailu disagrees with Prasenjit Duara's proposition that land investigations during the Guomindang reign produced no results. The estimated amount of uncovered black land in Huailu (5,000 mu) was close to what was uncovered in Hebei counties in the early 1940s (from 3,000 to 7,000 mu), which Duara believes to have been possible only under Japanese occupation (Duara 1988: 227–34).

5. The only exception was Anxia village, where the largest plot of black land was reportedly 6 mu, of which 2 mu were black land, the rest wasteland. That means that the cultivator needed to pay 4 yuan to legally own it.

Chapter 12

1. Conditions in south-central Hebei were of course much more complicated than this characterization. As the preceding chapters explained, community organizations in some villages were relatively weak. In the absence of communal cooperation in taxation, the xiangdi in those villages were responsible only for tax prompting, exactly as the xiangbao were in nineteenth-century Baodi county in northeastern Hebei. There were also some villages that appeared more like their counterparts in South China. Sibeichai village in Luancheng county (east of Huailu), for example, was similar to most other villages in south-central Hebei in its commercialized economy and strong lineage organization (P. Huang 1985: 174; Duara 1988: 105–6). The villagers in Sibeichai also showed a strong sense of corporate identity, evident in their restrictive conditions for village membership. A person was not considered a full member of the village unless three previous generations had lived there (Duara 1988: 212). However, unlike most villages in this area, Sibeichai was a highly differentiated community, where land was owned predominantly by absentee landlords, a situation typical of South China villages (Duara 1988: 174–75).

2. "Power" is defined as one's ability to "carry out his own will against the resistance of others" (Weber 1978: 63) or to "make a difference" in the result of a process (Giddens 1984: 14). In spite of the diverse conceptions of power, however, most modern analyses tend to emphasize the "communicative" aspect of power (Habermas 1984)—that is, the power or ability to communicate by speech, symbols, or other signs. I use the term *power* here to denote a person's ability to exert influence over others both by controlling material and institutional means and by using symbolic resources, especially the norms and values embedded in the community.

3. David Sabean's concept of community is illuminating here. As he puts it, "community is a matter of mediations and reciprocities. . . . What makes commu-

nity possible is the fact that it involves a series of mediated relationships. One central form of mediation is provided by property—the access to resources, the apportionment of rights and claims, and the acceptance of obligations and duties." On the central importance of discourse in the community, he notes, "what is common in community is not shared values or common understanding so much as the fact that members of a community are engaged in the same argument, the same *raisonnement*, the same *Rede*, the same discourse, in which alternative strategies, misunderstandings, conflicting goals and values are threshed out. What makes community is the discourse" (Sabean 1984: 29–30).

4. In his acclaimed study of marketing structure in rural China, G. William Skinner proposes the concept of a "standard marketing area," which he argues to be the "effective social field of the peasant." A typical marketing area, Skinner explains, encompassed about 1,500 households in eighteen or so villages over an area of about fifty square kilometers. At the center of this area was a marketing town where the peasant household traded its agricultural products and craft items (Skinner 1964–65).

5. This trend was even prevalent in the Yangzi delta, an area much more commercialized than south-central Hebei (P. Huang 1990).

6. In Weber's sociology, patrimonialism is a traditional form of political domination in which the ruler equates political power with his personal property and exercises his power arbitrarily in the absence of binding norms and regulations from the bureaucratic administration (Weber 1968: 1028–31). In general, Weber treats the Chinese government as a form of "patrimonialism." However, unlike the patrimonial state in a feudal society, which was undermined by the independence of aristocratic manors, the very absence of landed estates in premodern China made the Chinese state "the most consistent political form of patrimonialism" (ibid.: 1091). At the same time, Weber observes that the distinct practices in China's political life, in particular, literary education and the official qualifying examinations as the basis of office-holding, which radically broke with the typical patrimonial officialdom that rests on the ruler's personal discretion and favor. These practices, Weber believes, were specifically "bureaucratic," and to this extent China was "formally the most perfect representative of the modern, pacified and bureaucratized society" (ibid.: 1049, 1050). Taking into account both features outlined above, Weber characterized the Chinese state as representing "the purest type of patrimonial bureaucracy" (ibid.: 1063).

7. Given the central importance of this idea in their political thinking, it is no wonder that neo-Confucian scholars and bureaucrats enthusiastically promoted the *xiangyue* (community compacts or community covenant) system, a locally organized association to promote community welfare and ensure local public order and fulfillment of official obligations. As a form of self-administration, it combined local initiative and state control, and was embraced as a feasible way to bring about the Confucian ideal of government through education rather than regulation (de Bary 1983, 1998; Übelhör 1989; Duan 1996; Hauf 1996; Cao Guoqing 1997; Cheng Pengfei 2000; Hu Qingjun 2001).

8. As a practical administrator the magistrate did not necessarily and invariably

represent the interests of the state. Instead, he often manipulated his superiors and local communities to maximize his personal gain at minimal cost to himself. He played different roles in different circumstances. Formally, the magistrate represented the state in enforcing state policies and in public exchanges with his superiors or subjects. At the same time, he could engage in illegal practices to enrich his yamen and himself at the state's expense, as he did by printing and using "small deeds" in violation of the provincial government's regulation (Chapter 6). He could ignore the provincial governor's ordinances or treat them as a formality when they increased his administrative burden, as he did when ordered to investigate black land. He could also speak on behalf of local communities under his jurisdiction and openly reject the governor's orders when they would jeopardize his relations with the local elites whose support he relied on in his daily administration (Chapter 8). The magistrate's approach to local governance thus varied in different situations, often combining official policies and representations with informal and even illegal practices.

9. Although the increasing population and hence the expanding administrative expenditures prompted local officials to increase taxes using various excuses, Yongzheng emperor nevertheless attempted to regularize the collection of the irregular charges in order to limit the tax burden and set the newly regularized charges at a very low level for fear of violating the maxim of low taxation (Zelin 1984). In the last decades of the Qing, when military expenses and foreign indemnities skyrocketed, the ruler could only turn to other channels such as creating commercial taxes (e.g., lijin) and maritime custom duties, rather than increasing the land tax. As a result, the land tax remained reasonably low until the beginning of the twentieth century.

andi paichai　按地派差
Anxia　岸下(村)
anzhao cungui　按照村規
bachi jiaoquan　把持教權
bailinzhuang　柏林莊(村)
baiqi　白契
bangban xiangdi　幫辦鄉地
bangong pingyu　辦公平餘
bangong wusi　辦公無私
baocun jiugui　保存舊規
Baodi　寶坻(縣)
baojia　保甲
baolan　包攬
baoshou　包收
baoweituan　保衛團
baozheng　保正
bashan yishui yifentian　八山一水一分
　　田
Beiganzi　北甘子(村)
Beigucheng　北故城(村)
Beihu　北胡(村)
Beiqiema　北郄馬(村)
Beitongye　北銅冶(村)
Beixiangbei　北降北(村)
Beizai　北寨(村)
bingchai　兵差
bingzi gui　丙字櫃
bu an xiaode cungui xingshi　不按小的
　　村規行事
bupingdeng tiaoyue　不平等條約
buyi xianggui　不依鄉規

buzhengshi　佈政使
caizheng dongshi hui　財政董事會
caizheng suo　財政所
caizheng ting　財政廳
canshihui　參事會
caoqi　草契
ceshu　冊書
cha wu qiren　查無其人
chaiyao　差徭
chaiyao chu　差徭處
chaiyao diaocha suo　差徭調查所
chazhao jiuzhang　查照舊章
chengshuo　成說
chengxiang shenshi　城鄉紳士
chige　斥革
chuanpiao　串票
citang　祠堂
congying xiangdi, xi yixiang zhi lingxiu
　　充膺鄉地，係一**鄉**之領袖
cuiliang pibing　催糧批稟
cuiliang xiangdi　催糧鄉地
cuiquan　催勸
cungui　村規
cunshi　村事
cunzhang　村長
cunzhang xiangyue langbei weijian　村
　　長鄉約狼狽為奸
cunzheng　村正
cunzhong jiugui　村中舊規
Dabeiguan　大北關(村)
dachai　大差
Daguo　大郭

Daming 大名(縣)
diankuan 墊款
diankuan xiangdi 墊款鄉地
diantui 典推
diantui qishui 典推契稅
diaochayuan 調查員
dibao 地保
diding 地丁
difang 地方
dijuan 地捐
diliang 地糧
dilin 地鄰
dingce 丁冊
Dingxian 定縣
dingyi 丁役
Dingzhou 定州
dipi 地痞
Donghushenpu 東胡申鋪
Dongjiao 東焦(村)
Dongliangxiang 東良廂(村)
Dongpingtong 東平同(村)
Dongtongping 東同坪(村)
dongshi 董事
Dongxuying 東許營(村)
Dongying 東營(村)
Dongzhuang 東莊(村)
Duanzhuang 段莊(村)
ducui 督催
Fancun 范村
fang 房
fankang gongyi 反抗公議
fei gai xianggui buyi 非改鄉規不依
feisa 飛灑
fuhu 富戶
Fujiazhuang 符家莊
Fuyi quanshu 賦役全書
ganfu 干父
ganyu cungong 干預村公
ganyu waishi 干預外事
Gaojiaying 高家營(村)
Gaoqian 高遷(村)
Gaoyi 高邑(村)
ge na ge liang 各納各糧
gensui xiangdi qianwen 跟隨鄉地錢
　文

gongli 公立
gongshiqian 工食錢
gongsi yiti 公私一體
gongzheng heping 公正和平
guanban qizhi 官版契紙
guanchan ju 官產局
guanchan zongchu 官產總處
guandu shenquan 官督紳勸
guanfu yiwan 官賦易完
guanli 官立
guanshen hukong 官紳互控
guanzhi de jiaoyu 官治的教育
guanzhong 官中
guiji 詭寄
guishu zhizhang fanshi 櫃書紙張飯
　食
guize 規則
Gujiayu 谷家峪(村)
guoge chu 過割處
guojia zhuyi 國家主義
hai 害
hecun gongyi 闔村公議
hegong juang 河工捐
heidi 黑地
Hejintang 何錦堂
Hengshan 橫山(村)
heping liaoli 和平了理
hexiang gongju 闔鄉公舉
hexiang linju 闔鄉遴選
heyi shenmin bing xiangdi huahu
　rendeng 闔邑紳民並鄉地花戶人
　等
heyi xiangdi 闔邑鄉地
hongbo 紅薄
hongce 紅冊
hongming xiangdi 紅名鄉地
hongqi 紅契
Houjiaying 侯家營(村)
Houxiazhai 後夏寨(村)
huahu 花戶
Huailu 獲鹿(縣)
Huairou 懷柔(縣)
huaming 花名
huandui 換兌
huangchai 皇差

Huangyan 黃岩

hufang 戶房

huishou 會首

huohao 火耗

Huozhai 霍寨(村)

jiagong jisi 假公濟私

jianfang 柬房

jianjia xie qi, feisi wubi 減價寫契，
肥私舞弊

jiansheng 監生

jiaoyuhui 教育會

jingcha suo 警察所

jingcui 警催

jingqu 警區

Jingxian 景縣

Jingxing 井陘(縣)

jinhou haohao bangong 今後好好辦公

jintie 津貼

jinzheng jinjie 盡徵盡解

jiuding 舊丁

jiugui 舊規

jiuli 舊例

jiuxue 舊學

jizhuang di 寄莊地

ju shi kangwei 俱是抗違

juan 卷

juanban jigu 捐辦積谷

jubao 舉報

juehu 絕戶

jugong 舉貢

juzhong zishi 聚眾滋事

kaocheng 考成

kekao 科考

Kongjiahui 孔教會

Laiyang 萊陽(縣)

leling 勒令

Lengshuigou 冷水溝(村)

li 里

Liangjiazhuang 梁家莊(村)

liang sui di zhou 糧隨地走

liangchuan 糧串

Liangjiazhuang 梁家莊

liangyin 糧銀

liangzu zhengli weiyuanhui 糧租整理
委員會

Lianhuaying 蓮花營(村)

liaoliao wuji 寥寥無幾

liedang 逆黨

lijia 里甲

Lijiazhuang 李家莊(村)

lijin 厘金

lin 鄰

lingdi 嶺底(村)

lingju tuoren 遴舉妥人

Lingshou 靈壽(縣)

lishu 里書

lizhang 里長

Longwang tang 龍王堂

Loudi 樓底(村)

lü 閭

Luancheng 欒城(縣)

Luanxian 灤縣

lunliu menhu, annian huanchong 輪
流門戶，按年換充

lunliu menhu, zhou er fu shi 輪流門
戶，週而復始

lüzhang 閭長

Macun 馬村

maimai qishui 買賣契稅

mayan siqi, minyu saodi 罵言四起，
名譽掃地

Mazhuang 馬莊(村)

meijuan 煤捐

men 門

mentou 門頭

Michang 米廠(村)

minzheng ting 民政廳

mixin zhi naojin 迷信之腦筋

mujuan 畝捐

mulu 目錄

Nandu 南杜(村)

Nangu 南谷(村)

Nangucheng 南故城(村)

Nanguyi 南故邑(村)

Nanguo 南郭(村)

Nanhaishan 南海山(村)

Nanlonggui 南龍貴(村)

Nanpi 南皮(縣)

Nanqiema 南郄馬(村)

Nantongye 南同冶(村)

Nanwei　南位(村)

Nanxinzhuang　南新莊(村)

Nanzhai　南寨(村)

Nanzhuang　南莊(村)

neiwufu　內務府

neizheng　內政

nianli jingzhuang　年力精壯

nianli zhengqiang　年力正強

numa　怒罵

pai　牌

paigui　牌規

paijuan　派捐

paitou　牌頭

piaocui　票催

Pinggu　平谷(縣)

Pingshan　平山(縣)

pohuai cungui　破壞村規

pohuai xianggui, lanju xiangdi　破壞鄉規，濫舉**鄉**地

pohuai xuexiao　破壞學校

puji jiaoyu　普及教育

qiangquan　強權

Qianlianggezhuang　前梁各莊(村)

qidi　旗地

qidong　耆董

Qiejiazhuang　郄家莊(村)

qigen　契根

qingcha dimu shiwusuo　清查地畝事務所

qingfu zongju　清賦總局

qingjin xiangyi　親近鄉誼

Qinghe　清河(縣)

qingli nanrong　情理難容

qiren　旗人

qishui　契稅

qiwei　契尾

qizhi　契紙

qu　區

quanxian gongyi　全縣公議

quanxue suo　勸學所

quanxue suozhang　勸學所長

quanxue zongdong　勸學總董

quanxueyuan　勸學員

quanzong　全宗

qujing　區警

qunian lü zhang　去年閭長

qunian xiangdi　去年鄉地

qunian xiangzhang　去年鄉長

Quyang　曲陽(縣)

raoluan cungui　擾亂村規

raomin　擾民

renduo　人多

renpin duanzheng　人品端正

renxin dongyao　人心動搖

renzhi　仁治

Sanhe　三河(縣)

sanman wuji　散漫無稽

Shajing　沙井(村)

shanfei　膳費

Shangcheng gongmen, xiaying huahu　上承公門，下應花·

shangmang　上忙

Shangzhuang　上莊(村)

Shanhou　山後(村)

shanhou liangchuan　善後糧捐

Shanxiayin　山下尹(村)

shence　審冊

shendong　紳董

sheng yihui　省議會

shengyuan　生員

Shenhou　申后(村)

shenjin　紳衿

shenju yidi, weibian yingtao　身居異地，未便硬討

shenmin　紳民

shenshi　紳士

Shenze　深澤(縣)

sheshu　社書

shi wei juwen　視為俱文

shifan sheng　師範生

Shijiazhuang　石家莊(村)

Shijing　石井(村)

Shimen　石門(村)

shishen　士紳

shiye ting　實業廳

shoucui　守催

shoushi　首事

Shuangmiao　雙廟

shuji　書記

Shulu　束鹿(縣)

shuohe chengjiao　說合成交
Shunyi　順義(縣)
shuyin xiaoqi　屬印小契
si chou zhongyong　私抽中用
Sibeichai　寺北柴(村)
sili　私立
simai simai　私買私賣
siqi　私契
sishu　私塾
siyue　私約
sizhong　私中
Songcun　宋村
suan dazhang　算大賬
sufu xiangwang, bangong shuxi　素孚
　鄉望，辦公熟悉
suiliang daizheng　隨糧帶徵
Suncun　孫村
suosong zhi ren　唆訟之人
sushou　宿手
Taiping　太平(村)
Taitou　臺頭(村)
Tancun　談村
Tangxian　唐縣
tankuan　攤款
taochi junshi tejuan　討赤軍事特捐
taohu　逃戶
Tazong　塔冢(村)
techi　特斥
tianfu　田賦
tianfu qingli chu　田賦清理處
Tongxian　通縣
toupiao gongju　投票公舉
touxie　偷寫
tu　圖
tucheng　圖承
tugui　圖規
tugun　土棍
tuhao lieshen　土豪劣紳
Tumen　土門(村)
tushu　圖書
tutou　圖頭
wei de dazhong tongyi　未得大眾同意
Weitong　位同(村)
wenluan cungui　紊亂村規
wenluan jiugui　紊亂舊規

wenluan xianggui　紊亂鄉規
Wudian　吳店(縣)
wulai guntu　無賴土棍
wuwei　無為
wuzhi xiangyu　無知鄉愚
xiamang　下忙
xian　縣
xian yi/canshihui　縣議/參事會
xian zuzhifa　縣組織法
xianbao　現保
xiancheng　縣丞
xiang　鄉
xiang xi nian qing xian kuan　嚮係年
　清年款
xiangbao　鄉保
xiangdi　鄉地
xiangdi banzi　鄉地班子
xianggui　鄉規
Xianghe　香河(縣)
xiangmin dahui　鄉民大會
xiangyi　鄉誼
xiangyu wuzhi　鄉愚無知
xiangyue　鄉約
xiangzhang　鄉長
xiangzhen zhizi　鄉鎮自治
xiangzhen zhizi shixingfa　鄉鎮自治
　施行法
xiangzhong paijie　鄉眾排解
xiannian　現年
xianzheng huiyi　縣政會議
Xiaobi　小畢(村)
xiaochai　小差
xiaoma　笑罵
Xiaoyudi　小于底(村)
Xilonggui　西龍貴(村)
xinding　新丁
xingzheng　行政
xinshi shenshi　新式紳士
xinxue　新學
xinzheng　新政
Xiongxian　雄縣
Xiumen　休門(村)
xiushen　修身
Xixiu　西秀(村)
Xixuezhuang　西薛莊(村)

References

The Huailu county government archives, currently preserved in the Hebei Provincial Archives, are cited by category (*quanzong*) number, subcategory (*mulu*) number, file (*juan*) number, and year when the file was created (e.g., 656.2.852, 1926).

Andrew, Anita M., and John A. Rapp, eds. 2000. *Autocracy and China's Rebel Founding Emperors: Comparing Chairman Mao and Ming Taizu*. Lanham, Md.: Rowman and Littlefield.

Ardant, Gabriel. 1975. "Financial Policy and Economic Infrastructure of Modern States and Nations." In Charles Tilly, ed., *The Formation of National States in Western Europe*, pp. 380–455. Princeton, N.J.: Princeton University Press.

Averill, Stephen. 1987. "Party, Society and Local Elite in the Jiangxi Communist Movement," *Journal of Asian Studies* 46 (2): 279–303.

———. 1990. "Local Elites and Communist Revolution in the Jiangxi Hill Country." In Joseph Esherick and Mary Rankin, eds., *Chinese Local Elites and Patterns of Dominance*, pp. 282–304. Berkeley: University of California Press.

———. 1991. "Moral Economy and the Chinese Revolution," *Peasant Studies* 18 (2): 65–96.

Bai Jing'an 白靖安. 1988. "Ershi niandai Shijiazhuang jiaoxian de mianhua chanxiao qingkuang" 二十年代石家莊郊縣的棉花產銷情況 (The situation of cotton production and marketing in the neighboring counties of Shijiazhuang in the 1920s). In *Shijiazhuang wenshi ziliao* 石家莊文史資料 (Source materials on Shijiazhuang local history), vol. 8. Shijiazhuang, Hebei.

Baixiang xianzhi 柏鄉縣誌 (Gazetteer of Baixiang county). 1932.

Balazs, Etienne. 1964. *Chinese Civilization and Bureaucracy: Variations on a Theme*. New Haven, Conn.: Yale University Press.

Bastid, Marianne. 1985. "The Structure of the Financial Institutions of the State in the Late Qing." In S. R. Schram, ed., *The Scope of State Power in China*. New York: St. Martin's Press.

Baxter, James C. 1994. *The Meiji Unification through the Lens of Ishikawa Prefecture*. Cambridge, Mass.: Harvard University Press.

Beattie, Hilary. 1979. *Land and Lineage in China: A Study of T'ung-ch'eng County, Anhwei, in the Ming and Ch'ing Dynasties.* Cambridge, England: Cambridge University Press,

Berce, Yves-Marie. 1990. *History of Peasant Revolts: The Social Origins of Rebellion in Early Modern France.* Ithaca, N.Y.: Cornell University Press.

Bernhardt, Kathryn. 1992. *Rents, Taxes, and Peasant Resistances: The Lower Yangzi Region 1840–1950.* Stanford, Calif.: Stanford University Press.

Bourdieu, Pierre. 1977. *Outline of a Theory of Practice.* Cambridge, England: Cambridge University Press.

———. 1980. *The Logic of Practice.* Stanford, Calif.: Stanford University Press.

———. 1985. "The Social Space and the Genesis of Groups." *Social Science Information* 24 (2): 195–220.

———. 1986. "The Forms of Capital." In John G. Richardson, ed., *Handbook of Theory and Research for the Sociology of Education,* pp. 241–58. New York: Greenwood Press.

———. 1992. *An Invitation to Reflexive Sociology.* Chicago: University of Chicago Press.

Brandauer, Frederick P., and Chun-chieh Huang, eds. 1994. *Imperial Rulership and Cultural Change in Traditional China.* Seattle: University of Washington Press.

Braun, Rudolf. 1975. "Taxation, Sociopolitical Structure, and State-Building: Great Britain and Brandenburg-Prussia." In Charles Tilly, ed., *The Formation of National States in Western Europe,* pp. 380–455. Princeton, N.J.: Princeton University Press.

Buck, John Lossing. 1930. *Chinese Farm Economy: A Study of 2,866 Farms in Seventeen Localities and Seven Provinces in China.* Chicago: University of Chicago Press.

———. 1937a. *Land Utilization in China: A Study of 16,786 Farms in 168 Localities, and 38,256 Farm Families in Twenty-two Provinces in China, 1929–1933.* Shanghai: Commercial Press.

———. 1937b. *Land Utilization in China, Statistics.* Chicago: University of Chicago Press.

Cao Guoqing 曹國慶. 1997. "Mingdai xiangyue tuixing de tedian" 明代鄉約推行的特點 (Characteristics of the implementation of the xiangyue system in the Ming dynasty). *Zhongguo wenhua yanjiu* 中國文化研究 Spring.

Cao Shuji. 2001. "Qingdai beifang chengshi renkou yanjiu: jian yu Shijianya shangque" 清代北方城市人口研究：兼與施堅雅商榷 (A study of population in northern Chinese cities during the Qing: a dialogue with G. W. Skinner), *Zhongguo renkou kexue* 中國人口科學, no. 4.

Cartier, Carolyn. 2002. "Origins and Evolution of a Geographical Idea: The Macroregion in China." *Modern China* 28 (1).

Chang, Chung-li. 1955. *The Chinese Gentry: Studies on Their Role in Nineteenth-Century Chinese Society.* Seattle: University of Washington Press.

Chen Dengyuan 陳登原. 1938. *Zhongguo tianfu shi* 中國田賦史 (History of the land tax in China). Shanghai: shangwu yinshuguan.

Chen Feng 陳峰. 1999. "Qingchu qingyao bofu zhengce kaolun" 清初輕徭薄賦政策考論 (The light-tax policy in early Qing). *Wuhan daxue xuebao* 武漢大學學報, 2.

Chen, Fu-mei Chang, and Ramon H. Myers. 1976. "Customary law and the economic growth of China during the Ch'ing period." *Ch'ing-shih wen-t'i* 3 (5): 1–27.

Chen Han Seng. 1933. *The Present Agrarian Problem in China*. Shanghai: China Institute of Pacific Relations.

———. 1936. *Landlord and Peasant in China: A Study of the Agrarian Crisis in South China*. New York: International Publishers.

Chen, Jerome. 1969. "Historical Background." In Jack Gray, ed., *Modern China's Search for a Political Form*, pp. 1–40. London: Oxford University Press.

———. 1985. "Local government Finances in Republican China." *Republican China* 10 (2): 42–54.

———. 1992. *The Highlanders of Central China: A History, 1895–1937*. Armonk, N.Y.: M. E. Sharpe.

Chen, Shao-kwan. 1914. *The System of Taxation in China in the Tsing Dynasty, 1644–1911*. New York: Columbia University.

Chen, Yung-fa. 1986. *Making Revolution: The Communist Movement in Eastern and Central China, 1937–1945*. Berkeley: University of California Press.

Chen Zenghui 陳增輝. 2000. "Rujia minben sixiang yuanliu" 儒家民本思想源流 (The origin and development of the Confucian thought on people as the state's foundation). *Zhongzhou xuekan* 中州學刊, 3.

Chen Zhenhan 陳振漢. 1989. *Qingshilu jingji shi ziliao* 清實錄經濟史資料 (Materials of economic history from Qingshilu), 1644–1820. Beijing: Beijing daxue chubanshe.

Chen Zhiping 陳支平. 1988. *Qingdai fuyi zhidu yanbian xintan* 清代賦役制度演變新探 (A new inquiry into the involution of the tax system during the Qing). Xiamen: Xiamen daxue chubanshe.

Cheng Fang 程方. 1939. *Zhongguo xianzheng gailun* 中國縣政概論 (An outline of county administration in China). Shanghai: Shangwu yinshuguan.

Cheng Hanchang 成漢昌. 1994. *Ershi shiji qian banqi Zhongguo tudi zhidu yu tudi gaige* 二十世紀前半期中國土地制度與土地改革 (Land system and land reform in early twentieth-century China). Beijing: Zhongguo dang'an chubanshe.

Cheng Maoxing 程懋型. 1936. *Xianxing baojia zhidu* 現行保甲制度 (The current baojia system). Shanghai: Zhonghua shuju.

Cheng Pengfei 程鵬飛. 2000. "Wang Yangming zhixing heyi yu nangong xiangyue" 王陽明知行合一與南贛鄉約 (Wang Yangming's theory of unity of knowledge and practice and village covenants in southern Jiangxi), *Guizhou wenshi congkan* 貴州文史叢刊, 3.

Ch'ü, T'ung-tsu. 1962. *Local Government in China under the Ch'ing*. Cambridge, Mass: Harvard University Press.

Chugoku noson kanko chosa kankokai 中國農村慣行調查刊行會. 1952–58. *Chgoku noson kanko chosa* 中國農村慣行調查 (Investigations of customary practices in rural China). 6 vols. Tokyo: Iwanami.

Cong Hangxiang 從翰香. 1992. "Cong quyi jingji de jiaodu kan Qing mo Min chu Huabei pingyuan Ji-Lu-Yu san sheng de nongcun" 從區域經濟的角度看清末民初華北平原冀魯豫三省得農村 (Rural Hebei, Shandong, and Henan of the North China plain during the late Qing and early Republican period: a study of regional economy). In Ye Xian'en 葉顯恩, ed., *Qingdai quyi shehui jingji yanjiu* 清代區域社會經濟研究 (Studies on regional social economy during the Qing). Beijing: Zhonghua shuju.

———, ed. 1995. *Jindai Ji-Lu-Yu xiangcun* 近代冀魯豫鄉村 (The rural society of Hebei, Shandong, and Henan in the modern period). Beijing: Zhongguo shehui kexue chubanshe.

Daming xianzhi 大名縣誌 (Gazetteer of Daming county). 1934.

Daqing lüli 大清律例 (Qing Statutes and Substatutes). N.d.

de Bary, Wm. Theodore. 1983. *The Liberal Tradition in China*. Hong Kong: Chinese University Press.

———. 1998. *Asian Values and Human Rights: A Confucian Communitarian Perspective*. Cambridge, Mass.: Harvard University Press.

Dennerline, Jerry. 1988. "The New Hua Charitable Estate and Local Level Leadership in Wuxi County at the End of the Qing." In University of Chicago, *Papers from the Center for Far Eastern Studies* 4: 19–71.

Dier lishi dang'anguan 第二歷史檔案館. 1994. *Guomindang zhengfu zhengzhi zhidu dang'an shiliao xuanbian* 國民黨政府政治制度檔案史料選編 (Selected historical archives on the political system of the Guomindang government), vol. 2. Hefei: Anhui jiaoyu chubanshe.

Difang zizhi quanshu 地方自治全書 (A complete compendium of documents on local self-government). n.d. Shanghai: Gongmin shuju.

Dingxian zhi 定縣誌 (Gazetteer of Dingxian). 1934.

Downs, Anthony. 1957. *An Economic Theory of Democracy*. New York: Harper.

Duan Zichang 段自成. 1996. "Qingdai qianqi de xiangyue" 清代前期的鄉約 (The xiangyue in early Qing), *Nandu xuetan* 南都學壇 16 (5).

Duara, Prasenjit. 1988. *Culture, Power, and the State: Rural North China, 1900–1942*. Stanford, Calif.: Stanford University Press.

———. 1990. "Elites and the Structures of Authority in the Villages of North China, 1900–1949." In Joseph W. Esherick and Mary B. Rankin, eds., *Chinese Local Elites and Patterns of Dominance*. Berkeley: University of California Press.

———. 1995. *Rescuing History from the Nation: Questioning Narratives of Modern China*. Chicago: University of Chicago Press.

Dun Yuchun 敦玉春. 1989. "Qingmo wutanhua Dun Fengju" (清末武探花敦鳳舉). In *Shijiazhuang jiaoqu wenshi ziliao* 石家莊郊區文史資料 (Source materials on Shijiazhuang local history), 1: 49–51.

Durkheim, Emile. 1961. *Moral Education: A Study in the Theory and Application of the Sociology of Education*. New York: Free Press of Glencoe.

Eastman, Lloyd E. 1974. *The Abortive Revolution: China under Nationalist Rule, 1927–1937*. Cambridge, Mass.: Harvard University Press.

———. "State Building and the Revolutionary Transformation of Rural Society in North China," *Modern China* 16 (April): 226–34.

Ebrey, Patricia Buckley, and James L. Watson, eds. 1986. *Kinship Organization in Late Imperial China, 1000–1940*. Berkeley: University of California Press.

Endicott, Stephen. 1988. *Red Earth: Revolution in a Sichuan Village*. London: Tauris.

Esherick, Joseph W. 1976. *Reform and Revolution in China: The 1911 Revolution in Hunan and Hubei*. Berkeley: University of California Press.

———. 1987. *The Origins of the Boxer Uprising*. Berkeley: University of California Press.

Esherick, Joseph W., and Mary Backus Rankin, eds. 1990. *Chinese Local Elites and Patterns of Dominance*. Berkeley: University of California Press.

Fan Zhiyong 樊志勇. "Minjia lahui" 民間臘會 (The December carnival in local society). In *Shijiazhuang wenshi ziliao* 石家莊文史資料 (Source materials on Shijiazhuang local history), vol. 6. Shijiazhuang, Hebei.

Faure, David. 1976. "Land Tax Collection in Kiangsu Province in the Late Ch'ing Period," *Ch'ing-shih wen-t'i*, 3.6: 49–75.

———. 1985. "The Plight of the Farmers: A Study of the Rural Economy of Jiangnan and the Pearl River Delta, 1870–1937." *Modern China* 11 (January): 3–37.

———. 1989. *The Rural Economy of Pre-Liberation China: Trade Increase and Peasant Livelihood in Jiangsu and Guangdong, 1870–1937*. Hong Kong: Oxford University Press.

Fei Hsiao-Tung. 1939. *Peasant Life in China: A Field Study of Country Life in the Yangtze Valley*. New York: Dutton.

———. 1948. *Earthbound China: A Study of Rural Economy in Yunnan*. London: Routledge and Kegan Paul.

———. 1999 [1946–47]. "Xiangtu chongjian" 鄉土重建 (Reconstruction of rural society). In Fei Xiaotong, *Fei Xiaotong wenji* 費孝通文集 (Works of Fei Xiaotong), vol. 4. Beijing: Qunyan chubanshe.

Fei Kangcheng 費成康. 1998. *Zhongguo de jiafa zugui* 中国的家法族规 (Family laws and clan regulations in China). Shanghai: Shanghai shehui kexue chubanshe.

Finer, Samuel E. 1975. "State- and Nation-Building in Europe: The Role of the Military." In Charles Tilly, ed., *The Formation of National States in Western Europe*, pp. 380–455. Princeton, N.J.: Princeton University Press.

Foucault, Michel. 1978 [1976]. *The History of Sexuality*. Random House.

Freedman, Maurice. 1966. *Chinese Lineage and Society, Fukien and Kwangtung*. London: Athlone Press.

Fu, Zhengyuan. 1993. *Autocratic Tradition and Chinese Politics*. Cambridge, England: Cambridge University Press.

Gamble, Sidney D. 1954. *Ting Hsien: A North China Rural Community*. New York: Institute of Pacific Relations.

———. 1963. *North China Villages: Social, Political and Economic Activities before 1933*. Berkeley: University of California Press.

Gillin, Donald G. 1967. *Warlord: Yen Hsi-shan in Shansi Province, 1911–1949*. Princeton, N.J.: Princeton University Press.

Gu Zhun 顧準. 1982. *Xila chengbang zhidu* 希臘城邦制度 (The Greek city-states). Beijing: Zhongguo shehui kexue chubanshe.

———. 1999. *Minzhu yu "zhongji mudi"* 民主與"終極目的" (Democracy and the "ultimate end"). Beijing: Zhongguo qingnian chubanshe.

Gunde, Richard. 1976. "Land Tax and Social Change in Sichuan, 1925–35," *Modern China* 2 (1): 23–48.

Guomin zhengfu 國民政府. 1928. "Chengzhi tuhao lieshen tiaoli" 懲治土豪劣紳條例 (Regulations on the punishment of native bullies and evil gentry). In Dier lishi dang'anguan 第二歷史檔案館 (1994), pp. 610–12.

———. 1930. "Xian zuzhi fa" 縣組織法 (County reorganization act). In Dier lishi dang'anguan (1994), pp. 524–29.

Hardin, Russell. 1982. *Collective Action.* Baltimore: Johns Hopkins University Press.

Hauf, Kandice. 1996. "The Community Covenant in Sixteenth Century Ji'an Prefecture, Jiangxi," *Late Imperial China* 17 (2): 1–50.

HBSZ (Hebei sheng difangzhi bianzuan weiyuanhui 河北省地方誌編纂委員會). 1993. *Hebei shengzhi* 河北省誌 (Gazetteer of Hebei province), vol. 3. Shijiazhuang: Hebei kexue jishu chubanshe.

He Lianchang 何聯昌. 1986. "Nangaoyingcun kaiban Fanwenguan qianhou" 南高營村開辦法文館前後 (The creation of the French-language school in Nangaoying village). In *Shijiazhuang wenshi ziliao* 石家莊文史資料 (Source materials on Shijiazhuang local history), vol. 8. Shijiazhuang, Hebei.

He Ping 何平. 1998. *Qingdai fushui zhengce yanjiu* 清代賦稅政策研究 (A study of Qing tax policies). Beijing: Zhongguo shehui kexue chubanshe.

He Zifeng 何子豐. 1986. "Jiu shehui jianwen sanji" 舊社會見聞散記 (Random notes on events in the old society). In *Shijiazhuang wenshi ziliao* 石家莊文史資料 (Source materials on Shijiazhuang local history), vol. 5. Shijiazhuang, Hebei.

Hebei renmin chubanshe 河北人民出版社, ed. 1984. *Keai de Hebei* 可愛的河北 (The lovable Hebei). Shijiazhuang: Hebei renmin chubanshe.

Hebei sheng Minzhengting 河北省民政廳. 1933. *Hebei sheng ge xian gaikuang yilan* 河北省各縣概況一覽 (An outline of the conditions in individual counties of Hebei province). Baoding: Hebei sheng minzhengting.

Hebei tongzhi gao 河北通誌稿 (Manuscript of the gazetteer of Hebei province). 1993 [1931–37]. Beijing: Yanshan chubanshe.

Hechter, Michael. 1983. "A Theory of Group Solidarity." In Michael Hechter, ed., *The Microfoundations of Macrosociology.* Philadelphia: Temple University Press.

———. 1987. *Principles of Group Solidarity.* Berkeley: University of California Press.

———. 1990. "The Emergence of Cooperative Social Institutions." In Michael Hechter, ed., *Social Institutions: Their Emergence, Maintenance, and Effects.* New York: Aldine de Gruyter.

Hinton, Harold C. 1956. *The Grain Tribute System of China, 1845–1911.* Cambridge, Mass.: Harvard University Press.

Hokushi keizai chosajo 北支經濟調查所. 1940. *Noka keizai chosa hokoku: Kakuroku ken, 1939* 農家經濟調查報告：獲鹿縣 (Report on the investigation of peasant household economy: Huailu county, 1939). Beijing.

Hou Jianxin 侯建新. 2001a. "Ershi shiji shang banqi jizhong nongye shengchan tiaojian kaocha" 二十世紀上半期冀中農業生產條件攷察 (An examination of the conditions of agricultural production in central Hebei in the first half of the twentieth century). *Lishi jiaoxue* 歷史教學, 2.

———. 2001b. "Minguo nianjian jizhong nonghu laodong shengchanlü yanjiu" 民國年間冀中農戶勞動生產率研究 (A study of the labor productivity of rural households in central Hebei in the Republican period). *Zhongguo nongshi* 中國農史, 1.

Hou Wailu 侯外廬. 1979. *Zhongguo fengjian shehui shilu* 中國封建社會史論 (Papers on the history of feudal China). Beijing: renmin chubanshe.

Hsiao, Kung-chuan. 1960. *Rural China: Imperial Control in the Nineteenth Century*. Seattle: University of Washington Press.

Hu Chunfan 胡春帆. 1984. "Shilun Qing qianqi de juanmian zhengce" 試論清前期的蠲免政策 (The tax exemption policy in early Qing). *Qingshi yanjiu ji* 清史研究集, vol. 3.

Hu Rulei 胡如雷. 1979. *Zhongguo fengjian shehui xingtai yanjiu* 中國封建社會形態研究 (A study of the forms of feudal society in China). Beijing: Sanlian.

Hu Qingjun 胡慶鈞. 2001. "Cong Lantian xiangyue dao Chenggong xiangyue" 從藍田鄉約到呈貢鄉約 (From the Lantian village covenant to the Chenggong village covenant). *Yunnan shehui kexue* 云南社會科學, 3.

Hua Li 華立. 1988. "Qingdai baojia zhidu jianlun" 清代保甲制度簡論 (A brief study of the baojia system under the Qing). *Qingshi yanjiu ji* 清史研究集, vol. 6.

Huailu xianzhi 獲鹿縣誌 (Gazetteer of Huailu county). 1985 [1876]. Huailu: Huailu county government.

———. 1990 [1522–66]. Shanghai: Shanghai shudian.

———. 1998. Beijing: Zhongguo dang'an chubanshe.

Huang Fengxin 黃鳳新. 1998. "Lun Qingdai qidi zhanyou xingshi de yanbian" 論清代旗地佔有形式的演變(Evolution of the possession patterns of banner land in the Qing dynasty), *Jilin daxue shehui kexue xuebao* 吉林大學社會科學學報, 6.

Huang, Han Liang. 1918. *The Land Tax in China*. New York: Columbia University.

Huang, Philip C. C. 1985. *The Peasant Economy and Social Change in North China*. Stanford, California: Stanford University Press.

———. 1990. *The Peasant Family and Rural Development in the Yangzi Delta, 1350–1988*. Stanford, California: Stanford University Press.

———. 1996. *Civil Justice in China: Representation and Practice in the Qing*. Stanford, Calif.: Stanford University Press.

———. 2001. *Code, Custom, and Legal Practice in China: The Qing and the Republic Compared*. Stanford, Calif.: Stanford University Press.

Huangchao wenxian tongkao 皇朝文獻通考 (A comprehensive compendium of the literature of the dynasty [Qing]). 1901. Shanghai.

Hubu zeli 戶部則例 (Rules and Regulations of the Board of Revenue). N.d.

Jia Xiuyan 賈秀嚴. 1992. *Minguo jiage shi* 民國物價史 (Price history of Republican China). Beijing: Zhongguo wujia chubanshe.

Jiang Shijie 江士杰. 1944. *Lijia zhidu kaolue* 里甲制度考論 (An examination of the lijia system). Shanghai: Shangwu yinshuguan.

Jiang Taixin 江太新. 1991. "Qingdai Huailu xian renkou chutan" 清代獲鹿縣人口初探 (A preliminary study on the population of Huailu county in the Early Qing). *Zhongguo Jingjishi Yanjiu* 中國經濟史研究, vol. 2.

Jiao Shouzhi 焦受之. 1987. "Jiefangqian Zhengding liangmianhangye de xingshuai" 解放前正定糧棉行業的興衰 (The rise and fall of the grain and cotton trading business in Zhengding before the Liberation). In *Shijiazhuang wenshi ziliao* 石家莊文史資料 (Source materials on Shijiazhuang local history), vol. 8. Shijiazhuang, Hebei.

Jiaoyubu 教育部. 1912. "Gongbu xiaoxuexiao ling" (Promulgation of the ordinance on primary schools). In Qu Xingui 璩鑫圭 ed., 1991, *Zhongguo jindai jiaoyu shi ziliao huibian: xuezhi yanbian* 中国近代教育史资料彙編：學制演變 (A compendium of source materials on modern Chinese educational history: evolution of the educational system). Shanghai: Shanghai jiaoyu chubanshe.

———. 1914. "Zhengli jiaoyu fang'an cao'an" 整理教育方案草案 (A draft plan for educational consolidation). In Shu Xincheng 舒新城, ed., 1981, *Zhongguo jindai jiaoyu shi ziliao* 中国近代教育史资料 (Source materials on modern Chinese educational history). Beijing: Renmin jiaoyu chubanshe.

Jin Dequn 金德群, ed. 1991. *Zhongguo Guomindang tudi zhengce yanjiu* 中國國民黨土地政策研究 (A study of the land policy of Guomindang). Beijing: Haiyang chubanshe.

Jinghai xianzhi 靜海縣誌 (Gazetteer of Jinghai county). 1934.

Jingxian zhi 景縣誌 (Gazetteer of Jingxian). 1932.

Jingxing xianzhi 井陘縣誌 (Gazetteer of Jingxing county). 1875.

Jordan, Donald A. 1976. *The Northern Expedition: China's National Revolution of 1926–1928*. Honolulu: University Press of Hawaii.

Kahler, Miles, and David Lake. 2003. *Governance in a Global Economy*. Princeton, N.J.: Princeton University Press.

Kahoku sogo chosa kenkyujo 華北綜合調查研究所. 1944. *Sekimon shi kinko noson jittai chosa hokokusho* 石門市近郊農村實態調查報告書 (Report on the investigation of actual conditions in a village in the suburb of Shimen [Shijiazhuang] city). Beijing.

Kapp, Robert A. 1973. *Szechwan and the Chinese Republic: Provincial Militarism and Central Power, 1911–1938*. New Haven, Conn.: Yale University Press.

Katayama, Tsuyoshi 片山剛. 1982a. "Shinmatsu Kotosho shuko deruta no zukohyo to soreo meguru shomondai" 清末廣東省珠江でるたの圖甲表とそれをめぐる諸問題 (Problems concerning the tujia charts in the Pearl River Delta in Guangdong province during the late Qing period). *Shigaku zasshi* 史學雜誌 91 (4): 42–81.

———. 1982b. "Shindai Kotosho shuko deruta no zukosei ni tsuite" 清代廣東省珠江でるたの圖甲制について (The tujia system in the Pearl River delta in Guangdong province during the Qing dynasty), *Toyo gakuho* 東洋學報 63 (3–4): 1–34.

———. 1992. "Qingmo Zhujiang shanjiaozhou diqu tujia biao yu zongzu zuzhi de gaizu" 清末珠江三角洲地區圖甲表與宗族組織的改組 (The tujia charts and the transformation of clan organizations in the Pearl River delta in the late Qing). In Ye Xian'en 葉顯恩, ed., *Qingdai quyi shehui jingji yanjiu* 清代區域社會經濟研究 (Studies on regional social economy during the Qing). Beijing: Zhonghua shuju.

Kawakatsu Mamoru . 川勝守 1980. *Chugoku hoken kokka no shihai kozo* 中國封建國家の支配構造 (The administrative structure of the Chinese state). Tokyo: University of Tokyo Press.

Keating, Pauline. 1997. *Two Revolutions: Village Reconstruction and the Cooperative Movement in Northern Shaanxi, 1934–1945.* Stanford, Calif.: Stanford University Press.

Kong Qingtai 孔慶泰. 1998. *Guomindang zhengfu zhengzhi zhidu shi* 國民黨政府政治制度史 (History of the political system of the Guomindang government). Hefei: Anhui jiaoyu chubanshe.

Kuhn, Philip A. 1975. "Local Self-Government under the Republic: Problems of Control, Autonomy, and Mobilization." In Frederic Wakeman Jr. and Carolyn Grant, eds., *Conflict and Control in Late Imperial China*, pp. 257–98. Berkeley: University of California Press. .

———. 1978–79. "Local Taxation and Finance in Republican China." In *Select Papers from the Center for Far Eastern Studies* 3: 100–36.

———. 1986. "The Development of Local Government." In Denis Twitchett and John King Fairbank, eds., *The Cambridge History of China*, vol. 13: *Republican China, 1912–49*, part 2. Cambridge, England: Cambridge University Press.

———. 1990. *Soulstealers: The Chinese Sorcery Scare of 1768.* Cambridge, Mass.: Harvard University Press.

Lai Xinxia 來新夏, ed. 1983. *Beiyang junfa shigao* 北洋軍閥史話 (A history of the northern warlords). Wuhan: Hubei renmin chubanshe.

Lamb, Jefferson D. H. (Lin Tung-hai). 1931. *The Development of the Agrarian Movement and Agrarian Legislation in China, 1912–1930.* Peiping (Beijing): Yenching University.

Levine, Steven. 1987. *Anvil of Victory: The Communist Revolution in Manchuria, 1945–1948.* New York: Columbia University Press.

Li Dian 黎典 and Li Ming 李銘. 1986. *Hebei jindai dashi ji* 河北近代大事記 (Chronicle of Hebei in the modern period). Shijiazhuang: Hebei renmin chubanshe.

Li Hongyi 李鴻毅. 1977 [1934]. *Hebei tianfu zhi yanjiu* 河北田賦之研究 (A Study of land tax in Hebei). Taibei: Chengwen chubanshe.

Li, Huaiyin. 2000a. "Village Regulations at Work: Local Taxation in Huailu County, 1900–936," *Modern China* 26 (1): 79–109.

———. 2000b. "State and Village in Late Qing and Republican North China: Local Administration and Land Taxation in Huailu County, Hebei Province, 1875–1936." Ph.D. dissertation, University of California, Los Angeles.

———. 2003a. "Power, Discourse, and Legitimacy in Rural North China: Disputes over the Village Head Office in Huailu County in the 1910s and 1920s," *Twentieth-Century China* 28 (2): 73–110.

———. 2003b. "Zhongguo xiangcun zhili zhi chuantong xinshi: Hebei sheng Huailu xian zhi shili" 中國鄉村治理之傳統型式：河北省獲鹿縣之實例 (Patterns of village governance in traditional China: the case of Huailu county, Hebei province). In Philip Huang, ed., *Zhongguo xiangcun yanjiu* 中國鄉村研究 (Rural China), no. 1.

Li Jinghan 李景漢. 1933. *Dingxian shehui diaocha gaikuang* 景縣社會調查概況 (An outline of social survey in Jingxian). Beijing: Beijing daxue chubanshe.

Li Sanmou 李三謀 and Cao Jianqiang 曹建強. 2001. "Qingdai beifang nongdi shiyong fangshi" 清代北方農地使用方式 (The use of farming land in North China in the Qing dynasty), *Nongye kaogu* 農業考古, 3.

Li Wenzhi 李文治, ed. 1957. *Zhongguo jindai nongye shi ziliao* 中國近代農業史資料 (Source materials on the agricultural history of modern China), vol. 1: *1840–1911*. Beijing: Sanlian shudian.

Li Zhi'an 李治安 and Du Jiaji 杜家驥. 1993. *Zhongguo gudai guanliao zhengzhi: Zhongguo gudai xingzheng guanli ji guanliao bing pouxi* 中國古代官僚政治：中國古代行政管理及官僚病剖析 (Traditional Chinese bureaucracy: administrative management and bureaucratic disease in ancient China). Beijing: Shumu wenxian chubanshe.

Liang Yong 梁勇. 1986. "Shijiazhuang zaoqi de shangye" 石家莊早期的商業 (Commerce in the early history of Shijiazhuang), *Shijiazhuang wenshi ziliao* 石家莊文史資料 (Source materials on Shijiazhuang local history), vol. 8. Shijiazhuang, Hebei.

Liang Zhiping 梁治平. 1996. *Qingdai xiguanfa: shehui yu guojia* 清代習慣法:社会与国家 (Customary law in the Qing: society and state). Beijing: Zhongguo zhengfa daxue chubanshe.

Lingshou xianzhi 靈壽縣誌 (Gazetteer of Lingshou county). 1874.

Little, Daniel. 1989. *Understanding Peasant China: Case Studies in the Philosophy of Social Science*. New Haven: Yale University Press.

———. 1998. *Microfoundations, Method, and Causation*. New Brunswick, N.J.: Transaction.

Liu Chuanguang 劉傳廣. 2001. "Zhongguo gudai chuantong dezhi de yin yu guo" 中國古代傳統德治的因與果 (Reasons and results of the tradition of moral governance in ancient China). *Huanan shifan daxue xuebao* 華南師範大學學報, 4.

Liu Zhiwei 劉志偉. 1988. "Ming-Qing Zhujiang sanjiaozhou diqu lijiazhi zhong 'hu' de yanbian" 明清珠江三角洲地區里甲制中"戶"的衍變 (Changes in the term "household" under the lijia system in the Zhujiang delta during the Ming-Qing period). *Zhongshan daxue xuebao* 中山大學學報, 3.

———. 1997. *Zai guojia yu shehui zhijian: Ming-Qing Guangdong lijia fuyi zhidu yanjiu* 在國家與社會之間：明清廣東里甲賦役制度研究 (Between state and society: A study of the lijia tax system in Guangdong in the Ming and Qing periods). Guangzhou: Zhongshan daxue chubanshe.

Liu Ziyang 劉子揚. 1988. *Qingdai difang zhiguan kao* 清代地方職官考 (A study of local government posts in the Qing). Beijing: Zijincheng chubanshe.

Luancheng xianzhi 欒城縣誌 (Gazetteer of Luancheng county). 1872.

Luo Yuandao 羅遠道. 1994. "Shilun baojia zhi de yanbian jiqi zuoyong" 試論保甲制的演變及其作用 (The evolution and functions of the baojia system). *Zhongguo lishi wenwu* 中國歷史文物, 1.

Ma Daying 馬大英 et al. 1944. *Tianfu shi* 田賦史 (A history of land tax). Taiwan: Zhengzhong shuju.

MacKinnon, Stephen R. 1980. *Power and Politics in Late Imperial China: Yuan Shi-kai in Beijing and Tianjin, 1901–1908.* Berkeley: University of California Press.

Mann, Michael. 1986. *The Sources of Social Power: A History of Power from the Beginning to A.D. 1760.* Cambridge, England: Cambridge University Press.

———. 1988. *States, War, and Capitalism.* New York: Basil Blackwell.

Mann, Susan. 1987. *Local Merchants and the Chinese Bureaucracy, 1750–1950.* Stanford, Calif.: Stanford University Press.

Marx, Karl. 1951. "The Eighteenth Brumaire of Louis Bonaparte." In Karl Marx and Frederick Engels, *Selected Works,* vol. 1. Moscow: Foreign Languages Publishing House.

Mayhew, Leon. 1971. *Society: Institutions and Activity.* Glenview, Ill.: Scott, Foresman.

McKnight, Brian. 1971. *Village and Bureaucracy in Southern Sung China.* Chicago: University of Chicago Press.

Morita Akira 森田明. 1976. "Shindai no gito sei to sono haikei" 清代の"議圖"制とその背景 (The yitu system and its background in the Qing dynasty). *Shakai keizai shigaku* 社会經濟史學 42 (2): 1–23.

———. 1981. "Shindai gito sei saiko" 清代議圖制再考 (Reexamination of the Yitu system in the Qing period). *Toyo gakuho* 62 (3–4): 1–35.

Mosher, Stephen. 1983. *Broken Earth: The Rural Chinese.* New York: Free Press.

Myers, Ramon. 1970. *The Chinese Peasant Economy: Agricultural Development in Hopei and Shantung, 1890–1949.* Cambridge, Mass.: Harvard University Press.

Nangong xianzhi 南宮縣誌 (Gazetteer of Nanggong county). 1936.

Nanpi xianzhi 南皮縣誌 (Gazetteer of Nanpi county). 1932.

Nee, Victor. 1998. "Sources of the New Institutionalism." In Mary C. Brinton and Victor Nee, eds., *The New Institutionalism in Sociology,* pp. 1–16. Stanford, Calif.: Stanford University Press.

Nishimura Gensho 西村元照. 1976. "Shinsho no holan" 清初の包攬 (Baolan in the early Qing). *Toyoshi kenkyu* 東洋史研究 35 (3): 114–74.

North, Douglass. 1998. "Economic Performance Through Time." In Mary C. Brinton and Victor Nee, eds., *The New Institutionalism in Sociology,* pp. 247–57. Stanford, Calif.: Stanford University Press.

Olson, Mancur. 1965. *The Logic of Collective Action: Public Goods and the Theory of Groups.* Cambridge, Mass.: Harvard University Press, 1965.

———. 1971. *The Logic of Collective Action: Public Goods and the Theory of Groups.* Cambridge, Mass.: Harvard University Press.

Pan Zhe 潘哲 and Tang Shiru 唐世儒. 1984. "Huailu xian bianshence chubu yanjiu" 獲鹿縣編審冊初步研究 (A preliminary study of the cadastres of Huailu county). In Qingshi yanjiu suo 清史研究所, ed., *Qingshi yanjiu ji* 清史研究集, 3. Chengdu: Sichuan renmin chubanshe.

Parsons, Talcott. 1937. *The Structure of Social Action: A Study in Social Theory with Special Reference to a Group of Recent European Writers.* New York: McGraw-Hill.

Peng Houwen 彭厚文. 1998. "Shilun 30 niandai qianqi Guomindang daji tuhao lieshen de zhengce" 試論 30 年代前期打擊國民黨土豪劣紳的政策 (The Guomindang's attacking "local bullies and evil gentry" policy in the early 1930s). *Hubei daxue xuebao* 湖北大學學報, 1.

Perdue, Peter. 1987. *Exhausting the Earth: State and Peasant in Hunan, 1500–1850.* Cambridge, Mass.: Council on East Asian Studies, Harvard University.

Perkins, Dwight H. 1969. *Agricultural Development in China, 1368–1968.* Chicago: Aldine.

Perry, Elizabeth J. 1980. *Rebels and Revolutionaries in North China, 1845–1945.* Stanford, Calif.: Stanford University Press.

Pinggu xianzhi 平谷縣誌 (Gazetteer of Pinggu county). 1934.

Polanyi, Karl. 1957. *The Great Transformation.* Boston: Beacon Press.

Pomeranz, Kenneth. 1993. *The Making of a Hinterland: State, Society, and Economy in Inland North China, 1853–1937.* Berkeley: University of California Press.

Popkin, Samuel. 1979. *The Rational Peasant: The Political Economy of Rural Society in Vietnam.* Berkeley: University of California Press.

Prazniak, Roxann. 1980. "Tax Protest at Laiyang, Shandong, 1910." *Modern China* 6 (1): 41–71.

———. 1999. *Of Camel Kings and Other Things: Rural Rebels against Modernity in Late Imperial China.* Lanham, Md.: Rowman and Littlefield.

Qian Shifu 錢實甫. 1984. *Beiyang zhengfu shiqi de zhengzhi zhidu* 北洋政府時期的政治制度 (The Chinese political system during the northern warlord period). Beijing: Zhonghua shuju.

Qu Xingui 璩鑫圭 ed., 1991, *Zhongguo jindai jiaoyu shi ziliao huibian: xuezhi yanbian* 中国近代教育史资料彙編：學制演變 (A compendium of source materials on modern Chinese educational history: evolution of the educational system). Shanghai: Shanghai jiaoyu chubanshe.

Rankin, Mary Backus. 1972. *Elite Activism and Political Transformation in China: Zhejiang Province, 1865–1911.* Stanford, Calif.: Stanford University Press.

Rawski, Thomas G. 1989. *Economic Growth in Prewar China.* Berkeley: University of California Press.

Reed, Bradly. 2000. *Talons and Teeth: County Clerks and Runners in the Qing Dynasty.* Stanford, Calif.: Stanford University Press.

Robisheaux, Thomas. 1989. *Rural Society and the Search for Order in Early Modern Germany.* Cambridge, England: Cambridge University Press.

Rosenau, James. 1992. "Governance, Order, and Change in World Politics." In James Rosenau, ed., *Governance without Government: Order and Change in World Politics.* Cambridge, England: Cambridge University Press.

Rowe, William. 2001. *Saving the World: Chen Hongmou and Elite Consciousness in Eighteenth-Century China*. Stanford, Calif.: Stanford University Press.

Sabean, David. 1984. *Power in the Blood: Popular Culture and Village Discourse in Early Modern Germany*. Cambridge: Cambridge University Press.

Saeki Tomi 佐伯富. 1964. "Shindai no kyoyaku jiho ni tsuite" 清代の鄕約地保について (On the xiangyue and the dibao in the Qing time), *Tohogaku* 東方學, 28: 91–119.

———. 1965. "Shindai no risho" 清代の里書 (The lishu in the Qing dynasty), *Toyo gakuho* 東洋學報, 46.3: 67–77.

Schran, Peter. 1976. *Guerrilla Economy: The Development of the Shensi-Kansu-Ninghsia Border Region, 1937–1945*. Albany: State University of New York Press.

Schultz, Theodore W. 1964. *Transforming Traditional Agriculture*. New Haven, Conn.: Yale University Press.

Scott, James. 1976. *The Moral Economy of the Peasant: Rebellion and Subsistence in Southeast Asia*. New Haven, Conn.: Yale University Press.

———. 1985. *Weapons of the Weak: Everyday Forms of Peasant Resistance*. New Haven, Conn.: Yale University Press.

———. 1990. *Domination and the Arts of Resistance: Hidden Transcripts*. New Haven, Conn.: Yale University Press.

Shen, N. C. 1936. "The Local Government of China." *Chinese Social and Political Science Review*, pp.163–201.

Sheridan, James E. 1966. *Chinese Warlord: The Career of Feng Yu-hsiang*. Stanford, Calif.: Stanford University Press.

———. 1975. *China in Disintegration: The Republican Era in Chinese History, 1912–1949*. New York: Free Press.

Shi Zhihong 史志宏. 1984. "Cong huailu xian shence kan qingdai qianqi de tudi jizhong he tanding rudi gaige" 從獲鹿縣審冊看清代前期的土地集中和攤丁入地改革 (Land concentration and the reform of merging poll tax into land tax in early Qing as seen from the cadastres of Huailu county). *Hebeidaxue xuebao* 河北大學學報, 1.

Skinner, G. William. 1964–65. "Marketing and Social Structure in Rural China." *Journal of Asian Studies* 24 (1): 3–44; 24 (2): 195–228; 24 (3): 363–99.

———. 1971. "Chinese Peasants and the Closed Community: An Open and Shut Case." *Comparative Studies in Society and History* 13 (3): 270–81.

———. 1977. "Cities and the Hierarchy of Local Systems." In G. William Skinner, ed., *The City in Late Imperial China*, pp. 275–351. Stanford, Calif.: Stanford University Press.

Stapleton, Kristin. 1997. "County Administration in Late-Qing Sichuan. Conflicting Models of Rural Policing." *Late Imperial China* 18 (1): 100–132.

Sun Benwen 孫本文. 1943. *Xiandai Zhongguo shehui wenti* 現代中國社會問題 (Social problems in modern China). Shanghai: Shangwu yinshuguan.

Sun Haiquan 孫海泉. 1994. "Lun Qingdai cong lijia zhi dao baojia de yanbian" 論清代從里甲制到保甲的演變 (The evolution of the lijia system into the baojia in the Qing), *Zhongguo shi yanjiu* 中國史研究, 2.

Sweeten, Alan Richard. 1976. "The Ti-pao's Role in Local Government as Seen in Fukien Christian 'Cases,' 1863–69." *Ch'ing-shih wen-t'i* 3 (December): 1–25.

Tang Jun 唐軍. 2001. *Zhefu yu mianyan: dangdai Huabei cunluo jiazu de shengzhang licheng* 蟄伏與綿延：當代華北村落家族的生長歷程 (Dormancy and perpetuation: the growth of rural clans in contemporary North China). Beijing: Zhongguo shehui kexue chubanshe.

Tawney, R. H. 1932. *Land and Labor in China*. London: Allen and Unwin.

Talor, Michael. 1976. *Anarchy and Cooperation*. London: Wiley.

———. 1982. *Community, Anarchy and Liberty*. Cambridge: Cambridge University Press.

Tenshin jimusho chosaka 天津事務所調査課. 1936. *Kahoku sho nogyo chosa hokoku* 河北省農業調査報告 (Report on the investigation of agriculture in Hebei province). Tianjin.

Thaxton, Ralph A. 1983. *China Turned Rightside Up: Revolutionary Legitimacy in the Peasant World*. New Haven, Conn.: Yale University Press.

———. 1997. *Salt of the Earth: The Political Origins of Peasant Protest and Communist Revolution in China*. Berkeley: University of California Press.

Thompson, E. P. 1963. *The Making of the English Working Class*. New York: Vintage.

———. 1971. "The Moral Economy of the English Crowd in the Eighteenth Century," *Past and Present* 50: 71–136.

Tian Bofu 田伯伏. 1997. "Jing-Han tielu yu Shijiazhuang shi de xingqi" 京漢鐵路與石家莊市的興起 (The Beijing-Hankou railroad and the rise of Shijiazhuang city), *Hebei daxue xuebao* 河北大學學報 22 (2).

Tie Nan 鐵男. 1994. "Qingdai Hebei qidi chutan" 清代河北旗地初探 (A preliminary study of banner land in Hebei in the Qing). *Manzu yanjiu* 滿族研, 2.

Tien, Hung-mao. 1972. *Government and Politics in Kuomintang China, 1927–1937*. Stanford, Calif.: Stanford University Press.

Tilly, Charles. 1975a. "Reflections on the History of European State-Making." In Charles Tilly, ed., *The Formation of National States in Western Europe*, pp. 380–455. Princeton, N.J.: Princeton University Press.

———. 1975b. "Western State-Making and Theories of Political Transformation." In Charles Tilly, ed., *The Formation of National States in Western Europe*, pp. 380–455. Princeton, N.J.: Princeton University Press.

Tsin, Michael. 1999. *Nation, Governance, and Modernity in China: Canton, 1900–1927*. Stanford, Calif.: Stanford University Press.

Tudi weiyuanhui 土地委員會. 1937. *Quanguo tudi diaocha baogao gangyao* 全國土地調査報告綱要 (Abstract of the report on the nationwide land survey). Nanjing: Tudi weiyuanhui.

Übelhör, Monika. 1989. "The Community Compact (*Hsiang-yüeh*) of the Sung and Its Educational Significance." In Wm. Theodore de Bary and J. Chaffee, eds., *Neo-Confucian Education*. Berkeley: University of California Press.

Wakeman, Frederic, Jr. 1975. "Introduction: The Evolution of Local Control in Late Imperial China." In Frederic Wakeman Jr. and Carolyn Grant, eds.,

Conflict and Control in Late Imperial China, pp. 1–25. Berkeley: University of California Press.

Wan Guoding 萬國鼎. 1971 [1934]. *Jiangsu Wujin Nantong tianfu diaocha baogao* 江蘇武進南通田賦調查報告 (An investigation report on the land tax in Wujin and Nantong in Jiangsu). Taibei: Zhuanji wenxue chubanshe.

Wang Fuming 王福明. 1995. "Xiang yu cun de shehui jiegou" (Social structures of *xiang* and the village). In Cong Hanxiang 從翰香, ed., *Jindai Ji-Lu-Yu xiangcun* 近代冀魯豫鄉村 (The rural society of Hebei, Shandong, and Henan in the modern period), pp. 3–118. Beijing: Zhongguo shehui kexue chubanshe.

Wang Gaoxin 汪高鑫. 1995. "Zhu Xi zhengzhi sixiang chutan" 朱熹政治思想初探 (Preliminary research on Zhu Xi's political thought). *Anhui shixue* 安徽史學, 2.

Wang Rigen 王日根. 1997. "Ming-Qing jiceng shehui guanli zuzhi xitong lungang" 明清基層社會管理組織系統論綱 (The administrative organizations and systems of local society in the Ming and Qing periods). *Qingshi yanjiu* 清史研究, 2.

Wang Xinglai 王興來 and Zhu Xunxiao 朱訓曉. 1989. "Qianjin cun yu Tianzhujiao" 前進村與天主教 (Catholicism in Qianjin village), *Shijiazhuang jiaoqu wenshi ziliao* 石家莊郊區文史資料 (Source materials on suburban Shijiazhuang local history), vol. 1. Shijiazhuang: Hebei.

Wang, Yeh-chien. 1973a. *An Estimate of the Land-Tax Collection in China, 1753 and 1908*. Cambridge, Mass.: Harvard University Press.

———. 1973b. *Land Taxation in Imperial China, 1750–1911*. Cambridge, Mass.: Harvard University Press.

Wang Yuanbi 王元璧. 1935. "Tianfu zhengshou zhidu de gaige" 田賦征收制度的改革 (Reforms of the land taxation systems). *Dongfang zazhi* 東方雜誌 32 (7): 123–33.

Wanyan Shaoyuan 完颜绍元. 1994. *Fengjian yamen tanmi* 封建衙门探秘 (Behind the door of the Mandarin yamen). Tianjin: Tianjin jiaoyu chubanshe.

Waters, Neil L. 1983. *Japan's Local Pragmatists: The Transition from Bakumatsu to Meiji in the Kawasaki Region*. Cambridge, Mass.: Harvard University Press.

Watson, Rubie S. 1985. *Inequality among Brothers: Class and Kinship in South China*. Cambridge, England: Cambridge University Press.

———. 1990. "Corporate Property and Local Leadership in the Pearl River Delta, 1898–1941." In Joseph Esherick and Mary Rankin, eds., *Chinese Local Elites and Patterns of Dominance*, pp. 239–60. Berkeley: University of California Press.

Watt, John R. 1972. *The District Magistrate in Late Imperial China*. New York: Columbia University Press.

Weber, Max. 1951 [1922]. *The Religion of China: Confucianism and Taoism*. Glencoe, Ill.: Free Press.

———. 1968. *Economy and Society: An Outline of Interpretive Sociology*. 3 vols. New York: Bedminster Press.

Wei Guangqi 魏光奇. 1998a. "Difang zizhi yu Zhili si ju" 地方自治與直隸四局 (Self-government and the Four Offices in Zhili). *Lishi yanjiu* 歷史研究, 2.

————. 1998b. "Zhili difang zizhi zhong de xian caizheng" 直隸地方自治中的縣財政 (County finance in local self-government in Zhili). *Jindaishi yanjiu* 近代史研究 1: 62–80.

————. 2000a. "Qingdai Zhili de lishe yu xiangdi" 清代直隸的里社與鄉地 (The lishe and xiangdi in Zhili in the Qing). *Zhongguo shi yanjiu* 中國史研究, 1.

————. 2000b. "Qingdai Zhili de chaiyao" 清代直隸的差徭 (The chaiyao tax in Zhili in the Qing). *Qingshi yanjiu* 清史研究, 3.

Wei Qingyuan 韋慶遠. 2001. "Zhuangtou jiapu yu Qingdai dui qidi de guanli" 莊頭家譜與清代對旗地的管理 (The zhuangtou genealogy and banner land management in the Qing). *Zhongguo shehui jingjie shi yanjiu* 中國社會經濟史研究, 2.

Wen Juntian 聞鈞天. 1935. *Zhongguo baojia zhidu* 中國保甲制度 (The baojia system in China). Shanghai: Shangwu yinshuguan.

Wen'an xianzhi 文安縣誌 (Gazetteer of Wen'an county). 1922.

Will, Pierre-Etienne. 1998. "The 1744 Annual Audits of Magistrate Activity and Their Fate." *Late Imperial China* 18 (2): 1–50.

Wittfogel, Karl A. 1957. *Oriental Despotism: A Comparative Study of Total Power.* New Haven, Conn.: Yale University Press.

Wolf, Eric R. 1969. *Peasant Wars of the Twentieth Century.* New York: Harper and Row.

Wood, Alan. 1995. *Limits to Autocracy.* Honolulu: University of Hawaii Press.

Woon, Yuen-fong. 1984. *Social Organization in South China, 1911–1949.* Ann Arbor: Center for Chinese Studies, University of Michigan.

Wou, Odoric. 1994. *Mobilizing the Masses: Building Revolution in Henan.* Stanford, Calif.: Stanford University Press.

Wu Ding'an 吳定安. 2000. "Zhuzi shecang zhi fa jiqi yingxiang" 朱子社倉之法及其影響 (Zhu Xi's promotion of community granary and its consequences), *Jiangxi shehui kexue* 江西社會科學, 12.

Wu Ze 吳澤. 1993. *Dongfang shehui jingji xingtai shilun* 東方社會經濟形態史論 (Papers on the history of Oriental socioeconomic history). Shanghai: Shanghai renmin chubanshe.

Xiao Tian 小田. 1997. *Jiangnan xiangzhen shehui de jindai zhuanxing* 江南鄉鎮社會的近代轉型 (Modern transformation of the rural market-town society in Jiangnan). Beijing: Zhongguo shangye chubanshe.

Xie Feng 解峰 et al. 1990. *Dangdai Zhongguo de Hebei* 當代中國的河北 (Hebei in contemporary China). Beijing: Zhongguo shehui kexue chubanshe.

Xie Qinglin 解青林. 1988. "Shijiazhuang mianbu shi kaolue" 石家莊棉布史考略 (A history of cotton cloth in Shijiazhuang). In *Shijiazhuang wenshi ziliao* 石家莊文史資料 (Source materials on Shijiazhuang local history), vol. 8. Shijiazhuang: Hebei.

Xiongxian xinzhi 雄縣新誌 (New gazetteer of Xiongxian). 1929.

Xu Hao 徐浩. 1999. "Qingdai Huabei nongcun fengjian boxue he nonghu gongfuye shengchan zhuangkuang fenxi" 清代華北農村封建剝削和農戶工副業生產狀況分析 (An analysis of feudal exploitation, family industry, and sideline activities in rural North China in the Qing), *Shehui kexue zhanxian* 社會科學戰線, 5.

Xu Yushui 徐羽水. 1934. "Zhongguo tianfu zhi yi kaocha" 中國田賦之一攷察 (An examination of land tax in China). *Dongfang zazhi* 東方雜誌 31 (10): 55–65.

Xu Zhen'an 徐振安. 1984. "Shijiazhuang zhi renkou" 石家莊之人口 (Population in Shijiazhuang), *Shijiazhuang wenshi ziliao* 石家莊文史資料 (Source materials on Shijiazhuang local history), vol. 2. Shijiazhuang: Hebei.

Xuebu 學部. 1904. "Zouding chudeng xiaoxuetang zhangcheng" 奏定初等小學堂章程 (Memorial on the regulations on primary scholls). In Qu Xingui 璩鑫圭 ed., 1991, *Zhongguo jindai jiaoyu shi ziliao huibian: xuezhi yanbian* 中国近代教育史資料彙編: 學制演變 (A compendium of source materials on modern Chinese educational history: Evolution of the educational system), pp. 291–306. Shanghai: Shanghai jiaoyu chubanshe.

———. 1909. "Zouqing biantong chudeng xiaoxuetang zhangcheng zhe" 奏請變通初等小學堂章程摺 (Memorial on updating the regulations on primary schools). In Qu Xingui, 璩鑫圭 ed., 1991, *Zhongguo jindai jiaoyu shi ziliao huibian: xuezhi yanbian* 中国近代教育史資料彙編: 學制演變 (A compendium of source materials on modern Chinese educational history: Evolution of the educational system), pp. 543–46. Shanghai: Shanghai jiaoyu chubanshe.

———. 1910. "Gaiding Quanxuesuo zhangcheng" 改訂勸學所章程 (Revised regulations on the education promotion office). In Shu Xincheng 舒新城, ed., 1981, *Zhongguo jindai jiaoyu shi ziliao* 中国近代教育史資料 (Source materials on modern Chinese educational history), pp. 284–86. Beijing: Renmin jiaoyu chubanshe.

Xuxiu Jingxing xianzhi 續修井陘縣誌 (Updated edition of the gazetteer of Jingxing county). 1875.

Yamamoto Eishi 山本英史. 1977. "Shinsho ni okeru holan no tenkai" 清初における包攬の展開 (The development of baolan in the early Qing), *Toyo gakuho* 東洋學報 59 (1–2): 131–66.

———. 1980. "Sekkosho Tendaiken ni okeru toto ni tsuite" 浙江省天台縣における圖頭について (The tutou in Tiantai county, Zhejiang province), *Shigaku* 史學 50 (1–4): 421–49.

———. 1990. "Shinen ni yoru zeiryu holan to shincho kokka" 紳衿による稅糧包攬と清朝國家 (Proxy remittance of taxes by the gentry and the Qing state), *Toyoshi kenkyu* 東洋史研究 48 (4): 40–69.

Yang Junke 楊俊科. 1986. "Shijiazhuang zaoqi de zhuanyunye" 石家莊早期的轉運業 (Transport business in the early history of Shijiazhang). In *Shijiazhuang wenshi ziliao* 石家莊文史資料 (Source materials on Shijiazhuang local history), vol. 8. Shijiazhuang: Hebei.

Yang, Martin C. 1945. *A Chinese Village: Taitou, Shantung Province*. New York, Columbia University Press.

Yang Nianqun 楊念群. 2001. "Huabei Qingmiaohui de zuzhi jiegou yu gongneng yanbian: yi Xiekou cun, Huangtubeidian cun deng wei ge'an" 華北青苗會的組織結構與功能演變：以解口村、黃土北店村等為個案 (The organization and functional changes of Qingmiaohui in North China: the cases of Xiekou village and Huangtubeidian village). *Zhongzhou xuekan* 中州學刊, 3.

Yang Xuechen 楊學臣. 1963. "Qingdai qidi de xingzhi jiqi bianhua" 清代旗地的性質及其變化 (The nature and evolution of the banner land during the Qing period). *Lishi yanjiu* 歷史研究, 3: 175–95.

Yanshan xianzhi 鹽山縣誌 (Gazetteer of Yanshan county). 1916.

Yao Shusheng 姚樹聲. 1936. "Minguo yilai woguo tianfu zhi gaige" 民國以來我國田賦之改革 (Land tax reforms in our country since the founding of the Republic), *Dongfang zazhi* 33 (17): 77–88.

Ye Xian'en 葉顯恩 and Tan Dihua 譚棣華. 1985. "Guanyu Qing zhongye hou Zhujiang sanjiaozhou haozu de fuyi zhengshou wenti" 關於清中葉後珠江三角洲豪族的賦役征收問題 (Issues regarding tax collection among the strong descent groups in the Pearl River delta after mid-Qing). *Qingshi yanjiu tongxun* 清史研究通訊 2: 1–4.

Yi Zhongcai. 1929. *Difang zizhi xue yu cunzhi xue zhi jiyuan* (The age of self-government and the study of village systems). Hunan: Dangwu xunnian suo.

Young, Arthur N. 1965. *China's Wartime Finance and Inflation, 1937–1945.* Cambridge, Mass.: Harvard University Press.

———. 1971. *China's Nation-Building Effort, 1927–1937: The Financial and Economic Record.* Stanford, Calif.: Stanford University Press.

Yuanshi xianzhi 元氏縣誌 (Gazetteer of Yuansi county). 1931.

Zelin, Madeleine. 1984. *The Magistrate's Tael: Fiscal Reform in Eighteenth-Century Ch'ing China.* Berkeley: University of California Press.

Zhang Liwen. 2001. "Zhu Xi de 'wenzheng yi de' yu 'weizheng yi xing' de sixiang" 朱熹的"為政以德"與"為政以刑"的思想 (Zhu Xi's ideas on "governance by virtue" and "governance by punishment"). Beijing: *Guangming ribao* 光明日報, April 25.

Zhang Peiguo 張佩國. 1998. "Tudi ziyuan yu quanli wangluo: minguo shiqi de Huabei cunzhuang" 土地資源與權力網絡：民國時期的華北村莊 (Land resources and power network: North China villages in the Republican period). *Qilu xuekan* 齊魯學刊, 2.

———. 2000. *Diquan fenpei, nongjia jingjie, cunluo shequ: 1900–1945 nian de Shandong nongcun* 地權分配，農家經濟，村落社區：1900–1945年的山東農村 (Landholding distribution, peasant economy, and village communities: rural Shandong, 1900–1945). Jinan: Qilu shushe.

Zhang, Xin. 2000. *Social Transformation in Modern China: The State and Local Elites in Henan, 1900–1937.* Cambridge, England: Cambridge University Press.

Zhang Xingjiu 張星久. 2000. "Rujia wuwei sixiang de zhengzhi neihan yu shengcheng jizhi; jianlun Rujia ziyouzhuyi wenti" 儒家"無為"思想的政治內涵與生成機制：兼論儒家自由主義問題 (The genesis and political meanings of Confucian "non-action" ideas and Confucian liberalism). *Zhengzhixue yanjiu* 政治學研究, 2.

Zhang Xinyi 張心一. 1933. *Hebei sheng nongye gaikuang guji baogao* 河北省農業概況估計報告 (A report of estimates of the general condition of agriculture in Hebei province). Nanjing: Lifayuan tongjichu.

Zhang Youyi 章有義, ed. 1957. *Zhongguo jindai nongyeshi ziliao* 中國近代農業史資料 (Source materials on the agricultural history of modern China), vols. 2 and 3: 1912–27, 1927–37. Beijing: Sanlian shudian.

Zhang Youyu 張友漁 and Gao Chao 高潮. 1991. *Zhonghua lüling jicheng: Qing juan* 中華律令集成: 清卷 (Compendium of Chinese laws and regulations: the Qing volume). Changchun: Jilin renmin chubanshe.

Zhao Liaokong 趙了空. 1983. "Riben qinhua shiqi Shijiazhuang jige fandong huidaomen de neimu" 日本侵華時期石家莊幾個反動會道門的內幕 (Inside stories about the reactionary sects in Shijiazhuang during the Japanese occupation). In *Shijiazhuang wenshi ziliao* 石家莊文史資料 (Source materials on Shijiazhuang local history), vol. 1. Shijiazhuang: Hebei.

Zheng Qidong 鄭起東. 1992. "Qingdai Huabei de nongye gaizhi wenti" 清代華北的農業改制問題 (Agricultural transformation in North China during the Qing). In Ye Xian'en 葉顯恩, ed., *Qingdai quyi shehui jingji yanjiu* 清代區域社會經濟研究 (Studies on regional social economy during the Qing). Beijing: Zhonghua shuju.

Zhili Dingzhou zhi 直隸定州誌 (Gazetteer of Dingzhou county in Zhili). 1849.

Zhili quansheng caizheng shuomingshu 直隸全省財政說明書 (Report on the finance of the whole Zhili province). 1915. N.p.

Zhongguo nongmin yinhang jingji yanjiuhui 中國農民銀行經濟研究會. n.d. *Zhongguo ge zhongyao chengshi lingshou wujia zhishu yuebao* 中國各重要城市零售物價指數月報 (Monthly report on retail prices in the major cities of China). N.p.

Zhu Boneng 朱伯能. 1946. *Xian caizheng wenti* 縣財政問題 (Financial issues of county government). Shanghai: Zhengzhong shuju.

Zhu Dexin 朱德新. 1994. *Ershi shiji san sishi niandai Henan Jidong baojia zhidu yanjiu* 二十世紀三四十年代河南冀東保甲制度研究 (A study of the baojia system in Henan and Eastern Hebei in the 1930s and 1940s). Beijing: Zhongguo shehui kexue chubanshe.

Index

Index

administrative disputes, 5, 11; incidence of, 60, 274n1; magistrates in, 9; over the collection of chaiyao, 97–98; over the collection of land taxes, 99–107, 218–20; over deed taxes, 116–24; over the investigation of "black land," 248–49; over middlemen's commissions, 53–54; over positions of the Education Promotion Office, 180–82; over school funds, 58, 171–72; over school matters, 182–91; over tax burdens, 196–205; over tax liabilities, 127–30, 222, 223–28; over village head office, 136–62; over village funds, 229–32; over xiangdi service, 60, 66–91; village regulations in, 12
"after-war rehabilitation levy," 99; dispute over, 199–202
An Luohong, 173
ancestral hall, 64, 187–90
Andrew, Anita, 269n10
"anti-Reds military special contribution," 37, 200; resistance to, 202–5
Anxia village, 246, 249, 283n5
Ardant, Gabriel, 260
Averill, Stephen, 268n7

Bai Jing'an, 30
Bai Shulin, 156
bailiff. See tax collection
Balazs, Etienne, 7
banner land, 234–36

bannermen, 234–35
Baodi county, 42, 62, 279n2, 283n1
Baoding Circuit, 240
baojia, 6, 7, 8, 57, 125, 137, 251, 272n1; in "black land" investigation, 236; deterioration of, 43, 44; and land taxation, 42
baolan. See proxy remittance
baoshou. See tax-farming
baoweituan, 37; duties of, 212
baozhang, 236
Beattie, Hilary, 135
Beiganzi village, 278n7
Beigucheng village, 54, 173
Beihu village, 176, 177
Beijing government, 37, 120, 198, 203, 241; Ministry of Education, 168, 280n1, 280n2
Beijing-Hankou railroad, 25, 204
Beima village, 219
Beiqiema village, 118
Beitongye village, 59
Beixiangbei village, 52
Beiyang Law and Administrative School, 282n5
Beizai village, 127
"benevolent government," 258
Bernhardt, Kathryn, 44, 252, 268n7
Bi Chengqun, 249
bingchai. See military levy
"black land": investigation of, 5, 8, 18, 221, 236–49; origins of, 234–36

Wan Guoding, 64, 65
Wang Erbai, 245
Wang Faying, 75
Wang Fuming, 42, 57, 273n13, 279n2
Wang Guoxin, 108
Wang Kejian, 75–76
Wang Maishou, 80–81
Wang Shenxiu, 172
Wang Wanling, 248
Wang Wende, 116, 119
Wang Xi'ai, 245, 247
Wang Xijiu, 248
Wang, Yeh-chien, 2, 34, 35, 43, 44
Wang Yuanbi, 278n10
Wang Yulin, 104
Wang Yuyou, 276n11
Wang Zhan, 275n6
Wang Zhenzhong, 267n2
Wanyan Shaoyuan, 267n2
ward government, 15, 18; creation of,
    214. See also ward head; ward police
ward head: in administrative disputes,
    224–25, 229–30. See also ward govern-
    ment
ward informers: in "black land" investiga-
    tion, 244–50
ward office fee, 218
ward police, 78, 88, 194; in administrative
    disputes, 142, 145, 158–59; in "black
    land" investigation, 241, 250; in deed
    taxation, 117; duties of, 158; in land
    taxation, 96, 106, 216; in village head
    election, 280n5
Watson, Rubie, 136
Watt, John, 2
Weber, Max, 1, 6, 256–57, 269n12, 283n2,
    284n6
Wei Guangqi, 199
Wei Qingyuan, 235
Wei Yuanchang, 116
Weitong village, 86–89
"white deeds." See deeds
Wittfogel, Karl, 7
Wolf, Eric, 269n14
Wu Delian, 51

Wu Ding'an, 108
Wu Donglin, 178, 183, 184, 281n1
Wu Guilin, 183
Wu Kuliang, 176
Wu Liande, 53
Wu Molin, 183
Wu Peifu, 275n1
Wu Qingrui, 282n5
Wu Si, 267n2
Wu Weiyi, 101
Wu Ze, 269n10
wuwei, 258

xiang, 15, 209, 214; in Huailu county,
    272n4; supervisory committee of, 212,
    229. *See also* xiang government;
    xiangzhang
Xiang and Zhen Self-Government
    Implementation Act, 211
xiang government, 211–12; withdrawal of
    local elites from, 217. *See also*
    xiangzhang
xiangbao, 42, 57, 62, 273n13, 283n1
xiangdi, 8; abuse in tax collection,
    101–102; assistant to, 98; and the col-
    lection of enclave taxes, 106–107; in
    deed taxation, 111–14; in disputes over
    chaiyao, 97–98; in disputes over the
    village head office, 151–52; in land
    taxation, 8–9, 56–57; in local adminis-
    tration, 57–59; as middleman, 46,
    51–55, 66–67, 75–76, 83; origins of,
    41–46; performance in tax payment,
    61, 95; selection of, 46–51; tax-advanc-
    ing, 45; tax-prompting, 45, 102–105; as
    "unofficial middlemen," 115; and vil-
    lage head, 58; and xiangbao, 62. *See
    also* xiangdi service
xiangdi service: competition for, 66–67;
    disputes over, 60–61; evasion of, 67;
    funds for, 45, 137, 273n7; subsidy for,
    67, 151
xiangdi system. *See* xiangdi; xiangdi serv-
    ice
xianggui. See village regulations